WHITMAN'S & DICKINSON'S CONTEMPORARIES

AN ANTHOLOGY OF THEIR VERSE

Edited and with an Introduction by
Robert Bain

Southern Illinois University Press   *Carbondale and Edwardsville*

Library of Congress Cataloging-in-Publication Data

Whitman's and Dickinson's contemporaries : an anthology of their verse
/ edited and with an introduction by Robert Bain.
    p.   cm.
    Includes bibliographical references and index.
    1. American poetry—19th century.   2. Whitman, Walt, 1819–1892—
Contemporaries.   3. Dickinson, Emily, 1830–1886—Contemporaries.
I. Bain, Robert, 1932–
PS607.W455   1996
811'.308—dc20   95-9867
ISBN 0-8093-1721-4 (cloth). — ISBN 0-8093-2031-2 (pbk.)   CIP

For a new generation of readers,
Which includes our children and grandchildren—

Jenny Christine Giduz, William Luke Giduz,
Margaret Houren Somerville, Isaac Hugo Britt,
Margaret Woodbridge Roberts, Jesse Lee Roberts,
Henry Peronneau Roberts, Nell Clare Jensen Crumbley,
Audrey Charlotte Crockett, John Griffith Crockett,
Kimberly Blalock, Natalie Blalock,
Kelly Lynn McClanahan, Paige Marie McClanahan,
Davis Knox Brigman, and Tyler Addison Brigman

Contents

Contents

Contents   *xv*

Preface

Forgive, O Lord, my little jokes on Thee,
And I'll forgive Thy great big one on me.

—Robert Frost

History, like God in Frost's couplet, has played gigantic jokes on Whitman's and Dickinson's contemporary American poets. During their lifetimes, Walt Whitman had a small coterie of admirers, Emerson and Thoreau among them; only a few friends knew that Emily Dickinson wrote poetry. Many American poets commanding readers' attention during that time have suffered such a decline in reputation that their works are not easily available. This anthology presents the poetry of Whitman's and Dickinson's contemporaries so that readers can rediscover these authors, can reconstruct the poetic contexts of the age, and can better understand why Whitman and Dickinson now so overshadow other poets of their time.

From the middle of the nineteenth century until World War I, most Americans and Europeans identified American poetry not with Whitman or Dickinson, but with Henry Wadsworth Longfellow, James Russell Lowell, John Greenleaf Whittier, and Oliver Wendell Holmes. Ralph Waldo Emerson, better known as an essayist, and Edgar Allan Poe, better known as a short story writer, had also established reputations for their poetry. Joining these authors in the pantheon of poets were Lydia Huntley Sigourney, Ella Wheeler Wilcox, Alice and Phoebe Cary, Bayard Taylor, Thomas Bailey Aldrich, Paul Laurence Dunbar, Henry Timrod, Sidney Lanier, and many others. Readers would not rediscover such black poets as George Moses Horton and Frances Ellen Watkins Harper until after the middle of this century.

This anthology re-presents some of the period's poets. Scholars are looking with new eyes at these "lost" poets; they are finding good reasons for reading them again. David S. Reynolds' *Beneath the American Renaissance* (1988) and Cheryl Walker's *The Nightingale's Burden: Women Poets and American Culture Before 1900* (1982) re-examine works by these neglected authors to establish their relationship to writers most admired today. Understanding how history has played its jokes is always useful; such study also shows how these poets' works illuminate those of Whitman and Dickinson.

In looking again at Whitman's and Dickinson's contemporaries, we have discovered no poets who rival their genius, but we have discovered lively authors who address the issues of the day: slavery, the Civil War, religion, the relationship of self to society, Americans' consciousness of being different from Europeans, the status of women, and the artist's problems in American society.

We have arranged this anthology by the poets' birthdates. The earliest born was Lydia Huntley Sigourney (1791); the last was Paul Laurence Dunbar (1872), who died in 1906. The brief introductions present the particular poet's claim to fame in his or her own day, a biographical sketch, comments on major themes and forms, an estimate of the poet's importance today, a list of "Suggestions for Further Reading," and texts of the selected poems. An asterisk (*) following an entry in the "Suggestions for Further Reading" indicates that the item contains a useful bibliography of critical writings. Publication dates appear in parentheses at the end of each poem. When two dates appear, the first denotes periodical publication and the second identifies book publication; a single date signals book publication. In those instances where we have specified the year the poem was written, the second date indicates the year of first publication. Occasionally, dating becomes a problem; when that occurs, a question mark follows the date. We have kept our annotations to a minimum, noting mainly words, names, and events not available in a good desk dictionary.

Reading the poems in this anthology, along with those of Whitman and Dickinson (both available in inexpensive paper editions), will help students and teachers discover the "spirit of the age" and will perhaps suggest good reasons for reading these American poets again.

We thank heartily the following people at Southern Illinois University Press: Curtis Clark, who believed in our project; Tracey Moore, whose eagle eye saved us from embarrassments; and Carol A. Burns, who graciously ushered this book into the world. Finally, we thank Frances Coombs and Erika Lindemann for making the technical production of this book possible.

Introduction

This book reconstructs part of America's poetic landscape during the age of Whitman and Dickinson. The poets anthologized here speak to principal concerns of Whitman's and Dickinson's time; the poetry also tells of the age's taste in verse. That taste was largely not the taste of those who admire Whitman or Dickinson today.

The era's central historical events shaped much of the period's verse—the debate about slavery, the Civil War, social reforms, the westward expansion, the rise of the cities, women's struggles for suffrage, and the prospects for a reunited America emerging as a world power. Those killed in the Civil War numbered 620,000, more casualties than in all other American wars combined. Thousands more died of disease and wounds. Lincoln's assassination, a national tragedy, preoccupied dozens of poets. But these are not the only subjects that appear and reappear in the verse of Whitman's and Dickinson's contemporaries.

The Mexican War (1846–48) and the westward expansion before the Civil War elicited much verse. John Greenleaf Whittier and James Russell Lowell launched their poetic careers by opposing the Mexican War because they believed it was part of a Southern conspiracy to admit new slave states to the Union. Other poets also identified the Mexican War and the westward expansion with slavery. Henry David Thoreau spent a night in jail for failing to pay taxes to support the Mexican War, and Lowell fired off his *Biglow Papers (First Series)* condemning American involvement in that unpopular war. Whittier entered that controversy even earlier.

The Civil War and the debate over slavery reigned as the principal poetic topics before and during the war. Poets North and South debated these issues in inflammatory verses. Henry Timrod, Poet Laureate of the Confederacy, wrote his most moving verse about the birth of the Southern nation and about its "Lost Cause." Father Abram Ryan's "Conquered Banner" elegizes the flags in the dust of the defeated South. George Moses Horton, a slave and author of three volumes of poetry, recorded a black poet's anger and despair in "Division of an Estate" and other poems. Julia Ward Howe wrote the Union marching song, "The

Battle Hymn of the Republic," and many poets produced patriotic verses. Herman Melville's *Battle-Pieces* (1866) meditates upon the losses and waste of the war. Whitman wanted to capture the horror and heroism in his *Drum-Taps* (1865), but he feared no writer could get the war between a book's covers. He was probably right.

The Civil War's holocaust lingered long, but poets addressed other problems—problems that concerned Americans before the war and that grew more pressing afterwards.

One problem was the role of women in American society. The "Female Poets of America," to use the title of Rufus Griswold's 1849 anthology of their works, wrote voluminously about the problems of being a woman in a male-dominated American culture. After World War I, literary historians and critics—mainly advocates of the New Criticism—consigned these women's verses to the aesthetic slag-heap of sentimental claptrap. Recent critics have challenged that judgment. Women's poetry served a vital social function for those who wrote the poems and those who read them. Many women poets achieved celebrity and empowerment by publishing their work in a literary culture controlled by male editors and publishers. They also addressed subjects belonging to the "women's sphere": keeping a household, rearing children, dealing with men, and assuming responsibility for being moral guardians of their society, a role largely imposed by men and by a culture that viewed itself as Christian.

For years, literary historians and critics ignored the sizable body of work by American women poets, and as a result, students of American writing lost the sense of important issues these writers raised. But recently, such scholars as Cheryl Walker, Nina Baym, Emily Stipes Watts, and Alfred Habegger have re-examined works by women poets and fiction writers to discover their concerns about their identities as women. Those concerns included lack of suffrage, absence of economic opportunities, high infant mortality, risk of death in childbirth, temperance, and the consolation offered by religion, often a woman's only refuge in a society controlled by men. Though women were not the only ones to talk about temperance (Whitman published a temperance novel, *Franklin Evans*, in 1846), they often suffered most at the hands of drunken, abusive husbands and fathers. Only in the last decade or two have literary historians rediscovered these women's writings and what they say about the times.

Whitman and Dickinson wrote many poems about death—a subject that also preoccupied their contemporaries. For late twentieth-century readers, that preoccupation sometimes seems morbid, but the conditions of dying in the nineteenth century were quite different from those today. Most people in the nineteenth century died at home, not in hospitals or nursing homes. The "death watch," mainly the duty of women, brought death not only to the door, but inside the house. Its reality Whitman recorded in his *Drum-Taps* poems and Dickinson dealt with in dozens of poems—notably "Because I could not stop for Death—" (No. 712) and "I heard a Fly buzz—when I died—" (No. 465). Every poet in the century wrote on the subject because it was so central a part of living. And though much of the century's verse exhibits a Christian view of death and treats the subject sentimentally, it nevertheless expresses attitudes prevailing during the time.

From the earliest verses of Lydia Huntley Sigourney and William Cullen Bryant to those of Sidney Lanier and Lizette Woodworth Reese, nature inspired the century's poets. The vastness and variety of the American landscape evoked essentially three responses from the period's poets. Many poems simply picture the landscape or scene and record the poet's responses. Paul Hamilton Hayne wrote many pictorial poems; his "Aspects of the Pines" and "The Voice of the Pines" represent well this response to nature.

A second response to nature is the major one. In these poems, the poet reads nature allegorically, seeing in the natural event a correspondence to human events. Bryant's "To a Waterfowl" and Sigourney's "The Early Blue-Bird" typify this response to nature. Bryant sees the flight of the waterfowl as an allegory of life; at the end of his poem, he "tags" his meaning by pointing out the parallels between the lone waterfowl's flight and the journey through life. Sigourney likewise reads the coming of the early bluebird as an allegory of rebirth. She also "tags" her poem's meaning in the final stanza. In these poems, the poet not only records responses but also reads into the experience the meaning for the reader. Such nature poems abound in the period's verse.

Whitman and Dickinson excel at the third response to nature: the use of natural experience as a symbolic, not an allegorical, reading of nature. Whitman's sea and water imagery in "Song of Myself" and "Crossing Brooklyn Ferry" exemplify the symbolic representation of nature, as do Dickinson's poems about birds and bees. Whitman's and Dickinson's poems cross the line between allegory and symbol by suggesting multiple meanings for the natural experience. Comparing Dickinson's use of birds in "To hear an Oriole sing" (No. 526) and Bryant's use of the waterfowl or Sigourney's representation of the early bluebird illustrates dramatically the distinction between allegory and symbol in poetic language. Emerson's symbolic representation of nature in "The Snow-Storm" and Longfellow's allegorical rendering in "Hymn to the Night" also point graphically to this distinction.

Though the principal black authors of the period wrote primarily prose (Frederick Douglass, William Wells Brown, Charles W. Chesnutt, and W. E. B. Dubois), a number of poets published books of poems, and many more wrote verse that appeared in periodicals. Among the earliest was George Moses Horton, whose *Hope of Liberty* appeared in 1829 and whose last volume, *Naked Genius*, appeared in 1865. Horton's verse offers a version radically different from the moonlight-and-magnolia portrait of the South before the Civil War. Frances Ellen Watkins Harper and Henrietta Cordelia Ray, writing mainly after the war, recorded their private experience in their poems, but they also urged social reforms. Paul Laurence Dunbar's dialect poems earned him fame and a sizable readership at the end of the century. "We Wear the Mask" and "Sympathy" became key poems in critics' reassessments of African-American writing in this century. But it remained for the writers of the Harlem Renaissance in the 1920s to establish black authorship in the national consciousness.

Whitman's "To a Locomotive in Winter" and Dickinson's "I like to see it lap the Miles—" (No. 585) respond favorably to one of the era's concerns: rising industrialism. Melville in "A Utilitarian View of the *Monitor*'s Fight" and Emerson in his "Ode Inscribed to W. H. Channing" present somewhat different attitudes. Melville views the battle of the iron-clad *Monitor* and *Merrimack* as "plain mechanic power / Plied cogently in War now placed— / Where war belongs— / Among the trades and artisans" (lines 9–12). Such horror and impersonal power, he hopes, may make war "Less grand than Peace." Emerson chastizes the new industrialism and its accompanying greed for perverting people's values: "Things are in the saddle, / And ride mankind" (lines 50–51). In "Darius Greene and His Flying-Machine," John Townsend Trowbridge treats comically young Greene's Icarian ambitions to conquer gravity, but within a few years, the Wright brothers had done so.

That nostalgia for the lost, pastoral past fueled poets with subjects that appealed to popular audiences throughout the period. Poems like Longfellow's "My Lost Youth" and volumes like Whittier's *Snow-Bound* captured large readerships because they sought to recover in the collective consciousness memories of less complicated times. Published within a year after the Civil War's end, *Snow-Bound* earned Whittier ten thousand dollars, a huge sum for that day, and established him as one of the most-loved and read American poets. The appeal of James Whitcomb Riley's work evoked a similar response in Midwestern readers whose region was undergoing changes similar to those in the industrial Northeast a few decades earlier.

With the rise of industrialism and the cities during and after the Civil War came vast influxes of immigrants from China, Ireland, Russia, southern Europe, and Scandinavia. Added to these migrations were the large number of free blacks who moved to northern cities. Chinese immigrants came by the thousands to build the transcontinental railroad. Ben King, a white poet, captured the dialects and dreams of Negro migrants to Chicago; he also criticized the toll that poverty and misery took on people who moved to that stormy, bustling city in search of opportunity. Emma Lazarus, the daughter of Portuguese Jewish immigrants, wrote many poems about the hopes and fears of immigrants pouring into New York in the last quarter of the century. Lazarus's lines from "The New Colossus" adorn the base of the Statue of Liberty in New York Harbor: "Give me your tired, your poor, / Your huddled masses yearning to breathe free."

The westward expansion after the war captured the fancy of more fiction writers than poets, but the West also had its versifiers. Bret Harte in his "Truthful James" poems and Joaquin Miller in a voluminous body of verse recorded the western experience for the benefit of Eastern readers. Though Miller drew sympathetic and sometimes moving portraits of American Indians caught in the grasp of the white man's greed for land and wealth, both Harte and Miller romanticized the western experience as did the fiction writers of the period with their cardboard cowboys, Indians, and outlaws. In *Roughing It* (1872) and some short stories like "The Celebrated Jumping Frog of Calaveras County" (1865), Mark Twain captured the western experience more realistically, but Harte and Miller contributed to the early myths about the Wild West. They also enjoyed great popularity.

By the 1820s, American poets and prose writers discovered that they had a national past and folklore. In prose, James Fenimore Cooper created Natty Bumppo, the archetypal frontiersman who could not tolerate society's restrictions, and Washington Irving invented Ichabod Crane, the Connecticut Yankee schoolmaster who courted Katrina Van Tassel, a New York heiress of Dutch ancestry. But Longfellow and Whittier also tapped that lore for their verse. Whittier's "The Double-Headed Snake of Newbury" and Longfellow's *Song of Hiawatha* and *Evangeline* draw upon this Northern lore. In the South, William Gilmore Simms' novels and poems mined colonial Spanish and Revolutionary history. Poets filled their pages with events from the American past and from American folklore.

Whitman and Dickinson, more than most of their contempo-

rary poets, plumb the nature of consciousness and the uncon-
scious. Geoffrey Hartman has written that British romantic poets
wrote nature lyrics not to explore nature, but to examine the na-
ture of consciousness—how humans perceive, know, and cope
with an unknowable world. So did Emerson, Thoreau, Melville,
Hawthorne, and Poe. In poems such as "Crossing Brooklyn
Ferry" and "Out of the Cradle Endlessly Rocking," Whitman
tackles the question of the ways people know and intuit the un-
seen from the seen. Dickinson's "I felt a Funeral, in my Brain"
admirably typifies her obsession with consciousness. At the end
of that poem, the speaker says,

> And then a Plank in Reason, broke,
> And I dropped down, and down—
> And hit a World at every plunge,
> And Finished knowing—then—
>
> (No. 280, lines 17–20)

In radical ways, these writers anticipate twentieth-century preoc-
cupations with the nature of knowing and not knowing.

What separates Whitman and Dickinson from many of their
contemporaries is this concern with consciousness and the un-
conscious. Longfellow, Lowell, Whittier, and Holmes deal only
occasionally with this subject, and when they do, they usually
confirm the received ideas of their time about these mysterious
realms. Their visits to mysterious realms deal mainly with memo-
ries of the past, not explorations of consciousness and the uncon-
scious. Most of their contemporaries followed their lead.

But Poe pioneered in his poetry visits to dreamlands filled with
terror and mystery. His "The City in the Sea" creates a sur-
real landscape where light and air defy the laws of nature and
where "Death looks gigantically down" upon a ghastly, ghostly
world. "Dream-Land" recounts its speaker's visit by "a route ob-
scure and lonely" to "a wild weird clime that lieth, sublime, / Out
of SPACE—out of TIME" (lines 6–7). Emerson, Melville, and
Thoreau also journey to this place out of "time" and out of
"space," but for the most part, poets of the period ignored or
simply nibbled around the edges of this world.

Another subject central to Whitman and Dickinson—the role
of the poet in a democratic society—also commanded the atten-
tion of other writers. In his prefaces and in his poems, Whitman
advocated the role of poet-prophet who would inspire and lead
the people to new perceptions of themselves and the nobleness of
the democratic experiment in self-government. In her letters and
in dozens of poems about poetry, Dickinson measured poets and
poems by how they affected her as a reader, by how much what
she called "slant" truth a poem told (though she knew no poem

carried all the truth), and by how much a poem made readers perceive familiar things and events with new eyes.

Most poets wrote on this subject. In "Merlin," "Uriel," and "The Snow-Storm," Emerson contemplated the poet's mission, believing that the true bard scanned the skies and mounted "to paradise / By the stairway of surprise" (lines 37–38). That stairway led ultimately to man's awareness of his divinity. In "Israfel," Poe defined what he believed to be the poet's major job: to recover something of the heavenly music lost before man's fall. "To Helen" demonstrates how such poetry and beauty would elevate the reader's or perceiver's soul. George Moses Horton said in "The Art of a Poet" that "A bard must traverse o'er the world, / Where things concealed must rise unfurled, / And tread the foot of yore" (lines 19–21). He seems here to ask a poem to recover what William Faulkner called the "old verities."

Sexuality, usually a taboo topic in this era, received some attention from these poets. But unlike Whitman, who talked boldly about sexuality, most poets drew a genteel curtain between themselves and the subject. Dickinson, whom Thomas Wentworth Higginson described as a "virgin recluse," said more on this subject than Higginson dreamed. Modern readers have discovered in such poems as "Wild Nights—Wild Nights!" (No. 249), "Come slowly Eden" (No. 211), and "I started Early—took my Dog" (No. 520) a forthright, psychologically perceptive treatment of sexuality. Several poets included here—notably Emma Lazarus and Edith Wharton, who published a volume of poems when she was only sixteen—write of sexuality in ways similar to Whitman and Dickinson.

This brief catalog only hints at the topics Whitman's and Dickinson's contemporaries addressed. Like all poets in all times, they also wrote of love and marriage, of the relation of self to society, of human comedies and tragedies.

Though historical events ignited the era's poets, competing poetic theories dictated even more radically the themes and forms of their verse. Some writers like Emerson, Poe, Whitman, Lanier, and Dickinson articulated their theories in polished prose and in their poetry; other theories, less defined but nevertheless present in the period, carried even more weight in the poets' thinking about what a poem should be. Elements of these theories often overlap, but eight or nine identifiable notions about poetry account for the form and content of the era's poems.

Longfellow defined for most of his contemporaries what a poem should be and do. For Longfellow and his sizable number of followers, a poem should edify and inspire; he thus committed himself to a didactic poetry whose principal purpose was to inculcate a moral and to offer hope in a troublesome world. Like many of his contemporaries, Longfellow often tagged his poems so that readers would not miss his point. His lines from "The Day Is Done" state succinctly this view:

> Read from some humbler poet,
>   Whose songs gushed from his heart,
> As showers from the clouds of summer,
>   Or tears from the eyelids start;
>
> Who, through long days of labor,
>   And nights devoid of ease,
> Still heard in his soul the music
>   Of wonderful melodies.
>
> Such songs have power to quiet
>   The restless pulse of care
> And come like the benediction
>   That follows after prayer.
>
> (lines 25–36)

Longfellow's notion that poems should edify their readers is what Poe had in mind when he indicted "the heresy of *The Didactic*" in his essay, "The Poetic Principle" (1848, 1850). But Longfellow's view of poetry prevailed for most nineteenth-century poets and determined the kind of verse they wrote.

Many of the so-called sentimental, domestic poets—often women—espoused a theory akin to Longfellow's belief that a poem should edify, but with a different twist. In *The Nightingale's Burden: Women Poets and American Culture Before 1900*, Cheryl Walker has argued persuasively that many women poets filled their work with images of imprisoned birds longing to fly free. Walker reads these images as expressing the aspirations of women in a society ruled by men. These poems also often served for women the vital social function of reaffirming Christian values and of offering consolation and quiet resignation for their conditions. Lydia Huntley Sigourney, Alice Cary, and Phoebe Cary wrote many poems whose purpose was to counsel consolation and resignation. They also wrote other kinds of poems. Phoebe Cary's parodies of Longfellow's "The Day Is Done" and of Poe's "Annabel Lee" show the wit and humor often present in women's verse. But much domestic, sentimental poetry arose from a theory akin to Longfellow's didacticism.

In his "Lectures on Poetry" (1826), Bryant defined poetry not as an "imitative art," but as a "suggestive art" and compared the poet's goals with the painter's. Bryant believed that the painter's job was not to represent the scene photographically (though he did not use that word), but to suggest through the "indefiniteness" of language a "something" beyond the scene or event portrayed. He approached a symbolic view of poetry, but he seldom practiced his theory in his poems. More often he pointed specifically to his poem's "suggestiveness" by stating or tagging his meaning at the end. But in "The Prairies" and a few other poems, Bryant successfully followed his theory and in doing so wrote his best verse.

Poe wrote for his century a minority report about what a poem should be. In "The Philosophy of Composition," "The Poetic Principle," and dozens of reviews, he pummeled "the heresy of *The Didactic*" and theorized about how a poet creates a pure poem. Poe defined a poem as "*The Rhythmical Creation of Beauty*" whose effect on the reader should be a "pleasurable elevation, or excitement, *of the soul*" ("The Poetic Principle"). For him, the ideal poem was about one hundred lines long, attended to the music of language, had a melancholy tone, strove for indefiniteness rather than definiteness, and dealt with death, especially the death of a beautiful woman. He associated the death of a beautiful woman symbolically with the loss of Beauty and Eden ("The Philosophy of Composition"). Poe believed that a poem should exist for its own sake as a work of art rather than as moral teaching. He did not divorce art from morality, but he insisted that the grounds for judging a poem should be aesthetic rather than moral. He also emphasized the poet's role as creator of the poem rather than as one inspired by nature or by some other agency. Though Poe's theory never really caught on in his century, the New Criticism of the twentieth century has emphasized what he valued in a fine poem.

Whittier and Lowell represent well the theory that poetry's purpose is to promote social change by rousing readers to act against injustice. Whittier wrote that he "set a higher value on my name as appended to the Anti-Slavery Declaration of 1833 than on the title-page of any book." Lowell discerned one of his flaws as a poet in *A Fable for Critics* (1848). There he wrote of himself: "The top of the hill [Parnassus] he will ne'er come nigh reaching / Till he learns the distinction 'twixt singing and preaching" (lines 240–41). Whittier and Lowell wrote other kinds of poetry, but they also exemplify their era's impulse to view poetry's purpose as not only changing people's minds but also telling them how to act.

In his theory, Emerson believed poetry should be a "metre-making argument" and "organic," that its form should arise from the ideas and feelings the poet wished to express. "For it is not metres," he wrote in an essay, "but a metre-making argument that makes a poem,—a thought so passionate and alive that like the spirit of a plant or an animal it has an architecture of its own, and adorns nature with a new thing" ("The Poet," 1844). In

Emerson's organic theory, the poem's idea and form arise almost simultaneously; true poets do not allow verse and stanzaic conventions to control their work. They discover or invent new forms appropriate for the meaning they wish to convey. Simply filling old poetic forms with ideas from his own time was for Emerson slavish imitation and a way of committing artistic suicide.

Emerson's commitment to American democracy and to his belief that the poet had a special mission in such a society led him to look for a poet who best expressed American character and aspirations. Because true poets were seers (and see-ers) endowed with special insights, Emerson conceived of democratic poets as "liberating gods" who plumbed the national collective consciousness and who inspired and enlightened their countrymen. As namers and language-makers, Emerson's poets expressed what most Americans knew but could not put into their own words. Along with Whitman, Emerson insisted that America was a poem and that the national experience should provide grist for the American poet's mill. Sing your "own times and social circumstances," Emerson said in "The Poet." Emerson believed he had discovered that poet when he read the first edition of *Leaves of Grass* in 1855.

In *The Science of English Verse* (1880), Sidney Lanier articulated his theory that poetry was music. Though many of the period's writers compared poetry with music (Whitman, Poe, and Dickinson among them), Lanier carried his comparison far beyond that of his contemporaries. A trained musician and composer, he compared in detail the acoustics of language and music. Believing that the principal difference between the two was the use of "musical sounds" as opposed to "spoken words," Lanier noted the similarities in rhythm, duration, pitch, tone color, timbre, and rhyme. In some 150 pages, Lanier presented examples of English and American verse with musical annotations. Though critics in his day and ours have thought that Lanier strained his analogy to the breaking point, he practiced his theory successfully in such poems as "The Symphony," "Song of the Chattahoochee" and "The Marshes of Glynn." He also anticipated the technical interest in poetic acoustics by many poets of our time.

Another group of poets from the period looked upon their job as primarily providing entertainment. Though not many poets articulated this theory, a good many practiced it, among them Bret Harte and James Whitcomb Riley. These poets often wrote dialect poems about the quaintness of newly arrived Americans or of Americans from a particular region of the country. Much of the century's light verse, often appearing in newspapers, strove mainly to amuse and entertain. Most poets in the period wrote some light verse.

Emily Dickinson measured a poem by how it affected her, and in doing so, she developed in her letters and in her poems an "affective" theory of poetry. She told Thomas Wentworth Higginson, "If I read a book [and] it makes my whole body so cold that no fire can ever warm me, I know *that* is poetry. If I feel physically as if the top of my head were taken off, I know *that* is poetry. These are the only ways I know it. Is there any other way" (Letter from T. W. Higginson to his wife, 16 August 1870, in *Emily Dickinson: Selected Letters*, ed. Thomas H. Johnson [Cambridge: Belknap Press of Harvard UP, 1986] 208). Dickinson's poetry "Distills amazing sense / From ordinary Meanings—" (No. 448, lines 2–3). Affecting poets surprise readers by making the ordinary extraordinary and new through language:

> From the familiar species
> That perished by the Door—
> We wonder it was not Ourselves
> Arrested it—before—
>
> (No. 448, lines 5–8)

She associated poetry with possibility:

> I dwell in Possibility—
> A fairer House than Prose—
> More numerous of Windows—
> Superior—for Doors—
>
> (No. 657, lines 1–4)

The poet who succeeds in fulfilling Dickinson's expectations allows herself and her readers "The spreading wide my narrow Hands / To gather Paradise—" (No. 657, lines 11–12). Gary Lee Stonum in *The Dickinson Sublime* (Madison: U of Wisconsin P, 1990) describes Dickinson's notions about the relationship between author and reader thus: "According to Dickinson's affective understanding of poetry, moreover, the assertiveness of a writer's style plays a crucial role in provoking the reader's response. Beyond any momentary aggrandizement of the authorial self, it contributes centrally to a network of textual relations in which the author's part is never finally that of master" (23). Emily Dickinson entices her readers toward the sublime, says Stonum, by teasing, riddling, suggesting, and hesitantly nudging them toward truths told slantly. Several theorists of the era described "affective theories" of poetry, but none so eloquently as Dickinson.

The theories briefly summarized here shaped the way Whitman's and Dickinson's contemporaries thought about their art.

Many of those theories died with their authors, but those of Whitman, Dickinson, Poe, and Emerson still influence poets today. The theories of the so-called Fireside Poets or Schoolroom Poets (Longfellow, Whittier, Lowell, and Holmes) failed to fascinate the next generation of American poets—T. S. Eliot, Wallace Stevens, Amy Lowell, Edwin Arlington Robinson, Robert Frost, Ezra Pound. These new poets defined poetry in ways that would have puzzled most of Whitman's and Dickinson's contemporaries.

When Harriet Monroe founded *Poetry Magazine* in 1912 and Margaret Anderson began her *Little Review* in 1914, they entombed many nineteenth-century poets and their poetic theories. For Monroe, Anderson, and their contemporaries, Longfellow, Lowell, Whittier, and Holmes would not speak for the new century's poets. Whitman and Dickinson became the champions of the new generation; these poets forged new theories and wrote poems that often puzzled readers who admired the Fireside Poets. Monroe and Anderson published in their magazines the poems of Eliot, Stevens, Pound, Amy Lowell, Frost, and William Carlos Williams. The old era had ended, and the new one was aborning.

But until long after World War I, most Americans got their first taste of poetry by reading the writers included in this anthology. Rediscovering these poets will, we hope, be adventurous, informative, and rewarding—and may often surprise. These poems show that Whitman's and Dickinson's contemporaries felt the fire of their time and often translated that fire into memorable language that still moves and delights.

WHITMAN'S &
DICKINSON'S
CONTEMPORARIES

Lydia Huntley Sigourney
1791–1865

As the first and most popular
woman poet of the early nineteenth century, Lydia Huntley
Sigourney had, in her time, the single greatest influence on the
craft of women poets and their image as artists. Critics later rele-
gated her verse to the file of the "domestic sublime," along with
other work deemed sentimental, moralistic, and excessively ma-
ternal. Sigourney's image of the nurturing mother had a nostal-
gic appeal, but she also looked forward by showing that a
woman's province extended beyond crib and hearth to public
concerns. Her use of familiar verse forms created a common
ground for her readers, primarily women, while her poetry gave
them new ways of viewing themselves as participants in a democ-
racy.

Sigourney was born 1 September 1791 in Norwich, Connecti-
cut. Although the daughter of a poor gardener—she knew gen-
teel poverty as did many early nineteenth-century women po-
ets—Sigourney received an education and introduction to poetry
from the wife of her father's employer. Developing an early in-
terest in history, she offered a traditional male curriculum at a
Hartford women's school that she began in 1814 and ran for four
years. Her first book, *Moral Pieces, in Prose and Verse* (1815), came
out under her name; thereafter, she published anonymously at her
husband's insistence until his banking and hardware business de-
clined. Taking over the family finances, Sigourney began pub-
lishing in her own name again in 1833. Her 1834 *Poems*, cited by
Emily Stipes Watts as her best collection, had many reprintings.

Her drive for financial security in later life resulted in poems
that Watts has called "padded, pedantic, and prudish" (84).
While Sigourney fulfilled the stereotype of the profuse, amateur-
ish woman writer, she also earned the stature of a serious artist.
In 1849, her *Illustrated Poems* appeared in a series that included
Longfellow and Bryant. Writing for a half century, Sigourney
produced fifty-six volumes of poetry and prose and some two
thousand articles that made her ubiquitous in the magazines of
the day. She died on 10 June 1865 in Hartford, Connecticut, one
of the most well-known writers in America.

The subsequent notoriety of Sigourney's "funereal" poetry

obscured the range and function of her verse, say recent scholars. Sigourney's elegies, Watts notes, have more practical and realistic concerns than many of those written by her English and American contemporaries. Poems like "Death of an Infant" speak to the frequent nineteenth-century experience of infant mortality. Sigourney herself lost three children at birth. Rather than direct us to Bryant's philosophical view of death or to Whitman's embrace of the "low and delicious word death," Sigourney dwells in "Hebrew Dirge" on death's isolating effect on the living.

Nina Baym indicates that Sigourney's poems on death are, in fact, public, not private, forms; they offer "greeting card" formulas that meet the needs of a wide audience (388–89). The public dimension of Sigourney's work shows even more abundantly in her poetry on family life, nature, history, native Americans, and the woman author. "To a Shred of Linen" reveals her sensitivity to the conflict between motherhood and writing; the "Monody on Mrs. Hemans" considers the theme of "secret sorrow" that Cheryl Walker has found common to women poets of the time.

Called the "American Hemans," Sigourney, no doubt, was inspired by this popular English romantic writer, but she borrowed freely from many sources for her forms. Her "Pocahontas," written in a modifed Spenserian stanza, was the only epic undertaken by an American woman writer in her day. She also employed heroic couplets and tetrameter quatrains, and readers called her a "female Milton" for her use of blank verse. Sigourney wrote frequently in ballad stanzas, too, but never altered the form as did Dickinson.

Her facility with verse conventions—an expectation, not an objection, in the nineteenth century—helped her gain an unprecedented popularity as a woman poet. The value she gave to women's experience, not just in the domestic sphere, but in the wider contexts of nature, politics, and history, continues to interest students of women's issues and nineteenth-century American literary culture.

—*Wilson Somerville*

Suggestions for Further Reading

Baym, Nina. "Reinventing Lydia Sigourney." *American Literature* 62 (1990): 385–404.
Bowles, Dorothy A. "Lydia H. Sigourney." *American Magazine Journalists, 1741–1850*. Vol. 73 of *Dictionary of Literary Biography*. Ed. Sam G. Riley. Detroit: Gale, 1978. 264–74.
Haight, Gordon Sherman. *Mrs. Sigourney: The Sweet Singer of Hartford*. New Haven: Yale UP, 1930.

Walker, Cheryl. *The Nightingale's Burden: Women Poets and American Culture Before 1900.* Bloomington: Indiana UP, 1982.*

Watts, Emily Stipes. *The Poetry of American Women from 1632 to 1945.* Austin: U of Texas P, 1977.

TEXTS
Poems. 1827.
Poems. 1834.
Zinzendorff and Other Poems. 1835.
Pocahontas, and Other Poems. 1841.
Select Poems. 1845.

ꝺⲭⲉ

Death of an Infant[1]

Death found strange beauty on that polish'd brow,
And dash'd it out. There was a tint of rose
On cheek and lip. He touch'd the veins with ice,
And the rose faded.
            Forth from those blue eyes
There spake a wishful tenderness, a doubt
Whether to grieve or to sleep, which innocence
Alone may wear. With ruthless haste he bound
The silken fringes of those curtaining lids
For ever.
            There had been a murmuring sound
With which the babe would claim its mother's ear,   10
Charming her even to tears. The spoiler set
The seal of silence.
            But there beam'd a smile,
So fix'd, so holy, from that cherub brow,
Death gazed, and left it there. He dared not steal
The signet-ring of heaven.

                              (written 1824, 1827)

---

1. This poem appeared by mistake in an American edition of Felicia Hemans' work. See the note on authorship in Sigourney's London edition of *Pocahontas, and Other Poems* (1841) 71.

Hebrew Dirge

"Mourn for the *living*, and not for the *dead*."
                                        —Hebrew Dirge

I saw an infant, marble cold,
  Borne from the pillowing breast,
And in the shroud's embracing fold
  Laid down to dreamless rest;
And moved with bitterness I sighed,
  Not for the babe that slept,
But for the mother at its side,
  Whose soul in anguish wept.

They bare a coffin to its place,
  I asked them who was there?   10
And they replied "a form of grace,
  The fairest of the fair."
But for that blest one do ye moan,
  Whose angel-wing is spread?
No, for the lover pale and lone,
  His heart is with the dead.

I wandered to a new-made grave,
  And there a matron lay,
The love of Him who died to save,
  Had been her spirit's stay,   20
Yet sobs burst forth of torturing pain;
  Wail ye for her who died?
No, for that timid, infant train
  Who roam without a guide.

I murmur not for those who die,
  Who rise to glory's sphere,
I deem the tenants of the sky
  Need not our mortal tear,
Our woe seems arrogant and vain,
  Perchance it moves their scorn,   30
As if the slave beneath his chain,
  Deplored the princely born.

We live to meet a thousand foes,
  We shrink with bleeding breast,
Why shall we weakly mourn for those
  Who dwell in perfect rest?

Bound for a few sad, fleeting years
  A thorn-clad path to tread,
Oh! for the *living* spare those tears
  Ye lavish on the *dead*.

40
(1834)

The Indian's Welcome to the Pilgrim Fathers

Above them spread a stranger sky;
  Around, the sterile plain;
The rock-bound coast rose frowning nigh;
  Beyond,—the wrathful main:
Chill remnants of the wintry snow
  Still chok'd the encumbered soil,
Yet forth those Pilgrim Fathers go
  To mark their future toil.

'Mid yonder vale their corn must rise
  In Summer's ripening pride,   10
And there the church-spire woo the skies
  Its sister-school beside.
Perchance 'mid England's velvet green
  Some tender thought repos'd,
Though nought upon their stoic mien
  Such soft regret disclos'd.

When sudden from the forest wide
  A red-browed chieftain came,
With towering form, and haughty stride,
  And eye like kindling flame: 20
No wrath he breath'd, no conflict sought,
  To no dark ambush drew,
But simply *to the Old World brought*
  The welcome of the New.

That *welcome* was a blast and ban
  Upon thy race unborn.
Was there no seer, thou fated Man!
  Thy lavish zeal to warn?
Thou in thy fearless faith didst hail
  A weak, invading band,   30
But who shall heed thy children's wail
  Swept from their native land?

Lydia Huntley Sigourney

5

Thou gav'st the riches of thy streams,
    The lordship o'er thy waves,
The region of thine infant dreams
    And of thy fathers' graves,
But who to yon proud mansions piled
    With wealth of earth and sea,
Poor outcast from thy forest wild,
    Say, who shall welcome thee?   40

                                                        (1835)

The Early Blue-Bird[2]

Blue-Bird! on yon leafless tree,
Dost thou carol thus to me,
"Spring is coming! Spring is here?"
Says't thou so, my birdie dear?
What is that, in misty shroud,
Stealing from the darken'd cloud?
Lo! the snow-flakes' gathering mound
Settles o'er the whiten'd ground,
Yet thou singest, blithe and clear,
"Spring is coming! Spring is here!"   10

Strik'st thou not too bold a strain?
Winds are piping o'er the plain;
Clouds are sweeping o'er the sky
With a black and threatening eye;
Urchins, by the frozen rill,
Wrap their mantles closer still;
Yon poor man, with doublet old,
Doth he shiver at the cold?
Hath he not a nose of blue?
Tell me birdling, tell me true.   20

Spring's a maid of mirth and glee,
Rosy wreaths, and revelry:
Hast thou woo'd some winged love
To a nest in verdant grove?
Sung to her of greenwood bower,

_____

2. A word about the publication of poems listed with an 1841 date: "The Early Blue-Bird" appeared in both the New York and London editions of *Pocahontas, and Other Poems*; "Monody on Mrs. Hemans" appeared only in the New York edition.

Lydia Huntley Sigourney

Sunny skies that never lower?
Lured her with thy promise fair
Of a lot that knows no care?
Prythee, bird, in coat of blue,
Though a lover, tell her true.   30

Ask her if, when storms are long,
She can sing a cheerful song?
When the rude winds rock the tree,
If she'll closer cling to thee?
Then the blasts that sweep the sky,
Unappall'd shall pass thee by;
Though thy curtain'd chamber show
Siftings of untimely snow,
Warm and glad thy heart shall be,
Love shall make it Spring for thee.   40
                                                            (1841)

Monody on Mrs. Hemans[3]

Nature doth mourn for thee. There comes a voice
From her far solitudes, as though the winds
Murmured low dirges, or the waves complain'd,
Even the meek plant, that never sang before,
Save one brief requiem, when its blossoms fell,
Seems through its drooping leaves to sigh for thee,
As for a florist dead. The ivy wreathed
Round the gray turrets of a buried race,
And the proud palm-trees, that like princes rear
Their diadems 'neath Asia's sultry sky,   10
Blend with their ancient lore thy hallowed name.

Thy music, like baptismal dew, did make
Whate'er it touched more holy. The pure shell,
Pressing its pearly lips to ocean's floor,
The cloister'd chambers where the sea-gods sleep,
And the unfathom'd, melancholy main,
Lament for thee, through all the sounding deeps.

---

3. Felicia Hemans (1793–1835), an English romantic writer, was very popular
in America in her lifetime. This poem is a somewhat revised version of "Felicia
Hemans," written in 1835 and published in *Zinzendorff and Other Poems* (1835).

Hark! from sky piercing Himmaleh, to where
Snowdon doth wear his coronet of cloud,
From the scath'd pine-tree, near the red-man's hut,   20
To where the everlasting banian builds
Its vast columnar temple, comes a wail
For her who o'er the dim cathedral's arch,
The quivering sunbeam on the cottage wall,
Or the sere desert, pour'd the lofty chant
And ritual of the muse: who found the link
That joins mute nature to ethereal mind,
And made that link a melody.

                                    The vales
Of glorious Albion heard thy tuneful fame,
And those green cliffs, where erst the Cambrian bards   30
Swept their indignant lyres, exulting tell
How oft thy fairy foot in childhood climb'd
Their, rude romantic heights.⁴ Yet was the couch
Of thy last slumber in yon verdant isle,
Of song, and eloquence, and ardent soul,
Which, loved of lavish skies, though bann'd by fate,
Seem'd as a type of thine own varied lot,
The crown'd of genius, and the child of wo.
For at thy breast the ever-pointed thorn
Did girt itself in secret, mid the gush   40
Of such unstain'd, sublime, impassion'd song,
That angels, posing on some silver cloud,
Might listen mid the errands of the skies,
And linger all unblamed.

                                    How tenderly
Doth Nature draw her curtain round thy rest,
And, like a nurse, with finger on her lip,
Watch that no step disturb thee, and no hand
Profane thy sacred harp. Methinks she waits
Thy waking, as some cheated mother hangs
O'er the pale babe, whose spirit death hath stolen,   50
And laid it, dreaming, on the lap of Heaven.
Said we that thou art dead? We dare not. No.
For every mountain, stream, or shady dell
Where thy rich echoes linger, claim thee still,

---

4. Wales, the domain of the "Cambrian bards," was the early home of Mrs.
Hemans. Sigourney refers to the "prompting influences of romantic and sublime
scenery" in the Welsh landscape in her memoir of Mrs. Hemans. See *The Poetical
Works of Felicia Hemans, with a Memoir, by Mrs. L. H. Sigourney* (Boston:
Phillips, Sampson, 1853) 29.

Their own undying one. To thee was known
Alike the language of the fragile flower
And of the burning stars. God taught it thee.
So, from thy living intercourse with man,
Thou shalt not pass, until the weary earth
Drops her last gem into the doomsday flame.   60
Thou hast but taken thy seat with that bless'd choir,
Whose harmonies thy spirit learn'd so well
Through this low, darken'd casement, and so long
Interpreted for us.

                     Why should we say
Farewell to thee, since every unborn age
Shall mix thee with its household charities?
The hoary sire shall bow his deafen'd ear,
And greet thy sweet words with his benison;
The mother shrine thee as a vestal flame
In the lone temple of her sanctity;   70
And the young child who takes thee by the hand,
Shall travel with a surer step to Heaven.

                           (1841)

To a Shred of Linen

Would they swept cleaner!—
                   Here's a littering shred
Of linen left behind—a vile reproach
To all good housewifery. Right glad am I,
That no neat lady, train'd in ancient times
Of pudding-making, and of sampler-work,
And speckless sanctity of household care,
Hath happened here, to spy thee. She, no doubt,
Keen looking through her spectacles, would say,
"*This comes of reading books:*"—or some spruce beau,
Essenc'd and lily-handed, had he chanc'd   10
To scan thy slight superfices, 'twould be
"*This comes of writing poetry.*"—Well—well—
Come forth—offender!—hast thou aught to say?
Canst thou by merry thought, or quaint conceit,
Repay this risk, that I have run for thee?
—Begin at alpha, and resolve thyself
Into thine elements. I see thee stalk
And bright, blue flower of flax, which erst o'erspread
That fertile land, where mighty Moses stretch'd

His rod miraculous.[5] I see thy bloom
Tinging, too scantly, these New England vales.
But, lo! the sturdy farmer lifts his flail,
To crush thy bones unpitying, and his wife
With 'kerchief'd head, and eyes brimful of dust,
Thy fibrous nerves, with hatchel-tooth divides.
—I hear a voice of music—and behold!
The ruddy damsel singeth at her wheel,
While by her side the rustic lover sits.
Perchance, his shrewd eye secretly doth count
The mass of skeins, which, hanging on the wall,   30
Increaseth day by day. Perchance his thought,
(For men have deeper minds than women—sure!)
Is calculating what a thrifty wife
The maid will make; and how his dairy shelves
Shall groan beneath the weight of golden cheese,
Made by her dextrous hand, while many a keg
And pot of butter, to the market borne,
May, transmigrated, on his back appear,
In new thanksgiving coats.
                              Fain would I ask,
Mine own New England, for thy once loved wheel,   40
By sofa and piano quite displac'd.
Why dost thou banish from thy parlor-hearth
That old Hygeian harp, whose magic rul'd
Dyspepsia, as the minstrel-shepherd's skill
Exorcis'd Saul's ennui?[6] There was no need,
In those good times, of callisthenics, sure,
And there was less of gadding, and far more
Of home-born, heart-felt comfort, rooted strong
In industry, and bearing such rare fruit,
As wealth might never purchase.
                              But come back,   50
Thou shred of linen. I did let thee drop,
In my harangue, as wiser ones have lost
The thread of their discourse. What was thy lot
When the rough battery of the loom had stretch'd
And knit thy sinews, and the chemist sun
Thy brown complexion bleach'd?
                              Methinks I scan
Some idiosyncrasy, that marks thee out
A defunct pillow-case.—Did the trim guest,

---

5. Exodus 9:31 records that the plague of hail, which Moses called down from
Yahweh, destroyed Egypt's flax crop.

6. Hygeia was the Greek goddess of health. David's harp playing soothed
Saul's evil spirit (1 Samuel 16:23).

Lydia Huntley Sigourney

To the best chamber usher'd, e'er admire
The snowy whiteness of thy freshen'd youth   60
Feeding thy vanity? or some sweet babe
Pour its pure dream of innocence on thee?
Say, hast thou listen'd to the sick one's moan,
When there was none to comfort?—or shrunk back
From the dire tossings of the proud man's brow?
Or gather'd from young beauty's restless sigh
A tale of untold love?
                              Still, close and mute!—
Wilt tell no secrets, ha?—Well, then, go down,
With all thy churl-kept hoard of curious lore,
In majesty and mystery, go down   70
Into the paper mill, and from its jaws,
Stainless and smooth, emerge.—Happy shall be
The renovation, if on thy fair page
Wisdom and truth, their hallow'd lineaments
Trace for posterity. So shall thine end
Be better than thy birth, and worthier bard
Thine apotheosis immortalise.

                                        (1845)

William Cullen Bryant
1794–1878

Nineteenth-century American readers regarded William Cullen Bryant as one of their leading citizens and best poets. Known to recent generations as one of the Fireside Poets, Bryant wrote some of the first distinctively American poetry. As one of our earliest literary critics, he helped define an American poetics. Throughout his long career as a respected newspaper editor, he consistently championed liberal causes and social reform.

Bryant was born on 3 November 1794, in Cummington, an isolated frontier town in western Massachusetts. He began reading and writing at an early age, entering Williams College in 1810 as a sophomore; he left after one year, hoping to transfer to Yale. Because he lacked tuition money, Bryant read law instead, gaining admission to the bar before his twenty-first birthday in 1815. Before he began practicing law, Bryant wrote regularly, and beginning with his father's submission of "Thanatopsis" for publication in 1817, Bryant published regularly in leading periodicals for the next several years. In 1821, Bryant married Frances Fairchild and saw eight of his pieces, including the last revision of "Thanatopsis," published as *Poems of William Cullen Bryant.*

He moved his family to New York in 1825 and struggled in vain to make the *New York Review and Atheneum Magazine* a success. During his editorship of this failing magazine in 1825 and 1826, Bryant delivered four "Lectures on Poetry" to the New York Atheneum Society, offering one of the first American definitions of the nature of poetry. In 1832, Bryant collected for the first time most of his work in *Poems*; the publication was a success, selling 90 percent of its first printing within six months. Over the next four decades, his collected poems were reprinted numerous times, and with each successive printing until his death, he added new poems.

In 1827, Bryant began working for the *New York Evening Post,* and by 1829, he was editor-in-chief, a position he held until his death. In the 1840s and 1850s, he devoted his energies to the newspaper, exerting increasing influence on national politics. A long-time opponent of slavery, Bryant was one of the founders of the Republican Party in 1855, and he helped elect Lincoln in 1860. As involved as he was politically, he continued to write poetry. During the Civil War, when his newspaper was growing dramatically, Bryant prepared for publication a volume of his recent work, *Thirty Poems* (1864).

In his later years, Bryant became a national symbol because of his contribution to the American identity through his work as poet, journalist, and political activist. In 1876, he supervised the final edition of his collected poetry, *Poetical Works of William Cullen Bryant*. Bryant died on 12 June 1878 at the age of eighty-three; he is buried next to his wife in Roslyn, New York.

Throughout his career, Bryant explored the themes of death and human progress that he had first discovered in "Thanatopsis," "To a Waterfowl," and "The Prairies." In his explorations of both themes, he turned to nature for setting and subject (McLean 17, 48). Critics have characterized Bryant as the first American poet who used native scenes and native subjects to produce poetry of universal significance. Walt Whitman's description of Bryant in *Specimen Days* exemplifies that assessment:

> [P]ulsing the first interior verse—throbs of a mighty world—
> bard of the river and wood, ever conveying a taste of the open
> air, with scents as from hay fields, grapes, birch-borders . . .
> beginning and ending his long career with chants of death,
> with here and there through all, poems or passages of po-
> ems, touching the highest universal truths, enthusiasms, du-
> ties. (109)

Whitman recognized that Bryant's creative powers endured through the years. Though his earlier works earned him the most attention, Bryant's later poetry reflects the vision and the voice of a mature poet, not a fading voice from the past.

His sensitive rendering of the natural scene in "The Flood of Years" compares favorably with his earlier, more widely read poems. Instead of betraying "his inability to respond to the living forces of nature" as McLean and others argue (20), his later poems reflect how he responds differently, how the experiences of the years changed his creative imagination and his poetic vision. Bryant records his reconciliation with death in "The Flood of Years," revealing a poet who has benefited from his continued contemplation of that subject. Building on his earlier meditations in "To a Waterfowl" and "The Prairies," Bryant in later poems such as "The Death of Lincoln" and "The Flood of Years" continued to explore the inevitability and the cost of progress, a theme so inextricably a part of the American experiences of expansion, industrialization, and war.

Employing a variety of poetic forms, Bryant experimented with rhyme schemes and with different stanza arrangements. He masters the natural rhythms of blank verse in "Thanatopsis" and "The Prairies," and he demonstrates that same mastery in his later "The Flood of Years." His comfort with various rhyme schemes is evident in the rhymed quatrains of "To a Waterfowl" and "The Death of Lincoln." In all his work, he displays control and discipline, but not at the expense of emotion and imagination. In "The Poet," he warns against the "cold rhymer" who produces a "smooth array of phrase, / Artfully sought and ordered"; instead, he argues for a poet who will "Seize the great thought," invest the work with "feelings of calm power and mighty sweep," and "write / The words inspired by wonder and delight" (lines 13–14, 23, 35, 41–42).

Bryant's reputation as a poet has suffered most from the charge that he makes explicit the message or moral of his poems, violating a fundamental criterion of the New Criticism's definition of good poetry. However, as scholars have expanded their critical gaze, they have valued Bryant's poetry more fully. His current reputation rests solidly on his early work, but his later poems deserve reconsideration. They reflect both aspects of the man: the private, philosophic poet of nature and speculation and the public, political poet questioning the nation's values and future. Whitman and Dickinson benefited from Bryant's early work establishing American poetry in an American context. But Bryant continued to create while they were creating. While they forged indisputably new artistic constructions, he was fashioning further the work he had begun earlier. He deserves to be read in that context.

—*Glenn Blalock*

Suggestions for Further Reading

Brodwin, Stanley, Michael D'Innocenzo, and Joseph G. Astman, eds. *William Cullen Bryant and His America: Centennial Conference Proceedings, 1878–1978*. New York: AMS, 1983.

McLean, Albert E. *William Cullen Bryant*. Updated ed. Boston: Twayne, 1989.*

Rocks, James E. "William Cullen Bryant." *Fifteen American Authors Before 1900: Bibliographic Essays on Research and Criticism*. Ed. Earl N. Harbert and Robert A. Rees. Rev. ed. Madison: U of Wisconsin P, 1984. 55–79.*

Whitman, Walt. *Specimen Days*. New York: NAL, 1961.

TEXT
Poetical Works of William Cullen Bryant. 1876.

꙳

Thanatopsis

To him who in the love of Nature holds
Communion with her visible forms, she speaks
A various language; for his gayer hours
She has a voice of gladness, and a smile
And eloquence of beauty, and she glides
Into his darker musings, with a mild
And healing sympathy, that steals away
Their sharpness, ere he is aware. When thoughts
Of the last bitter hour come like a blight
Over thy spirit, and sad images   10
Of the stern agony, and shroud, and pall,
And breathless darkness, and the narrow house,
Make thee to shudder, and grow sick at heart;—
Go forth, under the open sky, and list
To Nature's teachings, while from all around—
Earth and her waters, and the depths of air—
Comes a still voice—Yet a few days, and thee
The all-beholding sun shall see no more
In all his course; nor yet in the cold ground,
Where thy pale form was laid, with many tears,   20
Nor in the embrace of ocean, shall exist
Thy image. Earth, that nourished thee, shall claim
Thy growth, to be resolved to earth again,
And, lost each human trace, surrendering up
Thine individual being, shalt thou go
To mix for ever with the elements,
To be a brother to the insensible rock
And to the sluggish clod, which the rude swain
Turns with his share, and treads upon. The oak
Shall send his roots abroad, and pierce thy mould.   30

Yet not to thine eternal resting-place
Shalt thou retire alone, nor couldst.thou wish
Couch more magnificent. Thou shalt lie down
With patriarchs of the infant world—with kings,
The powerful of the earth—the wise, the good,
Fair forms, and hoary seers of ages past,

All in one mighty sepulchre. The hills
Rock-ribbed and ancient as the sun,—the vales
Stretching in pensive quietness between;
The venerable woods—rivers that move
In majesty, and the complaining brooks   40
That make the meadows green; and, poured round all,
Old Ocean's gray and melancholy waste,—
Are but the solemn decorations all
Of the great tomb of man. The golden sun,
The planets, all the infinite host of heaven,
Are shining on the sad abodes of death,
Through the still lapse of ages. All that tread
The globe are but a handful to the tribes
That slumber in its bosom.—Take the wings
Of morning, pierce the Barcan wilderness,   50
Or lose thyself in the continuous woods
Where rolls the Oregon, and hears no sound,
Save his own dashings—yet the dead are there:
And millions in those solitudes, since first
The flight of years began, have laid them down
In their last sleep—the dead reign there alone.
So shalt thou rest, and what if thou withdraw
In silence from the living, and no friend
Take note of thy departure? All that breathe
Will share thy destiny. The gay will laugh   60
When thou art gone, the solemn brood of care
Plod on, and each one as before will chase
His favorite phantom; yet all these shall leave
Their mirth and their employments, and shall come
And make their bed with thee. As the long train
Of ages glides away, the sons of men,
The youth in life's green spring, and he who goes
In the full strength of years, matron and maid,
The speechless babe, and the gray-headed man—
Shall one by one be gathered to thy side,   70
By those, who in their turn shall follow them.

   So live, that when thy summons comes to join
The innumerable caravan, which moves
To that mysterious realm, where each shall take
His chamber in the silent halls of death,
Thou go not, like the quarry-slave at night,
Scourged to his dungeon, but, sustained and soothed
By an unfaltering trust, approach thy grave,
Like one who wraps the drapery of his couch
About him, and lies down to pleasant dreams.   80

(1817, 1876)

To a Waterfowl

Whither, midst falling dew,
While glow the heavens with the last steps of day,
Far, through their rosy depths, dost thou pursue
Thy solitary way?

Vainly the fowler's eye
Might mark thy distant flight to do thee wrong,
As, darkly seen against the crimson sky,
Thy figure floats along.

Seek'st thou the plashy brink
Of weedy lake, or marge of river wide,   10
Or where the rocking billows rise and sink
On the chafed ocean-side?

There is a Power whose care
Teaches thy way along that pathless coast—
The desert and illimitable air—
Lone wandering, but not lost.

All day thy wings have fanned,
At that far height, the cold, thin atmosphere,
Yet stoop not, weary, to the welcome land,
Though the dark night is near.   20

And soon that toil shall end;
Soon shalt thou find a summer home, and rest,
And scream among thy fellows; reeds shall bend,
Soon, o'er thy sheltered nest.

Thou'rt gone, the abyss of heaven
Hath swallowed up thy form; yet, on my heart
Deeply hath sunk the lesson thou hast given,
And shall not soon depart.

He who, from zone to zone,
Guides through the boundless sky thy certain flight,   30
In the long way that I must tread alone,
Will lead my steps aright.

(written 1815, 1876)

William Cullen Bryant   17

The Prairies

These are the gardens of the Desert, these
The unshorn fields, boundless and beautiful,
For which the speech of England has no name—
The Prairies. I behold them for the first,
And my heart swells, while the dilated sight
Takes in the encircling vastness. Lo! they stretch
In airy undulations, far away,
As if the Ocean, in his gentlest swell,
Stood still, with all his rounded billows fixed,
And motionless forever. Motionless?—   10
No—they are all unchained again. The clouds
Sweep over with their shadows, and, beneath,
The surface rolls and fluctuates to the eye;
Dark hollows seem to glide along and chase
The sunny ridges. Breezes of the South!
Who toss the golden and the flame-like flowers,
And pass the prairie-hawk that, poised on high,
Flaps his broad wings, yet moves not—ye have played
Among the palms of Mexico and vines
Of Texas, and have crisped the limpid brooks   20
That from the fountains of Sonora glide
Into the calm Pacific—have ye fanned
A nobler or a lovelier scene than this?
Man hath no part in all this glorious work:
The hand that built the firmament hath heaved
And smoothed these verdant swells, and sown their slopes
With herbage, planted them with island-groves,
And hedged them round with forests. Fitting floor
For this magnificent temple of the sky—
With flowers whose glory and whose multitude   30
Rival the constellations! The great heavens
Seem to stoop down upon the scene in love,—
A nearer vault, and of a tenderer blue,
Than that which bends above our Eastern hills.

As o'er the verdant waste I guide my steed,
Among the high rank grass that sweeps his sides
The hollow beating of his footstep seems
A sacrilegious sound. I think of those
Upon whose rest he tramples. Are they here—
The dead of other days?—and did the dust   40
Of these fair solitudes once stir with life
And burn with passion? Let the mighty mounds
That overlook the rivers, or that rise

In the dim forest crowded with old oaks,
Answer. A race, that long has passed away,
Built them; a disciplined and populous race
Heaped, with long toil, the earth, while yet the Greek
Was hewing the Pentelicus to forms
Of symmetry, and rearing on its rock
The glittering Parthenon. These ample fields   50
Nourished their harvests, here their herds were fed,
When haply by their stalls the bison lowed,
And bowed his manèd shoulder to the yoke.
All day this desert murmured with their toils,
Till twilight blushed, and lovers walked, and wooed
In a forgotten language, and old tunes,
From instruments of unremembered form,
Gave the soft winds a voice. The red-man came—
The roaming hunter-tribes, warlike and fierce,
And the mound-builders vanished from the earth.   60
The solitude of centuries untold
Has settled where they dwelt. The prairie-wolf
Hunts in their meadows, and his fresh-dug den
Yawns by my path. The gopher mines the ground
Where stood their swarming cities. All is gone;
All—save the piles of earth that hold their bones,
The platforms where they worshipped unknown gods,
The barriers which they builded from the soil
To keep the foe at bay—till o'er the walls
The wild beleaguerers broke, and, one by one,   70
The strongholds of the plain were forced, and heaped
With corpses. The brown vultures of the wood
Flocked to those vast uncovered sepulchres,
And sat, unscared and silent, at their feast.
Haply some solitary fugitive,
Lurking in marsh and forest, till the sense
Of desolation and of fear became
Bitterer than death, yielded himself to die.
Man's better nature triumphed then. Kind words
Welcomed and soothed him; the rude conquerors   80
Seated the captive with their chiefs; he chose
A bride among their maidens, and at length
Seemed to forget—yet ne'er forgot—the wife
Of his first love, and her sweet little ones,
Butchered, amid their shrieks, with all his race.

    Thus change the forms of being. Thus arise
Races of living things, glorious in strength,
And perish, as the quickening breath of God

Fills them, or is withdrawn. The red-man, too,
Has left the blooming wilds he ranged so long, 90
And, nearer to the Rocky Mountains, sought
A wilder hunting-ground. The beaver builds
No longer by these streams, but far away,
On waters whose blue surface ne'er gave back
The white man's face—among Missouri's springs,
And pools whose issues swell the Oregon—
He rears his little Venice. In these plains
The bison feeds no more. Twice twenty leagues
Beyond remotest smoke of hunter's camp,
Roams the majestic brute, in herds that shake 100
The earth with thundering steps—yet here I meet
His ancient footprints stamped beside the pool.

    Still this great solitude is quick with life.
Myriads of insects, gaudy as the flowers
They flutter over, gentle quadrupeds,
And birds, that scarce have learned the fear of man,
Are here, and sliding reptiles of the ground,
Startlingly beautiful. The graceful deer
Bounds to the wood at my approach. The bee,
A more adventurous colonist than man, 110
With whom he came across the eastern deep,
Fills the savannas with his murmurings,
And hides his sweets, as in the golden age,
Within the hollow oak. I listen long
To his domestic hum, and think I hear
The sound of that advancing multitude
Which soon shall fill these deserts. From the ground
Comes up the laugh of children, the soft voice
Of maidens, and the sweet and solemn hymn
Of Sabbath worshippers. The low of herds 120
Blends with the rustling of the heavy grain
Over the dark-brown furrows. All at once
A fresher wind sweeps by, and breaks my dream,
And I am in the wilderness alone.

                              (written 1832, 1876)

The Poet

    Thou, who wouldst wear the name
       Of poet mid thy brethren of mankind,

And clothe in words of flame
  Thoughts that shall live within the general mind!
Deem not the framing of a deathless lay
The pastime of a drowsy summer day.

But gather all thy powers,
  And wreak them on the verse that thou dost weave,
And in thy lonely hours,
  At silent morning or at wakeful eve,   10
While the warm current tingles through thy veins,
Set forth the burning words in fluent strains.

No smooth array of phrase,
  Artfully sought and ordered though it be,
Which the cold rhymer lays
  Upon his page with languid industry,
Can wake the listless pulse to livelier speed,
Or fill with sudden tears the eyes that read.

The secret wouldst thou know
  To touch the heart or fire the blood at will?   20
Let thine own eyes o'erflow;
  Let thy lips quiver with the passionate thrill;
Seize the great thought, ere yet its power be past,
And bind, in words, the fleet emotion fast.

Then, should thy verse appear
  Halting and harsh, and all unaptly wrought,
Touch the crude line with fear,
  Save in the moment of impassioned thought;
Then summon back the original glow, and mend
The strain with rapture that with fire was penned.   30

Yet let no empty gust
  Of passion find an utterance in thy lay,
A blast that whirls the dust
  Along the howling street and dies away;
But feelings of calm power and mighty sweep,
Like currents journeying through the windless deep.

Seek'st thou, in living lays,
  To limn the beauty of the earth and sky?
Before thine inner gaze
  Let all that beauty in clear vision lie;   40
Look on it with exceeding love, and write
The words inspired by wonder and delight.

Of tempests wouldst thou sing,
  Or tell of battles—make thyself a part
Of the great tumult; cling
  To the tossed wreck with terror in thy heart;
Scale, with the assaulting host, the rampart's height,
And strike and struggle in the thickest fight.

So shalt thou frame a lay
  That haply may endure from age to age,   50
And they who read shall say:
  "What witchery hangs upons this poet's page?
What art is his the written spells to find
That sway from mood to mood the willing mind!"

                                        (written 1864, 1876)

The Death of Lincoln

Oh, slow to smite and swift to spare,
  Gentle and merciful and just!
Who, in the fear of God, didst bear
  The sword of power, a nation's trust!

In sorrow by thy bier we stand,
  Amid the awe that hushes all,
And speak the anguish of a land
  That shook with horror at thy fall.

Thy task is done; the bond are free:
  We bear thee to an honored grave,   10
Whose proudest monument shall be
  The broken fetters of the slave.

Pure was thy life; its bloody close
  Hath placed thee with the sons of light,
Among the noble host of those
  Who perished in the cause of Right.

                                        (written 1865, 1876)

from The Flood of Years

A MIGHTY Hand, from an exhaustless Urn,
Pours forth the never-ending Flood of Years,

Among the nations. How the rushing waves
Bear all before them! On their foremost edge,
And there alone, is Life. The Present there
Tosses and foams, and fills the air with roar
Of mingled noises. There are they who toil,
And they who strive, and they who feast, and they
Who hurry to and fro. The sturdy swain—
Woodman and delver with the spade—is there,   10
And busy artisan beside this bench,
And pallid student with his written roll.
A moment on the mounting billow seen,
The flood sweeps over them and they are gone.

. . . .

Lo! next a kneeling crowd, and one who spreads
The hands in prayer, the engulfing wave o'ertakes
And swallows them and him. A sculptor wields
The chisel, and the stricken marble grows
To beauty; at his easel, eager-eyed,
A painter stands, and sunshine at his touch   20
Gathers upon his canvas, and life glows;
A poet, as he paces to and fro,
Murmurs his sounding lines. Awhile they ride
The advancing billow, till its tossing crest
Strikes them and flings them under, while their tasks
Are yet unfinished. See a mother smile
On her young babe that smiles to her again;
The torrent wrests it from her arms; she shrieks
And weeps, and midst her tears is carried down.
A beam like that of moonlight turns the spray   30
To glistening pearls; two lovers, hand in hand,
Rise on the billowy swell and fondly look
Into each other's eyes. The rushing flood
Flings them apart: the youth goes down; the maid
With hands outstretched in vain, and streaming eyes,
Waits for the next high wave to follow him.
An aged man succeeds; his bending form
Sinks slowly. Mingling with the sullen stream
Gleam the white locks, and then are seen no more.

Lo! wider grows the stream—a sea-like flood   40
Saps earth's walled cities; massive palaces
Crumble before it; fortresses and towers
Dissolve in the swift waters; populous realms
Swept by the torrent see their ancient tribes
Engulfed and lost; their very languages
Stifled, and never to be uttered more.

. . . .

Sadly I turn and look before, where yet

The Flood must pass, and I behold a mist
Where swarm dissolving forms, the brood of Hope,
Divinely fair, that rest on banks of flowers,   50
Or wander among rainbows, fading soon
And reappearing, haply giving place
To forms of grisly aspect such as Fear
Shapes from the idle air—where serpents lift
The head to strike, and skeletons stretch forth
The bony arm in menace. Further on
A belt of darkness seems to bar the way
Long, low, and distant, where the Life to come
Touches the Life that is. The Flood of Years
Rolls toward it near and nearer. It must pass   60
That dismal barrier. What is there beyond?
Hear what the wise and good have said. Beyond
That belt of darkness, still the Years roll on
More gently, but with not less mighty sweep.
They gather up again and softly bear
All the sweet lives that late were overwhelmed
And lost to sight, all that in them was good,
Noble, and truly great, and worthy of love—
The lives of infants and ingenuous youths,
Sages and saintly women who have made   70
Their households happy; all are raised and borne
By that great current on its onward sweep,
Wandering and rippling with caressing waves
Around green islands fragrant with the breath
Of flowers that never wither. So they pass
From stage to stage along the shining course
Of that bright river, broadening like a sea.
As its smooth eddies curl along their way
They bring old friends together; hands are clasped
In joy unspeakable; the mother's arms   80
Again are folded round the child she loved
And lost. Old sorrows are forgotten now,
Or but remembered to make sweet the hour
That overpays them; wounded hearts that bled
Or broke are healed forever. In the room
Of this grief-shadowed present, there shall be
A Present in whose reign no grief shall gnaw
The heart, and never shall a tender tie
Be broken; in whose reign the eternal Change
That waits on growth and action shall proceed   90
With everlasting Concord hand in hand.

(1876)

George Moses Horton
1797?–1883?

George Moses Horton, widely acknowledged as America's first professional black poet, the first Southern black to publish, and the first black to publish while a slave, has yet to be accepted by critics as a major black voice. Though early commentators viewed Horton as a minor and derivative poet, within the last decade critics have begun to treat Horton seriously. These critics read Horton's conventional language and themes as a cloak for his indictments of white social oppression.

Horton was probably born in 1797 on the William Horton plantation, close to present-day Rich Square in northeastern North Carolina. After moving to Chatham County in 1814, Horton discovered Chapel Hill, the university town where he spent most of the next fifty years. During Sunday market excursions, Horton encountered the pranks of university students who requested that he "spout" oratory before completing a sale (Walser, *Naked Genius* ii). To escape this humiliating ritual, Horton responded with poetry, changing his harassers' jeers to expressions of astonishment. Students soon began commissioning Horton to produce acrostics based on their sweethearts' names. On Sundays, he would dictate the verses he had composed "at the handle of the plow" (Walser, *Naked Genius* 22), earning income that purchased his release from farm work.

In 1829, Horton's first collection of poems, *The Hope of Liberty*, was published by Joseph Gales in Raleigh. Impetus for this project came through the efforts of the writer Caroline Lee Hentz, who lived in Chapel Hill for five years. Hentz "transcribed Horton's verse (he could not write until about 1832), tutored him in prosody, and sent his poems to the *Lancaster* [Mass.] *Gazette*" (Sherman 6). Proceeds from *The Hope of Liberty* were to finance the poet's emigration to Liberia, but sales were poor and Horton never realized his dream of purchasing his freedom.

During the next twenty years, Horton published another book of poetry and delivered two public speeches. In the summer of 1845, he secured a list of ninety-nine subscribers, eighty-one of whom were Chapel Hill students (Jackson 89), and brought out

The Poetical Works of George M. Horton, the Colored Bard of North Carolina. Asked by the students to give a Fourth of July Oration in 1849, Horton delivered a five-minute speech greeted by "repeated applause" (Walser, *Black Poet* 73). In his 1859 speech, purportedly given during commencement week, Horton wrote that "mankind" is "more fond of listening to what abuses recognized genius . . . particularly in one of low birth . . . than to expand the circle in which he stands" (ms., "The Stream of Liberty and Science").

Little is known of Horton's later years apart from his association with Captain William H. S. Banks of the Ninth Michigan Cavalry Volunteers and the fact that he ended his life in Philadelphia. When Banks mustered out of the Union Army on 21 July 1865, he and Horton traveled to Raleigh where they arranged for William B. Smith to publish *Naked Genius* (1865). Of the 134 poems it contained, all but three of the forty-five in *Poetical Works* were included, while only two were taken from *The Hope of Liberty*; most of the poems were written in the weeks Horton traveled with Banks' troops (Jackson 91). Horton spent his final eighteen years in Philadelphia, where he performed odd jobs and wrote prose narratives of Bible episodes for Sunday schools. Collier Cobb, a Chapel Hill geology professor, reported having seen Horton in 1883 and addressed him as "Poet," to which Horton replied, "That pleases me greatly, Professor Cobb . . . you are using my proper title . . . " (Walser, *Black Poet* 106). Cobb also reported that Horton died later that year.

Collier Cobb and Richard Walser, who represent the first generation of serious readers of Horton, acknowledge Horton's having accomplished a number of "firsts" and emphasize his having educated himself against great odds. As Blyden Jackson and Louis Rubin observe in *Black Poetry in America*, "The very fact that a slave could write poetry was all the justification needed for publication" (9). Recent critics like Joan R. Sherman and Blyden Jackson have explored the influence audience and market may have exerted on Horton's rhymes and his imperfect mimicking of classic and romantic writers.

Jackson identifies the starting point for future criticism when he writes that "whatever claims . . . may be advanced about the level of Horton's poetic accomplishment, . . . he was not a simple, or simple-minded, fellow whether as an individual in a social order or as a writer seeking the voice that suited him" (92). Understanding how voice and social position intertwine and inform one another may explain the tone of Horton's 1859 speech to Chapel Hill graduates. Perhaps Horton was "signifying" in the manner Henry Louis Gates Jr. describes as a self-reflexive use of language that indirectly comments on linguistic traditions and current usage through a form of self-conscious parody (105). Such sophistication would account for the commencement speech and also allow for the parody in "George Moses Horton, Myself," "The Obstructions of Genius," and "The Art of a Poet." Even Civil War poems like "The Union of Parties" and "The Spectator of the Battle of Belmont, November 6, 1863" can be read as critiques of the war rather than exaltations of the new peace it promised.

—*Paul Crumbley*

Suggestions for Further Reading

Cobb, Collier. "An American Man of Letters." *University Magazine* (North Carolina) ns 27 (Oct. 1909): 25–32.
Gates, Henry Louis, Jr. *The Signifying Monkey: A Theory of African-American Literary Criticism.* New York: Oxford UP, 1988.
Jackson, Blyden. *A History of Afro-American Literature.* Vol. 1. Baton Rouge: Louisiana State UP, 1989.
Jackson, Blyden, and Louis D. Rubin Jr.. *Black Poetry in America.* Baton Rouge: Louisiana State UP, 1974.*
Sherman, Joan R. *Invisible Poets.* 2nd ed. Urbana: U of Illinois P, 1989.
Walser, Richard. *The Black Poet.* New York: Philosophical Library, 1966.
———. Introduction. *Naked Genius.* By George Moses Horton. Greensboro: Greensboro Printing, 1982. i–vii.

TEXTS
The Hope of Liberty. 1829.
The Poetical Works of George M. Horton, the Colored Bard of North Carolina. 1845.
Naked Genius. 1865.

ӭχ€

On Liberty and Slavery

Alas! and am I born for this,
　　To wear this slavish chain?
Deprived of all created bliss,
　　Through hardship, toil and pain?

How long have I in bondage lain,
　　And languished to be free!

Alas! and must I still complain—
   Deprived of liberty.

Oh, Heaven! and is there no relief
   This side the silent grave—   10
To soothe the pain—to quell the grief
   And anguish of a slave?

Come Liberty, thou cheerful sound,
   Roll through my ravished ears!
Come, let my grief in joys be drowned,
   And drive away my fears.

Say unto foul oppression, Cease:
   Ye tyrants rage no more,
And let the joyful trump of peace,
   Now bid the vassel soar.   20

Soar on the pinions of that dove
   Which long has cooed for thee,
And breathed her notes from Afric's grove,
   The sound of Liberty.

Oh, Liberty! thou golden prize,
   So often sought by blood—
We crave thy sacred sun to rise,
   The gift of nature's God!

Bid slavery hide her haggard face,
   And barbarism fly: 30
I scorn to see the sad disgrace
   In which enslaved I lie.

Dear Liberty! upon thy breast,
   I languish to respire;
And like the swan unto her nest,
   I'd to thy smiles retire.

Oh, blest asylum—heavenly balm!
   Unto thy boughs I flee—
And in thy shades the storm shall calm,
   With songs of Liberty!   40
                    (1829)

Division of an Estate

It well bespeaks a man beheaded, quite
Divested of the laurel robe of life,
When ev'ry member struggles for its base;
The head, the power of order, now recedes,
Unheeded efforts rise on ev'ry side,
With dull emotion rolling through the brain
Of apprehending slaves. The flocks and herds
In sad confusion now run to and fro,
And seem to ask, distressed, the reason why
That they are thus prostrated. Howl, ye dogs!   10
Ye cattle low! Ye sheep astonished bleet!
Ye bristling swine trudge squealing thro' the glades
Void of an owner to impart you food.
Sad horses lift your head and neigh aloud,
And caper, frantic, from the dismal scene;
Mow the last food upon your grass clad lea,
And leave a solitary home behind.
In hopeless widowhood, no longer gay,
The traveling sun of gain his journey ends;
In unavailing pain he sets with tears—   20
A King, sequestered, sinking from his throne;
Succeeded by a train of busy friends,
Like stars which rise with smiles to mark the flight
Of awful Phoebus to another world.
Stars after stars in fleet succession rise;
Into the wide empire of fortune cleave,
Regardless of the donor of their lamps,
Like heirs forgetful of parental care,
Redound in reverence to expiring age.
But soon parental benediction flies   30
Like vivid meteors in a moment gone,
As though they ne'er had been; but O, the state,
The dark suspense in which poor vassels stand,
Each mind upon the spire of chance hangs, fluctuate,
The day of separation is at hand.
Imagination lifts her gloomy curtain
Like evening's mantle at the flight of day,
Through which the trembling pinnacle we spy,
On which we must stand with hopeful smiles,
Or apprehending frowns to tumble on   40
The right or left forever.

(1845)

George Moses Horton, Myself

I feel myself in need
   Of the inspiring strains of ancient lore,
My heart to lift, my empty mind to feed,
   And all the world explore.

I know that I am old
   And never can recover what is past,
But for the future may some light unfold
   And soar from ages blast.

I feel resolved to try,
   My wish to prove, my calling to pursue,   10
Or mount up from the earth into the sky,
   To show what heaven can do.

My genius from a boy,
   Has fluttered like a bird within my heart;
But could not thus her powers employ,
   Impatient to depart.

She like a restless bird,
   Would spread her wing, her power to be unfurl'd,
And let her songs be loudly heard,
   And dart from world to world.   20

             (1865)

The Obstructions of Genius

I am surveyed by envy's eye,
   By white and colored all the same,
Which oft draws out a secret sigh,
   To feel the ills that bother fame.

Throughout my life I've tried the path,
   Which seemed as leading out of gloom,
Beneath my feet still kindled wrath,
   Genius seemed leading to a tomb.

No cultivating hand was found,
   To urge the night improving slave,   10

Never by freedom's laurel crowned,
　　But pushed by hardship to the grave.

Has philanthropic vigor slept,
　　So long in cells of disregard,
While genius in his fetters wept,
　　Devoid of favors or reward.

They often fly to trivial pleas,
　　To interdict the important cause,
To crush the negligent disease,
　　And kill the force of humane laws.　　　　20

Why did the Gods of Afric sleep,
　　Forgetful of their guardian love,
When the white traitors of the deep,
　　Betray'd him in the palmy grove.

Let us the evil now forget,
　　Which darkened the Columbian shore,
Till sun shall fail to rise and set,
　　And slavery's cries are heard no more.

　　　　　　　　　　　　　　　　　　　(1865)

The Art of a Poet

True nature first inspires the man,
But he must after learn to scan,
　　And mark well every rule;
Gradual the climax then ascend,
And prove the contrast in the end,
　　Between the wit and fool.

A fool tho' blind, may write a verse,
And seem from folly to emerge,
　　And rhyme well every line;
One lucky, void of light, may guess,　　　　10
And safely to the point may press,
　　But this does not refine.

Polish mirror, clear to shine,
And streams must run if they refine,
　　And widen as they flow;

The diamonds water lies concealed,
Till polished it is ne'er revealed,
    Its glory bright to show.

A bard must traverse o'er the world,
Where things concealed must rise unfurled,   20
    And tread the foot of yore;
Tho' he may sweetly harp and sing,
But strictly prune the mental wing,
    Before the mind can soar.

                                                        (1865)

The Spectator of the Battle of Belmont, November 6, 1863

O, brother spectators, I long shall remember,
    The blood-crimson veil which spreads over the field,
When battle commenc'd on the sixth of November,
    With war-beaming aspect, the sword and the shield.

The sound of destruction breaks loud from the mortars,
    The watchman is tolling the death-tuning knell,
The heroes are clustering from quarter to quarter;
    What mortal, the fate of this combat shall tell?

Blood breaks from its vein like a stream from its fountain;
    Spectators the pain of the conflict explore;   10
The fugitives fly to the cave on the mountain,
    Betray'd by the vestige of blood in their gore.

The conflict begins from the twang of the drummer,
    And ends with the peal of a tragical tale;
O yes, it subsides like a storm into summer,
    No less for the dead shall the living bewail.

I've heard of the battles of many foreign nations;
    I've heard of the wonderful conflicts of Troy,
And battles, with bloodshed, thro' all generations,
    But nothing like this could my feelings annoy.   20

The dark dirge of destiny, sung by a spirit,
    Alone can the scene of the combat display,

For surely no dull earthly mortal can merit
A wonder to equal this tragical lay.

(1865)

Lincoln Is Dead

He is gone, the strong base of the nation,
   The dove to his covet has fled;
Ye heroes lament his privation,
   For Lincoln is dead.

He is gone down, the sun of the Union,
   Like Pheobus, that sets in the west;
The planet of peace and commotion,
   Forever has gone to his rest.

He is gone from a world of commotion,
   No equal succeeds in his stead;   10
His wonders extend with the ocean,
   Whose waves murmur, Lincoln is dead.

He is gone and can ne'er be forgotten,
   Whose great deeds eternal shall bloom;
When gold, pearls and diamonds are rotten,
   His deeds will break fresh from the tomb.

He is gone out of glory to glory,
   A smile with the tear may be shed;
O, then let us tell the sweet story,
   Triumphantly, Lincoln is dead.   20

(1865)

Peace at Home

'Tis when a storm subsides,
     And breathes a clement breeze behind,
     Such is the quiet stream of mind,
     Thus all things are to heaven resigned,
And friend with friend divides.

When peace is gone from home,
    A whirlwind resides in her stead,
    And all the laurel's leaves are shed,
    The willow droops her verdant head,
The chamber is a tomb.   10

Where peace forbears to dwell,
    Life from the hut or fleet away,
    Whose wife is pouting night or day,
    Oh, tortured man forbear to stay,
Her path leads unto hell.

A forward wife is death,
    Woman indeed is hard to find,
    Man to her end is ever blind,
    'Tis best to leave the wretch behind,
Nor spend with such a breath.   20

Why should one live on thorns,
    And yet a transient time to live,
    With one who will not take nor give,
    But will the dearest friend deceive,
And every favor scorn.

How pleasing is the hour,
    When a rude storm has passed away,
    And left the field and garden gay,
    Whilst lambent o'er the breast of May,
Play inoffensive flowers.   30

Never regret the flight,
    From one in her own folly left,
    Who frowns and tramples on a gift,
    Leave her alone herself to shift,
And vanish from her sight.

(1865)

George Moses Horton

Sarah Helen Whitman
(1803–1878)

Known as a poet who encouraged and imitated Edgar Allan Poe, Sarah Helen Whitman was an established poet well before she met Poe. In fact, Poe admired Whitman's poetry before he met her. After Poe's death, Whitman developed a style notable for its relatively unsentimental treatment of death and lost love and for its intelligent contemplation of contemporary issues like slavery and science. Today, Whitman is perhaps best known as the defender and one-time fiancée of Poe.

Sarah Helen Power was born 19 January 1803 in Providence, Rhode Island, to Nicholas and Anna Marsh Power. She married attorney John Winslow Whitman in 1828 and lived with him in Boston. In 1829, Whitman published her first poem, "Retrospective," in *Ladies' Magazine*, under the name "Helen." When her husband died in 1833, she returned to Providence and became active in Northeastern literary circles, publishing many magazine articles on spiritualism, transcendentalism, and literature, as well as poems. In Providence, she was thought to be somewhat extraordinary, given to communing with the spirits of the dead. Oral Sumner Coad, in his introduction to a 1949 limited edition of *Edgar Poe and His Critics*, wrote that Whitman "chose to surround her fragile beauty with floating veils and trailing shawls and a twilight atmosphere sometimes pervaded by the odor of ether, presumably used as a stimulant for her weak heart" (Whitman 9).

Whitman met Poe in 1848, after she wrote an intimate poem addressed to the author of "The Raven." Poe received a copy of Whitman's poem and was so inspired he wrote "To Helen" ("I saw thee once—once only—years ago") for its author. She returned his poem with another of her own, and the romance was on its way. Relinquishing her share of her family's small estate because of her mother's strong opposition to the match, Whitman became engaged to Poe on the condition that he give up liquor. But when he appeared at her house intoxicated, she broke off the engagement. Nevertheless, she remained Poe's good friend until his death a few months later. Her sonnet, "To ———" (1853)

perhaps expresses her regret at having rejected Poe. In 1860, she put her rebuttal of a slanderous obituary in writing, with *Edgar Poe and His Critics.*

Whitman devoted her later years to her sister Susan Anna, with whom she lived until the sister's death in 1877. Despite reportedly poor health throughout her life, Whitman lived to the age of seventy-five. She died 27 June 1878 and is buried in the North Burial Ground in Providence, Rhode Island.

Whitman did much more in her life than defend Poe. Her two volumes of poems, *Hours of Life, and Other Poems* (1853) and *Poems* (1879), a posthumous collection of the 1853 poems and newer works, were well received by critics and the public. Whitman's poems reflect her belief in the transcendentalist movement and her awareness of such current issues as abolition, educational reform, and social experiments. She did not ignore homelier themes; love and loss were prominent ones. Her poems also reflect her lifelong belief that her death was imminent.

In 1879, George William Curtis praised Whitman's poems as "strongly original," displaying an "affluence of extensive and rare cultivation . . . not often discovered in any volume of poems, and never before in those of an American woman" (*Putnam's Weekly*). George Ripley, in the New York *Tribune*, praised her weaving of "a profound and intense experience into the natural materials of song." Both critics noted especially Whitman's inspired descriptions of nature.

—*Lisa Carl*

Suggestions for Further Reading

Miller, John Carl, ed. *Poe's Helen Remembers.* Charlottesville: U of Virginia P, 1979.

Watts, Emily Stipes. *The Poetry of American Women: From 1632 to 1945.* Austin: U of Texas P, 1977. 188–89.

Whitman, Sarah Helen. *Edgar Poe and His Critics.* Ed. Oral Sumner Coad. New Brunswick, NJ: Rutgers UP, 1949.

TEXTS
Hours of Life, and Other Poems. 1853.
Poems. 1879.

from Sonnets
To Elizabeth Barrett Browning

II

> "Ad una vista
> D'un gran palazzo Michol ammirava
> Si come donna dispettosa e trista."[1]
>
> —*Il Purgatorio*

Sometimes I see thee, pale with scorn and sorrow,
At a great palace window, looking forth,
To-day on plumèd Florentines,—to-morrow
Upon the stern battalions of the North:
Sometimes o'er little children bending lowly,
To hear their cry, in the dark factories drowned;
Ah, then, thy pitying brow grows sweet and holy,
With a saint's aureole of sorrow crowned!
But most I love thee when that mystic glory—
Kindling at horrors that abhor the day—   10
Sheds a wild, stormy splendor over the story
Of the dark fugitive, who turned away
To death's cold threshold, calm in death's disdain,
From the 'White Pilgrim's Rock,' beside the western main.

                                        (1853, revised 1879)

III

> "Or discendiamo omai a maggior pieta."[2]
>
> —*L'Inferno*

Ay, most I love thee when thy starry song
Stoops to the plague-spot that we dare not name,
And bares with burning breath the envenomed wrong—
Our country's dark inheritance of shame.
When our blaspheming synods look thereon,
(Stifling God's law and Nature's noble ires
With the cold ashes of dead council-fires,)
That Gorgon Terror chills them into stone.
Yet, while they dream, another nobler heart,
Serene in love's great light and woman's ruth,   10
A woman, loyal to God's living truth,

---

1. "At the sight of a great palace, Michol admired it like a spiteful and sad woman."
2. "Now let us descend to greater pity."

Hath uttered calm, clear words whose rays shall dart,
Like sunbeams through our realm's Tartarean gloom,
Till freedom's holy law its Stygian depths illume.

(1853, revised 1879)

from Sonnets

To ———

IV

We met beneath September's gorgeous beams:
Long in my house of life thy star had reigned;—
Its mournful splendor trembled through my dreams,
Nor with the night's phantasmal glories waned.
We wandered thoughtfully o'er golden meads
To a lone woodland, lit by starry flowers,
Where a wild, solitary pathway leads
Through mouldering sepulchres and cypress bowers.
A dreamy sadness filled with autumnal air;—
By a low, nameless grave I stood beside thee,   10
My heart according to thy murmured prayer
The full, sweet answers that my lips denied thee.
O mournful faith, on that dread altar sealed—
Sad dawn of love in realms of death revealed!

(1853, revised 1879)

Night Wanes

Night wanes: the nation's travail, throe by throe,
Brings on the hour that shall absolve her sin;
And the great, solemn bells, now swinging slow,
  With tales of murder in their iron din,
  Shall ring the years of peace and freedom in.

Be patient, O my heart; look through the gloom
  Of the sad present, look through all the past,
And learn how, out of sin and death and doom,
  And mournful tragedies, august and vast,
  The world's great victories are achieved at last.   10

Look far away; count all the triumphs bought
  By martyred saints, found worthy to atone

For others' sin, see life from death outwrought,
  And know each blast from War's wild bugle blown
Shall melt in music round the "Great White Throne."

(written 1861, 1879)

from Christmas Eve
To My Little Friends at New Rochelle

Let fall the curtains, drop the shades;
Behind the hills the twilight fades;
The sullen rain-drops, heavily,
In the dank, drooping hemlocks lie;
The fir-trees in the rounding park
Loom statelier through the gathering dark,
And reddening in the starless night
The tall church windows blaze with light.
The north wind whistles down the glades;
Let fall the curtains, drop the shades,   10
And, while the fire-light's glowing gloom
Casts fitful shadows through the room,
Gather around the ruddy blaze
To welcome in the holidays.
. . . .
Sweet Christmas Eve! The holidays
May pass, the fire-light's cheerful blaze
Die out, the little waltzing feet
To other mazy measures beat,
And other Christmas Trees may spread
Their fragrant branches o'er my head,   20
And fairy fruit for us may fall
In many a distant bower and hall,
And Santa Claus at Christmas tide
May down the roaring chimneys ride,
And chapel bells with solemn chime
Ring in the Christ-child's holy time,
And tell to all the wondering Earth
The mystic story of his birth;
But memory long shall fondly dwell
On this blithe eve at New Rochelle,   30
And fairer deem our Christmas Tree
Than all that have been or may be,
And keep the birthnight it embalms
Sweet as the breath of heavenly palms.

(written December 1866, 1879)

The Portrait[3]

After long years I raised the folds concealing
That face, magnetic as the morning's beam:
While slumbering memory thrilled at its revealing,
Like Memnon wakening from his marble dream.

Again I saw the brow's translucent pallor,
The dark hair floating o'er it like a plume;
The sweet, imperious mouth, whose haughty valor
Defied all portents of impending doom.

Eyes planet calm, with something in their vision
That seemed not of earth's mortal mixture born;   10
Strange mystic faiths and fantasies Elysian,
And far, sweet dreams of "fairy lands forlorn."
. . . .
Oft has that pale, poetic presence haunted
My lonely musings at the twilight hour,
Transforming the dull earth-life it enchanted,
With marvel and with mystery and with power.

Oft have I heard the sullen sea-wind moaning
Its dirge-like requiems on the lonely shore,
Or listened to the Autumn woods intoning
The wild, sweet legend of the lost Lenore.   20
. . . .
Sweet, mournful eyes, long closed upon earth's sorrow,
Sleep restfully after life's fevered dream!
Sleep, wayward heart! till on some cool, bright morrow,
Thy soul, refreshed, shall bathe in morning's beam.

Though cloud and sorrow rest upon thy story,
And rude hands lift the drapery of thy pall,
Time, as a birthright, shall restore the glory,
And Heaven rekindle all the stars that fall.

(1870, 1879)

---

3. Presumably, this poem is a memory of Poe, with allusions to "The Raven"
and his requiem poem "Lenore."

Science

"The words 'vital force,' 'instinct,' 'soul,' are only ex-
pressions of our ignorance."

—Buckner[4]

While the dull Fates sit nodding at their loom,
Benumbed and drowsy with its ceaseless boom,
I hear, as in a dream, the monody
Of life's tumultuous, ever-ebbing sea;
The iron tramp of armies hurrying by
Forever and forever but to die;
The tragedies of time, the dreary years,
The frantic carnival of hopes and fears,
The wild waltz-music wailing through the gloom,
The slow death-agonies, the yawning tomb,   10
The loved ones lost forever to our sight,
In the wide waste of chaos and old night;
Earth's long, long dream of martyrdom and pain;
No God in heaven to rend the welded chain
Of endless evolution!
                        Is this *all?*
And mole-eyed "Science," gloating over bones,
The skulls of monkeys and the Age of Stones,
Blinks at the golden lamps that light the hall
Of dusty death, and answers: "It is all."   20

(written 1877, 1879)

---

4. Probably Ludwig Buchner (1824–99), physician and materialist philosopher.

Ralph Waldo Emerson
1803–1882

Ralph Waldo Emerson's influence on American poetry resonates everywhere. More than any of his contemporaries (before Whitman and Dickinson), Emerson consciously sought to create an American poetic voice in his poems and in his criticism. The rugged rhymes and rhythms of poems such as "Merlin" and the "Ode Inscribed to W. H. Channing" attempt to escape the inherited confines of British meters. In his criticism, he advocated an organic poetry of meter-making argument that chaunts American times and social circumstances. Emerson believed that a truly American poetry should draw upon its own myths, symbols, and legends; he argued that the American poet who sings well about his own times sings both nationally and universally.

Emerson touched his contemporaries and many who followed. Emily Dickinson admired his poems; Walt Whitman said he was "simmering, simmering, simmering" until Emerson brought him "to a boil" (Trowbridge 366–67). Hyatt Waggoner, a modern critic, argues that Emerson stands at the center of American poetic tradition from the Puritans to the present (*American Poets* xi–xvii). Author of only two volumes of poetry, Emerson knew he was not the American poet he described in his essay "The Poet" (1844). But he recognized Whitman as the real thing in *Leaves of Grass* (1855) and greeted him at the beginning of a great career. Though critics today regard Emerson as an essayist, a lecturer, and a social critic, his poems and essays about poetry still define what an American poem—or any poem, for that matter—might be.

Emerson was born 25 May 1803 in Boston, Massachusetts, the son of William and Ruth Haskins Emerson. He attended Boston Public Latin School (1812–17), graduated from Harvard College in 1821, taught school from 1821 to 1826, and entered Harvard's Divinity School in 1825. In 1829, after being ordained as a Unitarian minister of Boston's Second Church, Emerson married Ellen Tucker, who died of consumption in 1831. Resigning his pastorate in October 1832 after a controversy over Communion, he toured Europe and England (1832–33), where he met Carlyle, Wordsworth, and Coleridge.

Emerson began a new life in 1833. That year he lectured for a secular audience; in 1835, he married Lydia ("Lidian") Jackson and moved to Concord, Massachusetts. They had four children, three of whom lived to adulthood. A popular lecturer everywhere except the South, Emerson published *Nature* (1836), delivered his "American Scholar Address" at Harvard (1837), and riled Harvard's Divinity School faculty with his "Divinity School Address" (1838). From 1840 to 1844, he edited (with Margaret Fuller and Henry David Thoreau) *The Dial*, a transcendental magazine; in his Lyceum lectures, he established a pattern that accounted for most of his books: mining his *Journals* for ideas and images, trying out those ideas in lectures to live audiences, revising his lectures interminably, and finally publishing them as books.

And the books followed: *Essays* (First Series) (1841), *Essays* (Second Series) (1844), *Representative Men* (1850), *English Traits* (1856), *The Conduct of Life* (1860), *Society and Solitude* (1870), and *Letters and Social Aims* (1875), among others. Emerson lectured in England and toured France (1847–48), visited California (1871), and journeyed to Egypt, Rome, Paris, and London (1871–72). When he died at Concord on 27 April 1882, Emerson had earned recognition as a major critic of American culture, a spokesman for democracy, and an advocate for a distinctive American writing.

His two volumes of poems—*Poems* (1846) and *May-Day and Other Poems* (1867)—appeared twenty-one years apart. The first contained fifty-nine poems and the second forty-four. Emerson had written poetry since the 1820s, and his two books do not collect all of his verse. Several critics attacked *Poems* for its metrical irregularity and its obscurity; even Margaret Fuller, who believed Emerson took "the highest rank" among American poets, faulted *Poems* for its philosophical bent and for its failure to "wake far-off echoes in the heart" (qtd. in Allen 466). *May-Day* received similarly mixed reviews. Critics who admired this volume also pointed out that the poems were highly abstract.

Emerson's poems admirably gloss his prose, treating themes that pervade his essays: talent and genius, the individual and society, freedom and fate, feminine and masculine, reason and understanding, nature and human nature, consciousness and the unconscious, the material and the spiritual worlds, America and Europe, democracy and aristocracy, past and present. In his prose, he repeatedly explored the differences between looking and seeing, thinking and thought, and form and meaning.

Because his poems treat these subjects, they are, as his contemporary critics noted, often philosophical and abstract.

But in "The Snow-Storm," "Days," "Hamatreya," and "Brahma," Emerson often fused idea and image to create poems that readers and critics still admire. Readers who wish to understand the ideas Emerson explored in his prose would do well to peruse the poems for their succinct expression in verse. As F. O. Matthiessen argued fifty years ago, students of the nineteenth century must know Emerson's works if they wish to know about American culture in Emerson's time (xii).

—*Robert Bain*

Suggestions for Further Reading

Allen, Gay Wilson. *Waldo Emerson: A Biography*. New York: Viking, 1981.

Matthiessen, F. O. *American Renaissance: Art and Expression in the Age of Emerson and Whitman*. New York: Oxford UP, 1941.

Stovall, Floyd. "Ralph Waldo Emerson." *Eight American Authors: A Review of Research and Criticism*. Ed. James Woodress. New York: Norton, 1971. 37–83.*

Trowbridge, John Townsend. *My Own Story, with Recollections of Noted Persons*. Boston: Riverside Press, 1903.

Waggoner, Hyatt H. *American Poets: From the Puritans to the Present*. New York: Dell, 1968.

———. *Emerson as Poet*. Princeton: Princeton UP, 1974.

Woodress, James, et al., eds. *American Literary Scholarship: An Annual*. Durham, NC: Duke UP, 1965–Present.*

TEXT
Poems by Ralph Waldo Emerson. Boston: Houghton, 1904.

ᗧᕦ

Each and All

Little thinks, in the field, yon red-cloaked clown
Of thee from the hill-top looking down;
The heifer that lows in the upland farm,
Far-heard, lows not thine ear to charm;
The sexton, tolling his bell at noon,
Deems not that great Napoleon
Stops his horse, and lists with delight,

Whilst his files sweep round yon Alpine height;
Nor knowest thou what argument
Thy life to thy neighbor's creed has lent.   10
All are needed by each one;
Nothing is fair or good alone.
I thought the sparrow's note from heaven,
Singing at dawn on the alder bough;
I brought him home, in his nest, at even;
He sings the song, but it cheers not now,
For I did not bring home the river and sky;—
He sang to my ear,—they sang to my eye.
The delicate shells lay on the shore;
The bubbles of the latest wave   20
Fresh pearls to their enamel gave,
And the bellowing of the savage sea
Greeted their safe escape to me.
I wiped away the weeds and foam,
I fetched my sea-born treasures home;
But the poor, unsightly, noisome things
Had left their beauty on the shore
With the sun and the sand and the wild uproar.
The lover watched his graceful maid,
As 'mid the virgin train she strayed,   30
Nor knew her beauty's best attire
Was woven still by the snow-white choir.
At last she came to his hermitage,
Like the bird from the woodlands to the cage;—
The gay enchantment was undone,
A gentle wife, but fairy none.
Then I said, "I covet truth;
Beauty is unripe childhood's cheat;
I leave it behind with the games of youth:"—
As I spoke, beneath my feet   40
The ground-pine curled its pretty wreath,
Running over the club-moss burrs;
I inhaled the violet's breath;
Around me stood the oaks and firs;
Pine-cones and acorns lay on the ground;
Over me soared the eternal sky,
Full of light and of deity;
Again I saw, again I heard,
The rolling river, the morning bird;—
Beauty through my senses stole;   50
I yielded myself to the perfect whole.

(1846)

Hamatreya[1]

Bulkeley, Hunt, Willard, Hosmer, Meriam, Flint,[2]
Possessed the land which rendered to their toil
Hay, corn, roots, hemp, flax, apples, wool and wood.
Each of these landlords walked amidst his farm,
Saying, " 'Tis mine, my children's and my name's.
How sweet the west wind sounds in my own trees!
How graceful climb those shadows on my hill!
I fancy these pure waters and the flags
Know me, as does my dog: we sympathize;
And, I affirm, my actions smack of the soil."   10

Where are these men? Asleep beneath their grounds:
And strangers, fond as they, their furrows plough.
Earth laughs in flowers, to see her boastful boys
Earth-proud, proud of the earth which is not theirs;
Who steer the plough, but cannot steer their feet
Clear of the grave.
They added ridge to valley, brook to pond,
And sighed for all that bounded their domain;
"This suits me for a pasture; that's my park;
We must have clay, lime, gravel, granite-ledge,   20
And misty lowland, where to go for peat.
The land is well,—lies fairly to the south.
'Tis good, when you have crossed the sea and back,
To find the sitfast acres where you left them."
Ah! the hot owner sees not Death, who adds
Him to his land, a lump of mould the more.
Hear what the Earth says:—

Earth-Song

"Mine and yours
Mine, not yours.
Earth endures;   30
Stars abide—
Shine down in the old sea;
Old are the shores;
But where are old men?
I who have seen much,
Such have I never seen.

---

1. Probably from *Vishnu Purana* where Emerson read of the Hindu god
"Maitreya" or from the Greek for "Earth-Mother."
2. Last names of the first settlers of Concord, Massachusetts.

"The lawyer's deed
Ran sure,
In tail,
To them, and to their heirs   40
Who shall succeed,
Without fail,
Forevermore.

"Here is the land,
Shaggy with wood,
With its old valley,
Mound and flood.
But the heritors?—
Fled like the flood's foam.
The lawyer, and the laws,   50
And the kingdom,
Clean swept herefrom.

"They called me theirs,
Who so controlled me;
Yet every one
Wished to stay, and is gone,
How am I theirs,
If they cannot hold me,
But I hold them?"

When I heard the Earth-song   60
I was no longer brave;
My avarice cooled
Like lust in the chill of the grave.

                                               (1846)

The Rhodora[3]
On Being Asked, Whence Is the Flower?

In May, when sea-winds pierced our solitudes,
I found the fresh Rhodora in the woods,
Spreading its leafless blooms in a damp nook,
To please the desert and the sluggish brook.
The purple petals, fallen in the pool,
Made the black water with their beauty gay;
Here might the red-bird come his plumes to cool,
And court the flower that cheapens his array.

---

3. New England shrub akin to the rhododendron.

Rhodora! if the sages ask thee why
This charm is wasted on earth and sky,   10
Tell them, dear, that if eyes were made for seeing,
Then Beauty is its own excuse for being:
Why thou wert there, O rival of the rose!
I never thought to ask, I never knew:
But, in my simple ignorance, suppose
The self-same Power that brought me there brought you.

(1846)

The Snow-Storm

Announced by all the trumpets of the sky,
Arrives the snow, and, driving o'er the fields,
Seems nowhere to alight: the whited air
Hides hills and woods, the river, and the heaven,
And veils the farm-house at the garden's end.
The sled and traveller stopped, the courier's feet
Delayed, all friends shut out, the housemates sit
Around the radiant fireplace, enclosed
In a tumultuous privacy of storm.

Come see the north wind's masonry.   10
Out of an unseen quarry evermore
Furnished with tile, the fierce artificer
Curves his white bastions with projected roof
Round every windward stake, or tree, or door.
Speeding, the myriad-handed, his wild work
So fanciful, so savage, nought cares he
For number or proportion. Mockingly,
On coop or kennel he hangs Parian[4] wreaths;
A swan-like form invests the hidden thorn;
Fills up the farmer's lane from wall to wall,   20
Maugre the farmer's sighs; and at the gate
A tapering turret overtops the work.
And when his hours are numbered, and the world
Is all his own, retiring, as he were not,
Leaves, when the sun appears, astonished Art
To mimic in slow structures, stone by stone,
Built in an age, and mad wind's night-work,
The frolic architecture of the snow.

(1846)

---

4. A white marble from Paros, a Greek island. Used in Greek statues.

Ode Inscribed to W. H. Channing[5]

Though loath to grieve
The evil time's sole patriot,
I cannot leave   .
My honied thought
For the priest's cant,
Or statesman's rant.

If I refuse
My study for their politique,
Which at the best is trick,
The angry Muse   10
Puts confusion in my brain.

But who is he that prates
Of the culture of mankind,
Of better arts and life?
Go, blindworm, go,
Behold the famous States
Harrying Mexico
With rifle and with knife!

Or who, with accent bolder,
Dare praise the freedom-loving mountaineer?   20
I found by thee, O rushing Contoocook![6]
And in thy valleys, Agiochook![7]
The jackals of the negro-holder.

The God who made New Hampshire
Taunted the lofty land
With little men;—
Small bat and wren
House in the oak:—

If earth-fire cleave
The upheaved land, and bury the folk,   30
The southern crocodile would grieve.
Virtue palters; Right is hence;
Freedom praised, but hid;

---

5. A response to William Henry Channing (1810–84), an abolitionist and clergyman who questioned Emerson about his views on slavery and the Mexican War.

6. New Hampshire river.

7. Mountains in New Hampshire.

Funeral eloquence
Rattles the coffin-lid.

What boots thy zeal,
O glowing friend,
That would indignant rend
The northland from the south?
Wherefore? to what good end?   40
Boston Bay and Bunker Hill
Would serve things still;—
Things are of the snake.

The horseman serves the horse,
The neatherd serves the neat,
The merchant serves the purse,
The eater serves his meat;
'Tis the day of the chattel,
Web to weave, and corn to grind;
Things are in the saddle,   50
And ride mankind.

There are two laws discrete,
Not reconciled,—
Law for man, and law for thing;
The last builds town and fleet,
But it runs wild,
And doth the man unking.

'Tis fit the forest fall,
The steep be graded,
The mountain tunnelled,   60
The sand shaded,
The orchard planted,
The glebe tilled,
The prairie granted,
The steamer built.

Let man serve law for man;
Live for friendship, live for love,
For truth's and harmony's behoof;
The state may follow how it can,
As Olympus follows Jove.   70

    Yet do not I implore
The wrinkled shopman to my sounding woods,
Nor bid the unwilling senator

Ask votes of thrushes in the solitudes.
Every one to his chosen work;—
Foolish hands may mix and mar;
Wise and sure the issues are.
Round they roll till dark is light,
Sex to sex, and even to odd;—
The over-god   80
Who marries Right to Might,
Who peoples, unpeoples,—
He who exterminates
Races by stronger races,
Black by white faces,—
Knows to bring honey
Out of the lion;
Grafts gentlest scion
On pirate and Turk.

The Cossack eats Poland,   90
Like stolen fruit;
Her last noble is ruined,
Her last poet mute:
Straight, into double band
The victors divide;
Half for freedom strike and stand;—
The astonished Muse finds thousands at her side.

                                                        (1846)

Merlin[8]

I

Thy trivial harp will never please
Or fill my craving ear;
Its chords should ring as blows the breeze,
Free, peremptory, clear.
No jingling serenader's art,
Nor tinkle of piano strings,
Can make the wild blood start
In its mystic springs.
The kingly bard
Must smite the chords rudely and hard,   10

---

8. One of Emerson's names for the ideal poet and probably a reference to the
Merlin of King Arthur legends.

As with hammer or with mace;
That they may render back
Artful thunder, which conveys
Secrets of the solar track,
Sparks of the supersolar blaze.
Merlin's blows are strokes of fate,
Chiming with the forest tone,
When boughs buffet boughs in the wood;
Chiming with the gasp and moan
Of the ice-imprisoned flood;   20
With the pulse of manly hearts;
With the voice of orators;
With the din of city arts;
With the cannonade of wars;
With the marches of the brave;
And prayers of might from martyrs' cave.

Great is the art,
Great be the manners, of the bard.
He shall not his brain encumber
With the coil of rhythm and number;   30
But, leaving rule and pale forethought,
He shall aye climb
For his rhyme.
"Pass in, pass in," the angels say,
"In to the upper doors,
Nor count compartments of the floors,
But mount to paradise
By the stairway of surprise."

Blameless master of the games,
King of sport that never shames,   40
He shall daily joy dispense
Hid in song's sweet influence.
Forms more cheerly live and go,
What time the subtle mind
Sings aloud the tune whereto
Their pulses beat,
And march their feet,
And their members are combined.

By Sybarites beguiled,
He shall no task decline;   50
Merlin's mighty line
Extremes of nature reconciled,—
Bereaved a tyrant of his will,

And made the lion mild.
Songs can the tempest still,
Scattered on the stormy air,
Mould the year to fair increase,
And bring in poetic peace.

He shall not seek to weave,
In weak, unhappy times,   60
Efficacious rhymes;
Wait his returning strength.
Bird that from the nadir's floor
To the zenith's top can soar,—
The soaring orbit of the muse exceeds that journey's length.
Nor profane affect to hit
Or compass that, by meddling wit,
Which only the propitious mind
Publishes when 'tis inclined.
There are open hours   70
When the God's will sallies free,
And the dull idiot might see
The flowing fortunes of a thousand years;—
Sudden, at unawares,
Self-moved, fly-to the doors,
Nor sword of angels could reveal
What they conceal.

II

The rhyme of the poet
Modulates the king's affairs;
Balance-loving Nature   80
Made all things in pairs.
To every foot its antipode;
Each color with its counter glowed;
To every tone beat answering tones,
Higher or graver;
Flavor gladly blends with flavor;
Leaf answers leaf upon the bough;
And match the paired cotyledons.
Hands to hands, and feet to feet,
In one body grooms and brides;   90
Eldest rite, two married sides
In every mortal meet.
Light's far furnace shines,
Smelting balls and bars,

Forging double stars,
Glittering twins and trines.
The animals are sick with love,
Lovesick with rhyme;
Each with all propitious Time
Into chorus wove.   100

Like the dancers' ordered band,
Thoughts come also hand in hand;
In equal couples mated,
Or else alternated;
Adding by their mutual gage,
One to other, health and age.
Solitary fancies go
Short-lived wandering to and fro,
Most like to bachelors,
Or an ungiven maid,   110
Not ancestors,
With no posterity to make the lie afraid,
Or keep truth undecayed.
Perfect-paired as eagle's wings,
Justice is the rhyme of things;
Trade and counting use
The self-same tuneful muse;
And Nemesis,
Who with even matches odd,
Who athwart space redresses   120
The partial wrong,
Fills the just period,
And finishes the song.

Subtle rhymes, with ruin rife,
Murmur in the house of life,
Sung by the Sisters as they spin;[9]
In perfect time and measure they
Build and unbuild our echoing clay.
As the two twilights of the day
Fold us music-drunken in.   130
                                                       (1846)

---

9. In Greek and Roman mythology, the Fates were three sisters: Clotho, who spun the thread of life; Lachesis, who assigned humans their destiny; and Atropos, who cut the thread of life at death.

Bacchus[10]

Bring me wine, but wine which never grew
In the belly of the grape,
Or grew on vine whose tap-roots, reaching through,
Under the Andes to the Cape,
Suffer no savor of the earth to scape.

Let its grapes the morn salute
From a nocturnal root,
Which feels the acrid juice
Of Styx and Erebus;[11]
And turns the woe of Night,   10
By its own craft, to a more rich delight.

We buy ashes for bread;
We buy diluted wine;
Give me of the true,—
Whose ample leaves and tendrils curled
Among the silver hills of heaven
Draw everlasting dew;
Wine of wine,
Blood of the world,
Form of forms, and mould of statures,   20
That I intoxicated,
And by the draught assimilated,
May float at pleasure through all natures;
The bird-language rightly spell,
And that which roses say so well.

Wine that is shed
Like the torrents of the sun
Up the horizon walls,
Or like the Atlantic streams, which run
When the South Sea calls.   30

Water and bread,
Food which needs no transmuting,
Rainbow-flowing, wisdom-fruiting,
Wine which is already man,
Food which teach and reason can.

---

10. The Greek god of wine, often associated with an orgiastic religion celebrating the power and fertility of nature.

11. In Greek mythology, Erebus is the dark region beneath the earth through which the dead must pass before they reach Hades.

Wine which Music is,—
Music and wine are one,—
That I, drinking this,
Shall hear far Chaos talk with me;
Kings unborn shall walk with me;   40
And the poor grass shall plot and plan
What it will do when it is man.
Quickened so, will I unlock
Every crypt of every rock.

I thank the joyful juice
For all I know;—
Winds of remembering
Of the ancient being blow,
And seeming-solid walls of use
Open and flow.   50

Pour, Bacchus! the remembering wine;
Retrieve the loss of me and mine!
Vine for vine be antidote,
And the grape requite the lote!
Haste to cure the old despair,—
Reason in Nature's lotus drenched,
The memory of ages quenched;
Give them again to shine;
Let wine repair what this undid;
And where the infection slid,   60
A dazzling memory revive;
Refresh the faded tints,
Recut the aged prints,
And write my old adventures with the pen
Which on the first day drew,
Upon the tablets blue,
The dancing Pleiads and eternal men.

(1846)

Concord Hymn[12]

By the rude bridge that arched the flood,
    Their flag to April's breeze unfurled,

---

12. "Sung at the Completion of the Battle Monument, July 4, 1837." First
printed as a leaflet distributed on the poem's occasion.

Here once the embattled farmers stood
   And fired the shot heard round the world.

The foe long since in silence slept;
   Alike the conqueror silent sleeps;
And Time the ruined bridge has swept
   Down the dark stream which seaward creeps.

On this green bank, by this soft stream,
   We set to-day a votive stone;   10
That memory may their deed redeem,
   When, like our sires, our sons are gone.

Spirit, that made those heroes dare
   To die, and leave their children free,
Bid Time and Nature gently spare
   The shaft we raise to them and thee.

                                     (1846)

Brahma[13]

If the red slayer think he slays,
   Or if the slain think he is slain,
They know not well the subtle ways
   I keep, and pass, and turn again.

Far or forgot to me is near;
   Shadow and sunlight are the same;
The vanished gods to me appear;
   And one to me are shame and fame.

They reckon ill who leave me out;
   When me they fly, I am the wings;   10
I am the doubter and the doubt,
   And I the hymn the Brahmin sings.

The strong gods pine for my abode,
   And pine in vain the sacred Seven;
But thou, meek lover of the good!
   Find me, and turn thy back on heaven.

                                     (1867)

---

13. In Hindu theology, the supreme being.

Days

Daughters of Time, the hypocritic Days,
Muffled and dumb like barefoot dervishes,
And marching single in an endless file,
Bring diadems and fagots in their hands.
To each they offer gifts after his will,
Bread, kingdoms, stars, and the sky that holds them all.
I, in my pleached garden, watched the pomp,
Forgot my morning wishes, hastily
Took a few herbs and apples, and the Day
Turned and departed silent. I, too late,   10
Under her solemn fillet saw the scorn.

                                                    (1867)

William Gilmore Simms

1806–1870

As Mary Ann Wimsatt describes
him, "William Gilmore Simms epitomizes the literary and cul-
tural life of the antebellum South. From 1825 to 1870 he produced
poetry, fiction, drama, histories, biographies, essays, and ora-
tions, [in] . . . nearly 80 books" (395). A staunch supporter of
Southern nationalism, his personal prosperity and national popu-
larity peaked in the 1840s and 1850s just before the Civil War that
destroyed both.

William Gilmore Simms was born on 17 April 1806 to a less-
than-prominent Charleston, South Carolina, family. His mother
died in childbirth two years later, and his father moved to the
Southwestern frontier, leaving Simms to be reared by his mater-
nal grandmother. He was educated in the Charleston city schools,
at the College of Charleston, and as a medical apprentice to a
local druggist before he finally settled on the law as a career. By
the time he was admitted to the bar in 1827, he had traveled ex-
tensively in frontier Mississippi while visiting his father and
knew well the Tidewater culture of antebellum South Carolina.
He had also published his first poem, the long "Monody, on the
Death of Gen. Charles Cotesworth Pinckney" (1825). He pub-
lished five more books of verse during the next seven years, sug-
gesting the ready fluency and productivity that would mark his
entire career. By the end of the 1830s, he had begun to concen-
trate on the long historical romances that would earn him fi-
nancial security and lasting fame. Widowed once, he married
Chevilette Eliza Roach in 1836, forming an alliance with her
wealthy lowland family. His plantation home, Woodlands, be-
came the base for an influential literary and political life.

Simms' ardent support of Southern nationalism (and of
Southern poets like Timrod and Hayne) made the disappoint-
ments of the war years all the more bitter. A series of personal
losses culminated in the 1863 death of his wife, and a fire de-
stroyed his beloved Woodlands in 1865. Although he (unlike
Timrod) survived the ravages of the war, he was reduced to hack
writing for poorly paying journals in order to support his large

family. His health eventually gave way, and he died in Charleston on 11 June 1870.

Simms wrote over fifteen books of poetry in a impressive array of styles and forms. A sense of brooding, latent violence pervades his description of "the terrible, the beautiful, the strange" Southern world in "The Edge of the Swamp" (line 38). The speaker of the poem regards an alien landscape— "ghastly . . . dank [and] . . . monstrous" (lines 11–16)—a landscape that the speaker is tempted to flee rather than celebrate. Louis D. Rubin, Jr., has called this poem "an allegory of the writer in the South" (52) because of this sense of alienation. "The Lost Pleiad," written over ten years earlier, anticipates the sense of loss and doubt that later permeates "the edge of the swamp."

Despite Simms' poetic ability, he continues to be known primarily as a romancer in the tradition of Scott and Cooper. Only in the last twenty years has renewed interest in Simms the man sparked a reevaluation of Simms the poet.

—*Terry Roberts*

Suggestions for Further Reading

Guilds, John Caldwell, ed. *"Long Years of Neglect": The Work and Reputation of William Gilmore Simms*. Fayetteville: U of Arkansas P, 1988.

Kibler, James E., Jr. *The Poetry of William Gilmore Simms: An Introduction and Bibliography*. Spartanburg, SC: Reprint Company, 1979.*

Rubin, Louis D., Jr. *The Edge of the Swamp: A Study in the Literature and Society of the Old South*. Baton Rouge: Louisiana State UP, 1989.

The Selected Poems of William Gilmore Simms. Ed. James Everett Kibler, Jr. Athens: U of Georgia P, 1990.

Wimsatt, Mary Ann. "William Gilmore Simms." *Fifty Southern Writers Before 1900*. Ed. Robert Bain and Joseph M. Flora. New York: Greenwood, 1987. 395–415.*

TEXT

Poems Descriptive, Dramatic, Legendary and Contemplative. 1853.

The Lost Pleiad[1]

I

Not in the sky,
Where it was seen
So long in eminence of light serene,—
Nor on the white tops of the glistering wave,
Nor down, in mansions of the hidden deep,
Though beautiful in green
And crystal, its great caves of mystery,—
Shall the bright watcher have
Her place, and, as of old, high station keep!

II

Gone! gone!   10
Oh! never more, to cheer
The mariner, who holds his course alone
On the Atlantic, through the weary night,
When the stars turn to watchers, and do sleep,
Shall it again appear,
With the sweet-loving certainty of light,
Down shining on the shut eyes of the deep!

III

The upward-looking shepherd on the hills
Of Chaldea, night-returning, with his flocks,
He wonders why his beauty doth not blaze,   20
Gladdening his gaze,—
And, from his dreary watch along the rocks,
Guiding him homeward o'er the perilous ways!
How stands he waiting still, in a sad maze,
Much wondering, while the drowsy silence fills
The sorrowful vault!—how lingers, in the hope that night
May yet renew the expected and sweet light,
So natural to his sight!

---

1. The pleiades are a cluster of stars in the constellation Taurus, six of which
are readily visible and the seventh "lost." According to Greek mythology, they
represent the daughters of Atlas and Pleione, placed by Zeus in the heavens.

IV

And lone,
Where, at the first, in smiling love she shone,   30
Brood the once happy circle of bright stars:
How should they dream, until her fate was known,
That they were ever confiscate to death?
That dark oblivion the pure beauty mars,
And, like the earth, its common bloom and breath,
That they should fall from high;
Their lights grow blasted by a touch, and die,—
All their concerted springs of harmony
Snapt rudely, and the generous music gone!

V

Ah! still the strain   40
Of wailing sweetness fills the saddening sky;
The sister stars, lamenting in their pain
That one of the selectest ones must die,—
Must vanish, when most lovely, from the rest!
Alas! 'tis ever thus the destiny.
Even Rapture's song hath evermore a tone
Of wailing, as for bliss too quickly gone.
The hope most precious is the soonest lost,
The flower most sweet is first to feel the frost.
Are not all short-lived things the loveliest?   50
And, like the pale star, shooting down the sky,
Look they not ever brightest, as they fly
From the lone sphere they blest!

                                              (1828, 1829)

The Edge of the Swamp

'Tis a wild spot, and even in summer hours,
With wondrous wealth of beauty and a charm
For the sad fancy, hath the gloomiest look,
That awes with strange repulsion. There, the bird
Sings never merrily in the sombre trees,
That seem to have never known a term of youth,
Their young leaves all being blighted. A rank growth
Spreads venomously round, with power to taint;
And blistering dews await the thoughtless hand

That rudely parts the thicket. Cypresses,   10
Each a great ghastly giant, eld and gray,
Stride o'er the dusk, dank tract,—with buttresses
Spread round, apart, not seeming to sustain,
Yet link'd by secret twines, that, underneath,
Blend with each arching trunk. Fantastic vines,
That swing like monstrous serpents in the sun,
Bind top to top, until the encircling trees
Group all in close embrace. Vast skeletons
Of forests, that have perish'd ages gone,
Moulder, in mighty masses, on the plain;   20
Now buried in some dark and mystic tarn,
Or sprawl'd above it, resting on great arms,
And making, for the opossum and the fox,
Bridges, that help them as they roam by night.
Alternate stream and lake, between the banks,
Glimmer in doubtful light: smooth, silent, dark,
They tell not what they harbor; but, beware!
Lest, rising to the tree on which you stand,
You sudden see the moccasin snake heave up
His yellow shining belly and flat head   30
Of burnish'd copper. Stretch'd at length, behold
Where yonder Cayman, in his natural home,
The mammoth lizard, all his armor on,
Slumbers half-buried in the sedgy grass,
Beside the green ooze where he shelters him.
The place, so like the gloomiest realm of death,
Is yet the abode of thousand forms of life,—
The terrible, the beautiful, the strange,—
Winged and creeping creatures, such as make
The instinctive flesh with apprehension crawl,   40
When sudden we behold. Hark! at our voice
The whooping crane, gaunt fisher in these realms,
Erects his skeleton form and shrieks in flight,
On great white wings. A pair of summer ducks,
Most princely in their plumage, as they hear
His cry, with senses quickening all to fear,
Dash up from the lagoon with marvellous haste,
Following his guidance. See! aroused by these,
And startled by our progress o'er the stream,
The steel-jaw'd Cayman, from his grassy slope,   50
Slides silent to the slimy green abode,
Which is his province. You behold him now,
His bristling back uprising as he speeds
To safety, in the centre of the lake,
Whence his head peers alone,—a shapeless knot,

That shows no sign of life; the hooded eye,
Nathless, being ever vigilant and sharp,
Measuring the victim. See! a butterfly,
That, travelling all the day, has counted climes
Only by flowers, to rest himself a while,   60
And, as a wanderer in a foreign land,
To pause and look around him ere he goes,
Lights on the monster's brow. The surly mute
Straightway goes down; so suddenly, that he,
The dandy of the summer flowers and woods,
Dips his light wings, and soils his golden coat,
With the rank waters of the turbid lake.
Wondering and vex'd, the plumed citizen
Flies with an eager terror to the banks,
Seeking more genial natures,—but in vain.   70
Here are no gardens such as he desires,
No innocent flowers of beauty, no delights
Of sweetness free from taint. The genial growth
He loves, finds here no harbor. Fetid shrubs,
That scent the gloomy atmosphere, offend
His pure patrician fancies. On the trees,
That look like felon spectres, he beholds
No blossoming beauties; and for smiling heavens,
That flutter his wings with breezes of pure balm,
He nothing sees but sadness—aspects dread,   80
That gather frowning, cloud and fiend in one,
As if in combat, fiercely to defend
Their empire from the intrusive wing and beam.
The example of the butterfly be ours.
He spreads his lacquer'd wings above the trees,
And speeds with free flight, warning us to seek
For a more genial home, and couch more sweet
Than these drear borders offer us tonight.

(1840)

Henry Wadsworth Longfellow
1807–1882

From 1850 until World War I, Henry Wadsworth Longfellow reigned as *the* national poet. Critics on both sides of the Atlantic praised his narrative poems, his musical lyrics, his translations, his use of the American and European past, and his technical virtuosity; publishers reprinted his works by the dozens. After World War I, Longfellow's reputation plummeted. Critics castigated his work for its optimism, its failure to plumb the tragic, its didacticism and shallowness, and for the poet's belief that verse should edify. Scholars recently reassessing Longfellow's poetry have been kinder. Lawrence Buell, in *Henry Wadsworth Longfellow: Selected Poems* (1988), concludes, "No one can fully comprehend the literary culture of nineteenth-century America without coming to terms with his work" (xxxii).

Henry Wadsworth Longfellow was born 27 February 1807 in Portland, Maine, the son of Zilpah Wadsworth and Stephen Longfellow, a lawyer and politician. Entering Bowdoin College at age fifteen, he graduated in 1825 and spent three years (1826–29) studying literature and languages in France, Italy, Germany, and Spain. On his return, he taught at Bowdoin College (1829–35) and married Mary Storer Potter in 1831. When Mary died after a miscarriage during a trip to Germany in 1835, Longfellow grieved greatly. He returned to teach at Harvard College (1836–54), earning accolades as a teacher and scholar. In 1843, he married Frances Appleton; they had six children, five of whom survived to maturity. Fanny died in 1861 when her dress caught fire in a household accident. "The Cross of Snow" records his loss. After resigning from Harvard in 1854, Longfellow devoted the rest of his life to writing and translating. In Europe in 1868, he received international acclaim and honorary degrees from Oxford and Cambridge. When he died on 24 March 1882, Longfellow was the most-read American poet.

While a student at Bowdoin, he published poems and essays in magazines. With the publication of his volumes *Voices of the Night* (1839) and *Ballads and Other Poems* (1841), Longfellow became an immediate and popular favorite. Six editions of *Voices* appeared in two years. *Poems on Slavery* (1842) added little to his fame. But *The Belfry of Bruges* (1845), *Evangeline, A Tale of Acadie* (1847), which had six printings in nine weeks, *The Seaside and the Fireside* (1850), which sold thirty thousand copies in five years, and *The Song of Hiawatha* (1855), which sold fifty thousand copies in eighteen months, firmly established Longfellow's popularity in America and Europe.

The Courtship of Miles Standish (1858) and *Tales of a Wayside Inn* (1863) brought Longfellow further fame. He published other volumes of shorter poems: *Flower-de-Luce* (1866), *Keramos and Other Poems* (1878), *Ultima Thule* (1880), and *In the Harbor* (1882). After the Civil War he turned his attention mainly to longer works and translations. Among these works are two more parts of *Tales of a Wayside Inn* (1872, 1873); his three-volume translation of Dante's *Divine Comedy* (1867); *Christus: A Mystery* (1872), a long verse drama in three parts; and *The Masque of Pandora and Other Poems* (1875). He also wrote several volumes of prose and edited prolifically.

Longfellow experimented with verse forms more than any poet of his time. He wrote odes, elegies, ballads, hymns, sonnets, narratives, dramatic verse, blank verse, and heroic couplets; he wrote poems in iambic, trochaic, anapestic, and dactylic meters in poetic feet ranging from dimeter and hexameter to eight-stress lines. He was one of the first poets in English to write in unrhymed trochaic tetrameter (*The Song of Hiawatha*) and in unrhymed hexameters (*Evangeline* and *The Courtship of Miles Standish*). In short poems, Longfellow improvised upon stanzaic forms, but in his longer works, the verse paragraph governs structure, as it does in Whitman's poetry.

Longfellow's themes do not range as widely as his verse experiments. The words "genial" and "mild melancholy" describe the emotional range of his themes. His belief that poetry should edify seems always to temper his poems about loss, death, mutability, nature, art, and the human condition. Longfellow loved the past, and though dreams and myths fascinated him, he worked mainly, as Howard Nemerov notes, through allegory, personification, and anecdote rather than symbol, metaphor, and myth (25–26). But his best poems do employ metaphor and myth; the music and story of "The Tide Rises, the Tide Falls," "Snow-Flakes," "My Lost Youth," and more than twenty other lyrics still haunt. Unlike the major romantic writers, Longfellow nibbled around the unconscious rather than plunging into it.

Critics have not settled the matter of Longfellow's reputation, though the latest returns relegate him to "minor poet" or "major minor poet." Since the New Criticism, lyric poetry has prevailed and long narratives have become unfashionable. Perhaps a new

generation of critics may find reasons to admire Longfellow
again. Perhaps.

—*Robert Bain*

Suggestions for Further Reading

Arvin, Newton. *Longfellow: His Life and Work.* 1963. Boston: Little,
Brown, 1977.*

Buell, Lawrence, ed. *Henry Wadsworth Longfellow: Selected Poems.*
New York: Penguin, 1988.*

Nemerov, Howard, ed. *Longfellow: Selected Poetry.* New York:
Laurel, 1959.

Rust, Richard Dilworth. "Henry Wadsworth Longfellow." *Fifteen
American Authors Before 1900: Biographical Essays on Research and
Criticism.* Ed. Earl N. Harbert and Robert A. Rees. Rev. ed. Madi-
son: U of Wisconsin P, 1984. 357–78.*

TEXT
The Complete Poetical Works of Henry Wadsworth Longfellow. Boston:
Houghton, 1902.

᠔ᢟᠮ

A Psalm of Life
What the Heart of the Young Man Said to the Psalmist

Tell me not, in mournful numbers,
 Life is but an empty dream!—
For the soul is dead that slumbers,
 And things are not what they seem.

Life is real! Life is earnest!
 And the grave is not its goal;
Dust thou art, to dust returnest,
 Was not spoken of the soul.

Not enjoyment, and not sorrow,
 Is our destined end or way;   10
But to act, that each tomorrow
 Find us farther than to-day.

Art is long, and Time is fleeting,
 And our hearts, though stout and brave,

Still, like muffled drums, are beating
    Funeral marches to the grave.

In the world's broad field of battle,
    In the bivouac of Life,
Be not like dumb, driven cattle!
    Be a hero in the strife!   20

Trust no Future, howe'er pleasant!
    Let the dead Past bury its dead!
Act,—act in the living Present!
    Heart within, and God o'erhead!

Lives of great men all remind us
    We can make our lives sublime,
And, departing, leave behind us
    Footprints on the sands of time;

Footprints, that perhaps another,
    Sailing o'er life's solemn main,   30
A forlorn and shipwrecked brother,
    Seeing, shall take heart again.

Let us, then, be up and doing,
    With a heart for any fate;
Still achieving, still pursuing,
    Learn to labor and to wait.

                                                    (1839)

Hymn to the Night
Ἀσπασίη,τρίλλιστος[1]

I heard the trailing garments of the Night
    Sweep through her marble halls!
I saw her sable skirts all fringed with light
    From the celestial walls!

I felt her presence, by its spell of might,
    Stoop e'er me from above;
The calm, majestic presence of the Night,
    As of the one I love.

---

1. "Welcome, thrice prayed for." From the *Iliad*, 8. 488.

I heard the sounds of sorrow and delight,
   The manifold, soft chimes,   10
That fill the haunted chambers of the Night,
   Like some old poet's rhymes.

From the cool cisterns of the midnight air
   My spirit drank repose;
The fountain of perpetual peace flows there,—
   From those deep cisterns flows.

O holy Night! from thee I learn to bear
   What man has borne before!
Thou layest thy finger on the lips of Care,
   And they complain no more.   20

Peace! Peace! Orestes-like I breathe this prayer![2]
   Descend with broad-winged flight,
The welcome, the thrice-prayed for, the most fair,
   The best-loved Night!

                                                          (1839)

The Slave Singing at Midnight

Loud he sang the psalm of David!
He, a Negro and enslavèd,
Sang of Israel's victory,
Sang of Zion, bright and free.

In that hour, when night is calmest,
Sang he from the Hebrew Psalmist,
In a voice so sweet and clear
That I could not choose but hear,

Songs of triumph, and ascriptions,
Such as reached the swart Egyptians,   10
When upon the Red Sea coast
Perished Pharaoh and his host.

And the voice of his devotion
Filled my soul with strange emotion;

---

2. In Aeschylus' *The Eumenides*, Orestes prays that the Furies will cease
tormenting him.

For its tones by turns were glad,
Sweetly solemn, wildly sad.

Paul and Silas, in their prison,[3]
Sang of Christ, the Lord arisen.
And an earthquake's arm of might
Broke their dungeon-gates at night.   20

But, alas! what holy angel
Brings the Slave this glad evangel?
And what earthquake's arm of might
Breaks his dungeon-gates at night?

(1842)

The Arsenal at Springfield[4]

This is the Arsenal. From floor to ceiling,
    Like a huge organ, rise the burnished arms;
But from their silent pipes no anthem pealing
    Startles the villages with strange alarms.

Ah! what a sound will rise, how wild and dreary,
    When the death-angel touches those swift keys!
What loud lament and dismal Miserere[5]
    Will mingle with their awful symphonies!

I hear even now the infinite fierce chorus,
    The cries of agony, the endless groan,   10
Which, through the ages that have gone before us,
    In long reverberations reach our own.

On helm and harness rings the Saxon hammer,
    Through Cimbric forest roars the Norseman's song,
And loud, amid the universal clamor,
    O'er distant deserts sounds the Tartar gong.

I hear the Florentine, who from his palace
    Wheels out his battle-bell with dreadful din,

---

3. See Acts 16:16–40.
4. The Arsenal at Springfield, Massachusetts. Longfellow visited there in 1843.
5. "Miserere mei, Domine" ("Have mercy on me, O Lord"). See Psalms 31.

And Aztec priests upon their teocallis
    Beat the wild war-drums made of serpent's skin;   20

The tumult of each sacked and burning village;
    The shout that every prayer for mercy drowns;
The soldiers' revels in the midst of pillage;
    The wail of famine in beleaguered towns;

The bursting shell, the gateway wrenched asunder,
    The rattling musketry, the clashing blade;
And ever and anon, in tones of thunder
    The diapason of the cannonade.

Is it, O man, with such discordant noises,
    With such accursed instruments as these,   30
Thou drownest Nature's sweet and kindly voices,
    And jarrest the celestial harmonies?

Were half the power that fills the world with terror,
    Were half the wealth bestowed on camps and courts,
Given to redeem the human mind from error,
    There were no need of arsenals or forts:

The warrior's name would be a name abhorrèd!
    And every nation, that should lift again
Its hand against a brother, on its forehead
    Would wear forevermore the curse of Cain!   40

Down the dark future, through long generations,
    The echoing sounds grow fainter and then cease;
And like a bell, with solemn, sweet vibrations,
    I hear once more the voice of Christ say, "Peace!"

Peace! and no longer from its brazen portals
    The blast of War's great organ shakes the skies!
But beautiful as songs of the immortals,
    The holy melodies of love arise.

                                        (1846)

The Day Is Done

The day is done, and the darkness
    Falls from the wings of Night,

As a feather is wafted downward
    From an eagle in his flight.

I see the lights of the village
    Gleam through the rain and the mist,
And a feeling of sadness comes o'er me
    That my soul cannot resist:

A feeling of sadness and longing,
    That is not akin to pain,   10
And resembles sorrow only
    As the mist resembles the rain.

Come, read to me some poem,
    Some simple and heartfelt lay,
That shall soothe this restless feeling,
    And banish the thoughts of day.

Not from the grand old masters,
    Not from the bards sublime,
Whose distant footsteps echo
    Through the corridors of Time.   20

For, like strains of martial music,
    Their mighty thoughts suggest
Life's endless toil and endeavor;
    And to-night I long for rest.

Read from some humbler poet,
    Whose songs gushed from his heart,
As showers from the clouds of summer,
    Or tears from the eyelids start;

Who, through long days of labor,
    And nights devoid of ease,   30
Still heard in his soul the music
    Of wonderful melodies.

Such songs have power to quiet
    The restless pulse of care,
And come like the benediction
    That follows after prayer.

Then read from the treasured volume
    The poem of thy choice,

And lend to the rhyme of the poet
  The beauty of thy voice.   40

And the night shall be filled with music,
  And the cares, that infest the day,
Shall fold their tents, like the Arabs,
  And as silently steal away.

                                                    (1846)

Seaweed

When descends on the Atlantic
    The gigantic
Storm-wind of the equinox,
Landward in his wrath he scourges
    The toiling surges,
Laden with seaweed from the rocks:

From Bermuda's reefs; from edges
    Of sunken ledges,
In some far-off, bright Azore;
From Bahama, and the dashing,   10
    Silver-flashing
Surges of San Salvador;

From the tumbling surf, that buries
    The Orkneyan skerries,
Answering the hoarse Hebrides;
And from wrecks of ships, and drifting
    Spars, uplifting
On the desolate, rainy seas;—

Ever drifting, drifting, drifting
    On the shifting   20
Currents of the restless main;
Till in sheltered coves, and reaches
    Of sandy beaches,
All have found repose again.

So when storms of wild emotion
    Strike the ocean
Of the poet's soul, erelong
From each cave and rocky fastness,

In its vastness,
Floats some fragment of a song: 30

From the far-off isles enchanted,
    Heaven has planted
With the golden fruit of Truth;
From the flashing surf, whose vision
    Gleams Elysian
In the tropic clime of Youth;

From the strong Will, and the Endeavor
    That forever
Wrestle with the tides of Fate;
From the wreck of Hopes far-scattered,   40
    Tempest-shattered,
Floating waste and desolate;—

Ever drifting, drifting, drifting
    On the shifting
Currents of the restless heart;
Till at length in books recorded,
    They, like hoarded
Household words, no more depart.
                                                (1850)

from The Song of Hiawatha
Hiawatha's Childhood

Downward through the evening twilight,
In the days that are forgotten,
In the unremembered ages,
From the full moon fell Nokomis,
Fell the beautiful Nokomis,
She a wife, but not a mother.
    She was sporting with her women,
Swinging in a swing of grape-vines,
When her rival the rejected,
Full of jealousy and hatred,   10
Cut the leafy swing asunder,
Cut in twain the twisted grape-vines,
And Nokomis fell affrighted
Downward through the evening twilight,
On the Muskoday, the meadow,
On the prairie full of blossoms.
"See! a star falls!" said the people;

"From the sky a star is falling!"
There among the ferns and mosses,
There among the prairie lilies,   20
On the Muskoday, the meadow,
In the moonlight and the starlight,
Fair Nokomis bore a daughter.
And she called her name Wenonah,
As the first-born of her daughters.
And the daughter of Nokomis
Grew up like the prairie lilies,
Grew a tall and slender maiden,
With the beauty of the moonlight,
With the beauty of the starlight.   30
    And Nokomis warned her often,
Saying oft, and oft repeating,
"Oh, beware of Mudjekeewis,
Of the West-Wind, Mudjekeewis;
Listen not to what he tells you;
Lie not down upon the meadow,
Stoop not down among the lilies,
Lest the West-Wind come and harm you!"
    But she heeded not the warning,
Heeded not those words of wisdom,   40
And the West-Wind came at evening,
Walking lightly o'er the prairie,
Whispering to the leaves and blossoms,
Bending low the flowers and grasses,
Found the beautiful Wenonah,
Lying there among the lilies,
Wooed her with his words of sweetness,
Wooed her with his soft caresses,
Till she bore a son in sorrow,   50
Bore a son of love in sorrow.
    Thus was born my Hiawatha,
Thus was born the child of wonder;
But the daughter of Nokomis,
Hiawatha's gentle mother,
In her anguish died deserted
By the West-Wind, false and faithless,
By the heartless Mudjekeewis.
    For her daughter long and loudly
Wailed and wept the sad Nokomis;   60
"Oh that I were dead!" she murmured,
"Oh that I were dead, as thou art!
No more work, and no more weeping,
Wahonowin! Wahonowin!"

By the shores of Gitche Gumee,
By the shining Big-Sea-Water,
Stood the wigwam of Nokomis,
Daughter of the Moon, Nokomis.
Dark behind it rose the forest,
Rose the black and gloomy pine-trees,   70
Rose the firs with cones upon them;
Bright before it beat the water,
Beat the clear and sunny water,
Beat the shining Big-Sea-Water.
    There the wrinkled old Nokomis
Nursed the little Hiawatha,
Rocked him in his linden cradle,
Bedded soft in moss and rushes,
Safely bound with reindeer sinews;
Stilled his fretful wail by saying,   80
"Hush! the Naked Bear will hear thee!"
Lulled him into slumber, singing,
"Ewa-yea! my little owlet!
Who is this, that lights the wigwam?
With his great eyes lights the wigwam?
Ewa-yea! my little owlet!"
    Many things Nokomis taught him
Of the stars that shine in heaven;
Showed him Ishkoodah, the comet,
Ishkoodah, with fiery tresses;   90
Showed the Death-Dance of the spirits,
Warriors with their plumes and war-clubs,
Flaring far away to northward
In the frosty nights of Winter;
Showed the broad white road in heaven,
Pathway of the ghosts, the shadows,
Running straight across the heavens,
Crowded with the ghosts, the shadows.
    At the door on summer evenings,
Sat the little Hiawatha;   100
Heard the whispering of the pine-trees,
Heard the lapping of the waters,
Sounds of music, words of wonder;
"Minne-wawa!" said the pine-trees,
"Mudway-aushka!" said the water.
    Saw the fire-fly, Wah-wah-taysee,
Flitting through the dusk of evening,
With the twinkle of its candle
Lighting up the brakes and bushes,
And he sang the song of children,   110

Sang the song Nokomis taught him:
"Wah-wah-taysee, little fire-fly,
Little, flitting, white-fire insect,
Little, dancing, white-fire creature,
Light me with your little candle,
Ere upon my bed I lay me,
Ere in sleep I close my eyelids!"
  Saw the moon rise from the water
Rippling, rounding from the water,
Saw the flecks and shadows on it,   120
Whispered, "What is that, Nokomis?"
And the good Nokomis answered:
"Once a warrior, very angry,
Seized his grandmother, and threw her
Up into the sky at midnight;
Right against the moon he threw her;
'Tis her body that you see there."
  Saw the rainbow in the heaven,
In the eastern sky, the rainbow,
Whispered, "What is that, Nokomis?"   130
And the good Nokomis answered:
" 'Tis the heaven of flowers you see there;
All the wild-flowers of the forest,
All the lilies of the prairie,
When on earth they fade and perish,
Blossom in that heaven above us."
  When he heard the owls at midnight,
Hooting, laughing in the forest,
"What is that?" he cried in terror,
"What is that," he said, "Nokomis?"   140
And the good Nokomis answered:
"That is but the owl and owlet,
Talking in their native language,
Talking, scolding at each other. "
  Then the little Hiawatha
Learned of every bird its language,
Learned their names and all their secrets,
How they built their nests in Summer,
Where they hid themselves in Winter,
Talked with them whene'er he met them,   150
Called them "Hiawatha's Chickens."
  Of all beasts he learned the language,
Learned their names and all their secrets,
How the beavers built their lodges,
Where the squirrels hid their acorns,
How the reindeer ran so swiftly,

Why the rabbit was so timid,
Talked with them whene'er he met them,
Called them "Hiawatha's Brothers."
    Then Iagoo, the great boaster, 160
He the marvellous story-teller,
He the traveller and the talker,
He the friend of old Nokomis,
Made a bow for Hiawatha;
From a branch of ash he made it,
From an oak-bough made the arrows,
Tipped with flint, and winged with feathers,
And the cord he made of deer-skin.
    Then he said to Hiawatha:
"Go, my son, into the forest, 170
Where the red deer herd together,
Kill for us a famous roebuck,
Kill for us a deer with antlers!"
    Forth into the forest straightway
All alone walked Hiawatha
Proudly, with his bow and arrows;
And the birds sang round him, o'er him,
"Do not shoot us, Hiawatha!"
Sang the robin, the Opechee,
Sang the bluebird, the Owaissa, 180
"Do not shoot us, Hiawatha!"
    Up the oak-tree, close beside him,
Sprang the squirrel, Adjidaumo,
In and out among the branches,
Coughed and chattered from the oak-tree,
Laughed, and said between his laughing,
"Do not shoot me, Hiawatha!"
    And the rabbit from his pathway
Leaped aside, and at a distance
Sat erect upon his haunches, 190
Half in fear and half in frolic,
Saying to the little hunter,
"Do not shoot me, Hiawatha!"
    But he heeded not, nor heard them,
For his thoughts were with the red deer;
On their tracks his eyes were fastened,
Leading downward to the river,
To the ford across the river,
And as one in slumber walked he.
    Hidden in the alder-bushes, 200
There he waited till the deer came,
Till he saw two antlers lifted,

Saw two eyes look from the thicket,
Saw two nostrils point to windward,
And a deer came down the pathway,
Flecked with leafy light and shadow.
And his heart within him fluttered,
Trembled like the leaves above him,
Like the birch-leaf palpitated,
As the deer came down the pathway.   210
   Then, upon one knee uprising,
Hiawatha aimed an arrow;
Scarce a twig moved with his motion,
Scarce a leaf was stirred or rustled,
But the wary roebuck started,
Stamped with all his hoofs together,
Listened with one foot uplifted,
Leaped as if to meet the arrow;
Ah! the singing, fatal arrow,
Like a wasp it buzzed and stung him!   220
   Dead he lay there in the forest,
By the ford across the river;
Beat his timid heart no longer,
But the heart of Hiawatha
Throbbed and shouted and exulted,
As he bore the red deer homeward,
And Iagoo and Nokomis
Hailed his coming with applauses.
   From the red deer's hide Nokomis
Made a cloak for Hiawatha,   230
From the red deer's flesh Nokomis
Made a banquet to his honor.
All the village came and feasted,
All the guests praised Hiawatha,
Called him Strong-Heart, Soan-ge-taha!
Called him Loon-Heart, Mahn-go-taysee!

                                                         (1855)

My Lost Youth

   Often I think of the beautiful town[6]
      That is seated by the sea;
   Often in thought go up and down
   The pleasant streets of that dear old town,

   ---
   6. Longfellow's birthplace, Portland, Maine.

And my youth comes back to me.
    And a verse of a Lapland song[7]
Is haunting my memory still:
"A boy's will is the wind's will,
And the thoughts of youth are long, long thoughts."

I can see the shadowy lines of its trees,   10
    And catch, in sudden gleams,
The sheen of the far-surrounding seas,
And islands that were the Hesperides
    Of all my boyish dreams.
    And the burden of that old song,
    It murmurs and whispers still:
    "A boy's will is the wind's will,
And the thoughts of youth are long, long thoughts."

I remember the black wharves and the slips,
    And the sea-tides tossing free;   20
And Spanish sailors with bearded lips,
And the beauty and mystery of the ships,
    And the magic of the sea.
    And the voice of that wayward song
    Is singing and saying still:
    "A boy's will is the wind's will,
And the thoughts of youth are long, long thoughts."

I remember the bulwarks by the shore,
    And the fort upon the hill;
The sunrise gun, with its hollow roar,   30
The drumbeat repeated o'er and o'er,
    And the bugle wild and shrill.
    And the music of that old song
    Throbs in my memory still:
    "A boy's will is the wind's will,
And the thoughts of youth are long, long thoughts."

I remember the sea-fight far away,[8]
    How it thundered o'er the tide!
And the dead captains, as they lay
In their graves, o'erlooking the tranquil bay   40
    Where they in battle died.
    And the sound of that mournful song

---

7. A Lapland folksong translated by Johann Gottfried Herder (1744–1803), a German poet.
    8. Reference to the 1813 battle between the American *Enterprise* and the British *Boxer*. The Americans won, but both captains were killed and were buried side by side in the cemetery on Mountjoy.

Goes through me with a thrill:
"A boy's will is the wind's will,
And the thoughts of youth are long, long thoughts."

I can see the breezy dome of groves,
    The shadows of Deering's Woods;
And the friendships old and the early loves
Come back with a Sabbath sound, as of doves
    In quiet neighborhoods.   50
        And the verse of that sweet old song,
        It flutters and murmurs still:
        "A boy's will is the wind's will,
And the thoughts of youth are long, long thoughts."

I remember the gleams and glooms that dart
    Across the school-boy's brain;
The song and the silence in the heart,
That in part are prophecies, and in part
    Are longings wild and vain.
        And the voice of that fitful song   60
        Sings on, and is never still:
        "A boy's will is the wind's will,
And the thoughts of youth are long, long thoughts."

There are things of which I may not speak;
    There are dreams that cannot die;
There are thoughts that make the strong heart weak,
And bring a pallor into the cheek,
    And a mist before the eye.
        And the words of that fatal song
        Come over me like a chill: 70
        "A boy's will is the wind's will,
And the thoughts of youth are long, long thoughts."

Strange to me now are the forms I meet
    When I visit the dear old town;
But the native air is pure and sweet,
And the trees that o'ershadow each well-known street,
    As they balance up and down,
        Are singing the beautiful song,
        Are sighing and whispering still:
        "A boy's will is the wind's will,   80
And the thoughts of youth are long, long thoughts."

And Deering's Woods are fresh and fair,
    And with joy that is almost pain

My heart goes back to wander there,
And among the dreams of the days that were,
  I find my lost youth again.
    And the strange and beautiful song,
    The groves are repeating it still:
    "A boy's will is the wind's will,
And the thoughts of youth are long, long thoughts."   90
                                                       (1858)

Snow-Flakes

    Out of the bosom of the Air,
      Out of the cloud-folds of her garments shaken,
    Over the woodlands brown and bare,
      Over the harvest fields forsaken,
        Silent, and soft, and slow
        Descends the snow.

    Even as our cloudy fancies take
      Suddenly shape in some divine expression,
    Even as the troubled heart doth make
      In the white countenance confession,   10
        The troubled sky reveals
        The grief it feels.

    This is the poem of the air,
      Slowly in silent syllables recorded;
    This is the secret of despair,
      Long in its cloudy bosom hoarded,
        Now whispered and revealed
        To wood and field.

                                                     (1863)

Chaucer

    An old man in a lodge within a park;
      The chamber walls depicted all around
      With portraitures of huntsman, hawk, and hound,
      And the hurt deer. He listeneth to the lark,
    Whose song comes with the sunshine through the dark
      Of painted glass in leaden lattice bound:

He listeneth and he laugheth at the sound,
  Then writeth in a book like any clerk.
He is the poet of the dawn, who wrote
  The Canterbury Tales, and his old age   10
  Made beautiful with song; and as I read
I hear the crowing cock, I hear the note
  Of lark and linnet, and from every page
  Rise odors of ploughed field or flowery mead.

                                                          (1875)

Milton

I pace the sounding sea-beach and behold
  How the voluminous billows roll and run,
  Upheaving and subsiding, while the sun
  Shines through their sheeted emerald far unrolled,
And the ninth wave, slow gathering fold by fold[9]
  All its loose-flowing garments into one,
  Plunges upon the shore, and floods the dun
  Pale reach of sands, and changes them to gold.
So in majestic cadence rise and fall
  The mighty undulations of thy song,   10
  O sightless bard, England's Maeonides![10]
And ever and anon, high over all
  Uplifted, a ninth wave superb and strong,
  Floods all the soul with its melodious seas.

                                                          (1875)

The Cross of Snow

In the long, sleepless watches of the night,
  A gentle face—the face of one long dead—[11]
  Looks at me from the wall, where round its head
  The night-lamp casts a halo of pale light.
Here in this room she died; and soul more white
  Never through martyrdom of fire was led
  To its repose; nor can in books be read

---

9. The ninth wave is supposed to be the strongest in the cycle hitting the shore.
10. Homer, like Milton, was blind.
11. Longfellow refers to Fanny, his second wife, who died in 1861.

The legend of a life more benedight.
There is a mountain in the distant West
  That, sun-defying, in its deep ravines   10
  Displays a cross of snow upon its side.
Such is the cross I wear upon my breast
  These eighteen years, through all the changing scenes
  And seasons, changeless since the day she died.

(written 1879, 1886)

The Tide Rises, the Tide Falls

The tide rises, the tide falls,
The twilight darkens, the curlew calls;
Along the sea-sands damp and brown
The traveller hastens toward the town,
  And the tide rises, the tide falls.

Darkness settles on roofs and walls,
But the sea, the sea in the darkness calls;
The little waves, with their soft, white hands,
Efface the footprints in the sands,
  And the tide rises, the tide falls.   10

The morning breaks; the steeds in their stalls
Stamp and neigh, as the hostler calls;
The day returns, but nevermore
Returns the traveller to the shore,
  And the tide rises, the tide falls.

(1880)

John Greenleaf Whittier

1807–1892

Editor, journalist, abolitionist, and author of some twenty volumes of poetry, John Greenleaf Whittier rivalled Longfellow as America's most popular nineteenth-century poet. Early in his career, Whittier published fiery abolitionist poems and verses drawing upon New England folklore. A devout Quaker, he wrote much religious poetry. Whittier's occasional verse includes many tributes to his contemporaries, among them Alice Cary, Lydia Huntley Sigourney, Bayard Taylor, Henry Wadsworth Longfellow, James Russell Lowell, and Oliver Wendell Holmes. His nature, occasional, and narrative poems earned him avid readers, but his mature anti-slavery poetry and his reminiscences of childhood proved his most fertile subjects. *Snow-Bound* (1866) and *The Tent on the Beach* (1867), which sold twenty thousand copies in three weeks, established Whittier as one of his day's favorite poets. Though critics today believe that only "possibly forty" of his poems deserve attention (Pickard 133), his contemporaries consumed and quoted his poetry.

The son of John and Abigail Hussey Whittier, poor and devout Quakers, Whittier was born on 17 December 1807 on a farm near Haverhill, Massachusetts. With little early formal schooling and two terms at Haverhill Academy (1827–28), he published his first poem in 1826 in the *Newburyport Free Press*, a newspaper edited by William Lloyd Garrison. By the time he was twenty, eighty poems had appeared in newspapers.

Whittier's association with Garrison and the anti-slavery movement led him into politics and to several newspaper editorships. Always frail, he resigned his editorship of the *New England Review* in 1832, served as a delegate to the first American Anti-Slavery Convention (1833), and won a seat in the Massachusetts legislature (1835). After his father's death in 1830, Whittier sold the Haverhill farm in 1836 and moved with his mother and sisters to nearby Amesbury, his home for most of his remaining years. He edited the *Pennsylvania Freeman* (1838–40) and the *Middlesex Standard* (Lowell, Massachusetts, 1844–45) before becoming a corresponding editor of Garrison's *National Era* in 1847, a position he held until 1860.

Though he never married, Whittier had platonic relationships with several women. After his mother's death in 1857, he concentrated on writing poetry; the death of his beloved sister Elizabeth in 1864 deprived him of his life's companion. His famous seventieth birthday party in 1877 assembled New England's notables; on that occasion Mark Twain delivered a hilarious comic address that portrayed three con-men posing as Emerson, Longfellow, and Holmes. In Mark Twain's speech, the con-men invade a California miner's cabin, eat his food, steal his boots, and misquote the poets' verse. The New England notables (Whittier included), according to Henry Nash Smith, were only politely amused (92–112). Whittier received an Honorary Degree from Harvard in 1886 and saw to completion the seven-volume edition of his poems in 1888–89. Following a stroke, he died on 7 September 1892 at Hampton Falls, New Hampshire. He was buried in the family plot at Amesbury.

Whittier published two books—*Legends of New-England* (1831), containing verse and prose, and an anti-slavery tract entitled *Justice and Expediency* (1833)—before collecting his *Poems* (1838). *Lays of My Home* (1843), *Voices of Freedom* (1846), and *Songs of Labor* (1850) followed, along with his only novel, *Margaret Smith's Journal* (1848–49). *Songs* contained "Ichabod!," his indictment of Daniel Webster's vote on the Fugitive Slave Act. Whittier continued issuing books of poems regularly: *The Chapel of Hermits* (1853), *The Panorama* (1856), *Home Ballads* (1860), and *In War Time* (1864). *Home Ballads* collected his best poems of the 1850s: "Skipper Ireson's Ride" and "The Double-Headed Snake of Newbury." *Snow-Bound* and *The Tent on the Beach* not only secured Whittier's popularity but they also earned him money. Later volumes include *Among the Hills* (1869), *The Pennsylvania Pilgrim* (1872), *The Vision of Echard* (1878), *The King's Missive* (1881), *The Bay of Seven Islands* (1883), and *Saint Gregory's Guest* (1886). Whittier printed his last collection of poems, *At Sundown* (1890), privately.

Believing that poetry's purpose was to make people better, Whittier wrote that he "set a higher value on my name as appended to the Anti-Slavery Declaration of 1833 than on the title-page of any book" (qtd. in von Frank 193). This view of poetry—alien to Poe's, but the prevailing view of his century—emphasized its social functions rather than its possibilities for exploring the human psyche and the unconscious. This attitude also forced Whittier to rely on inherited verse forms, especially the ballad (the form of his more successful poems). He also had little sympathy for Walt Whitman's *Leaves of Grass*; he purportedly threw Whitman's book in the fire (Wagenknecht 20), though biographers dispute this point. New Criticism nailed Whittier to the mast of poetic sloppiness, simplicity, and naive optimism, but the Quaker conscience that created his best work still appeals. A poet of the commonplace without Dickinson's or Frost's sense of playfulness, Whittier may today be the most important of New England's "schoolroom" or "genteel" poets.

—*Robert Bain*

Suggestions for Further Reading

Keller, Karl. "John Greenleaf Whittier." *Fifteen American Authors Before 1900: Biographical Essays on Research and Criticism.* Ed. Earl N. Harbert and Robert A. Rees. Rev. ed. Madison: U of Wisconsin P, 1984. 468–99.*

Pickard, John B. *John Greenleaf Whittier: An Introduction and Interpretation.* New York: Barnes and Noble, 1961.*

Smith, Henry Nash. *Mark Twain: The Development of a Writer.* New York: Atheneum, 1967.

von Frank, Albert J. "John Greenleaf Whittier." *The American Renaissance in New England.* Vol. 1 of *Dictionary of Literary Biography.* Ed. Joel Myerson. Detroit: Gale, 1978. 191–200.

Wagenknecht, Edward. *John Greenleaf Whittier: A Portrait in Paradox.* New York: Oxford UP, 1967.*

TEXT
The Complete Poetical Works of John Greenleaf Whittier. 1892.

⁂

Ichabod![1]

So fallen! so lost! the light withdrawn
        Which once he wore!
The glory from his gray hairs gone
        Forevermore!

Revile him not,—the Tempter hath
        A snare for all;
And pitying tears, not scorn and wrath,
        Befit his fall!

---

1. Ichabod is a Hebrew name meaning "glory is departed." Whittier refers to Daniel Webster, a Massachusetts senator who voted for passage of the 1850 Fugitive Slave Act. See also 1 Samuel 4:21.

O, dumb be passion's stormy rage,
    When he who might   10
Have lighted up and led his age,
    Falls back in night.

Scorn! would the angels laugh, to mark
    A bright soul driven,
Fiend-goaded, down the endless dark,
    From hope and heaven!

Let not the land once proud of him
    Insult him now,
Nor brand with deeper shame his dim,
    Dishonored brow.   20

But let its humbled sons, instead,
    From sea to lake,
A long lament, as for the dead,
    In sadness make.

Of all we loved and honored, naught
    Save power remains,—
A fallen angel's pride of thought,
    Still strong in chains.

All else is gone; from those great eyes
    The soul has fled: 30
When faith is lost, when honor dies,
    The man is dead!

Then, pay the reverence of old days
    To his dead fame;
Walk backward, with averted gaze,[2]
    And hide the shame!

               (1850)

Skipper Ireson's Ride

Of all the rides since the birth of time,
Told in story or sung in rhyme,—
On Apuleius's Golden Ass,[3]

---

2. See Genesis 9:20–23.
3. Roman satirist Lucius Apuleius (second century B.C.) wrote *The Golden Ass*.

Or one-eyed Calender's horse of brass,[4]
Witch astride of a human back,
Islam's prophet on Al-Borák,—[5]
The strangest ride that ever was sped
Was Ireson's, out from Marblehead!
   Old Floyd Ireson, for his hard heart,
     Tarred and feathered and carried in a cart   10
       By the women of Marblehead!

Body of turkey, head of owl,
Wings a-droop like a rained-on fowl,
Feathered and ruffled in every part,
Skipper Ireson stood in the cart.
Scores of women, old and young,
Strong of muscle, and glib of tongue,
Pushed and pulled up the rocky lane,
Shouting and singing the shrill refrain:
   "Here's Flud Oirson, fur his horrd horrt,   20
     Torr'd an' futherr'd an' corr'd in a corrt
       By the women o' Morble'ead."

Wrinkled scolds with hands on hips,
Girls in bloom of cheek and lips,
Wild-eyed, free-limbed, such as chase
Bacchus round some antique vase,
Brief of skirt, with ankles bare,
Loose of kerchief and loose of hair,
With conch-shells blowing and fish-horns' twang,
Over and over the Maenads sang: 30
   "Here's Flud Oirson, fur his horrd horrt,
     Torr'd an' futherr'd an' corr'd in a corrt
       By the women o' Morble'ead!"

Small pity for him!—He sailed away
From a leaking ship, in Chaleur Bay,—
Sailed away from a sinking wreck,
With his own town's-people on her deck!
"Lay by! lay by!" they called to him.
Back he answered, "Sink or swim!
Brag of your catch of fish again!"   40
And off he sailed through the fog and rain!
   Old Floyd Ireson, for his hard heart,

---

4. From *The Arabian Nights*. A calender is a dervish.
5. Winged animal that carried Mohammed to heaven.

Tarred and feathered and carried in a cart
By the women of Marblehead!

Fathoms deep in dark Chaleur
That wreck shall lie forevermore.
Mother and sister, wife and maid,
Looked from the rocks of Marblehead
Over the moaning and rainy sea,—
Looked for the coming that might not be!   50
What did the winds and the sea-birds say
Of the cruel captain who sailed away?—
    Old Floyd Ireson, for his hard heart,
    Tarred and feathered and carried in a cart
    By the women of Marblehead!

Through the street, on either side,
Up flew windows, doors swung wide;
Sharp-tongued spinsters, old wives gray,
Treble lent the fish-horn's bray.
Sea-worn grandsires, cripple-bound,   60
Hulks of old sailors run aground,
Shook head, and fist, and hat, and cane,
And cracked with curses the hoarse refrain:
    "Here's Flud Oirson, fur his horrd horrt,
    Torr'd an' futherr'd an' corr'd in a corrt
    By the women o' Morble'ead!"

Sweetly along the Salem road
Bloom of orchard and lilac showed.
Little the wicked skipper knew
Of the fields so green and the sky so blue.   70
Riding there in his sorry trim,
Like an Indian idol glum and grim,
Scarcely he seemed the sound to hear
Of voices shouting, far and near:
    "Here's Flud Oirson, fur his horrd horrt,
    Torr'd an' futherr'd an' corr'd in a corrt
    By the women o' Morble'ead!"

"Hear me, neighbors!" at last he cried,—
"What to me is this noisy ride?
What is the shame that clothes the skin   80
To the nameless horror that lives within?
Waking or sleeping, I see a wreck,
And hear a cry from a reeling deck!

Hate me and curse me,—I only dread
The hand of God and the face of the dead!"
    Said old Floyd Ireson, for his hard heart,
    Tarred and feathered and carried in a cart
        By the women of Marblehead!

Then the wife of the skipper lost at sea
Said, "God has touched him!—why should we!"   90
Said an old wife mourning her only son,
"Cut the rogue's tether and let him run!"
So with soft relentings and rude excuse,
Half scorn, half pity, they cut him loose,
And gave him a cloak to hide him in,
And left him alone with his shame and sin.
    Poor Floyd Ireson, for his hard heart,
    Tarred and feathered and carried in a cart
        By the women of Marblehead!

                                        (1857, 1860)

The Double-Headed Snake of Newbury[6]

Far away in the twilight time
Of every people, in every clime,
Dragons and griffins and monsters dire,
Born of water, and air, and fire,
Or nursed, like the Python, in the mud
And ooze of the old Deucalion flood,
Crawl and wriggle and foam with rage,
Through dusk tradition and ballad age.
So from the childhood of Newbury town
And its time of fable the tale comes down   10
Of a terror which haunted bush and brake,
The Amphisbaena, the Double Snake!

Thou who makest the tale thy mirth,
Consider that strip of Christian earth
On the desolate shore of a sailless sea,
Full of terror and mystery,

---

6. "Concerning ye Amphisbaena, as soon as I received your commands, I
made diligent inquiry:. . . . he assures me yt it had really two heads, one at each
end; two mouths, two stings or tongues." Rev. Christopher Toppan to Cotton
Mather. [Whittier's note]

Half redeemed from the evil hold
Of the wood so dreary, and dark, and old,
Which drank with its lips of leaves the dew
When Time was young, and the world was new,   20
And wove its shadows with sun and moon,
Ere the stones of Cheops[7] were squared and hewn.
Think of the sea's dread monotone,
Of the mournful wail from the pine-wood blown,
Of the strange, vast splendors that lit the North,
Of the troubled throes of the quaking earth,
And the dismal tales the Indian told,
Till the settler's heart at his hearth grew cold,
And he shrank from the tawny wizard boasts,
And the hovering shadows seemed full of ghosts,   30
And above, below, and on every side,
The fear of his creed seemed verified;—
And think, if his lot were now thine own,
To grope with terrors nor named nor known,
How laxer muscle and weaker nerve
And a feebler faith thy need might serve;
And own to thyself the wonder more
That the snake had two heads, and not a score!

Whether he lurked in the Oldtown fen
Or the gray earth-flax of the Devil's Den,   40
Or swam in the wooded Artichoke,
Or coiled by the Northman's Written Rock,
Nothing on record is left to show;
Only the fact that he lived, we know,
And left the cast of a double head
In the scaly mask which he yearly shed.
For he carried a head where his tail should be,
And the two, of course, could never agree,
But wriggled about with main and might,
Now to the left and now to the right;   50
Pulling and twisting this way and that,
Neither knew what the other was at.

A snake with two heads, lurking so near!—
Judge of the wonder, guess at the fear!
Think what ancient gossips might say,

---

7. Cheops, whose original name was Khu-fu, was a king of Egypt during the
fourth dynasty (2900?–2877 B.C.). He erected the Great Pyramid.

Shaking their heads in their dreary way,
Between the meetings on Sabbath-day!
How urchins, searching at day's decline
The Common Pasture for sheep or kine,
The terrible double-ganger heard   60
In leafy rustle or whir of bird!
Think what a zest it gave to the sport,
In berry-time, of the younger sort,
As over pastures blackberry-twined,
Reuben and Dorothy lagged behind,
And closer and closer, for fear of harm,
The maiden clung to her lover's arm;
And how the spark, who was forced to stay,
By his sweetheart's fears, till the break of day,
Thanked the snake for the fond delay!   70

Far and wide the tale was told,
Like a snowball growing while it rolled.
The nurse hushed with it the baby's cry;
And it served, in the worthy minister's eye,
To paint the primitive serpent by.
Cotton Mather came galloping down
All the way to Newbury town,
With his eyes agog and his ears set wide,
And his marvellous inkhorn at his side;
Stirring the while in the shallow pool   80
Of his brains for the lore he learned at school,
To garnish the story, with here a streak
Of Latin, and then another of Greek:
And the tales he heard and the notes he took,
Behold! are they not in his Wonder-Book?

Stories, like dragons, are hard to kill.
If the snake does not, the tale runs still
In Byfield Meadows, on Pipestave Hill.
And still, whenever husband and wife
Publish the shame of their daily strife,   90
And, with mad cross-purpose, tug and strain
At either end of the marriage-chain,
The gossips say, with a knowing shake
Of their gray heads, "Look at the Double Snake!
One in body and two in will,
The Amphisbaena is living still!"

                                              (1859, 1860)

from Snow-Bound[8]
A Winter Idyl

> Announced by all the trumpets of the sky,
> Arrives the snow; and, driving o'er the fields,
> Seems nowhere to alight; the whited air
> Hides hills and woods, the river and the heaven
> And veils the farm-house at the garden's end.
> The sled and traveller stopped, the courier's feet
> Delayed, all friends shut out, the housemates sit
> Around the radiant fireplace, enclosed
> In a tumultuous privacy of storm.
>
> —Emerson

The sun that brief December day
Rose cheerless over hills of gray,
And, darkly circled, gave at noon
A sadder light than waning moon.
Slow tracing down the thickening sky

---

8. "To the Memory of The Household It Describes This Poem Is Dedicated by the Author." [Whittier's note beneath the subtitle]

"As the Spirits of Darkness be stronger in the dark, so Good Spirits which be Angels of Light are augmented not only by the Divine light of the Sun, but also by our common Wood Fire: and as the Celestial Fire drives away dark spirits, so also this our Fire of Wood doth the same."—Cor. Agrippa, Occult Philosophy, Book 1, ch. 5. [Whittier's note]

"The inmates of the family at the Whittier homestead who are referred to in the poem were my father, mother, my brother and two sisters, and my uncle and aunt, both unmarried. In addition, there was the district school master, who boarded with us. . . .

"In my boyhood, in our lonely farm-house, we had scanty sources of information; few books and only a small weekly newspaper. Our only annual was the Almanac. Under such circumstances story-telling was a necessary resource in the long winter evenings. My father when a young man had traversed the wilderness to Canada, and could tell us of his adventures with Indians and wild beasts, and of his sojourn in the French villages. My uncle was ready with his record of hunting and fishing and, it must be confessed, with stories which he at least half believed, of witchcraft and apparitions. My mother, who was born in the Indian-haunted region of Somersworth, New Hampshire, between Dover and Portsmouth, told us of the inroads of the savages, and the narrow escape of her ancestors. She described strange people who lived on the Piscataqua and Cocheco, among whom was Bantam the sorcerer. I have in my possession the wizard's 'conjuring book,' which he solemnly opened when consulted. It is a copy of Cornelius Agrippa's *Magic*, printed in 1651, dedicated to Dr. Robert Child, who, like Michael Scott, had learned 'the art of glammorie / In Padua beyond the sea,' and who is famous in the annals of Massachusetts, where he was at one time a resident, as the first man who dared petition the General Court for liberty of conscience. The full title of the book is *Three Books of Occult Philosophy, by Henry Cornelius Agrippa, Knight, Doctor of both Laws, Counsellor to Caesar's Sacred Majesty and Judge of the Prerogative Court*." [Whittier's note, appended later]

Its mute and ominous prophecy,
A portent seeming less than threat,
It sank from sight before it set.
A chill no coat, however stout,
Of homespun stuff could quite shut out,   10
A hard, dull bitterness of cold,
    That checked, mid-vein, the circling race
    Of life-blood in the sharpened face,
The coming of the snow-storm told.
The wind blew east; we heard the roar
Of Ocean on his wintry shore,
And felt the strong pulse throbbing there
Beat with low rhythm our inland air.

Meanwhile we did our nightly chores,—
Brought in the wood from out of doors,   20
Littered the stalls, and from the mows
Raked down the herd's-grass for the cows:
Heard the horse whinnying for his corn;
And, sharply clashing horn on horn,
Impatient down the stanchion rows
The cattle shake their walnut bows;
While, peering from his early perch
Upon the scaffold's pole of birch,
The cock his crested helment bent
And down his querulous challenge sent.   30

Unwarmed by any sunset light
The gray day darkened into night,
A night made hoary with the swarm,
And whirl-dance of the blinding storm,
As zigzag wavering to and fro
Crossed and recrossed the wingèd snow:
And ere the early bedtime came
The white drift piled the window-frame,
And through the glass the clothes-line posts
Looked in like tall and sheeted ghosts.   40

So all night long the storm roared on:
The morning broke without a sun;
In tiny spherule traced with lines
Of Nature's geometric signs,
In starry flake, and pellicle,
All day the hoary meteor fell;
And, when the second morning shone,
We looked upon a world unknown,

On nothing we could call our own.
Around the glistening wonder bent   50
The blue walls of the firmament,
No cloud above, no earth below,—
A universe of sky and snow!
The old familiar sights of ours
Took marvellous shapes; strange domes and towers
Rose up where sty or corn-crib stood,
Or garden-wall, or belt of wood;
A smooth white mound the brush-pile showed,
A fenceless drift what once was road;
The bridle-post an old man sat   60
With loose-flung coat and high cocked hat;
The well-curb had a Chinese roof;
And even the long sweep, high aloof,
In its slant splendor, seemed to tell
Of Pisa's leaning miracle.

A prompt, decisive man, no breath
Our father wasted: "Boys, a path!"
Well pleased, (for when did farmer boy
Count such a summons less than joy?)
Our buskins on our feet we drew;   70
   With mittened hands, and caps drawn low,
   To guard our necks and ears from snow,
We cut the solid whiteness through.
And, where the drift was deepest, made
A tunnel walled and overlaid
With dazzling crystal: we had read
Of rare Aladdin's wondrous cave,
And to our own his name we gave,
With many a wish the luck were ours
To test his lamp's supernal powers.   80
We reached the barn with merry din,
And roused the prisoned brutes within.
The old horse thrust his long head out,
And grave with wonder gazed about;
The cock his lusty greeting said,
And forth his speckled harem led;
The oxen lashed their tails, and hooked,
And mild reproach of hunger looked;
The horned patriarch of the sheep,
Like Egypt's Amun roused from sleep,   90
Shook his sage head with gesture mute,
And emphasized with stamp of foot.

All day the gusty north-wind bore
The loosening drift its breath before;
Low circling round its southern zone,
The sun through dazzling snow-mist shone.
No church-bell lent its Christian tone
To the savage air, no social smoke
Curled over woods of snow-hung oak.
A solitude made more intense   100
By dreary-voiced elements,
The shrieking of the mindless wind,
The moaning tree-boughs swaying blind,
And on the glass the unmeaning beat
Of ghostly finger-tips of sleet.
Beyond the circle of our hearth
No welcome sound of toil or mirth
Unbound the spell, and testified
Of human life and thought outside.
We minded that the sharpest ear   110
The buried brooklet could not hear,
The music of whose liquid lip
Had been to us companionship,
And, in our lonely life, had grown
To have an almost human tone.

As night drew on, and, from the crest
Of wooded knolls that ridged the west,
The sun, a snow-blown traveller, sank
From sight beneath the smothering bank,
We piled, with care, our nightly stack   120
Of wood against the chimney-back,—
The oaken log, green, huge, and thick,
And on its top the stout back-stick;
The knotty forestick laid apart,
And filled between with curious art
The ragged brush; then, hovering near,
We watched the first red blaze appear,
Heard the sharp crackle, caught the gleam
Of whitewashed wall and sagging beam,
Until the old, rude-furnished room   130
Burst, flower-like, into rosy bloom;
While radiant with a mimic flame
Outside the sparkling drift became,
And through the bare-boughed lilac tree
Our own warm hearth seemed blazing free.
The crane and pendent trammels showed,

The Turks' heads on the andirons glowed;
While childish fancy, prompt to tell
The meaning of the miracle,
Whispered the old rhyme: "*Under the tree*   140
When fire outdoors burns merrily,
There the witches are making tea."
The moon above the eastern wood
Shone at its full; the hill-range stood
Transfigured in the silver flood,
Its blown snows flashing cold and keen,
Dead white, save where some sharp ravine
Took shadow, or the sombre green
Of hemlocks turned to pitchy black
Against the whiteness at their back.   150
For such a world and such a night
Most fitting that unwarming light,
Which only seemed where'er it fell
To make the coldness visible.

Shut in from all the world without,
We sat the clean-winged hearth about,
Content to let the north-wind roar
In baffled rage at pane and door,
While the red logs before us beat
The frost-line back with tropic heat;   160
And ever, when a louder blast
Shook beam and rafter as it passed,
The merrier up its roaring draught
The great throat of the chimney laughed,
The house-dog on his paws outspread
Laid to the fire his drowsy head,
The cat's dark silhouette on the wall
A couchant tiger's seemed to fall;
And, for the winter fireside meet,
Between the andirons' straddling feet,   170
The mug of cider simmered slow,
The apples sputtered in a row,
And, close at hand, the basket stood
With nuts from brown October's wood.

What matter how the night behaved?
What matter how the north-wind raved?
Blow high, blow low, not all its snow
Could quench our hearth-fire's ruddy glow.
O Time and Change!—with hair as gray,
As was my sire's that winter day,   180

How strange it seems, with so much gone
Of life and love, to still live on!
Ah, brother! only I and thou
Are left of all that circle now,—
The dear home faces whereupon
That fitful firelight paled and shone.
Henceforward, listen as we will,
The voices of that hearth are still;
Look where we may, the wide earth o'er
Those lighted faces smile no more.   190
We tread the paths their feet have worn,
    We sit beneath their orchard trees,
    We hear, like them, the hum of bees
And rustle of the bladed corn;
We turn the pages that they read,
    Their written words we linger o'er,
But in the sun they cast no shade,
No voice is heard, no sign is made,
    No step is on the conscious floor!
Yet Love will dream, and Faith will trust,   200
(Since He who knows our need is just,)
That somehow, somewhere, meet we must.
Alas for him who never sees
The stars shine through his cypress-trees!
Who, hopeless, lays his dead away,
Nor looks to see the breaking day
Across the mournful marbles play!
Who hath not learned, in hours of faith,
    The truth to flesh and sense unknown,
That Life is ever lord of Death,   210
    And Love can never lose its own!

We sped the time with stories old,
Wrought puzzles out, and riddles told,
Or stammered from our school-book lore
"The Chief of Gambia's golden shore."[9]
How often since, when all the land
Was clay in Slavery's shaping hand,
As if a far-blown trumpet stirred
The languorous, sin-sick air, I heard:
"Does not the voice of reason cry,   220
    Claim the first right which Nature gave,
From the red scourge of bondage fly,

---

9. From "The African Chief," an abolitionist poem by Sarah Morton
(1759–1846). Whittier quotes from the poem in lines 220–23.

Nor deign to live a burdened slave!"
Our father rode again his ride
On Memphremagog's wooded side;
Sat down again to moose and samp
In trapper's hut and Indian camp;
Lived o'er the old idyllic ease
Beneath St Francois' hemlock-trees;
Again for him the moonlight shone   230
On Norman cap and bodiced zone;
Again he heard the violin play
Which led the village dance away,
And mingled in its merry whirl
The grandam and the laughing girl.
Or, nearer home, our steps he led
Where Salisbury's level marshes spread
    Mile-wide as flies the laden bee;
Where merry mowers, hale and strong,
Swept, scythe on scythe, their swaths along,   240
    The low green prairies of the sea.
We shared the fishing off Boar's Head,
    And round the rocky Isles of Shoals
    The hake-broil on the drift-wood coals;
The chowder on the sand-beach made,
Dipped by the hungry, steaming hot,
With spoons of clam-shell from the pot.
We heard the tales of witchcraft old,
And dream and sign and marvel told
To sleepy listeners as they lay   250
Stretched idly on the salted hay,
Adrift along the winding shores,
When favoring breezes deigned to blow
The square sail of the gundelow
And idle lay the useless oars.

Our mother, while she turned her wheel
Or run the new-knit stocking-heel,
Told how the Indian hordes came down
At midnight on Cochecho town,
And how her own great-uncle bore   260
His cruel scalp-mark to fourscore.
Recalling, in her fitting phrase,
    So rich and picturesque and free,
    (The common unrhymed poetry
Of simple life and country ways,)
The story of her early days,—
She made us welcome to her home;

Old hearths grew wide to give us room;
We stole with her a frightened look
At the gray wizard's conjuring book,[10]   270
The fame whereof went far and wide
Through all the simple countryside;
We heard the hawks at twilight play,
The boat-horn on Piscataqua,
The loon's weird laughter far away;
We fished her little trout-brook, knew
What flowers in wood and meadow grew,
What sunny hillsides autumn-brown
She climbed to shake the ripe nuts down,
Saw where in sheltered cove and bay   280
The ducks' black squadron anchored lay,
And heard the wild geese calling loud
Beneath the gray November cloud.

Then, haply, with a look more grave,
And soberer tone, some tale she gave
From painful Sewel's ancient tome,[11]
Beloved in every Quaker home,
Of faith fire-winged by martyrdom,
Or Chalkley's Journal, old and quaint,—[12]
Gentlest of skippers, rare sea-saint!   290
Who, when the dreary calms prevailed,
And water-butt and bread-cask failed,
And cruel, hungry eyes pursued
His portly presence mad for food,
With dark hints muttered under breath
Of casting lots for life or death,
Offered, if Heaven withheld supplies,
To be himself the sacrifice.
Then, suddenly, as if to save
The good man from his living grave,   300
A ripple on the water grew,
A school of porpoise flashed in view.
"Take, eat," he said, "and be content;
These fishes in my stead are sent
By Him who gave the tangled ram
To spare the child of Abraham."

Our uncle, innocent of books,
Was rich in lore of fields and brooks,

---

10. Agrippa's *Occult Philosophy* (1651).
11. William Sewel (1650–1725) wrote a *History of the Quakers* (1717).
12. Captain Thomas Chalkley (1675–1741) wrote a *Journal* (1747).

The ancient teachers never dumb
Of Nature's unhoused lyceum.   310
In moons and tides and weather wise,
He read the clouds as prophecies,
And foul or fair could well divine,
By many an occult hint and sign,
Holding the cunning-warded keys
To all the woodcraft mysteries;
Himself to Nature's heart so near
That all her voices in his ear
Of beast or bird had meanings clear,
Like Apollonius of old,   320
Who knew the tales of sparrows told,
Or Hermes who interpreted
What the sage cranes of Nilus said;
A simple, guileless, childlike man,
Content to live where life began;
Strong only on his native grounds,
The little world of sights and sounds
Whose girdle was the parish bounds,
Whereof his fondly partial pride
The common features magnified,   330
As Surrey hills to mountains grew
In White of Selbornes's loving view,—[13]
He told how teal and loon he shot,
And how the eagle's eggs he got,
The feats on pond and river done,
The prodigies of rod and gun;
Till, warming with the tales he told,
Forgotten was the outside cold,
The bitter wind unheeded blew,
From ripening corn the pigeons flew,   340
The partridge drummed i' the wood, the mink
Went fishing down the river-brink.
In fields with bean or clover gay,
The woodchuck, like a hermit gray,
    Peered from the doorway of his cell;
The muskrat plied the mason's trade,
And tier by tier his mud-walls laid;
And from the shagbark overhead
    The grizzled squirrel dropped his shell.

Next, the dear aunt, whose smile of cheer   350
And voice in dreams I see and hear,—

---

13. *Natural History of Selbourne* (1798), by Gilbert White (1720–93), an
Englishman.

John Greenleaf Whittier

The sweetest woman ever Fate
Perverse denied a household mate,
Who, lonely, homeless, not the less
Found peace in love's unselfishness,
And welcome wheresoe'er she went,
A calm and gracious element,
Whose presence seemed the sweet income
And womanly atmosphere of home,—
Called up her girlhood memories,   360
The huskings and the apple-bees,
The sleigh-rides and the summer sails,
Weaving through all the poor details
And homespun warp of circumstance
A golden woof-thread of romance.
For well she kept her genial mood
And simple faith of maidenhood;
Before her still a cloud-land lay,
The mirage loomed across her way;
The morning dew, that dries so soon   370
With others, glistened at her noon;
Through years of toil and soil and care,
From glossy tress to thin gray hair,
All unprofaned she held apart
The virgin fancies of the heart.
Be shame to him of woman born
Who hath for such but thought of scorn.

There, too, our elder sister plied
Her evening task the stand beside;
A full, rich nature, free to trust,   380
Truthful and almost sternly just,
Impulsive, earnest, prompt to act,
And make her generous thought a fact,
Keeping with many a light disguise
The secret of self-sacrifice.
O heart sore-tried! thou has the best
That Heaven itself could give thee,—rest,
Rest from all bitter thoughts and things!
    How many a poor one's blessing went
    With thee beneath the low green tent   390
Whose curtain never outward swings!

As one who held herself a part
Of all she saw, and let her heart
    Against the household bosom lean,
Upon the motley-braided mat

Our youngest and our dearest sat,
Lifting her large, sweet, asking eyes,
   Now bathed in the unfading green
And holy peace of Paradise.
Oh, looking from some heavenly hill,   400
   Or from the shade of saintly palms,
   Or silver reach of river calms,
Do those large eyes behold me still?
With me one little year ago:—
The chill weight of the winter snow
   For months upon her grave has lain;
And now, when summer south-winds blow
   And brier and harebell bloom again,
I tread the pleasant paths we trod,
I see the voilet-sprinkled sod   410
Whereon she leaned, too frail and weak
The hillside flowers she loved to seek,
Yet following me where'er I went
With dark eyes full of love's content.
The birds are glad; the brier-rose fills
The air with sweetness; all the hills
Stretch green to June's unclouded sky;
But still I wait with ear and eye
For something gone which should be nigh,
A loss in all familiar things,   420
A flower that blooms, and bird that sings.
And yet, dear heart! remembering thee,
   Am I not richer than of old?
Safe in thy immortality
   What change can reach the wealth I hold?
   What chance can mar the pearl and gold
Thy love hath left in trust with me?
And while in life's late afternoon,
   Where cool and long the shadows grow,
I walk to meet the night that soon   430
   Shall shape and shadow overflow,
I cannot feel that thou art far,
Since near at need the angels are;
And when the sunset gates unbar,
   Shall I not see thee waiting stand,
And, white against the evening star,
   The welcome of thy beckoning hand?

Brisk wielder of the birch and rule,
The master of the district school
Held at the fire his favored place,   440

Its warm glow lit a laughing face
Fresh-hued and fair, where scarce appeared
The uncertain prophecy of beard.
He teased the mitten-blinded cat,
Played cross-pins on my uncle's hat,
Sang songs, and told us what befalls
In classic Dartmouth's college halls.
Born the wild Northern hills among,
From whence his yeoman father wrung
By patient toil subsistence scant,   450
Not competence and yet not want,
He early gained the power to pay
His cheerful, self-reliant way;
Could doff at ease his scholar's gown
To peddle wares from town to town;
Or through the long vacation's reach
In lonely lowland districts teach,
Where all the droll experience found
At stranger hearths in boarding round,
The moonlit skater's keen delight,   460
The sleigh-drive through the frosty night,
The rustic party, with its rough
Accompaniment of blind-man's-bluff,
And whirling-plate, and forfeits paid,
His winter task a pastime made.
Happy the snow-locked homes wherein
He tuned his merry violin,
Or played the athlete in the barn,
Or held the good dame's winding-yarn,
Or mirth-provoking versions told   470
Of classic legends rare and old,
Wherein the scenes of Greece and Rome
Had all the commonplace of home,
And little seemed at best the odds
'Twixt Yankee pedlers and old gods;
Where Pindus-born Arachthus[14] took
The guise of any grist-mill brook,
And dread Olympus at his will
Became a huckleberry hill.

A careless boy that night he seemed;   480
    But at his desk he had the look
And air of one who wisely schemed,

---

14. "Pindus" refers to a mountain range in northwest Greece, and
"Arachthus" is an ancient name for the Aras River in Turkey.

And hostage from the future took
In trained thought and lore of book.
Large-brained, clear-eyed, of such as he
Shall Freedom's young apostles be,
Who, following in War's bloody trail,
Shall every lingering wrong assail;
All chains from limb and spirit strike,
Uplift the black and white alike;   490
Scatter before their swift advance
The darkness and the ignorance,
The pride, the lust, the squalid sloth,
Which nurtured Treason's monstrous growth,
Made murder pastime, and the hell
Of prison-torture possible;
The cruel lie of caste refute,
Old forms remould, and substitute
For Slavery's lash the freeman's will,
For blind routine, wise-handed skill;   500
A school-house plant on every hill,
Stretching in radiate nerve-lines thence
The quick wires of intelligence;
Till North and South together brought
Shall own the same electric thought,
In peace a common flag salute,
And, side by side in labor's free
And unresentful rivalry,
Harvest the fields wherein they fought.
. . . .
At last the great logs, crumbling low,   510
Sent out a dull and duller glow,
The bull's-eye watch that hung in view,
Ticking its weary circuit through,
Pointed with mutely warning sign
Its black hand to the hour of nine.
That sign the pleasant circle broke:
My uncle ceased his pipe to smoke,
Knocked from its bowl the refuse gray,
And laid it tenderly away;
Then roused himself to safely cover   520
The dull red brands with ashes over.
And while, with care, our mother laid
The work aside, her steps she stayed
One moment, seeking to express
Her grateful sense of happiness
For food and shelter, warmth and health,
And love's contentment more than wealth,

With simple wishes (not the weak,
Vain prayers which no fulfilment seek,
But such as warm the generous heart,   530
O'er-prompt to do with Heaven its part)
That none might lack, that bitter night,
For bread and clothing, warmth and light.

Within our beds awhile we heard
The wind that round the gables roared,
With now and then a ruder shock,
Which made our very bedsteads rock.
We heard the loosened clapboards tost,
The board-nails snapping in the frost;
And on us, through the unplastered wall,   540
Felt the light sifted snow-flakes fall.
But sleep stole on, as sleep will do
When hearts are light and life is new;
Faint and more faint the murmurs grew,
Till in the summer-land of dreams
They softened to the sound of streams,
Low stir of leaves, and dip of oars,
And lapsing waves on quiet shores.

Next morn we wakened with the shout
Of merry voices high and clear;   550
And saw the teamsters drawing near
To break the drifted highways out.
Down the long hillside treading slow
We saw the half-buried oxen go,
Shaking the snow from heads uptost,
Their straining nostrils white with frost.
Before our door the straggling train
Drew up, an added team to gain.
The elders threshed their hands a-cold,
    Passed, with the cider-mug, their jokes   560
    From lip to lip; the younger folks
Down the loose snow-banks, wrestling, rolled,
Then toiled again the cavalcade
    O'er windy hill, through clogged ravine,
    And woodland paths that wound between
Low drooping pine-boughs winter-weighed.
From every barn a team afoot,
At every house a new recruit,
Where, drawn by Nature's subtlest law,
Haply the watchful young men saw   570
Sweet doorway pictures of the curls

And curious eyes of merry girls,
Lifting their hands in mock defence
Against the snow-ball's compliments,
And reading in each missive tost
The charm with Eden never lost.

We heard once more the sleigh-bells' sound;
   And, following where the teamsters led,
The wise old Doctor went his round,
Just pausing at our door to say,   580
In the brief autocratic way
Of one who, prompt at Duty's call,
Was free to urge her claim on all,
   That some poor neighbor sick abed
At night our mother's aid would need.
For, one in generous thought and deed,
   What mattered in the sufferer's sight
   The Quaker matron's inward light,
The Doctor's mail of Calvin's creed?
All hearts confess the saints elect   590
   Who, twain in faith, in love agree,
And melt not in an acid sect
   The Christian pearl of charity!

So days went on: a week had passed
Since the great world was heard from last.
The Almanac we studied o'er,
Read and reread our little store
Of books and pamphlets, scarce a score;
One harmless novel, mostly hid
From younger eyes, a book forbid,   600
And poetry, (or good or bad,
A single book was all we had,)
Where Ellwood's meek, drab-skirted Muse,[15]
   A stranger to the heathen Nine,
   Sang, with a somewhat nasal whine,
The wars of David and the Jews.
At last the floundering carrier bore
The village paper to our door.
Lo! broadening outward as we read,
To warmer zones the horizon spread;   610
In panoramic length unrolled
We saw the marvels that it told.

---

15. Thomas Ellwood (1639–1714), an English Quaker who wrote *Davideis*
(1712).

Before us passed the painted Creeks,[16]
    And daft McGregor on his raids
    In Costa Rica's everglades.[17]
And up Taygetos winding slow
Rode Ypsilanti's Mainote Greeks,[18]
A Turk's head at each saddle-bow!
Welcome to us its week-old news,
Its corner for the rustic Muse,   620
    Its monthly gauge of snow and rain,
Its record, mingling in a breath
The wedding bell and dirge of death:
Jest, anecdote, and love-lorn tale,
The latest culprit sent to jail;
Its hue and cry of stolen and lost,
Its vendue sales and goods at cost,
    And traffic calling loud for gain.
We felt the stir of hall and street,
The pulse of life that round us beat;   630
The chill embargo of the snow
Was melted in the genial glow;
Wide swung again our ice-locked door,
And all the world was ours once more!

Clasp, Angel of the backwood look
    And folded wings of ashen gray
    And voice of echoes far away,
The brazen covers of thy book;
The weird palimpsest old and vast,
Wherein thou hid'st the spectral past;   640
Where, closely mingling, pale and glow
The characters of joy and woe;
The monographs of outlived years,
Or smile-illumed or dim with tears,
    Green hills of life that slope to death,
And haunts of home, whose vistaed trees
Shade off to mournful cypresses
    With the white amaranths underneath.
Even while I look, I can but heed
    The restless sands' incessant fall,   650
Importunate hours that hours succeed,

---

16. The Creek Indian War of 1813–14 and the moving of these tribes to the Oklahoma Territory.

17. Gregor MacGregor, an Englishman, attempted to colonize and conquer Costa Rica in 1819. He failed.

18. Alexander Ypsilanti (1792–1828), a leader of Greek soldiers in the war against the Turks in 1820.

Each clamorous with its own sharp need,
    And duty keeping pace with all.
Shut down and clasp the heavy lids;
I hear again the voice that bids
The dreamer leave his dream midway
For larger hopes and graver fears:
Life greatens in these later years,
And century's aloe flowers to-day!

Yet, haply, in some lull of life,   660
Some Truce of God which breaks its strife,
The worldling's eyes shall gather dew,
    Dreaming in throngful city ways
Of winter joys his boyhood knew;
And dear and early friends—the few
Who yet remain—shall pause to view
    These Flemish pictures of old days;
Sit with me by the homestead hearth,
And stretch the hands of memory forth
    To warm them at the wood-fire's blaze!   670
And thanks untraced to lips unknown
Shall greet me like the odors blown
From unseen meadows newly mown,
Or lilies floating in some pond,
Wood-fringed, the wayside gaze beyond;
The traveller owns the grateful sense
Of sweetness near, he knows not whence,
And, pausing, takes with forehead bare
The benediction of the air.

                                            (1866)

Edgar Allan Poe

1809–1849

Edgar Allan Poe has weathered many critical vicissitudes during his varied career as poet, critic, theorist, editor, and fiction writer. Emerson called him the "jingle man"; Rufus Griswold, his earliest biographer, maligned his art and morality; French poet and critic Charles Baudelaire praised his poems. Able to defend himself in any combat, Poe called the Bostonians "Frogpondians" (Silverman 269–70), chastized contemporary poets for committing the "heresy of *The Didactic*" ("The Poetic Principle"), and wrote ironically of the "so-called poetry of the so-called transcendentalists" ("The Philosophy of Composition"). Though he wrote only a few more than fifty poems, his poems and critical writings about poetry have established him as a major poet. In his literary theory and practice, Poe "helped to create the modern literary imagination" (Carlson, "Edgar Allan Poe" 365) by championing art for its own value and by symbolically centering his work in the maelstrom of the unconscious.

The son of itinerant actors Elizabeth Arnold and David Poe, Jr., Edgar Poe was born 19 January 1809 in Boston, Massachusetts. Soon orphaned, he moved to the household of John and Frances Allan (hence Poe's middle name) of Richmond, Virginia. Allan, a merchant, never legally adopted Poe, but while conducting business in England, Allan educated the boy in British schools (1815–20) and sent him to the University of Virginia in 1826. Poe left school the following year because of gambling debts. After a sojourn in Boston, he served briefly in the army before Allan secured him an appointment to the U.S. Military Academy at West Point in July 1830.

Poe left West Point for New York City in February 1831 and then moved to Baltimore where he lived with Mrs. Maria Clemm, his aunt, and her daughter Virginia. By that time, he had published three volumes of poetry: *Tamerlane and Other Poems* (1827); *Al Aaraaf, Tamerlane, and Minor Poems* (1829); and *Poems by Edgar A. Poe* (1831), which included "To Helen," "The City in the Sea," and "Israfel."

Discouraged by the reception of his poems, Poe began in 1831 to write prose tales for magazines. After serving successfully as assistant editor of the *Southern Literary Messenger* (1835–36) in Richmond and after marrying his thirteen-year-old cousin Virginia Clemm on 16 May 1836, he moved again to New York where he struggled for a living. Moving to Philadelphia, Poe coedited *Burton's Gentleman's Magazine* in 1839 and later held an editorial position with *Graham's Magazine* (1841–42). During this time, he wrote a few poems and some of his best fiction: "Ligeia" (1838); his only novel, *The Narrative of Arthur Gordon Pym* (1838); and twenty-five tales in two volumes entitled *Tales of the Grotesque and Arabesque* (1840).

The 1840s were both painful and productive for Poe. He agonized much about Virginia, who ruptured a blood vessel in 1842, never fully recovered her health, and died of tuberculosis on 30 January 1847. Always plagued by drinking problems and the need for money, Poe moved in April 1844 to New York to work briefly for the *Evening Mirror* and then to purchase his own paper, the *Broadway Journal*, which he edited from 25 October 1845 to 3 January 1846. "The Raven" appeared in the *Evening Mirror* on 29 January 1845, and he published a poem by Walter Whitman ("Art Singing and Heart Singing") in his *Journal* on 29 November 1845. In addition to dozens of reviews (including his attack on Longfellow), essays, and tales, he published two books in 1845: *The Raven and Other Poems* and *Tales by Edgar A. Poe*.

After Virginia's death, he suffered severe depression. Recovering, he later formed romantic attachments to Annie Richmond and Sarah Helen Whitman, the latter a poet and author of *Edgar Poe and His Critics* (1860), a book defending his work and character. In his last years, Poe attempted unsuccessfully to finance his ideal magazine, to be called *The Stylus*. He also wrote *Eureka: A Prose Poem* (1848), a long philosophical treatise on the nature of the universe. On a return trip from Richmond to publicize *The Stylus*, Poe stopped in Baltimore, where he was found semiconscious on the street and taken to a hospital. He died 7 October 1849 of "congestion of the brain" (Carlson, "Edgar Allan Poe" 370).

In "The Philosophy of Composition," "The Poetic Principle," and other essays, Poe insisted that poetry should be the rhythmical creation of beauty, that the poem should exist for its own sake and not for didactic purposes, and that a true poem should elevate the reader's soul. He often associated poetry with music. "To Helen" and "Israfel" illustrate in verse the theory he forwarded in his essays. To create the music of his verse, Poe employed conventional rhythms and verse forms. But thematically, his poems represent radical explorations of the surreal world of the psyche. His recurrent themes include dreams as reality, the hunger for supernal beauty, the lost Eden, death and the world's dark powers, nightmare visions and the demonic self, and ideal love and beauty as redemptive (Carlson, *Introduction* vi-vii). In "The Raven," "Dream-Land," and other poems, Poe presents abnormal psychological studies of their speakers. He was, as critics have noted, a conscious symbolist.

Often called the father of the modern short story and the modern detective story, Poe's poetry influenced greatly such French symbolists as Baudelaire, whose followers influenced the American imagists of the early twentieth century. More important, Poe has been a popular poet for serious critics and general readers from his day to ours. Though he still has his detractors, his reputation today seems secure.

—Robert Bain

Suggestions for Further Reading

Carlson, Eric W. "Edgar Allan Poe." *Fifty Southern Writers Before 1900.* Ed. Robert Bain and Joseph M. Flora. New York: Greenwood, 1987. 365–88.*

———, ed. *Introduction to Poe: A Thematic Reader.* Glenview, IL: Scott, Foresman, 1967.

Hubbell, Jay B. "Edgar Allan Poe." *Eight American Authors: A Review of Research and Criticism.* Ed. James Woodress. New York: Norton, 1971. 3–36.*

Quinn, Arthur Hobson. *Edgar Allan Poe: A Critical Biography.* New York: Appleton-Century, 1941; New York: Cooper Square, 1970.

Silverman, Kenneth. *Edgar A. Poe: Mournful and Never-Ending Remembrance.* New York: HarperCollins, 1991.

Stovall, Floyd. *Edgar Poe the Poet: Essays Old and New on the Man and His Work.* Charlottesville: UP of Virginia, 1969.

Thomas, Dwight, and David K. Jackson. *The Poe Log: A Documentary Record of the Life of Edgar Allan Poe, 1980–1849.* Boston: Hall, 1987.*

Woodress, James, et al. *American Literary Scholarship: An Annual.* Durham, NC: Duke UP, 1965–Present.*

TEXTS
The Raven and Other Poems. 1845.
The Poems of Edgar Allan Poe. Ed. Floyd Stovall. Charlottesville: UP of Virginia, 1965.

Sonnet—To Science

SCIENCE! true daughter of Old Time thou art!
Who alterest all things with thy peering eyes.
Why preyest thou thus upon the poet's heart,
    Vulture, whose wings are dull realities?
How should he love thee? or how deem thee wise,
    Who wouldst not leave him in his wandering
To seek for treasure in the jewelled skies,
    Albeit he soared with an undaunted wing?
Hast thou not dragged Diana from her car?
    And driven the Hamadryad from the wood   10
To seek a shelter in some happier star?
    Hast thou not torn the Naiad from her flood,
The Elfin from the green grass, and from me
The summer dream beneath the tamarind tree?

(1829, 1845)

Romance

Romance, who loves to nod and sing,
With drowsy head and folded wing,
Among the green leaves as they shake
Far down within some shadowy lake,
To me a painted paroquet
Hath been—a most familiar bird—
Taught me my alphabet to say—
To lisp my very earliest word
While in the wild wood I did lie
A child—with a most knowing eye.   10

Of late, eternal Condor years
So shake the very Heaven on high
With tumult as they thunder by,
I have not time for idle cares
Through gazing on the unquiet sky.
And when an hour with calmer wings
Its down upon my spirit flings—
That little time with lyre and rhyme
To while away—forbidden things!
My heart would feel to be a crime   20
Unless it trembled with the strings.

(1829, 1845)

To Helen

Helen, thy beauty is to me
    Like those Nicean barks of yore,
That gently, o'er a perfumed sea,
    The weary, way-worn wanderer bore
    To his own native shore.

On desperate seas long wont to roam,
    Thy hyacinth hair, thy classic face,
Thy Naiad airs have brought me home
    To the glory that was Greece,
    And the grandeur that was Rome. 10

Lo! in yon brilliant window-niche
    How statue-like I see thee stand,
The agate lamp within thy hand!
    Ah, Psyche, from the regions which
    Are Holy-Land!

              (1831, 1845)

Israfel[1]

In Heaven a spirit doth dwell
"Whose heart-strings are a lute;"
None sing so wildly well
As the angel Israfel,
And the giddy stars (so legends tell)
Ceasing their hymns, attend the spell
Of his voice, all mute.

Tottering above
    In her highest noon,
    The enamoured moon 10
Blushes with love,
    While, to listen, the red levin
    (With the rapid Pleiads, even,
    Which were seven,)
Pauses in Heaven.

---

1. "And the angel Israfel, whose heart-strings are a lute, and who has the sweetest voice of all God's creatures.—Koran." [Poe's note] Poe here quotes from George Sale's "Preliminary Discourse" in his edition of the *Koran* (1764): "the angel Israfel, who has the most melodious voice of all God's creatures."

And they say (the starry choir
   And the other listening things)
That Israfeli's fire
Is owing to that lyre
   By which he sits and sings—   20
The trembling living wire
Of those unusual strings.

But the skies that angel trod,
   Where deep thoughts are a duty—
Where Love's a grown up God—
   Where the Houri glances are
Imbued with all the beauty
   Which we worship in a star.

Therefore, thou art not wrong,
   Israfeli, who despisest   30
An unimpassioned song;
To thee the laurels belong,
   Best bard, because the wisest!
Merrily live, and long!

The ecstasies above
   With thy burning measures suit—
Thy grief, thy joy, thy hate, thy love,
   With the fervour of thy lute—
Well may the stars be mute!

Yes, Heaven is thine; but this   40
   Is a world of sweets and sours;
   Our flowers are merely—flowers,
And the shadow of thy perfect bliss
   Is the sunshine of ours.

If I could dwell
Where Israfel
   Hath dwelt, and he where I,
He might not sing so wildly well
   A mortal melody,
While a bolder note than this might swell   50
   From my lyre within the sky.

                                (1831, 1845)

The City in the Sea[2]

Lo! Death has reared himself a throne
In a strange city lying alone
Far down within the dim West,
Where the good and the bad and the worst and the best
Have gone to their eternal rest.
There shrines and palaces and towers
(Time-eaten towers that tremble not!)
Resemble nothing that is ours.
Around, by lifting winds forgot,
Resignedly beneath the sky   10
The melancholy waters lie.

No rays from the holy heaven come down
On the long night-time of that town;
But light from out the lurid sea
Streams up the turrets silently—
Gleams up the pinnacles far and free—
Up domes—up spires—up kingly halls—
Up fanes—up Babylon-like walls—
Up shadowy long-forgotten bowers
Of sculptured ivy and stone flowers—   20
Up many and many a marvellous shrine
Whose wreathèd friezes intertwine
The viol, the violet, and the vine.

Resignedly beneath the sky
The melancholy waters lie.
So blend the turrets and shadows there
That all seem pendulous in air,
While from a proud tower in the town
Death looks gigantically down.

There open fanes and gaping graves   30
Yawn level with the luminous waves;
But not the riches there that lie
In each idol's diamond eye—
Not the gaily-jewelled dead
Tempt the waters from their bed;
For no ripples curl, alas!
Along that wilderness of glass—
No swellings tell that winds may be

---

2. Earlier titles for this poem were "The Doomed City" (1831) and "The City
of Sin" (1836).

Upon some far-off happier sea—
No heavings hint that winds have been   40
On seas less hideously serene.

But lo, a stir is in the air!
The wave—there is a movement there!
As if the towers had thrust aside,
In slightly sinking, the dull tide—
As if their tops had feebly given
A void within the filmy Heaven.
The waves have now a redder glow—
The hours are breathing faint and low—
And when, amid no earthly moans,   50
Down, down that town shall settle hence.
Hell, rising from a thousand thrones,[3]
Shall do it reverence.

                                        (1831, 1845)

The Haunted Palace[4]

In the greenest of our valleys
    By good angels tenanted,
Once a fair and stately palace—
    Radiant palace—reared its head.
In the monarch Thought's dominion—
    It stood there!
Never seraph spread a pinion
    Over fabric half so fair!

Banners yellow, glorious, golden,
    On its roof did float and flow,   10
(This—all this—was in the olden
    Time long ago,)
And every gentle air that dallied,
    In that sweet day,
Along the ramparts plumed and pallid,
    A wingèd odour went away.

Wanderers in that happy valley,
    Through two luminous windows, saw

---

3. See Isaiah 14:9.
4. Poe published "The Haunted Palace" in his story "The Fall of the House of Usher" (1839).

Spirits moving musically,
  To a lute's well-tuned law,   20
Round about a throne where, sitting
  (Porphyrogene!)⁵
In state his glory well befitting,
  The ruler of the realm was seen.

And all with pearl and ruby glowing
  Was the fair palace door,
Through which came flowing, flowing, flowing,
  And sparkling evermore,
A troop of Echoes, whose sweet duty
  Was but to sing,   30
In voices of surpassing beauty,
  The wit and wisdom of their king.

But evil things, in robes of sorrow,
  Assailed the monarch's high estate.
(Ah, let us mourn!—for never [m]orrow⁶
  Shall dawn upon him desolate!)
And round about his home the glory
  That blushed and bloomed,
Is but a dim-remembered story
  Of the old time entombed.   40

And travellers, now, within that valley,
  Through the red-litten windows see
Vast forms, that move fantastically
  To a discordant melody,
While, like a ghastly rapid river,
  Through the pale door
A hideous throng rush out forever
  And laugh—but smile no more.

                                              (1839, 1845)

The Conqueror Worm⁷

Lo! 'tis a gala night
  Within the lonesome latter years!

---

5. "Born to the purple" or of royal birth.
6. The 1845 text reads "sorrow." Ensuing editors have emended the text to read "morrow."
7. Poe published this poem in his story "Ligeia" (1845).

An angel throng, bewinged, bedight
  In veils, and drowned in tears,
Sit in a theatre, to see
  A play of hopes and fears,
While the orchestra breathes fitfully
  The music of the spheres.

Mimes, in the form of God on high,
  Mutter and mumble low,   10
And hither and thither fly—
  Mere puppets they, who come and go
At bidding of vast formless things
  That shift the scenery to and fro,
Flapping from out their Condor wings
  Invisible Wo!

The motley drama—oh, be sure
  It shall not be forgot!
With its Phantom chased for evermore,
  By a crowd that seize it not,   20
Through a circle that ever returneth in
  To the self-same spot,
And much of Madness, and more of Sin,
  And Horror the soul of the plot.

But see, amid the mimic rout
  A crawling shape intrude!
A blood-red thing that writhes from out
  The scenic solitude!
It writhes!—it writhes!—with mortal pangs
  The mimes become its food,   30
And the angels sob at vermin fangs
  In human gore imbued.

Out—out are the lights—out all!
  And, over each quivering form,
The curtain, a funeral pall,
  Comes down with the rush of a storm,
And the angels, all pallid and wan,
  Uprising, unveiling, affirm
That the play is the tragedy, "Man,"
  And its hero the Conqueror Worm.   40
                     (1839, 1845)

Dream-Land

By a route obscure and lonely,
Haunted by ill angels only,
Where an Eidolon, named NIGHT,
On a black throne reigns upright,
I have reached these lands but newly
From an ultimate dim Thule—
From a wild weird clime that lieth, sublime,
  Out of SPACE—out of TIME.

  Bottomless vales and boundless floods,
And chasms, and caves, and Titan woods,   10
With forms that no man can discover
For the dews that drip all over;
Mountains toppling evermore
Into seas without a shore;
Seas that restlessly aspire,
Surging, unto skies of fire;
Lakes that endlessly outspread
Their lone waters—lone and dead,—
Their still waters, still and chilly
With the snows of the lolling lily.   20

By the lakes that thus outspread
Their lone waters, lone and dead,—
Their sad waters, sad and chilly
With the snows of the lolling lily,—
By the mountains—near the river
Murmuring lowly, murmuring ever,—
By the grey woods,—by the swamp
Where the toad and the newt encamp,—
By the dismal tarns and pools
  Where dwell the Ghouls,—   30
By each spot the most unholy—
In each nook most melancholy,—
There the traveller meets aghast
Sheeted Memories of the Past—
Shrouded forms that start and sigh
As they pass the wanderer by—
White-robed forms of friends long given,
In agony, to the Earth—and Heaven.

For the heart whose woes are legion
'Tis a peaceful, soothing region—   40

For the spirit that walks in shadow
'Tis—oh, 'tis an Eldorado!
But the traveller, travelling through it,
May not—dare not openly view it;
Never its mysteries are exposed
To the weak human eye unclosed;
So wills its King, who hath forbid
The uplifting of the fringèd lid;
And thus the sad Soul that here passes
Beholds it but through darkened glasses.   50

By a route obscure and lonely,
Haunted by ill angels only,
Where an Eidolon, named NIGHT,
On a black throne reigns upright,
I have wandered home but newly
From this ultimate dim Thule.

                                        (1844, 1845)

The Raven

Once upon a midnight dreary, while I pondered, weak and
        weary,
Over many a quaint and curious volume of forgotten lore,
While I nodded, nearly napping, suddenly there came a
        tapping,
As of some one gently rapping, rapping at my chamber door.
" 'Tis some visiter," I muttered, "tapping at my chamber
        door—
                Only this, and nothing more."

Ah, distinctly I remember it was in the bleak December,
And each separate dying ember wrought its ghost upon the
        floor,
Eagerly I wished the morrow;—vainly I had sought to
        borrow
From my books surcease of sorrow—sorrow for the lost
        Lenore—   10
For the rare and radiant maiden whom the angels name
        Lenore—
                Nameless here for evermore.

And the silken sad uncertain rustling of each purple curtain
Thrilled me—filled me with fantastic terrors never felt
    before;
So that now, to still the beating of my heart, I stood
    repeating
" 'Tis some visiter entreating entrance at my chamber
    door—
Some late visiter entreating entrance at my chamber door;—
              This it is, and nothing more."

Presently my soul grew stronger; hesitating then no longer,
"Sir," said I, "or Madam, truly your forgiveness I implore; 20
But the fact is I was napping, and so gently you came
    rapping,
And so faintly you came tapping, tapping at my chamber
    door,
That I scarce was sure I heard you"—here I opened wide
    the door;—
              Darkness there, and nothing more.

Deep into that darkness peering, long I stood there
    wondering, fearing,
Doubting, dreaming dreams no mortal ever dared to dream
    before;
But the silence was unbroken, and the darkness gave no
    token,
And the only word there spoken was the whispered word
    "Lenore!"
This I whispered, and an echo murmured back the word
    "Lenore!"
              Merely this, and nothing more.   30

Back into the chamber turning, all my soul within me
    burning,
Soon I heard again a tapping somewhat louder than before.
"Surely," said I, "surely that is something at my window
    lattice;
Let me see, then, what thereat is, and this mystery explore—
Let my heart be still a moment and this mystery explore;—
              'Tis the wind and nothing more.

Open here I flung the shutter, when, with many a flirt and
    flutter,
In there stepped a stately raven of the saintly days of yore;
Not the least obeisance made he; not an instant stopped or
    stayed he;

But, with mien of lord or lady, perched above my chamber
    door—   40
Perched upon a bust of Pallas[8] just above my chamber
    door—
                Perched, and sat, and nothing
    more.

Then this ebony bird beguiling my sad fancy into smiling,
By the grave and stern decorum of the countenance it wore,
"Though thy crest be shorn and shaven, thou," I said, "art
    sure no craven,
Ghastly grim and ancient raven wandering from the Nightly
    shore—
Tell me what thy lordly name is on the Night's Plutonian[9]
    shore!"
                Quoth the raven, "Nevermore."

Much I marvelled this ungainly fowl to hear discourse so
    plainly,
Though its answer little meaning—little relevancy bore;   50
For we cannot help agreeing that no living human being
Ever yet was blessed with seeing bird above his chamber
    door—
Bird or beast upon the sculptured bust above his chamber
    door,
                With such name as "Nevermore."

But the raven, sitting lonely on the placid bust, spoke only
That one word, as if his soul in that one word he did
    outpour.
Nothing farther then he uttered—not a feather then he
    fluttered—
Till I scarcely more than muttered "Other friends have
    flown before—
On the morrow *he* will leave me, as my hopes have flown
    before."
                Then the bird said "Nevermore." 60

Startled at the stillness broken by reply so aptly spoken,
"Doubtless," said I, "what it utters is its only stock and store
Caught from some unhappy master whom unmerciful
    Disaster

8. In Greek mythology, the patron goddess of Athens and the patron of
health, learning, and wisdom.
9. Pluto ruled Hades, the place of the dead, in Roman mythology.

Followed fast and followed faster till his songs one burden
    bore—
Till the dirges of his Hope that melancholy burden bore
              Of 'Never—nevermore.' "

But the raven still beguiling all my sad soul into smiling,
Straight I wheeled a cushioned seat in front of bird, and
    bust and door;
Then, upon the velvet sinking, I betook myself to linking
Fancy unto fancy, thinking what this ominous bird of
    yore—   70
What this grim, ungainly, ghastly, gaunt, and ominous bird
    of yore
              Meant in croaking "Nevermore."

This I sat engaged in guessing, but no syllable expressing
To the fowl whose fiery eyes now burned into my bosom's
    core;
This and more I sat divining, with my head at ease reclining
On the cushion's velvet lining that the lamplight gloated o'er,
But whose velvet violet lining with the lamplight gloating
    o'er,
              She shall press, ah, nevermore!

Then, methought, the air grew denser, perfumed from an
    unseen censer,
Swung by angels whose faint foot-falls tinkled on the tufted
    floor.   80
"Wretch," I cried, "thy God hath lent thee—by these angels
    he hath sent thee
Respite—respite and nepenthe from thy memories of
    Lenore!
Quaff, oh quaff this kind nepenthe and forget this lost
    Lenore!"
              Quoth the raven, "Nevermore."

"Prophet!" said I, "thing of evil!—prophet still, if bird or
    devil!—
Whether Tempter sent, or whether tempest tossed thee here
    ashore,
Desolate yet all undaunted, on this desert land enchanted—
On this home by Horror haunted—tell me truly, I implore—
Is there—*is* there balm in Gilead?[10] —tell me—tell me, I
    implore—
             Quoth the raven, "Nevermore." 90

---

10. A medicine made from the resin of trees growing in Gilead in Jordan.

"Prophet!" said I, "thing of evil—prophet still, if bird or
　　devil!
By that Heaven that bends above us—by that God we both
　　adore—
Tell this soul with sorrow laden if, within the distant
　　Aidenn,[11]
It shall clasp a sainted maiden whom the angels name
　　Lenore—
Clasp a rare and radiant maiden whom the angels name
　　Lenore."
　　　　　　　　　　Quoth the raven, "Nevermore."

"Be that word our sign of parting, bird or fiend!" I
　　shrieked, upstarting—
"Get thee back into the tempest and the Night's Plutonian
　　shore!
Leave no black plume as a token of that lie thy soul hath
　　spoken!
Leave my loneliness unbroken!—quit the bust above my
　　door!　　　　　　　　　　　　　　　　　　　　　　100
Take thy beak from out my heart, and take thy form from
　　off my door!"
　　　　　　　　　　Quoth the raven, "Nevermore."

And the raven, never flitting, still is sitting, still is sitting
On the pallid bust of Pallas just above my chamber door;
And his eyes have all the seeming of a demon's that is
　　dreaming,
And the lamp-light o'er him streaming throws his shadow
　　on the floor;
And my soul from out that shadow that lies floating on the
　　floor
　　　　　　　　　　Shall be lifted—nevermore!

　　　　　　　　　　　　　　　　　(1845)

---

11. Eden.

Oliver Wendell Holmes
1809–1894

Scientist, wit, and fierce critic of New England Calvinism, Dr. Oliver Wendell Holmes entertained his contemporaries with lyric and occasional poems. Today his literary reputation rests mainly on his three volumes of *Autocrat* essays and his novels. Though he is now considered a minor poet, a half century ago most American schoolchildren could recite lines from two of his most famous poems: "Old Ironsides" and "The Chambered Nautilus."

Born in Cambridge, Massachusetts, on 29 August 1809, Holmes was the son of Sarah Wendell and Abiel Holmes, minister of the First Church in Cambridge. Educated at Phillips Academy (1824–25) and Harvard College (1825–29), Holmes read law for a year before studying medicine in Paris from 1833 to 1835. After receiving his M.D. from Harvard in 1836, he taught at Dartmouth Medical College (1838–40). Holmes married Amelia Jackson in 1840; they had three children, the oldest of whom, Oliver Wendell Holmes, Jr., became a justice of the U.S. Supreme Court. Holmes practiced medicine in Boston before joining the Harvard Medical School faculty in 1847, a position he held until 1882. Throughout these years, Holmes earned distinction for his medical writings on malaria fever, puerperal fever ("childbed fever"), and the philosophy and psychology of medicine. He toured England in 1886 and collected his writings in thirteen volumes for the 1891 Riverside Edition. Holmes died in Cambridge on 10 October 1894, a much-revered scientist and man of letters.

Holmes began writing poetry while a Harvard student. He later collected his work in a volme entitled *Poems* (1836), which included "Old Ironsides." Holmes provided the name for *The Atlantic Monthly*, founded in 1857, and wrote for it *The Autocrat of the Breakfast-Table* essays, which he published in book form in 1858. He ended these essays with poems, chief among them "The Deacon's Masterpiece; or, The Wonderful 'One-Hoss Shay,' " his satire on Jonathan Edwards and New England Calvinism. Holmes continued this series in *The Professor at the Breakfast-Table* (1860) and *The Poet at the Breakfast-Table* (1872). He again collected his poems in *Songs in Many Keys* (1862) and wrote three novels: *Elsie Venner* (1861), *The Guardian Angel* (1867), and *A Mortal Antipathy* (1885). His later volumes of poetry included *Songs of Many Seasons* (1875), *The Iron Gate* (1880), *Before the Curfew* (1887), and *Over the Teacups* (1891). Holmes also wrote a biography of historian John Lathrop Motley (1879) and of Emerson (1885).

Although Holmes "left no distinctive mark on any single literary form" (Menikoff, *Dictionary* 106), within those forms he wrote with vigor. Accused by some critics of dilettantism, he defined New England brahminism in his poems and prose and wrote on such themes as nature and nurture, the search for truth, the foibles of his time, and the nature of art. He dealt with these themes with wit and insight. Critics today regard much of his lyric poetry as ordinary and conventional, but in his occasional poems and his light verse, Holmes still occupies an important place among the poets of his day.

—*Robert Bain*

Suggestions for Further Reading

Menikoff, Barry. "Oliver Wendell Holmes." *The American Renaissance in New England.* Vol. 1 of *Dictionary of Literary Biography.* Ed. Joel Myerson. Detroit: Gale, 1978. 106–13.

———. "Oliver Wendell Holmes." *Fifteen American Authors Before 1900: Biographical Essays on Research and Criticism.* Ed. Earl N. Harbert and Robert A. Rees. Rev. ed. Madison: U of Wisconsin P, 1984. 281–305.*

Tilton, Eleanor M. *Amiable Autocrat: A Biography of Dr. Oliver Wendell Holmes.* New York: H. Schuman, 1947.*

TEXT
The Poetical Works of Oliver Wendell Holmes. Boston: Houghton, 1902.

ꙅꚍꙅ

Old Ironsides[1]

Ay, tear her tattered ensign down!
   Long has it waved on high,
And many an eye has danced to see
   That banner in the sky;

1. Holmes wrote this poem in response to plans to dismantle the U.S. *Constitution*, the frigate that defeated the British *Guerriere* in the War of 1812. The ship was saved.

Beneath it rung the battle shout,
   And burst the cannon's roar;—
The meteor of the ocean air
   Shall sweep the clouds no more!

Her deck, once red with heroes' blood,
   Where knelt the vanquished foe,   10
When winds were hurrying o'er the flood,
   And waves were white below,
No more shall feel the victor's tread,
   Or know the conquered knee;—
The harpies of the shore shall pluck
   The eagle of the sea!

O better that her shattered hulk
   Should sink beneath the wave;
Her thunders shook the mighty deep,
   And there should be her grave;   20
Nail to the mast her holy flag,
   Set every threadbare sail,
And give her to the god of storms,
   The lightning and the gale!

                           (1836)

The Last Leaf[2]

I saw him once before,
As he passed by the door,
   And again
The pavement stones resound,
As he totters o'er the ground
   With his cane.

They say that in his prime,
Ere the pruning-knife of Time
   Cut him down,
Not a better man was found   10

2. The "last leaf" was Major Thomas Melville (1759–1832), grandfather of Herman Melville. "This poem was suggested by the appearance in one of our streets of a venerable relic of the Revolution, said to be one of the party who threw the tea overboard in Boston Harbor. He was a fine monumental specimen in his cocked hat and knee britches, with his buckled shoes and his sturdy cane. . . . an honored fellow-citizen whose costume was out of date, but whose patriotism never changed with years." [Holmes' note]

By the Crier on his round
        Through the town.

But now he walks the streets,
And looks at all he meets
        Sad and wan,
And he shakes his feeble head,
That it seems as if he said,
        "They are gone."

The mossy marbles rest
On the lips that he has prest   20
        In their bloom,
And the names he loved to hear
Have been carved for many a year
        On the tomb.

My grandmamma has said—
Poor old lady, she is dead
        Long ago—
That he had a Roman nose,
And his cheek was like a rose
        In the snow.   30

But now his nose is thin,
And it rests upon his chin
        Like a staff,
And a crook is in his back,
And a melancholy crack
        In his laugh.

I know it is a sin
For me to sit and grin
        At him here;
But the old three-cornered hat,   40
And the breeches, and all that,
        Are so queer!

And if I should live to be
The last leaf upon the tree
        In the spring,
Let them smile, as I do now,
At the old forsaken bough
        Where I cling.

                                        (1836)

The Chambered Nautilus

This is the ship of pearl, which, poets feign,
    Sails the unshadowed main,—
    The venturous bark that flings
On the sweet summer wind its purpled wings
In gulfs enchanted, where the Siren sings,
    And coral reefs lie bare,
Where the cold sea-maids rise to sun their streaming hair.

Its webs of living gauze no more unfurl;
    Wrecked is the ship of pearl!
    And every chambered cell,   10
Where its dim dreaming life was wont to dwell,
As the frail tenant shaped his growing shell,
    Before thee lies revealed,—
Its irised ceiling rent, its sunless crypt unsealed!

Year after year beheld the silent toil
    That spread his lustrous coil;
    Still, as the spiral grew,
He left the past year's dwelling for the new,
Stole with soft step its shining archway through,
    Built up its idle door,   20
Stretched in his last-found home, and knew the old no more.

Thanks for the heavenly message brought by thee,
    Child of the wandering sea,
    Cast from her lap, forlorn!
From thy dead lips a clearer note is born
Than ever Triton blew from wreathed horn!
    While on mine ear it rings,
Through the deep caves of thought I hear a voice that
    sings:—

Build thee more stately mansions, O my soul,
    As the swift seasons roll!   30
    Leave thy low-vaulted past!
Let each new temple, nobler than the last,
Shut thee from heaven with a dome more vast,
    Till thou at length art free,
Leaving thine outgrown shell by life's unresting sea!
          (1857, 1858)

The Deacon's Masterpiece;
or, The Wonderful "One-Hoss Shay"

A Logical Story

Have you heard of the wonderful one-hoss shay,
That was built in such a logical way
It ran a hundred years to the day,
And then, of a sudden, it—ah, but stay,
I'll tell you what happened without delay,
Scaring the parson into fits,
Frightening people out of their wits,—
Have your ever heard of that, I say?

Seventeen hundred and fifty-five.
Georgius Secundus was then alive,—   10
Snuffy old drone from the German hive.
That was the year when Lisbon-town
Saw the earth open and gulp her down,
And Braddock's army was done so brown,
Left without a scalp to its crown.
It was on the terrible Earthquake-day
That the Deacon finished the one-hoss shay.

Now in building of chaises, I tell you what,
There is always *somewhere* a weakest spot,—
In hub, tire, felloe, in spring or thill,   20
In panel, or crossbar, or floor, or sill,
In screw, bolt, thoroughbrace,—lurking still,
Find it somewhere you must and will,—
Above or below, or within or without,—
And that's the reason, beyond a doubt,
That a chaise *breaks down*, but doesn't *wear out*.

But the Deacon swore, (as Deacons do,
With an "I dew vum," or an "I tell *yeou*,")
He would build one shay to beat the taown
'n' the keounty 'n' all the kentry raoun';   30
It should be so built that it *couldn'* break daown:
—"Fur," said the Deacon, " 't's mighty plain
Thut the weakes' place mus' stan' the strain;
'n' the way t' fix it, uz I maintain,
        Is only jest
T' make that place uz strong uz the rest."

So the Deacon inquired of the village folk
Where he could find the strongest oak,
That couldn't be split nor bent nor broke,—
That was for spokes and floor and sills;   40
He sent for lancewood to make the thills;
The crossbars were ash, from the straightest trees,
The panels of white-wood, that cuts like cheese,
But lasts like iron for things like these;
The hubs of logs from the "Settler's ellum,"—
Last of its timber,—they couldn't sell 'em,
Never an axe had seen their chips,
And the wedges flew from between their lips,
Their blunt ends frizzled like celery-tips;
Step and prop-iron, belt and screw,   50
Spring, tire, axle, and linchpin too,
Steel of the finest, bright and blue;
Thoroughbrace bison-skin, thick and wide;
Boot, top, dasher from tough old hide
Found in the pit when the tanner died.
That was the way he "put her through."—
"There!" said the Deacon, "naow she'll dew!"

Do! I tell you, I rather guess
She was a wonder, and nothing less!
Colts grew horses, beards turned gray,   60
Deacon and deaconess dropped away,
Children and grandchildren—where were they?
But there stood the stout old one-hoss shay
As fresh as on Lisbon-earthquake-day!

EIGHTEEN HUNDRED;—it came and found
The Deacon's masterpiece strong and sound.
Eighteen hundred increased by ten;—
"Hahnsum kerridge" they called it then.
Eighteen hundred and twenty came;—
Running as usual; much the same.   70
Thirty and forty at last arrive,
And then come fifty, and FIFTY-FIVE.

Little of all we value here
Wakes on the morn of its hundredth year
Without both feeling and looking queer.
In fact, there's nothing that keeps its youth,
So far as I know, but a tree and truth.

(This is a moral that runs at large;
Take it.—You're welcome.—No extra charge.)

FIRST OF NOVEMBER,—the Earthquake-day— 80
There are traces of age in the one-hoss shay,
A general flavor of mild decay,
But nothing local, as one may say.
There couldn't be,—for the Deacon's art
Had made it so like in every part
That there wasn't a chance for one to start.
For the wheels were just as strong as the thills,
And the floor was just as strong as the sills,
And the panels just as strong as the floor,
And the whipple-tree neither less nor more, 90
And the back-crossbar as strong as the fore,
And the spring and axle and hub *encore*.
And yet, *as a whole*, it is past a doubt
In another hour it will be *worn out*!

First of November, 'Fifty-five!
This morning the parson takes a drive.
Now, small boys, get out of the way!
Here comes the wonderful one-hoss shay,
Drawn by a rat-tailed, ewe-necked bay.
"Huddup!" said the parson.—Off they went. 100
The parson was working his Sunday's text,—
Had got to *fifthly*, and stopped perplexed
At what the—Moses—was coming next.
All at once the horse stood still,
Close by the meet'n'-house on the hill.
—First a shiver, and then a thrill,
Then something decidedly like a spill,—
And the parson was sitting upon a rock,
At half past nine by the meet'n'-house clock,—
Just the hour of the Earthquake shock! 110
—What do you think the parson found,
When he got up and stared around?
The poor old chaise in a heap or mound,
As if it had been to the mill and ground!
You see, of course, if you're not a dunce,
How it went to pieces all at once,—
All at once, and nothing first,—
Just as bubbles do when they burst.

End of the wonderful one-hoss shay. 120
Logic is logic. That's all I say.

(1857, 1858)

Oliver Wendell Holmes

Jones Very

1813–1880

Jones Very presents an enigmatic figure: an anointed transcendentalist poet who never considered himself a transcendentalist; who claimed to take dictation from the Holy Spirit yet used demanding poetic forms; who was believed during his lifetime to be both a lunatic and a genius. Very wrote well over eight hundred poems, many appearing in newspapers and magazines, but published only one book of verse in his lifetime. Ralph Waldo Emerson selected and edited the poems for it and found the book a publisher. Were it not for his connection with Emerson, Very would scarcely be remembered at all, yet his verse is often quite good and strangely moving.

Jones Very was born in Salem, Massachusetts, on 28 August 1813. His father, a sea captain, was often away, and died when Very was eleven; Very was raised by his mother. The furtively quiet and high-strung young man's remarkable studiousness impressed an uncle, who offered to send him to Harvard. Very distinguished himself there, and subsequently at Harvard's divinity school.

Very's college years coincided with the emergence of the Harvard-centered transcendentalist movement. Amidst that religious and quasi-religious excitement, Very experienced a "change of heart," by which he felt himself compelled to eradicate his individual will and act only as the Holy Spirit instructed him. He had apparently always had religious inclinations despite his mother's outspoken atheism; the "change" lay in this deliberate renunciation of will, which he made his life's guiding principle. In so doing, he joined a tradition shared by the Antinomians and the Quakers, and aligned in principle with his transcendentalist contemporaries.

Very was particularly influenced by Emerson, who in 1838 informed the Divinity School senior class that "God incarnates himself in man" ("The Divinity School Address"). In that year Very proclaimed that he had become a "perfected being," speaking and acting entirely by divine direction, even in actions as simple as rising from his chair. He was given to making prophetic announcements to his friends (once informing Elizabeth

Peabody that he had "come to baptize [her] with the Holy Ghost and with fire"), and was once confined to an asylum for a month (Buell 315).

Such utterances earned Very a reputation among the transcendentalists as the embodiment of Emerson's poet-prophet. He had begun writing poems as early as 1833, and by this time was producing nearly a poem a day, claiming for these the same divine inspiration as for other aspects of his life. "I value these verses, not because they are *mine*," he declared, "but because they are *not*" (Gittleman). Emerson edited Very's *Essays and Poems*, published by Charles C. Little and James Brown in 1839.

The intensity of Very's inspiration seems to have been greatest before 1840. The remaining forty years of his life, during which he served as a minister in Salem, passed essentially without event. He was retiring, though not reclusive, and continued to write poems until his death on 8 May 1880. He is buried in the Old South Burial Ground in Salem.

Very was no formal innovator—the great majority of his poems are Shakespearean sonnets—but he mastered his chosen form. Most of his poems express his personal religious vision, in terms at once intense and austere. They usually present a single idea: the death-in-life of the materialistic in "The Grave-Yard"; passive receptivity to God's commands in "The Hand and Foot." Many of the poems in manuscript appear hastily written and virtually without punctuation, as if they had indeed been dictated to their author (causing a frustrated Emerson to ask while editing them, "cannot the Spirit parse and spell?") (qtd. in Miller 341).

Such a characterization, however, belies the degree of craft the poems reflect. Very's diction is consciously Biblical in its abundance of one- and two-syllable words, its use of the most common objects of everyday life to convey abstract spiritual concepts (see for example his fine poem "The Presence"), and its uncompromising air. He makes effective use of poetic personae, adopting the role of prophet, penitent, and even of God.

Scholars generally concur that Very's "effective years" were over by 1840—his poetic power having waned along with his acute spiritual excitement—but he continued to write for another four decades. While continuing to cover the religious territory staked out by the earlier work, Very wrote increasingly on topical issues as well. Though he produced a fair amount of forgettable occasional poetry, some of his later poems may have been unjustly ignored. At the least, they evince a passion about prevailing social issues with which Very is seldom credited.

After Very's death, two volumes of his poetry appeared. William P. Andrews edited a well-chosen selection in 1883. James Freeman Clarke's 1886 *Poems and Essays*, though not authoritative, is still the most complete collection. William Irving Bartlett reproduces nearly all of the previously unpublished poems surviving in manuscript. Until recently, critical interest in Very took the form of periodic "rediscoveries." He has lately received considerably greater scholarly interest, though his poetry is probably too restricted in style and subject matter to attract a much wider audience. Nevertheless, if Very's poetry does not often elicit affection, it does command respect.

—*Harry Crockett*

Suggestions for Further Reading

Buell, Lawrence. *Literary Transcendentalism*. Ithaca, NY: Cornell UP, 1973. See esp. 312–30.

Deese, Helen R., ed. *Jones Very: The Complete Poems*. Athens, GA: U of Georgia P, 1993.*

Gittleman, Edwin. *Jones Very: The Effective Years*. New York: Columbia UP, 1967.

Lyons, Nathan. *Jones Very: Selected Poems*. New Brunswick, NJ: Rutgers UP, 1966. See esp. introduction.

Miller, Perry, ed. *The Transcendentalists*. Cambridge: Harvard UP, 1950.

TEXTS
Essays and Poems. 1839.

Poems by Jones Very. 1883.

Poems and Essays by Jones Very: Complete and Revised Edition. 1886.

Jones Very: Emerson's "Brave Saint." Ed. William Irving Bartlett. Durham, NC: Duke UP, 1942.

꘎

The Garden

I saw the spot where our first parents dwelt;
And yet it wore to me no face of change,
For while amid its fields and groves I felt
As if I had not sinned, nor thought it strange;
My eye seemed but a part of every sight,
My ear heard music in each sound that rose,
Each sense forever found a new delight,
Such as the spirit's vision only knows;
Each act some new and ever-varying joy
Did by my Father's love for me prepare;   10

To dress the spot my ever fresh employ,
And in the glorious whole with Him to share;
No more without the flaming gate to stray,
No more for sin's dark stain the debt of death to pay.

(1838, 1839)

The Presence

I sit within my room, and joy to find
That Thou who always lov'st art with me here,
That I am never left by Thee behind,
But by thyself Thou keep'st me ever near;
The fire burns brighter when with Thee I look,
And seems a kinder servant sent to me;
With gladder heart I read Thy holy book,
Because Thou art the eyes by which I see;
This aged chair, that table, watch and door
Around in ready service ever wait;   10
Nor can I ask of Thee a menial more
To fill the measure of my large estate,
For Thou thyself, with all a father's care,
Where'er I turn, art ever with me there.

(1839, 1839)

The Grave-Yard

My heart grows sick before the wide-spread death
That walks and speaks in seeming life around;
And I would love the corse without a breath,
That sleeps forgotten 'neath the cold, cold ground;
For these do tell the story of decay,
The worm and rotten flesh hide not nor lie;
But this, though dying too from day to day,
With a false show doth cheat the longing eye;
And hide the worm that gnaws the core of life,
With painted cheek and smooth deceitful skin;   10
Covering a grave with sights of darkness rife,
A secret cavern filled with death and sin;
And men walk o'er these graves and know it not,
For in the body's health the soul's forgot.

(1839, 1839)

Terror

There is no safety! fear has seized the proud;
The swift run to and fro but cannot fly;
Within the streets I hear no voices loud,
They pass along with low, continuous cry;
Lament! bring forth the mourning garments now,
Prepare a solemn fast, for ye must morn;
Strip every leaf from off the boastful bough,
Let every robe from hidden deeds be torn;
Bewail! bewail! great Babylon must fall!
Her sins have reached to heaven; her doom is sealed;   10
Upon the Father now of mercies call,
For the great day of secrets is revealed!
Repent! why do ye still uncertain stand,
The kingdom of My Son is nigh at hand!

(1839, 1839)

The Hand and Foot

The hand and foot that stir not, they shall find
Sooner than all the rightful place to go;
Now in their motion free as roving wind,
Though first no snail more limited and slow;
I mark them full of labor all the day,
Each active motion made in perfect rest;
They cannot from their path mistaken stray,
Though 'tis not theirs, yet in it they are blest;
The bird has not their hidden track found out,
Nor cunning fox, though full of art he be;   10
It is the way unseen, the certain route,
Where ever bound, yet thou art ever free;
The path of Him, whose perfect law of love
Bids spheres and atoms in just order move.

(1839, 1883)

Yourself

'Tis to yourself I speak; you cannot know
Him whom I call in speaking such an one,
For thou beneath the earth liest buried low,

Which he alone as living walks upon;
Thou mayst at times have heard him speak to you,
And often wished perchance that you were he;
And I must ever wish that it were true,
For then thou couldst hold fellowship with me;
But now thou hear'st us talk as strangers, met
Above the room wherein thou liest abed;   10
A word perhaps loud spoken thou mayst get,
Or hear our feet when heavily they tread;
But he who speaks, or him who's spoken to,
Must both remain as strangers still to you.

                                        (1839, 1883)

The Silent

There is a sighing in the wood,
    A murmur in the beating wave;
The heart has never understood
    To tell in words the thoughts they gave.

Yet oft it feels an answering tone,
    When wandering on the lonely shore;
And could the lips its voice make known,
    'T would sound as does the ocean's roar.

And oft beneath the wind-swept pine,
    Some chord is struck the strain to swell;   10
Nor sounds nor language can define,
    'Tis not for words or sounds to tell.

'Tis all unheard; that Silent Voice,
    Whose goings forth unknown to all,
Bids bending reed and bird rejoice,
    And fills with music Nature's hall.

And in the speechless human heart
    It speaks, where'er man's feet have trod;
Beyond the lips' deceitful art,
    To tell of Him, the Unseen God.   20
                                        (1839, 1883)

The Strangers

Each care-worn face is but a book
    To tell of houses bought or sold;
Or filled with words that mankind took
    From those who lived and spoke of old.

I see none whom I know, for they
    See other things than him they meet;
And though they stop me by the way,
    'Tis still some other one to greet.

There are no words that reach my ear
    Those speak who tell of other things   10
Than what they mean for me to hear,
    For in their speech the counter rings.

I would be where each word is true,
    Each eye sees what it looks upon;
For here my eye has seen but few,
    Who in each act that act have done.

                (1840, 1876)

The Wild Rose of Plymouth

Upon the Plymouth shore the wild rose blooms
As when the Pilgrims lived beside the bay,
And scents the morning air with sweet perfumes;
Though new this hour, more ancient far than they;
More ancient than the wild yet friendly race
That roved the land before the Pilgrims came,
And here for ages found a dwelling-place,
Of whom our histories tell us but the name!
Though new this hour, out from the past it springs,
Telling this summer morning of earth's prime;   10
And happy visions of the future brings
That reach beyond, e'en to the verge of time;
Wreathing earth's children in one flowery chain
Of love and beauty, ever to remain.

                (1855, 1883)

Freedom and Union

By deeds, not words, we prove our inmost mind,
For things, not names, we labor and contend;
In noble souls the two are still combined,
And each to each a nobleness they lend!
Freedom and Union are not names, but things;
By deeds our fathers proved for them their love;
In vain with words like these the country rings
If to the things themselves we recreant prove.
In this alone all patriots agree,
To labor for their country's highest good;   10
And by the fruit it bears to judge the tree,
However party names are understood.
'Tis not the title that makes good the claim,
But nobler deeds, which justify the name.

(1860, 1886)

Hath the Rain a Father?
Or, Who Hath Begotten the Drops of Dew?
Job 38. 28

We say, "it rains." An unbelieving age!
Its very words its unbelief doth show;
Forgot the lessons of the sacred page,
Spoken by men of faith so long ago!
No farther than they see men's faith extends;
The mighty changes of the earth and sky
To them are causeless all, where Science ends;
An Unseen Cause they know not or deny.
They hear not in the whirlwind, or the storm,
The mighty Voice which spake to man of old;   10
They see not in the clouds of heaven His form,
Nor in His ceaseless works his power behold;
Who maketh small the countless drops of rain,
And sendeth showers upon the springing grain.

(1866, 1886)

The New World

The night that has no star lit up by God,
The day that round men shines who still are blind,
The earth their grave-turned feet for ages trod,

And sea swept over by His mighty wind,—
All these have passed away; the melting dream
That flitted o'er the sleepers' half-shut eye,
When touched by morning's golden-darting beam;
And he beholds around the earth and sky
What ever real stands; the rolling spheres,
And heaving billows of the boundless main,   10
That show, though time is past, no trace of years,
And earth restored he sees as his again,
The earth that fades not, and the heavens that stand,
Their strong foundations laid by God's right hand!

                                                        (1883)

The Freedmen of the Mississippi Valley

Wakeful I think upon the suffering race
That, fled from bondage, claim our fostering care;
What tongue their want can tell, or pen can trace,
Or who the story of their woes could bear?
The mother with her child, the aged one,
Now unprotected from the wintry blast;
Soon, soon for them the winter will be gone,
Soon, without aid, their sufferings here be past!
Help. till the storms of winter shall be o'er,
When their own hands abundance will supply;   10
Give all thou canst, food, raiment, from thy store,
Nor aught thou hast these suffering ones deny;
Lest they, escaped from slavery's hateful chain,
Should find but graves in freedom's fair domain.

                                                        (1886)

The New Man

The hands must touch and handle many things,
The eyes long waste their glances all in vain;
The feet course still in idle, mazy rings,
Ere man himself, the lost, shall back regain
The hand that ever moves, the eyes that see,
While day holds out his shining lamp on high,
And, strait as flies the honey-seeking bee,
Direct the feet to unseen flowers they spy;
These, when they come, the man revealed from heaven,

Shall labor all the day in quiet rest,   10
And find at eve the covert duly given,
Where with the bird they find sweet sleep and rest,
That shall their wasted strength to health restore,
And bid them seek with morn the hills and fields once more.

(1886)

John Godfrey Saxe

1816–1887

John Godfrey Saxe has retained
a fraction of the renown he once enjoyed as a writer of light verse
and a lyceum lecturer. The few scholars interested in his work
today discuss him as a Vermont poet, as a participant in the
lyceum movement, and as a member of the later Knickerbocker
Group. Saxe's ownership of the *Burlington* [Vermont] *Sentinel* es-
tablished his reputation as a commentator on current affairs. Af-
ter leaving Vermont in 1856, he devoted his life to literary pursuits
and speaking engagements. He regularly published poems in
leading periodicals and spoke at graduations and fraternal cele-
brations in addition to lecturing on the lyceum circuit. Saxe com-
bined his imposing six-foot-two frame with a robust and lively
delivery that made him a favorite with audiences.

Saxe was born in Highgate, Vermont, 2 June 1816, the second
of four sons of Peter and Elizabeth Saxe. At nineteen, Saxe en-
tered Wesleyan University but transferred to Middlebury College
after one year. Upon graduating from Middlebury in 1839, he
studied law, first in Lockport, New York, and then at St. Albans,
Vermont. In 1841, while engaged in these studies, he married
Sarah Newell Sollace and had his first poems published in the
Knickerbocker Magazine. Two years later, he passed the Vermont
bar and began a law practice that would never command the
whole of his energies. Neither his brief stints as school superin-
tendent and state's attorney for Chittenden County nor his bids
for governor in 1859 and 1860 distracted him from a growing de-
votion to letters. He purchased the *Burlington Sentinel* in 1850 and
further developed his interest in politics and language.

By the time Saxe sold the *Sentinel* and moved to Albany, New
York, in 1856, he had acquired a reputation as a punster and sati-
rist. His first two volumes, *Progress: A Satirical Poem* (1846) and
Humorous and Satirical Poems (1850), were followed by six other
volumes: *The Money-King and Other Poems* (1860); *The Fly-ing
Dutchman; or, the Wrath Herr Vonstoppelnoze* (1862); *Clever Stories
of Many Nations Rendered in Rhyme* (1865); *The Masquerade and
Other Poems* (1866); *Fables and Legends of Many Countries Ren-
dered in Rhyme* (1872); and *Leisure-Day Rhymes* (1875). Numerous

editions of his collected poems began to appear as early as 1850. Selling well, these volumes earned Saxe recognition as one of the day's most popular poets. Saxe enjoyed his celebrity until his youngest daughter died of tuberculosis in 1874. The following year he suffered brain damage in a railroad accident, and the next six years brought the deaths of his wife and three of his four remaining children. He never fully recovered from these losses.

Saxe's work seldom deviates from predictable rhyme schemes and metrical patterns. His meter is predominantly iambic, and he commonly wrote his longer poems in couplets. His shorter pieces are usually quatrains with *abab* rhyme or stanzas of up to eight lines with equally regular patterns. The poems for which Saxe was most famous during his lifetime were "Progress," "The Proud Miss MacBride," and "The Money-King," all three poems attacking contemporary excesses. In later books, Saxe wrote about the lore of other countries. His "The Blind Men and the Elephant" is the most well known of his adaptations of fables from around the world. The *Boston Post* cited Saxe as one of the most eagerly sought of all lyceum speakers during the late 1850s. When he died of a heart attack on 31 March 1887, Saxe was still enormously popular.

Recent studies of regional cultures and the literary atmosphere in America have raised questions about the popular mind that Saxe may be helpful in answering. His reactionary response to transcendentalism and female education in "Progress" betrays a fear that too much of the freedom advocated by Emerson and Whitman would lead America into anarchy. Read as a compendium of common fears, Saxe's satiric verse communicates an unremitting resistance to liberal ideas. For this reason, future readers of Saxe may find his work useful as a means of clarifying the conservative climate out of which Whitman and Dickinson wrote.

—*Paul Crumbley*

Suggestions for Further Reading

Dictionary of American Biography. Vol. 8. Ed. Dumas Malone. New York: Scribner's, 1935. 399–400.
Selected texts. Middlebury College. Starr Library. Special Collections. Bob Buckeye, Archivist. Middlebury, VT.

TEXT
The Poetical Works of John Godfrey Saxe. 1892.

Rhyme of the Rail

Singing through the forests,
    Rattling over ridges,
Shooting under arches,
    Rumbling over bridges,
Whizzing through the mountains,
    Buzzing o'er the vail,—
Bless me! this is pleasant,
    Riding on the Rail!

Men of different "stations"
    In the eye of Fame   10
Here are very quickly
    Coming to the same.
High and lowly people,
    Birds of every feather,
On a common level
    Traveling together!

Gentleman in shorts,
    Looming very tall;
Gentleman at large,
    Talking very small;   20
Gentleman in tights,
    With a loose-ish mien;
Gentleman in gray,
    Looking rather green.

Gentleman quite old,
    Asking for the news;
Gentleman in black,
    In a fit of blues;
Gentleman in claret,
    Sober as a vicar;   30
Gentleman in Tweed,
    Terribly in liquor!

Stranger on the right,
    Looking very sunny,
Obviously reading
    Something rather funny.
Now the smiles are thicker,
    Wonder what they mean?

John Godfrey Saxe

Faith he's got the *Knicker-*
Bocker Magazine!   40

Stranger on the left,
    Closing up his peepers;
Now he snores amain,
    Like the Seven Sleepers;
At his feet a volume
    Gives the explanation,
How the man grew stupid
    From "Association"!

Ancient maiden lady
    Anxiously remarks,   50
That there must be peril
    'Mong so many sparks!
Roguish-looking fellow,
    Turning to the stranger,
Says it's his opinion
    She is out of danger!

Woman with her baby,
    Sitting *vis-a-vis*;
Baby keeps a squalling;
    Woman looks at me;   60
Asks about the distance,
    Says its tiresome talking,
Noises of the cars
    Are so very shocking!

Market-woman careful
    Of the precious casket,
Knowing eggs are eggs,
    Tightly holds her basket;
Feeling that a smash,
    If it came would surely   70
Send her eggs to pot
    Rather prematurely!

Singing through the forests,
    Rattling over ridges,
Shooting under arches,
    Rumbling over bridges,
Whizzing through the mountains,
    Buzzing o'er the vale,—

Bless me! this is pleasant,
  Riding on the Rail!

(1850)

from The Proud Miss MacBride
A Legend of Gotham

I

O, terribly proud was Miss MacBride,
The very personification of Pride,
As she minced along in Fashion's tide,
Adown Broadway,—on the proper side,—
  When the golden sun was setting;
There was pride in the head she carried so high,
Pride in her lip and pride in her eye,
And a world of pride in the very sigh
  That her stately bosom was fretting;

II

A sigh that a pair of elegant feet,   10
Sandaled in satin, should kiss the street,—
The very same that the vulgar greet
In common leather not over "neat,"—
  For such is the common booting;
(And Christian tears may well be shed,
That even among our gentlemen bred,
The glorious day of Morocco is dead,
And Day and Martin¹ are reigning instead,
  On a much inferior footing!)

III

O, terribly proud was Miss MacBride,   20
Proud of her beauty, and proud of her pride,
And proud of fifty matters beside,
  That wouldn't have borne dissection;
Proud of her wit and proud of her walk,
Proud of her teeth and proud of her talk,
Proud of "knowing cheese from chalk,"
  On a very slight inspection!

---

1. Day and Martin were popular shoe brands and manufacturers.

IX

And yet the pride of Miss MacBride,
Although it had fifty hobbies to ride,
   Had really no foundation; 30
But, like the fabrics that gossips devise,—
Those single stories that often arise
And grow till they reach a four-story size,
   Was merely a fancy creation!

XII

Her birth, indeed, was uncommonly high,
For Miss MacBride first opened her eye
Through a skylight dim, on the light of the sky;
   But pride is a curious passion,
And in talking about her wealth and worth
She always forgot to mention her birth, 40
   To people of rank and fashion!

XIII

Of all the notable things on earth,
The queerest one is pride of birth,
   Among our "fierce Democracie"!
A bridge across a hundred years,
Without a prop to save it from sneers,—
Not even a couple of rotten peers,—
A thing for laughter, fleers, and jeers,
   Is American aristocracy!

XXXVIII

And now the unhappy Miss MacBride, 50
The merest ghost of her early pride,
   Bewails her lowly position;
Cramped in the very narrowest niche,
Above the poor, and below the rich,
   Was ever a worse condition?

Moral

Because you flourish in worldly affairs,
Don't be haughty, and put on airs,
   With insolent pride of station!

           John Godfrey Saxe

Don't be proud and turn up your nose
At poorer people in plainer clo'es,   60
But learn, for the sake of your soul's repose,
That wealth's a bubble, that comes,—and goes!
And that all Proud Flesh, wherever it grows,
    Is subject to irritation!

(1850)

from The Money-King[2]

    As landsmen, sitting in luxurious ease,
Talk of the dangers of the stormy seas;
As fireside travelers, with portentous mien,
Tell tales of countries they have never seen;
As parlor-soldiers, graced with fancy-scars,
Rehearse their bravery in imagined wars;
As arrant dunces have been known to sit
In grave discourse of wisdom and of wit;
As paupers, gathered in congenial flocks,
Babble of banks, insurances, and stocks;   10
As each is oftenest eloquent of what
He hates or covets, but possesses not;—
As cowards talk of pluck; misers, of waste;
Scoundrels, of honor; country clowns, of taste;—
I sing of MONEY!—no ignoble theme,
But loftier than poetasters dream,
Whose fancies, soaring to their native moon,
Rise like a bubble or a gay balloon,
Whose orb aspiring takes a heavenward flight,
Just in proportion as it's thin and light!   20
. . . .
Great was King Alfred; and if history state
His actions truly, good as well as great.
Great was the Norman; he whose martial hordes
Taught law and order to the Saxon lords,
With gentler thoughts their rugged minds imbued,
And raised the nation whom he first subdued.
Great was King Bess!—I see the critic smile,
As though the Muse mistook her proper style;
But to her purpose she will stoutly cling,
The royal maid was "every inch a king!"   30

---

2. "A poem delivered before the Phi Beta Kappa Society of Yale College, 1854." [Saxe's note]

Great was Napoleon,—and I would that fate
Might prove his namesake-nephew half as great;
Meanwhile this hint I venture to advance:—
What France admires is good enough for France!
Great princes were they all; but greater far
Than English King, or mighty Russian Czar,
Or Pope of Rome, or haughty Queen of Spain,
Baron of Germany, or Royal Dane,
Or Gallic Emperor, or Persian Khan,
Or any other merely mortal man,   40
Is the great monarch that my Muse would sing,
That mighty potentate, the Money-King!
His kingdom vast extends o'er every land,
And nations bow before his high command,
The weakest tremble, and his power obey,
The strongest honor, and confess his sway.
He rules the rulers!—e'en the tyrant Czar
Asks his permission ere he goes to war;
The Turk, submissive to his royal might,
By his decree has gracious leave to fight;   50
Whilst even Britannia makes her humblest bow
Before her Barings, not her Barons now,
Or on the Rothschild suppliantly calls
(Her affluent "uncle" with the golden balls),
Begs of the Jew that he will kindly spare
Enough to put her trident in repair,
And pawns her diamonds, while she humbly craves
The Money-King's consent to "rule the waves!"

. . . .

    To me the boon may gracious Heaven assign,—
No Cringing suppliant at Mammon's shrine,[3]   60
Nor slave of Poverty,—with joy to share
The happy mean expressed in Agur's prayer:—[4]
A house (my own) to keep me safe and warm,
A shade in sunshine, and a shield in storm;
A generous board, and a fitting raiment, clear
Of debts and duns throughout the circling year;
Silver and gold, in moderate store, that I
May purchase joys that only these can buy;
Some gems of art, a cultured mind to please,

---

3. Mammon refers to the false god of riches and avarice.
4. Reference to Agur probably derives from the Roman religious official
whose responsibility it was to predict the future on the basis of omens. Prior to
reading the omens, the augur would supplicate the gods in behalf of the
community.

Books, pictures, statues, literary ease. 70
That "time is money" prudent Franklin shows
In rhyming couplets and sententious prose.
Oh, had he taught the world in prose and rhyme,
The higher truth that Money may be Time!
And showed the people in his pleasant ways,
The art of coining dollars into days!
Days for improvement, days for social life,
Days for your God, your children, and your wife;
Some days for pleasure, and an hour to spend
In genial converse with an honest friend. 80
Such days be mine!—and grant me, Heaven, but this,
With blooming health, man's highest earthly bliss,—
And I will read without a sigh or frown,
The startling news that stocks are going down;
Hear without envy that a stranger hoards
Or spends more treasure than a mint affords;
See my next neighbor pluck a golden plum,
Calm and content with my cottage-home;
Take for myself what honest thrift may bring,
And for his kindness bless the Money-King! 90

(1860)

The Blind Men and the Elephant
A Hindoo Fable

I

It was six men of Indostan
  To learning much inclined,
Who went to see the Elephant
  (Though all of them were blind),
That each by observation
  Might satisfy his mind.

II

The *First* approached the Elephant,
  And happening to fall
Against his broad and sturdy side,
  At once began to bawl: 10
"God bless me! but the Elephant
  Is very like a wall!"

III

The *Second*, feeling of the tusk,
   Cried, "Ho! what have we here
So very round and smooth and sharp?
   To me 'tis mighty clear
This wonder of an Elephant
   Is very like a spear!"

IV

The *Third* approached the animal,
   And happening to take   20
The squirming trunk within his hands,
   Thus boldly up and spake:
"I see," quoth he, "the Elephant
   Is very like a snake!"

V

The *Fourth* reached out his eager hand,
   And felt about the knee.
"What most this wondrous beast is like
   Is mighty plain," quoth he;
" 'Tis clear enough the Elephant
   Is very like a tree!"   30

VI

The *Fifth*, who chanced to touch the ear,
   Said: "E'en the blindest man
Can tell what this resembles most;
   Deny the fact who can,
This marvel of an Elephant
   Is very like a fan!"

VII

The *Sixth* no sooner had begun
   About the beast to grope,
Than, seizing on the swinging tail
   That fell within his scope,   40
"I see," quoth he, "the Elephant
   Is very like a rope!"

Moral

So oft in theologic wars,
  The disputants, I ween,
Rail on in utter ignorance
  Of what each other mean,
And prate about an Elephant
  Not one of them has seen!

(1872)

Henry David Thoreau

1817–1862

The author of *A Week on the Concord and Merrimack Rivers*, "Civil Disobedience," and *Walden*, Henry David Thoreau longed early in his career to be a poet. He wrote in his *Journal* in August 1842: "My life hath been a poem I would have writ, / But I could not both live and live to utter it." Thoreau's formal verse, however, cannot rival the poetic prose of *Walden* or his *Journal*. Walter Harding and Michael Meyer note that of his two hundred poems, the significant ones "can be numbered on the fingers of both hands, if not one" (69–70). But in *Walden*, his *Journal*, and his essays, Thoreau lived a poet's life and uttered a poet's language.

The son of Cynthia Dunbar and John Thoreau, Henry David Thoreau was born in Concord, Massachusetts, on 12 July 1817. Educated at Concord Academy and Havard University (1833–37), he began his *Journal* in 1837 and opened a private school in Concord in 1838. Though he never married, he proposed in 1840 to Ellen Sewall, who declined. Thoreau published his first essay and his first poem ("Sympathy") in the *Dial* in 1840 and thereafter contributed regularly to that magazine. Thoreau spent two weeks in 1839 exploring the Concord and Merrimack Rivers with his brother John, who died of lockjaw in 1842. He moved to Walden Pond on 4 July 1845 where he lived for two years, two months, and two days (until September 1847) and where he worked on *A Week* (1849). Jailed overnight in 1846 for failing to pay taxes in protest against the Mexican War and slavery, he published "Resistance to Civil Government" (retitled "Civil Disobedience" after Thoreau's death) in 1849.

A traveler and surveyor by trade and temperament, Thoreau visited the Maine woods (1846, 1853, 1857), Cape Cod (1849, 1850, 1855, 1857), Canada (1850), Mount Monadnock (1858, 1860), and Minnesota (1861). These excursions supplied him with material for numerous essays published in magazines. *Walden* appeared in 1854. An admirer of Whitman's "Sun-Down" poem (an early title for "Crossing Brooklyn Ferry"), Thoreau met its author in 1856 in Brooklyn. An ardent opponent of slavery, he published in 1859 two essays on John Brown. He died on 6 May 1862 in Concord, where he had traveled "a good deal."

Thoreau's major poetic themes—nature, the self, the problems of the artist, and the transcendental experience—often illuminate in miniature those motifs appearing in his prose. Poems like "Light-Winged Smoke, Icarian Bird," "Woof of the Sun, Ethereal Gauze," and "I Am a Parcel of Vain Strivings Tied" show Thoreau at his best but seldom achieve the lyric or symbolic language of his prose. Influenced principally by earlier British poets (among them John Skelton and the metaphysical poets), Thoreau employed inherited verse forms. He never collected his poems in a book; editors gathered his poems in 1895, 1943, and 1964. Critics today rank him among the period's minor poets. But Thoreau stands in the first rank of his century's prose writers, and in that work, he diminished the distinctions between poetry and prose by writing poetic prose about his symbolic journeys into nature and into the self. His formal poems are footnotes to that noble work.

—*Robert Bain*

Suggestions for Further Reading

Harding, Walter, and Michael Meyer. *The New Thoreau Handbook.* New York: New York UP, 1980.*

Journal of Henry David Thoreau. Ed. Bradford Torry and Francis H. Allen. Vols. 7–20 in *The Writings of Henry David Thoreau.* 20 vols. Boston: Houghton, 1906.

Leary, Lewis. "Henry David Thoreau." *Eight American Authors: A Review of Research and Criticism.* Ed. James Woodress. New York: Norton, 1971. 129–71.*

Woodress, James, et al., eds. *American Literary Scholarship: An Annual.* Durham, NC: Duke UP, 1965–present.*

TEXT
Collected Poems of Henry Thoreau. Ed. Carl Bode. Baltimore: Johns Hopkins UP, 1964.

ꝺᵡꞓ

I Am a Parcel of Vain Strivings Tied[1]

I am a parcel of vain strivings tied
  By a chance bond together,
  Dangling this way and that, their links

---

1. Titles appeared on Thoreau's poems in their first publication in the *Dial* or in the first collected edition of 1895. "Sic Vita" was the title of this poem.

Were made so loose and wide,
        Methinks,
    For milder weather.

A bunch of violets without their roots,
        And sorrel intermixed,
    Encircled by a wisp of straw
        Once coiled about their shoots,   10
            The law
        By which I'm fixed.

A nosegay which Time clutched from out
        Those fair Elysian fields,
    With weeds and broken stems, in haste,
        Doth make the rabble rout
            That waste
        The day he yields.

And here I bloom for a short hour unseen,
        Drinking my juices up,   20
    With no root in the land
        To keep my branches green,
            But stand
        In a bare cup.

Some tender buds were left upon my stem
        In mimicry of life,
    But ah! the children will not know,
        Till time has withered them,
            The woe
        With which they're rife.   30

But now I see I was not plucked for naught,
        And after in life's vase
    Of glass set while I might survive,
        But by a kind hand brought
            Alive
        To a strange place.

That stock thus thinned will soon redeem its hours,
        And by another year,
    Such as God knows, with freer air,
        More fruits and fairer flowers   40
            Will bear,
        While I droop here.

(1841, 1895)

Great God, I Ask Thee for No Meaner Pelf[2]

Great God, I ask thee for no meaner pelf
Than that I may not disappoint myself,
That in my action I may soar as high,
As I can now discern with this clear eye.

And next in value, which thy kindness lends,
That I may greatly disappoint my friends,
Howe'er they think or hope that it may be,
They may not dream how thou'st distinguished me.

That my weak hand may equal my firm faith,
And my life practice more than my tongue saith;   10
That my low conduct may not show,
Nor my relenting lines,
That I thy purpose did not know,
Or overrated thy designs.

                                        (1842, 1895)

Light-Winged Smoke, Icarian Bird[3]

Light-winged Smoke, Icarian bird,
Melting thy pinions in thy upward flight,
Lark without song, and messenger of dawn,
Circling above the hamlets as thy nest;
Or else, departing dream, and shadowy form
Of midnight vision, gathering up thy skirts;
By night star-veiling, and by day
Darkening the light and blotting out the sun;
Go thou my incense upward from this hearth,
And ask the gods to pardon this clear flame.   10
                                        (1843, 1895)

Woof of the Sun, Ethereal Gauze[4]

Woof of the sun, ethereal gauze,
Woven of Nature's richest stuffs,

---

2. "My Prayer" was the title of this poem.
3. "Smoke" was this poem's title.
4. "Haze" was this poem's title.

Visible heat, air-water, and dry sea,
Last conquest of the eye;
Toil of the day displayed, sun-dust,
Aerial surf upon the shores of earth,
Ethereal estuary, frith of light,
Breakers of air, billows of heat,
Fine summer spray on inland seas;
Bird of the sun, transparent-winged   10
Owlet of noon, soft-pinioned,
From heath or stubble rising without song;
Establish thy serenity o'er the fields.

(1843, 1895)

William Ellery Channing II
1817–1901

"With him, thy name is Channing,"
Bronson Alcott once remarked of the mercurial poet and friend
of the transcendentalists, William Ellery Channing II (Buell 240).
Channing's inability to hold regular jobs, his love for long, me-
andering walks away from household duties, and his insistence
on being a poet led most Concord citizens to consider him, along
with Thoreau, a failure. While Ralph Waldo Emerson, Margaret
Fuller, and Henry David Thoreau recognized Channing's ability
to describe nature in poetry, they expected more from his talent
and waited patiently for him to produce polished, rhythmical po-
etry with transcendental themes. They waited in vain. Although
much of his early poetry appeared with favorable notice in
Fuller's *Dial*, his later poetry showed no significant advances.
Rather than illustrating metaphysical discoveries, Channing's
poetry simply conveyed emotional and intellectual responses to
nature as seen by a naturalist-poet. And apparently that was
enough for him.

When William Ellery Channing II was born 29 November
1817 to Dr. Walter Channing and Barbara Perkins Channing in
Boston, Massachusetts, he entered a family that emphasized duty
and achievement. To such a family, which included famous Uni-
tarian minister William Ellery Channing the elder, Channing the
younger soon became a source of worry and disappointment. Af-
ter entering and leaving Harvard in 1834, Channing tried home-
stead farming in Illinois and then moved to Cincinnati where he
began sending poetry to the *Dial*, the transcendental journal
based in Boston and edited by Margaret Fuller. In 1841, he mar-
ried Fuller's sister, Ellen, and settled in Concord. There he began
lifelong friendships with Emerson and Thoreau. The next years
saw Channing publish *Poems* (1843), *Poems: Second Series* (1847),
and *The Woodman and Other Poems* (1849) while briefly working
for Horace Greeley's *New York Tribune*. In 1853, Channing sepa-
rated from Ellen, who feared his volatile temper. Although they
reunited in 1855, Ellen died in 1856. Channing received a second
blow when Thoreau died six years later; his biography *Thoreau:
The Poet-Naturalist* (1873) bears witness to their friendship.

Channing published four more poetry collections, including *Near Home* (1858), *The Wanderer* (1871), *Eliot, A Poem* (1885), and *John Brown and the Heroes* (1886). He died 23 December 1901 in Concord.

Considered Concord's poet by Thoreau and a poet-naturalist by Emerson, Channing treats the New England landscape and the seasons in idyllic lyrics and meditative narratives. In poems such as "October" and "To One Complaining," Channing depicts the poet as a teacher who awakens the reader to nature's power. "Inscription for a Garden" and the exuberant "Sonnet XI" reveal Channing's belief that the truly alive individual is one who lives close to nature. Other poems such as "Walden Spring" assert that industrialization—here exemplified by a railroad—injures humanity by marring the landscape. Much of Channing's poetry displays a healthy egotism and notes the correspondence between the self's spiritual and emotional condition and nature. Channing is above all a poet of feeling, one who expresses the wonder and joy of being alive and aware of nature, one who shows anger at those oblivious to the outside world and its value.

Critical response to Channing has not been kind. Most critics regard him as a minor poet who wrote far too much, an inferior imitator of Emerson and Thoreau. Others ignore his writing and focus on his friendship with members of the transcendental circle. Yet, despite such criticism, readers may still appreciate Channing's poetry for its sincere meditations dressed in the colors and music of nature.

—Mary K. Edmonds

Suggestions for Further Reading

Buell, Lawrence. "Ellery Channing: The Major Phase of a Minor Poet." *Literary Transcendentalism: Style and Vision in the American Renaissance*. Ithaca, NY: Cornell UP, 1973. 239–64.

Hudspeth, Robert N. *Ellery Channing*. New York: Twayne, 1973.

McGill, Frederick T., Jr. *Channing of Concord: A Life of William Ellery Channing II*. New Brunswick: Rutgers UP, 1967.

TEXT

The Collected Poems of William Ellery Channing the Younger, 1817–1901. Gainesville, FL: Scholars' Facsimile & Reprints, 1967.

A Poet's Hope

Flying,—flying beyond all lower regions,
Beyond the light called day, and night's repose,
Where the untrammelled soul, on her wind-pinions
Fearlessly sweeping, defies my earthly woes;—
There,—there, upon that infinitest sea,
Lady, thy hope,—so fair a hope, summons me.

Fall off, ye garments of my misty weather,
Drop from my eyes, ye scales of time's applying;
Am I not godlike? meet not here together
A past and future infinite, defying,   10
The cold, still, callous moment of to-day?
Am I not master of the calm alway?

Would I could summon from the deep, deep mine,
Glutted with shapely jewels, glittering bright,
One echo of that splendor, call it thine,
And weave it in the strands of living light;
For it is in me, and the sea smiles fair,
And thitherward I rage, on whirling air.

Unloose me, demons of dull care and want,
I will not stand your slave, I am your king;   20
Think not within your meshes vile I pant
For the wild liberty of an unclipt wing;
My empire is myself, and I defy
The external; yes! I rule the whole, or die.

All music that the fullest breeze can play
In its melodious whisperings in the wood,
All modulations which entrance the day
And deify a sunlight solitude;
All anthems that the waves sing to the ocean
Are mine for song, and yield to my devotion.   30

And mine the soft glaze of a loving eye,
And mine the pure shapes of the human form,
And mine the bitterest sorrow's witchery,
And spells enough to make a snow-king warm;
For an undying hope thou breathest me,—
Hope which can ride the tossing, foaming sea.

Lady, there is a hope that all men have,
Some mercy for their faults, a grassy place
To rest in, and a flower-strown, gentle grave;
Another hope which purifies our race,   40
That when that fearful bourne[1] forever past,
They may find rest,—and rest *so* long to last.

I seek it not, I ask no rest for ever,
My path is onward to the farthest shores,—
Upbear me in your arms, unceasing river,
That from the soul's clear fountain swiftly pours,
Motionless not, until the end is won,
Which now I feel hath scarcely felt the sun.

To feel, to know, to soar unlimited,
Mid throngs of light-winged angels sweeping far,   50
And pore upon the realms unvisited,
That tesselate[2] the unseen unthought star,
To be the thing that now I feebly dream
Flashing within my faintest, deepest gleam.

Ah! caverns of my soul! how thick your shade,
Where flows that life by which I faintly see,—
Wave your bright torches, for I need your aid,
Golden-eyed demons of my ancestry!
Your son though blinded hath a light within,
A heavenly fire which ye from suns did win.   60

And, lady, in thy hope my life will rise
Like the air-voyager, till I upbear
These heavenly curtains of my filmy eyes,
Into a lighter, more celestial air;
A mortal's hope shall bear me safely on,
Till I the higher region shall have won.

O Time! O death! I clasp you in my arms,
For I can soothe an infinite cold sorrow,
And gaze contented on your icy charms,
And that wild snow-pile, which we call to-morrow;   70
Sweep on, O soft, and azure-lidded sky,
Earth's waters to your gentle gaze reply.

---

1. A boundary, goal, or destination.
2. To combine so as to form a mosaic.

I am not earth-born, though I here delay;
Hope's child, I summon infiniter powers,
And laugh to see the mild and sunny day
Smile on the shrunk and thin autumnal hours;
I laugh, for hope hath happy place with me,
If my bark sinks, 'tis to another sea.

(1843)

Inscription for a Garden

The spirit builds his house in the least flowers,—
A beautiful mansion; how the colors live,
Intricately delicate. Every night
An angel, for this purpose, from the heavens
With his small urn of ivory-like hue drops
A globular world of the purest element
In the flower's midst, feeding its tender soul
With lively inspiration. Wonder 'tis
That man will still want knowledge; is not here,
Spread in amazing wealth, a form too rare,   10
A soul so inward, that with open heart
Tremulous and tender, we must ever fear
Not to see near enough, of these deep things?

(1843)

October

Dry leaves with yellow ferns, they are
Fit wreath of Autumn, while a star
Still, bright, and pure, our frosty air
          Shivers in twinkling points
          Of thin, celestial hair,
And thus one side of heaven anoints.

I am beneath the moon's calm look,
Most quiet in this sheltered nook,
From trouble of the frosty wind
          That curls the yellow blade;   10
          Though in my covered mind
A grateful sense of change is made.

To wandering men how dear this sight,
Of a cold, tranquil autumn night,
In its majestic, deep repose.
        Thus shall their genius be,
        Not buried in high snows,
Though of as mute tranquillity.

An anxious life they will not pass,
Nor, as the shadow on the grass,   20
Leave no impression there to stay;
        To them all things are thought;
        The blushing morn's decay,
Our death, our life, by this is taught.

O find in every haze that shines
A brief appearance without lines,
A single word,—no finite joy;
        For present is a Power
        Which we may not annoy,
Yet love him stronger every hour.   30

I would not put this sense from me,
If I could some great sovereign be;
Yet will not task a fellow man
        To feel the same glad sense;
        For no one living can
Feel, save for his given influence.

                                                    (1843)

Sonnet XI

I love the universe,—I love the joy
Of every living thing. Be mine the sure
Felicity, which ever shall endure;
While passion whirls the madmen, as they toy,

To hate, I would my simple being warm
In the calm pouring sun; and in that pure
And motionless silence, ever would employ
My best true powers, without a thought's annoy.

See and be glad! O high imperial race,
Dwarfing the common altitude of strength,   10

Learn that ye stand on an unshaken base;
Your powers will carry you to any length.
Up! earnestly feel the gentle sunset beams;
Be glad in woods, o'er sands,—by marsh, or streams.

(1843)

To One Complaining

Go to the waving tree,
    The level circle's golden round,
Or on the margin of the Sea,
    List to the sound.

I bid thee from the roof,
    Where underneath the dreary day,
Puts thy frail spirit to the proof,
    To turn away.

Speak not beneath the wall,
    God hears thee not while thou art there,   10
But make thy consecrated hall
    The endless air.

Ride on the wild wind's mane
    When scornful Autumn hisses loud,
Sing like the heavy Summer's rain,
    So stately proud.

Have never-failing Hate,
    And be forbidden in thy deed,
And make thyself all desolate,
    Nor sate thy need.   20

Then when thy rage is spent,
    Thou shalt sit down to tell the tale,
And as thou see'st the way thou went,
    Be clad in mail.

Bad memories shall be,
    The storehouse of thy present worth,
The Past shall win this stake for thee,
    Another birth.

(1846)

Walden Spring

Whisper ye leaves your lyrics in my ear,
Carol thou glittering bird thy summer song,
And flowers, and grass, and mosses on the rocks,
And the full woods, lead me in sober aisles,
And may I seek this happy day the Cliffs,
When fluid summer melts all ores in one,
Both in the air, the water, and the ground.
And so I walked beyond the last, gray house,
And o'er the upland glance, and down the mead,
Then turning went into the oaken copse,—   10
Heroic underwoods that take the air
With freedom, nor respect their parent's death.
Yet a few steps, then welled a cryptic spring,
Whose temperate nectar palls not on the taste,
Dancing in yellow circles on the sand,
And carving through the ooze a crystal bowl.
Here sometime have I drank a bumper rare,
Wetting parched lips, from a sleek, emerald leaf,
Nursed at the fountain's breast, and neatly filled
The forest-cup, filled by a woodland hand,   20
That from familiar things draws sudden use,
Strange to the civic eye, to Walden plain.
And resting there after my thirst was quenched,
Beneath the curtain of a civil oak,
That muses near this water and the sky,
I tried some names with which to grave this fount.
And as I dreamed of these, I marked the roof,
Then newly built above the placid spring,
Resting upon some awkward masonry.
In truth our village has become a butt   30
For one of these fleet railroad shafts, and o'er
Our peaceful plain, its soothing sound is—Concord,
Four times and more each day a rumbling train
Of painted cars rolls on the iron road,
Prefigured in its advent by sharp screams
That Pandemonium satisfied should hear.
The steaming tug athirst, and lacking drink,
The railroad eye direct with fatal stroke
Smote the spring's covert, and by leaden drain
Thieved its cold crystal for the engine's breast.   40
Strange! that the playful current from the woods,
Should drag the freighted train, chatting with fire,
And point the tarnished rail with man and trade.

                                        (1848)

James Russell Lowell
1819–1891

Better known today as a critic than a poet, James Russell Lowell also earned fame in his time as a humorist, editor, essayist, teacher, abolitionist, reformer, and diplomat. Lowell delighted readers with the dialect verses in *The Biglow Papers* (*First Series*) (1848), his satiric attack on slavery and the Mexican War. In *A Fable for Critics* (1848), Lowell wrote playfully and tellingly about the leading authors of his day, among them William Cullen Bryant, Edgar Allan Poe, Ralph Waldo Emerson, and Margaret Fuller. He also wrote lyric poems and long occasional verse.

Born on 22 February 1819 in Cambridge, Massachusetts, James Russell Lowell was the son of the Reverend Charles Lowell, pastor of West Church, Boston, and Harriet Traill Spence. Educated at Cambridge School (1827–34) and Harvard College (1834–38), Lowell earned his Harvard law degree in 1840, but soon returned to his first love—literature. In 1844 he married Maria White, with whom he had four children; two survived infancy. After Maria's death in 1853, he married Frances Dunlap (1823–85) in 1857; they had no children. As a magazinist, Lowell edited three journals: *The Pioneer* (1843), and two influential periodicals: the *Atlantic Monthly* (1857–61), and the *North American Review* (1864–72). After studying in Europe in 1851–52 and 1855–56, he succeeded Henry Wadsworth Longfellow as a professor of modern languages at Harvard. Lowell received an honorary degree from Oxford University (1873) and served as Minister to Spain (1877–80) and England (1880–85). Before his death on 12 August 1891 in Cambridge, Lowell saw through the press the ten-volume Riverside Edition of his works.

Lowell's early poems appeared in the *Southern Literary Messenger* in 1839. *A Year's Life* (1841), his first volume, *Poems* (1843), and *Conversations on Some of the Old Poets* (1845) soon followed. The *Boston Courier* of 17 June 1846 printed his first *Biglow Paper*, but 1848 was Lowell's "annus mirabilis" (Duberman 89–117): that year saw publication of *Poems: Second Series* (published at the end of 1847), *The Biglow Papers* (*First Series*), *A Fable for Critics*, and *The Vision of Sir Launfal*. These volumes established Lowell as a poet-critic and commentator on his times. *Poems* (1849), published when Lowell was thirty, completed a remarkable decade of poetic productivity.

Though Lowell turned his attention to prose, criticism, teaching, and politics in the 1850s, he published *Ode Recited at the Commemoration of the Living and Dead Soldiers of Harvard University* (1865), *The Biglow Papers (Second Series)* (1867), *Under the Willows and Other Poems* (1869), *The Cathedral* (1870), *Three Memorial Poems* (1877), and *Heartsease and Rue* (1888). Horace E. Scudder's edition of Lowell's *Complete Poetical Works* contains some three hundred poems in 440 pages.

Critics today regard Lowell's lyric poems as marred by "technical infelicities and irregularities, didacticism, obscurity, and excessive literosity" (Wortham 127). As a prosodist, Lowell relied chiefly on traditional verse forms: odes, hymns, ballads, sonnets, blank verse, and rhyming couplets. But in *The Biglow Papers (First Series)*, he created Hosea Biglow and Birdofredum Sawin, cracker-barrel philosophers who spoke wittily in Yankee dialect about slavery and other injustices. Besides social injustices, Lowell explored thematically nature's beauty and God's benevolence, the importance of individual conscience, the necessity of striving "toward the Ideal," the heart's superiority over the intellect, and the need to make the past serve the present (Duberman 92–93). In *A Fable for Critics*, he judiciously recognized his penchant to preach; he wrote of himself: "The top of the hill [Parnassus] he will ne'er come nigh reaching / Till he learns the distinction 'twixt singing and preaching" (lines 240–41).

Lowell's most memorable work for modern critics remains *A Fable for Critics* and *The Biglow Papers (First Series)*. Even today, *A Fable for Critics* introduces readers intelligently to the period, and in *The Biglow Papers*, Lowell cloaks his moral indignation about slavery and the Mexican War effectively with humor and satire. Those achievements are not small.

—*Robert Bain*

Suggestions for Further Reading

Duberman, Martin. *James Russell Lowell*. Boston: Houghton, 1966.*

Rees, Robert A. "James Russell Lowell." *Fifteen American Authors Before 1900: Biographical Essays on Research and Criticism*. Ed. Earl N. Harbert and Robert A. Rees. Rev. ed. Madison: U of Wisconsin P, 1984. 468–99.*

Wortham, Thomas. "James Russell Lowell." *The American Renaissance in New England*. Vol. 1 of *The Dictionary of Literary Biography*. Ed. Joel Myerson. Detroit: Gale, 1978. 126–31.

TEXT

The Complete Poetical Works of James Russell Lowell. Boston: Houghton, 1896.

ꙮ

from The Biglow Papers
(First Series)

Thrash away, you'll *hev* to rattle
   On them kittle-drums o' yourn,—
'Taint a knowin' kind o' cattle
   Thet is ketched with mouldy corn;
Put in stiff, you fifer feller,
   Let folks see how spry you be,—
Guess you'll toot till you are yeller
   'Fore you git ahold o' me!

Thet air flag's a leetle rotten,
   Hope it aint your Sunday's best;—   10
Fact! it takes a sight o' cotton
   To stuff out a soger's chest:
Sence we farmers hev to pay fer 't,
   Ef you must wear humps like these,
S'posin' you should try salt hay fer 't,
   It would du ez slick ez grease.

'Twouldn't suit them Southern fellers,
   They're a dreffle graspin' set,
We must ollers blow the bellers
   Wen they want their irons het;   20
May be it's all right ez preachin',
   But *my* narves it kind o' grates,
Wen I see the overreachin'
   O' them nigger-drivin' States.

Them thet rule us, them slave-traders,
   Haint they cut a thunderin' swarth
(Helped by Yankee renegaders),
   Thru the vartu o' the North!
We begin to think it's nater
   To take sarse an' not be riled;—   30
Who'd expect to see a tater
   All on eend at bein' biled?

Ez fer war, I call it murder,—
    There you hev it plain an' flat;
I don't want to go no furder
    Than my Testyment fer that;
God hez sed so plump an' fairly,
    It's ez long ez it is broad,
An' you've gut to git up airly
    Ef you want to take in God.   40

'Taint your eppyletts an' feathers
    Make the thing a grain more right;
'Taint afollerin' your bell-wethers[1]
    Will excuse ye in His sight;
Ef you take a sword an' dror it,
    An go stick a feller thru,
Guv'ment aint to answer for it,
    God'll send the bill to you.

Wut's the use o' meetin'-goin'
    Every Sabbath, wet or dry,   50
Ef it's right to go amowin'
    Feller-men like oats an' rye?
I dunno but wut it's pooty
    Trainin' round in bobtail coats,—
But it's curus Christian dooty
    This 'ere cuttin' folks's throats.

They may talk o' Freedom's airy
    Tell they're pupple in the face,—
It's a grand gret cemetary
    Fer the barthrights of our race;   60
They jest want this Californy
    So's to lug new slave-states in
To abuse ye, an' to scorn ye,
    An' to plunder ye like sin.

Aint it cute to see a Yankee
    Take sech everlastin' pains,
All to get the Devil's thankee
    Helpin' on 'em weld their chains?
Wy, it's jest ez clear ez figgers,
    Clear ez one an' one make two,   70
Chaps thet make black slaves o' niggers
    Want to make wite slaves o' you.

---

1. A ram that leads a flock.

Tell ye jest the eend I've come to
    Arter cipherin' plaguy smart,
An' it makes a handy sum, tu,
    Any gump could larn by heart;
Laborin' man an' laborin' woman
    Hev one glory an' one shame.
Ev'y thin' thet's done inhuman
    Injers all on 'em the same.   80

'Taint by turnin' out to hack folks
    You're agoin' to git your right,
Nor by lookin' down on black folks
    Coz you're put upon by wite;
Slavery aint o' nary color,
    'Taint the hide thet makes it wus,
All it keers fer in a feller
    'S jest to make him fill its pus.

Want to tackle *me* in, du ye?
    I expect you'll hev to wait;   90
Wen cold lead puts daylight thru ye
    You'll begin to kal'late;
S'pose the crows wun't fall to pickin'
    All the carkiss from your bones,
Coz you helped to give a lickin'
    To them poor half-Spanish drones?

Jest go home an' ask our Nancy
    Wether I'd be sech a goose
Ez to jine ye,—guess you'd fancy
    The etarnal bung wuz loose!   100
She wants me fer home consumption,
    Let alone the hay's to mow,—
Ef you're arter folks o' gumption,
    You've a darned long row to hoe.

Take them editors thet's crowin'
    Like a cockerel three months old,—
Don't ketch any on 'em goin',
    Though they *be* so blasted bold;
Aint they a prime lot o' fellers?
    'Fore they think on 't guess they'll sprout   110
(Like a peach thet's got the yellers),
    With the meanness bustin' out.

Wal, go 'long to help 'em stealin'
    Bigger pens to cram with slaves,

James Russell Lowell   173

Help the men thet's ollers dealin'
   Insults on your fathers' graves;
Help the strong to grind the feeble,
   Help the many agin the few,
Help the men thet call your people
   Witewashed slaves an' peddlin' crew!   120

Massachusetts, God forgive her,
   She's akneelin' with the rest,
She, thet ough' to ha' clung forever
   In her grand old eagle-nest;
She thet ough' to stand so fearless
   W'ile the wracks are round her hurled,
Holdin' up a beacon peerless
   To the oppressed of all the world!

Ha'n't they sold your colored seamen?
   Ha'n't they made your env'ys w'iz?   130
Wut'll make ye act like freemen?
   Wut'll git your dander riz?
Come, I'll tell ye wut I'm thinkin'
   Is our dooty in this fix,
They'd ha' done 't ez quick ez winkin'
   In the days o' seventy-six.

Clang the bells in every steeple,
   Call all true men to disown
The tradoocers of our people,
   The enslavers o' their own;   140
Let our dear old Bay State proudly
   Put the trumput to her mouth,
Let her ring this messidge loudly
   In the ears of all the South:—

"I'll return ye good fer evil
   Much ez we frail mortils can,
But I wun't go help the Devil
   Makin' man the cus o' man;
Call me coward, call me traiter,
   Jest ez suits your mean idees,—   150
Here I stand a tyrant-hater,
   An' the friend o' God an' Peace!"

Ef I'd *my* way I hed ruther
   We should go to work an' part,
They take one way, we take t'other,
   Guess it wouldn't break my heart;

Men hed ough' to put asunder
　　Them thet God has noways jined;
An' I shouldn't gretly wonder
　　Ef there's thousands o' my mind.　　　　　　　160
　　　　　　　　　　　　　　　　　　　　　　　(1848)

　　　　　　　　—*Hosea Biglow*

from A Fable for Critics[2]

　　There comes Emerson first, whose rich words, every one,
Are like gold nails in temples to hang trophies on,
Whose prose is grand verse, while his verse, the Lord
　　knows,
Is some of it pr—— No, 'tis not even prose;
I'm speaking of metres; some poems have welled
From those rare depths of soul that have ne'er been excelled;
They're not epics, but that doesn't matter a pin,
In creating, the only hard thing's to begin;
A grass-blade's no easier to make than an oak;　　　　　10
If you've once found the way, you've achieved the grand
　　stroke;
In the worst of his poems are mines of rich matter,
But thrown in a heap with a crash and a clatter;
Now it is not one thing nor another alone
Makes a poem, but rather the general tone,
The something pervading, uniting the whole,
The before unconceived, unconceivable soul,
So that just in removing this trifle or that, you
Take away, as it were, a chief limb of the statue;
Roots, wood, bark, and leaves singly perfect may be,　　20
But, clapt hodge-podge together, they don't make a tree.

　　"But, to come back to Emerson (whom, by the way,
I believe we left waiting,)—his is, we may say,
A Greek head on right Yankee shoulders, whose range
Has Olympus for one pole, for t'other the Exchange;
He seems, to my thinking (although I'm afraid
The comparison must, long ere this, have been made),
A Plotinus-Montaigne,[3] where the Egyptian's gold mist
And the Gascon's shrewd wit cheek-by-jowl coexist;

---

2. The speaker in Lowell's *Fable* is Apollo, the Greek god of the sun,
prophecy, music, medicine, and poetry.
　　3. Plotinus (205?–270?) was a Greek idealist philosopher born in Egypt, and
Montaigne (1533–92) was a French essayist and skeptic.

All admire, and yet scarcely six converts he's got   30
To I don't (nor they either) exactly know what;
For though he builds glorious temples, 'tis odd
He leaves never a doorway to get in a god.
'Tis refreshing to old-fashioned people like me
To meet such a primitive Pagan as he,
In whose mind all creation is duly respected
As parts of himself—just a little projected;
And who's willing to worship the stars and the sun,
A convert to—nothing but Emerson.
So perfect a balance there is in his head,   40
That he talks of things sometimes as if they were dead;
Life, nature, love, God, and affairs of that sort,
He looks at as merely ideas; in short,
As if they were fossils stuck round in a cabinet,
Of such vast extent that our earth's a mere dab in it;
Composed just as he is inclined to conjecture her,
Namely, one part pure earth, ninety-nine parts pure lecturer;
You are filled with delight at his clear demonstration,
Each figure, word, gesture, just fits the occasion,
With the quiet precision of science he'll sort 'em,   50
But you can't help suspecting the whole a *post mortem.*

. . . .

   "He has imitators in scores, who omit
Not part of the man but his wisdom and wit,—
Who go carefully o'er the sky-blue of his brain,
And when he has skimmed it once, skim it again;
If at all they resemble him, you may be sure it is
Because their shoals mirror his mists and obscurities,
As a mud-puddle seems deep as heaven for a minute,
While the cloud that floats o'er is reflected within it.

   "There comes————,⁴ for instance; to see him's rare
      sport,   60
Tread in Emerson's tracks with legs painfully short;
How he jumps, how he strains, and gets red in the face,
To keep step with the mystagogue's natural pace!
He follows as close as a stick to a rocket,
His fingers exploring the prophet's each pocket.
Fie, for shame, brother bard; with good fruit of your own,
Can't you let Neighbor Emerson's orchards alone?
Beside, 'tis no use, you'll not find e'en a core,—
———— has picked up all the windfalls before.
They might strip every tree, and E. never would
      catch 'em,   70

---

4. Lowell here refers to Henry David Thoreau.

His Hesperides[5] have no rude dragon to watch 'em;
When they send him a dishful, and ask him to try 'em,
He never suspects how the sly rogues came by 'em;
He wonders why 'tis there are none such his trees on,
And thinks 'em the best he has tasted this season.
. . . .
    "There is Bryant, as quiet, as cool, and as dignified,
As a smooth, silent iceberg, that never is ignified,
Save when by reflection 'tis kindled 'o nights
With a semblance of flame by the chill Northern Lights.
He may rank (Griswold[6] says so) the first bard of your
    nation   80
(There's no doubt that he stands in supreme iceolation),
Your topmost Parnassus he may set his heel on,
But no warm applauses come, peal following peal on,—
He's too smooth and too polished to hang any zeal on:
Unqualified merits, I'll grant, if you choose, he has 'em,
But he lacks the one merit of kindling enthusiasm;
If he stir you at all, it is just, on my soul,
Like being stirred up with the very North Pole.

    "He is very nice reading in summer, but *inter
Nos*,[7] we don't want *extra* freezing in winter;   90
Take him up in the depth of July, my advice is,
When you feel an Egyptian devotion to ices.
But, deduct all you can, there's enough that's right good in
    him,
He has a true soul for the field, river, and wood in him;
And his heart, in the midst of brick walls, or where'er it is,
Glows, softens, and thrills with the tenderest charities—
To you mortals that delve in this trade-ridden planet?
No, to old Berkshire's hills, with their limestone and granite.
. . . .
    "But, my dear little bardlings, don't prick up your ears
Nor suppose I would rank you and Bryant as peers;   100
If I call him an iceberg, I don't mean to say
There is nothing in that which is grand in its way;
He is almost the one of your poets that knows
How much grace, strength, and dignity lie in Repose;
If he sometimes fall short, he is too wise to mar
His thought's modest fulness by going too far;
'Twould be well if your authors should all make a trial
Of what virtue there is in severe self-denial,

---

5. In Greek mythology, the daughters of Hesperus, who with a dragon
watched over the golden apples in the Isles of the Blest.
6. Rufus Griswold (1815–57), American author, editor, and critic.
7. Between us.

And measure their writings by Hesiod's staff,
Which teaches that all has less value than half.   110

    "There is Whittier, whose swelling and vehement heart
Strains the strait-breasted drab of the Quaker apart,
And reveals the live Man, still supreme and erect,
Underneath the bemummying wrappers of sect;
There was ne'er a man born who had more of a swing
Of the true lyric bard and all that kind of thing;
And his failures rise (though he seem not to know it)
From the very same cause that has made him a poet,—
A fervor of mind which knows no separation
'Twixt simple excitement and pure inspiration,   120
As my Pythoness[8] erst sometimes erred from not knowing
If 'twere I or mere wind through her tripod was blowing;
Let his mind once get head in its favorite direction
And the torrent of verse bursts the dams of reflection,
While, borne with a rush of the metre along,
The poet may chance to go right or go wrong,
Content with the whirl and delirium of song;
Then his grammar's not always correct, nor his rhymes,
And he's prone to repeat his own lyrics sometimes,
Not his best, though, for those are struck off at white-
          heats   130
When the heart in his breast like a trip-hammer beats,
And can ne'er be repeated again any more
Than they could have been carefully plotted before:
Like old what's-his-name there at the battle of Hastings
(Who, however, gave more than mere rhythmical bastings),
Our Quaker leads off metaphorical fights
For reform and whatever they call human rights,
Both singing and striking in front of the war,
And hitting his foes with the mallet of Thor;
Anne haec,[9] one exclaims, on beholding his knocks,   140
Vestis filii tui,[10] O leather-clad Fox?[11]
Can that be thy son, in the battle's mid din,
Preaching brotherly love and then driving it in
To the brain of the tough old Goliath of sin,
With the smoothest of pebbles from Castaly's spring[12]
Impressed on his hard moral sense with a sling?

---

8. "Pythoness" refers to a priestess of Apollo at Delphi.
9. *Anne haec* is a Latin phrase usually introducing a question and translated
as "What's that."
10. *Vestis filii tui* translates from the Latin as "in the clothing of your son."
11. George Fox (1624–91), English Quaker religious leader.
12. A spring on Mount Parnassus, a mountain in southern Greece sacred to
Apollo (the god of poetry) and the Muses.

"All honor and praise to the right-hearted bard
Who was true to The Voice when such service was hard,
Who himself was so free he dared sing for the slave
When to look but a protest in silence was brave;   150
All honor and praise to the women and men
Who spoke out for the dumb and the down-trodden then!
It needs not to name them, already for each
I see History preparing the statue and niche;
They were harsh, but shall *you* be so shocked at hard words
Who have beaten your pruning-hooks up into swords,
Whose rewards and hurrahs men are surer to gain
By the reaping of men and of women than grain?
Why should *you* stand aghast at their fierce wordy war, if
You scalp one another for Bank or for Tariff?   160
Your calling them cut-throats and knaves all day long
Doesn't prove that the use of hard language is wrong;
While the World's heart beats quicker to think of such men
As signed Tyranny's doom with a bloody steel-pen,
While on Fourth-of-Julys beardless orators fright one
With hints at Harmodius and Aristogeiton,[13]
You need not look shy at your sisters and brothers
Who stab with sharp words for the freedom of others;—
No, a wreath, twine a wreath for the loyal and true
Who, for sake of the many, dared stand with the few,   170
Not of blood-spattered laurel for enemies braved,
But of broad, peaceful oak-leaves for citizens saved!
. . . .

    "There comes Poe, with his raven, like Barnaby Rudge,[14]
Three fifths of him genius and two fifths sheer fudge,
Who talks like a book of iambs and pentameters,
In a way to make people of common sense damn metres,
Who has written some things quite the best of their kind,
But the heart somehow seems all squeezed out by the mind,
Who— But hey-day! What's this? Messieurs Mathews[15] and
    Poe,
You mustn't fling mud-balls at Longfellow so,   180
Does it make a man worse that his character's such

---

13. Harmodius (d. 514 B.C.) was an Athenian murderer, who with Aristogeiton
in 514 B.C. murdered Hipparchus, the younger brother of the "tyrant" Hippias.
They meant to kill Hippias, but Harmodius was killed and Aaristogeiton, who
fled, was later captured and executed. Later both were regarded as patriotic
martyrs and received divine honors.
    14. Charles Dickens published the novel *Barnaby Rudge* in 1841; the novel's
title character owned a raven named Grip.
    15. Cornelius Mathews (1817–89), American author and critic who attacked
Longfellow's poetry, as did Poe.

As to make his friends love him (as you think) too much?
Why, there is not a bard at this moment alive
More willing than he that his fellows should thrive;
While you are abusing him thus, even now
He would help either one of you out of a slough;
You may say that he's smooth and all that till you're hoarse,
But remember that elegance also is force;
After polishing granite as much as you will,
The heart keeps its tough old persistency still;   190
Deduct all you can, *that* still keeps you at bay;
Why, he'll live till men weary of Collins and Gray.[16]
I'm not over-fond of Greek metres in English,
To me rhyme's a gain, so it be not too jinglish,
And your modern hexameter verses are no more
Like Greek ones than sleek Mr. Pope[17] is like Homer;
As the roar of the sea to the coo of a pigeon is,
So, compared to your moderns, sounds old Melesigenes;[18]
I may be too partial, the reason, perhaps o'tis
That I've heard the old blind man recite his own
            rhapsodies,   200
And my ear with that music impregnate may be,
Like the poor exiled shell with the soul of the sea,
Or as one can't bear Strauss[19] when his nature is cloven
To its deeps within deeps by a stroke of Beethoven;[20]
But, set that aside, and 'tis truth that I speak,
Had Theocritus[21] written in English, not Greek,
I believe that his exquisite sense would scarce change a line
In that rare, tender, virgin-like pastoral Evangeline.
That's not ancient nor modern, its place is apart
Where time has no sway, in the realm of pure Art,   210
'Tis a shrine of retreat from Earth's hubbub and strife
As quiet and chaste as the author's own life."
. . . .

   "There's Holmes, who is matchless among you for wit;
A Leyden-jar always full-charged, from which flit
The electrical tingles of hit after hit;
In long poems 'tis painful sometimes, and invites
A thought of the way the new Telegraph writes,
Which pricks down its little sharp sentences spitefully

---

16. British poets William Collins (1721–59) and Thomas Gray (1716–71),
author of "Elegy Written in a Country Churchyard" (1751).
17. British poet Alexander Pope (1688–1744).
18. Homer.
19. Viennese composer Johann Strauss (1804–49), famous for his waltzes.
20. Ludwig van Beethoven (1770–1827), German composer.
21. Third century B.C. Greek author of pastoral poetry.

As if you got more than you'd title to rightfully,
And you find yourself hoping its wild father Lightning   220
Would flame in for a second and give you a fright'ning.
He has perfect sway of what I call a sham metre,
But many admire it, the English pentameter,
And Campbell,[22] I think, wrote most commonly worse,
With less nerve, swing, and fire in the same kind of verse,
Nor e'er achieved aught in 't so worthy of praise
As the tribute of Holmes to the grand *Marseillaise*.
You went crazy last year over Bulwer's New Timon;—[23]
Why, if B., to the day of his dying, should rhyme on,
Heaping verses on verses and tomes upon tomes,   230
He could ne'er reach the best point and vigor of Holmes.
His are just the fine hands, too, to weave you a lyric
Full of fancy, fun, feeling, or spiced with satiric
In a measure so kindly you doubt if the toes
That are trodden upon are your own or your foes'.

   "There is Lowell, who's striving Parnassus to climb
With a whole bale of *isms* tied together with rhyme,
He might get on alone, spite of brambles and boulders,
But he can't with that bundle he has on his shoulders,
The top of the hill he will ne'er come nigh reaching   240
Till he learns the distinction 'twixt singing and preaching;
His lyre has some chords that would ring pretty well,
But he'd rather by half make a drum of the shell,
And rattle away till he's old as Methusalem,
At the head of a march to the last new Jerusalem."

                                                    (1848)

---

22. Thomas Campbell (1777–1844), Scottish poet and author.
23. Edward Bulwer-Lytton (1802–73) was a popular British writer who
published the poem "The New Timon" in 1846.

Josiah Gilbert Holland

1819–1881

Josiah Gilbert Holland, extremely popular during his day, wrote five sentimental novels, two collections of morally instructive fictional letters, several collections of essays, and five volumes of poems. His staunchly moralistic, openly didactic writings caused biographer Harry Houston Peckham to label him "the major prophet of the unsophisticated, the supreme apostle to the naive" (2).

Josiah Holland was born in rural western Massachusetts on 24 July 1819. After a number of professional false starts, he earned his M.D. from the Berkshire Medical College in 1843. Although his attempts to build a medical practice failed, he was known throughout his life as "Doctor" Holland. In 1845, he married Elizabeth Luna Chapman. After seeking for a number of years to supplement his income by writing, in 1849 he joined Samuel Bowles as coeditor of the *Springfield Republican*. He gained a popular following in western Massachusetts while writing for the *Republican*, notably as the author of the "Timothy Titcomb" letters. In 1858 he capitalized on this hard-won popularity with the publication of the first of his book-length poems, *Bittersweet*, the success of which he immediately followed with a series of seasonal lecture tours. He went on to publish four more books of poetry—*Kathrina* (1867), *The Marble Prophecy and Other Poems* (1872), *The Mistress of the Manse* (1874) and *The Puritan's Guest* (1877)—which were collected under the title *Garnered Sheaves* in 1879. His popularity as a lecturer and author of moral tales and poems grew steadily. After selling his interest in the *Republican* in 1857, he edited the new *Scribner's Magazine* from 1870 until his death on 12 October 1881 in Springfield. His obituaries celebrated his Christian goodness, the sincerity of which had inspired a national following.

Holland's nineteenth-century popularity, based on didactic and devotional poems like "Alone!," "Gradatim," and "Intimations," was far greater than Whitman's. Holland criticized Whitman's verse in an essay entitled "Is It Poetry?" (*Every-Day Topics* 126–34), objecting strenuously to Whitman's lack of regular meter and form. Holland's relationship to Emily Dickinson is perhaps even more interesting. Although Mrs. Holland was one of Dickinson's closest friends and Dickinson mentions Holland often in her letters, Holland was evidently unaware of her unpublished poetry.

Holland's ignorance of Dickinson's poetry and his stout rejection of Whitman's has become all the more ironic as modern readers study Dickinson and Whitman and ignore Holland. The simpleminded faith and easy accessability that attracted so many nineteenth-century readers has long since lost its appeal.

— Terry Roberts

Suggestions for Further Reading

Holland, Josiah Gilbert. *Every-Day Topics*. Second Series. New York: Scribners, 1882.
———. *Timothy Titcomb's Letters to Young People*. New York: Scribners, 1858.
Peckham, Harry Houston. *Josiah Gilbert Holland in Relation to His Times*. Philadelphia: U of Pennsylvania P, 1940.

TEXT
Garnered Sheaves; The Complete Poetical Writings of J. G. Holland. 1873.

ꙅꚛꙅ

Alone!

All alone in the world! all alone!
With a child on my knee, or a wife on my breast,
Or, sitting beside me, the beautiful guest
Whom my heart leaps to greet as its sweetest and best,
Still alone in the world! all alone!

With my visions of beauty, alone!
Too fair to be painted, too fleet to be scanned,
Too regal to stay at my feeble command,
They pass from the grasp of my impotent hand:
Still alone in the world! all alone!   10

Alone with my conscience, alone!
Not an eye that can see when its finger of flame
Points my soul to its sin, or consumes it with shame!

Not an ear that can hear its low whisper of blame!
    Still alone in the world! all alone!

        In my visions of self, all alone!
The weakness, the meanness, the guilt that I see,
The fool or the fiend I am tempted to be,
Can only be seen and repented by me:
    Still alone in the world! all alone!   20

        Alone in my worship, alone!
No hand in the universe, joining with mine,
Can lift what it lays on the altar divine,
Or bear what it offers aloft to its shrine:
    Still alone in the world! all alone!

        In the valley of death, all alone!
The sighs and the tears of my friends are in vain,
For mine is the passage, and mine is the pain,
And mine the sad sinking of bosom and brain:
    Still alone in the world! all alone!   30

        Not alone! never, never alone!
There is one who is with me by day and by night,
Who sees and inspires all my visions of light,
And teaches my conscience its office aright:
    Not alone in the world! not alone!

        Not alone! never, never alone!
He sees all my weakness with pitying eyes,
He helps me to lift my faint heart to the skies,
And in my last passion he suffers and dies:
    Not alone! never, never alone!

                                                          (1872)

Gradatim

Heaven is not reached at a single bound;
        But we build the ladder by which we rise
        From the lowly earth to the vaulted skies,
And we mount to its summit round by round.

I count this thing to be grandly true:
        That a noble deed is a step toward God,—

WHERE IS THE POET GOING

The Road Not Taken

Two roads diverged in a yellow wood,
And sorry I could not travel both
And be one traveler, long I stood
And looked down one as far as I could
(5) To where it bent in the undergrowth;

Then took the other, as just as fair,
And having perhaps the better claim,
Because it was grassy and wanted wear;
Though as for that, the passing there
(10) Had worn them really about the same,

And both that morning equally lay
In leaves no step had trodden back.
Oh, I kept the first for another day!
Yet knowing how way leads on to way,
(15) I doubted if I should ever come back.

I shall be telling this with a sigh
Somewhere ages and ages hence:
Two roads diverged in a wood, and I—
I took the one less traveled by,
(20) And that has made all the difference.

"The Road Not Taken," by Robert Frost.

Lifting the soul from the common clod
To a purer air and a broader view.

We rise by the things that are under feet;
  By what we have mastered of good and gain; 10
  By the pride deposed and the passion slain,
And the vanquished ills that we hourly meet.

We hope, we aspire, we resolve, we trust,
  When the morning calls us to life and light,
  But our hearts grow weary, and, ere the night,
Our lives are trailing the sordid dust.

We hope, we resolve, we aspire, we pray,
  And we think that we mount the air on wings
  Beyond the recall of sensual things,
While our feet still cling to the heavy clay. 20

Wings for the angels, but feet for men!
  We may borrow the wings to find the way—
  We may hope, and resolve, and aspire, and pray;
But our feet must rise, or we fall again.

Only in dreams is a ladder thrown
  From the weary earth to the sapphire walls;
  But the dreams depart, and the vision falls,
And the sleeper wakes on his pillow of stone.

Heaven is not reached at a single bound;
  But we build the ladder by which we rise 30
  From the lowly earth to the vaulted skies,
And we mount to its summit, round by round.

          (1872)

Intimations[1]

What glory then! What darkness now!
  A glimpse, a thrill, and it is flown!
  I reach, I grasp, but stand alone,
With empty arms and upward brow!

---

1. Holland's "Intimations" was doubtlessly inspired by Wordsworth's "Ode: Intimations of Immortality." Compare in particular line 26 of Holland to lines 178–79 of Wordsworth's poem.

Ye may not see, O weary eyes!
　　The band of angels, swift and bright,
　　That pass, but cannot wake your sight,
Down trooping from the crowded skies.

O heavy ears! Ye may not hear
　　The strains that pass my conscious soul,　　10
　　And seek, but find no earthly goal,
Far falling from another sphere.

Ah! soul of mine! Ah! soul of mine!
　　Thy sluggish senses are but bars
　　That stand between thee and the stars,
And shut thee from the world divine.

For something sweeter far than sound,
　　And something finer than the light
　　Comes through the discord and the night
And penetrates, or wraps thee round.　　20

Nay, God is here, couldst thou but see;
　　All things of beauty are of Him;
　　And heaven, that holds the cherubim,
As lovingly embraces thee!

If thou hast apprehended well
　　The tender glory of a flower,
　　Which moved thee, by some subtle power
Whose source and sway thou couldst not tell;

If thou hast kindled to the sweep
　　Of stormy clouds across the sky,　　30
　　Or gazed with tranced and tearful eye,
And swelling breast, upon the deep;

If thou hast felt the throb and thrill
　　Of early day and happy birds,
　　While peace, that drowned thy chosen words
Has flowed from thee in glad good-will,

Then hast thou drunk the heavenly dew;
　　Then have thy feet in rapture trod
　　The pathway of a thought of God;
And death can show thee nothing new.　　40

For heaven and beauty are the same,—
　　Of God the all-informing thought,

To sweet, supreme expression wrought,
And syllabled by sound and flame.

The light that beams from childhood's eyes,
    The charm that dwells in summer woods,
    The holy influence that broods
O'er all things under twilight skies,—

The music of the simple notes
    That rise from happy human homes,   50
    The joy in life of all that roams
Upon the earth, and all that floats,

Proclaim that heaven's sweet providence
    Enwraps the homely earth in whole,
    And finds the secret of the soul
Through channels subtler than the sense.

O soul of mine! Throw wide thy door,
    And cleanse thy paths from doubt and sin;
    And the bright flood shall enter in
And give thee heaven for evermore!   60
                      (1872)

Herman Melville

1819–1891

Although best known in his day
and ours as a novelist, Herman Melville devoted the last three
decades of his literary career almost exclusively to poetry. The
man who made the sea a major subject in his novels also excelled
at writing sea poetry. Like many of his contemporaries, he also
found poetic inspiration in the Civil War, creating a realistic view
of modern war in what many critics consider his finest volume of
verse, *Battle-Pieces and Aspects of the War* (1866). Out of his long
and troubled quest for a religious faith that could withstand the
pressures of the age and the challenges of his own intellect grew
Clarel: A Poem and Pilgrimage in the Holy Land, an eighteen-thou-
sand-line philosophical poem that represents a major poetic
achievement even though it has yet to win the attention it de-
serves. Despite the quantity and quality of Melville's poetic out-
put, his contemporaries did not regard him as a significant poet.
Only in recent years have critics begun to appreciate the power,
depth, and artistry of his verse.

Born on 1 August 1819 in New York City, Melville grew up in
a distinguished and once-prosperous family fallen on hard times.
When Melville was twelve, his father died, leaving his family
destitute. The boy had to leave school at fifteen, finding various
jobs as a bank clerk, a farmhand, and a teacher until shipping for
Liverpool as a cabin boy in 1839. After four months he returned,
but went to sea again in December of 1840 on a whaling ship
bound for the South Pacific. He jumped ship in the Marquesa Is-
lands eighteen months later and lived for a month as the captive
of a cannibal tribe. Eventually he made his way to Tahiti and
then to Honolulu, where he enlisted as an ordinary seaman on an
American naval frigate. In October of 1844, nearly four years
after his departure, Melville returned to the United States and
began writing novels based on his adventures at sea.

Melville scored immediate successes with *Typee* (1846) and
Omoo (1847), his first two novels. The allegorical novel *Mardi*
(1849) puzzled and disappointed his readers, but they greeted
Melville's return to writing adventure novels—*Redburn* (1849)

and *White-Jacket* (1850)—with enthusiasm. Having apparently established an ability to earn a living as a writer, Melville married Elizabeth Shaw, an old family friend, in 1847. They settled first in New York and then in Pittsfield, Massachusetts, where he formed an influential friendship with Nathaniel Hawthorne during 1850–51. There he wrote his masterpiece, *Moby-Dick* (1851), which he dedicated to the older writer. His popularity began to wane with this novel, and with the subsequent publication of *Pierre* (1852), *Israel Potter* (1855), *Piazza Tales* (1856) and *The Confidence Man* (1857), Melville all but lost his popular audience. Exhausted and discouraged by his literary efforts and plagued by spiritual yearnings he could not satisfy, Melville seemed destined for serious mental and physical illness. As a restorative, his father-in-law sponsored a trip to Europe and the Holy Land in 1856–57, out of which emerged his long poem *Clarel* nineteen years later. After his return, Melville tried lecturing for three years, moved his family back to New York, and in 1866 accepted a job as customs inspector, a position he held for almost twenty years.

Except for *Billy Budd*, Melville wrote no more fiction, but by 1860 he had prepared a volume of poetry for publication. He found no publisher for it, but Harper & Brothers published a subsequent collection, entitled *Battle-Pieces and Aspects of the War*, in August of 1866. Inspired by the fall of Richmond, the poetic sequence covers many significant events of the war as well as incidents leading up to it ("The Portent") and a vision of the new state rising up afterwards. The book closes with a prose supplement urging fair and generous treatment of the South. Critics gave the work considerable attention, but its unconventional style led many of them to regard it as flawed. Despite the public's neglect, Melville continued to write verse, publishing the volume *Clarel* in 1876. He privately printed two other volumes: *John Marr and Other Sailors* (1888), a collection of sea poems, and *Timoleon* (1891), a collection of poems about travel, art, and history. At his death in New York on 28 September 1891, he left behind a substantial body of poetry, including several collections in progress.

Reviewers faulted Melville's poetry for its "crudities," its "fearful rhymes" and "epileptic meters" (rev., *American Literary Gazette* 190) and its "disregard of the laws of verse" (rev., *Round Table* 108–9). But Melville had great respect for form, as poems such as "Greek Architecture" attest. Far from rejecting traditional poetic forms, Melville wrote epigrams, epitaphs, ballads, verse epistles, dramatic monologues, panoramic and didactic narratives, prose-verse medleys like "Tom Deadlight," and Pindaric-like odes such as "The Conflict of Convictions." He did, however, violate traditional "laws of verse" by distorting stresses or varying tempos in unsettling ways and by blending prosaic or casual language with some of his loftiest expressions. Long viewed as evidence of his technical incompetence, these violations in fact generally enhance the theme of the poem, as in "A Utilitarian View of the *Monitor*'s Fight." His use of harsh diction and technical terminology in this poem also shows Melville's interest in what constitutes poetic language. In embracing restrictive poetic forms while deliberately violating traditional expectations of poetry, Melville resembles Emily Dickinson, and his verse suffered the same fate as hers at the hands of early critics.

Although diverse in subject matter, Melville's poetry, which he regarded as a vehicle for serious philosophical contemplation, deals with recurrent themes: the endless quest after truth, humankind's innate depravity, the nature of nature, the role of necessity in history, alienation and materialism as responses to modern life, and the high emotional costs of pursuing artistic and other intellectual endeavors. The failure of his verse to gain a following in his day is hardly surprising, since Melville had explored many of these same themes earlier in his philosophical fiction that had so disappointed the public. Even though modern readers may be more comfortable than his contemporaries were with the inconclusiveness and obscurity of much of his poetry, it has yet to excite anything approaching the degree of critical interest that his fiction has generated since the Melville revival of the 1920s. Recent critics nevertheless show a more sophisticated understanding of Melville's style, as well as a greater appreciation of his sensitive probing of the human psyche, his persistent and courageous searching after truth, and his sympathetic treatment of human suffering.

—*Ellen Gidu*ʒ

Suggestions for Further Reading

Bryant, John, ed. *A Companion to Melville Studies*. New York: Greenwood, 1986. See chapters entitled "Melville's Poems: The Late Agenda" by William H. Shurr (351–74) and "*Clarel*" by Vincent Kenny (375–406).*

Garner, Stanton. *The Civil War World of Herman Melville*. Manhattan: U of Kansas P, 1993.

Hook, Andrew. "Melville's Poetry." *Herman Melville: Reassessments*. Ed. A. Robert Lee. Totowa, NJ: Barnes, 1984. 176–98.

Lee, A. Robert. " 'Eminently Adapted for Unpopularity'? Melville's Poetry." *Nineteenth-Century American Poetry*. Ed. A. Robert Lee. London: Vision Press, 1987. 118–45.

Rev. of *Battle-Pieces*. *American Literary Gazette and Publishers' Circular* 1 Sept. 1866: 190.
Rev. of *Battle-Pieces*. *Round Table* (New York) 15 Sept. 1866: 108–9.
Robillard, Douglas, ed. "Symposium: Melville the Poet." *Essays in Arts and Sciences* (New Haven) 5 (July 1976).
Shurr, William H. *The Mystery of Iniquity: Melville as Poet, 1857–1891*. Lexington: UP of Kentucky, 1972.
Stein, William Bysshe. *The Poetry of Melville's Later Years: Time, History, Myth, and Religion*. Albany: SUNY P, 1972.

TEXTS

Battle-Pieces and Aspects of the War. 1866.
Collected Poems of Herman Melville. Ed. Howard P. Vincent. Chicago: Hendricks House, 1947.
Norman Eugene Jarrard. *Poems by Herman Melville: A Critical Edition of the Published Verse*. Diss. U of Texas, 1960.

இஃஇ

The Portent
(1859)

Hanging from the beam,
   Slowly swaying (such the law),
Gaunt the shadow on your green,
   Shenandoah!
The cut is on the crown
   (Lo, John Brown),[1]
And the stabs shall heal no more.

Hidden in the cap
   Is the anguish none can draw;
So your future veils its face,   10
   Shenandoah!
But the streaming beard is shown
   (Weird[2] John Brown),
The meteor[3] of the war.

(1866)

---

1. John Brown was hanged for treason and inciting a slave uprising in the fertile and peaceful Shenandoah Valley in northern Virginia on 2 December 1859 following his raid on the United States Arsenal at Harper's Ferry two months earlier. This was one of the most provocative events leading up to the Civil War.
2. "Weird" can mean having the power to direct fate.
3. Meteors were commonly regarded as omens.

Ball's Bluff[4]
A Reverie
(October, 1861)

One noonday, at my window in the town,
    I saw a sight—saddest that eyes can see—
    Young soldiers marching lustily
        Unto the wars,
With fifes, and flags in mottoed pageantry;
      While all the porches, walks, and doors
Were rich with ladies cheering royally.

They moved like Juny morning on the wave,
    Their hearts were fresh as clover in its prime
    (It was the breezy summer time),   10
        Life throbbed so strong,
How should they dream that Death in a rosy clime
      Would come to thin their shining throng?
Youth feels immortal, like the gods sublime.

Weeks passed; and at my window, leaving bed,
    By night I mused, of easeful sleep bereft,
    On those brave boys (Ah War! thy theft);
        Some marching feet
Found pause at last by cliffs Potomac cleft;
      Wakeful I mused, while in the street   20
Far footfalls died away till none were left.

                       (1866)

A Utilitarian View of the *Monitor*'s Fight[5]

Plain be the phrase, yet apt the verse,
    More ponderous than nimble;
For since grimed War here laid aside
His Orient pomp, 'twould ill befit

---

4. On 21 October 1861, Federal troops undertook a disastrous raid against the Confederates stationed along the Potomac at Ball's Bluff, Virginia, and lost one-thousand men in the ensuing massacre.

5. On 9 March 1862 in Hampton Roads, Virginia, the Federal warship *Monitor* met the Confederate warship *Virginia* (formerly the *Merrimack*) in the first battle between ironclads. The four-hour engagement ended in a draw, but it demonstrated the superiority of the ironclad and effectively closed the era of the wooden battleship.

        Overmuch to ply
    The rhyme's barbaric cymbal.

Hail to victory without the gaud
    Of glory; zeal that needs no fans
Of banners; plain mechanic power
Plied cogently in War now placed—   10
        Where War belongs—
    Among the trades and artisans.

Yet this was battle, and intense—
    Beyond the strife of fleets heroic;
Deadlier, closer, calm 'mid storm;
No passion; all went on by crank,
        Pivot, and screw,
    And calculations of caloric.

Needless to dwell; the story's known.
    The ringing of those plates on plates   20
Still ringeth round the world—
The clangor of that blacksmith's fray.
        The anvil-din
    Resounds this message from the Fates:

War shall yet be, and to the end;
    But war-paint shows the streaks of weather;
War yet shall be, but warriors
Are now but operatives; War's made
        Less grand than Peace,
    And a singe runs through lace and feather.

                                                        (1866)

Shiloh[6]
A Requiem
(April, 1862)

    Skimming lightly, wheeling still,
        The swallows fly low
    Over the field in clouded days,
        The forest-field of Shiloh—
    Over the field where April rain

---

6. The Battle of Shiloh, fought 6–7 April 1862 near Pittsburg Landing,
Tennessee, claimed the lives of twenty-three thousand men but gained nothing
for either side.

Solaced the parched ones stretched in pain
Through the pause of night
That followed the Sunday fight
    Around the church of Shiloh—
The church so lone, the log-built one,   10
That echoed to many a parting groan
        And natural prayer
    Of dying foemen mingled there—
Foemen at morn, but friends at eve—
    Fame or country least their care:
(What like a bullet can undeceive!)
    But now they lie low,
While over them the swallows skim,
    And all is hushed at Shiloh.

                                                    (1866)

Malvern Hill[7]
(July, 1862)

Ye elms that wave on Malvern Hill
    In prime of morn and May,
Recall ye how McClellan's men
        Here stood at bay?
While deep within yon forest dim
    Our rigid comrades lay—
Some with the cartridge in their mouth,
Others with fixed arms lifted South—
        Invoking so
The cypress glades? Ah wilds of woe!   10

The spires of Richmond, late beheld
    Through rifts of musket-haze,
Were closed from view in clouds of dust
        On leaf-walled ways,
Where streamed our wagons in caravan;
    And the Seven Nights and Days
Of march and fast, retreat and fight,
Pinched our grimed faces to ghastly plight—

---

7. The battle at Malvern Hill on 1 July 1862, part of McClellan's unsuccessful Peninsular Campaign against Richmond, was the last of the Seven Days Fight referred to in line 16.

Does the elm wood
Recall the haggard beards of blood?   20

The battle-smoked flag, with stars eclipsed,
　　We followed (it never fell!)—
In silence husbanded our strength—
　　Received their yell;
Till on this slope we patient turned
　　With cannon ordered well;
Reverse we proved was not defeat;
But ah, the sod what thousands meet!—
　　Does Malvern Wood
Bethink itself, and muse and brood?   30

　　　We elms of Malvern Hill
　　　　Remember every thing;
　　　But sap the twig will fill:
　　　Wag the world how it will,
　　　　Leaves must be green in Spring.

                                                                       (1866)

The House-Top
A Night Piece
(July, 1863)[8]

No sleep. The sultriness pervades the air
And binds the brain—a dense oppression, such
As tawny tigers feel in matted shades,
Vexing their blood and making apt for ravage.
Beneath the stars the roofy desert spreads
Vacant as Libya. All is hushed near by.
Yet fitfully from far breaks a mixed surf
Of muffled sound, the Atheist roar of riot.
Yonder, where parching Sirius set in drought,
Balefully glares red Arson—there—and there.   10
The Town is taken by its rats—ship-rats
And rats of the wharves. All civil charms
And priestly spells which late held hearts in awe—

---

8. Upon the enactment of the Conscription Act, white rioters who resented being drafted to fight for the freedom of slaves attacked blacks, looted, and burned a black church and orphanage in New York City in July 1863. To Melville, this incident rendered absurd the notion than humans are naturally good.

Fear-bound, subjected to a better sway
Than sway of self; these like a dream dissolve,
And man rebounds whole aeons back in nature.
Hail to the low dull rumble, dull and dead,
And ponderous drag that shakes the wall.
Wise Draco⁹ comes, deep in the midnight roll
Of black artillery; he comes, though late;   20
In code corroborating Calvin's creed
And cynic tyrannies of honest kings;
He comes, nor parlies; and the Town, redeemed,
Gives thanks devout; nor, being thankful, heeds
The grimy slur on the Republic's faith implied,
Which holds that Man is naturally good,
And—more—is Nature's Roman, never to be scourged.

(1866)

The Apparition
(A Retrospect)

Convulsions came; and, where the field
    Long slept in pastoral green,
A goblin-mountain was upheaved
(Sure the scared sense was all deceived),
    Marl-glen and slag-ravine.

The unreserve of Ill was there,
    The clinkers¹⁰ in her last retreat;
But, ere the eye could take it in,
Or mind could comprehension win,
    It sunk!—and at our feet.   10

So, then, Solidity's a crust—
    The core of fire below;
All may go well for many a year,
But who can think without a fear
    Of horrors that happen so?

(1866)

---

9. Draco, or Dracon, an Athenian lawgiver, drew up a code of law and punishment in 621 B.C. so harsh (he recommended capital punishment for even petty crimes) that most of it was repealed by Solon.
10. Masses of slag or hardened volcanic rock.

The Aeolian Harp[11]
At the Surf Inn

List the harp in window wailing
   Stirred by fitful gales from sea:
Shrieking up in mad crescendo—
   Dying down in plaintive key!

Listen: less a strain ideal
   Than Ariel's rendering of the Real.[12]
What that Real is, let hint
   A picture stamped in memory's mint.—

Braced well up, with beams aslant,
Betwixt the continents sails the *Phocion*,   10
For Baltimore bound from Alicant.
Blue breezy skies white fleeces fleck
Over the chill blue white-capped ocean:
From yard-arm comes—"Wreck ho, a wreck!"

   Dismasted and adrift,
   Long time a thing forsaken;
   Overwashed by every wave
   Like the slumbering kraken;
   Heedless if the billow roar,
   Oblivious of the lull,   20
   Leagues and leagues from shoal or shore,
   It swims—a levelled hull:
   Bulwarks gone—a shaven wreck,
   Nameless, and a grass-green deck.
   A lumberman: perchance, in hold
   Prostrate pines with hemlocks rolled.

   It has drifted, waterlogged,
   Till by trailing weeds beclogged:
      Drifted, drifted, day by day,
      Pilotless on pathless way.   30

---

11. Used by transcendentalists and romantic poets as a symbol of the artist or agent upon whom inspiration acts, the aeolian harp is a musical instrument consisting of a box of wood in which strings are stretched. It is usually placed in a window where the wind "plays" it by blowing across the strings. The force of the wind determines the kind and amount of sound it makes.

12. In Shakespeare's *Tempest*, Ariel creates a harmless storm at sea. His "rendering of the real" is deceptive, because storms at sea are in reality dangerous.

It has drifted till each plank
Is oozy as the oyster-bank:
    Drifted, drifted, night by night,
    Craft that never shows a light;
Nor ever, to prevent worse knell,
Tolls in fog the warning bell.

From collision never shrinking,
Drive what may through darksome smother;
Saturate, but never sinking,
Fatal only to the *other*!   40
    Deadlier than the sunken reef
Since still the snare it shifteth,
    Torpid in dumb ambuscade
Waylayingly it drifteth.

O, the sailors—O, the sails!
O, the lost crews never heard of!
Well the harp of Ariel wails
Thoughts that tongue can tell no word of!

                                            (1888)

The Maldive Shark

About the Shark, phlegmatical one,
Pale sot of the Maldive sea,
The sleek little pilot-fish, azure and slim,
How alert in attendance be.
From his saw-pit of mouth, from his charnel of maw
They have nothing of harm to dread,
But liquidly glide on his ghastly flank
Or before his Gorgonian head;
Or lurk in the port of serrated teeth
In white triple tiers of glittering gates,   10
And there find a haven when peril's abroad,
An asylum in jaws of the Fates!
They are friends; and friendly they guide him to prey,
Yet never partake of the treat—
Eyes and brains to the dotard lethargic and dull,
Pale ravener of horrible meat.

                                            (1888)

In a Garret

Gems and jewels let them heap—
    Wax sumptuous as the Sophi:[13]
For me, to grapple from Art's deep
    One dripping trophy!

                         (1891)

Monody[14]

To have known him, to have loved him
    After loneness long;
And then to be estranged in life,
    And neither in the wrong;
And now for death to set his seal—
    Ease me, a little ease, my song!

By wintry hills his hermit-mound
    The sheeted snow-drifts drape,
And houseless there the snow-bird flits
    Beneath the fir-trees' crape: 10
Glazed now with ice the cloistral vine
    That hid the shyest grape.

                         (1891)

Art

In placid hours well-pleased we dream
Of many a brave unbodied scheme.
But form to lend, pulsed life create,
What unlike things must meet and mate:
A flame to melt—a wind to freeze;
Sad patience—joyous energies;
Humility—yet pride and scorn;

---

13. A title of the supreme ruler of Persia.

14. Written upon the death of Nathaniel Hawthorne, whose friendship and intelligent appreciation of his work meant a great deal to Melville. Some critics claim that the reserved Hawthorne found Melville too intense, but the estrangement mentioned in line 3 may simply refer to their lessened contact over the years after each moved away from Pittsfield.

Instinct and study; love and hate;
Audacity—reverence. These must mate,
And fuse with Jacob's mystic heart,   10
To wrestle with the angel—Art.[15]

(1891)

Greek Architecture

Not magnitude, not lavishness,
But Form—the Site;
Not innovating wilfulness,
But reverence for the Archetype.

(1891)

---

15. According to Genesis 32:22–32, Jacob struggled with an angel and managed to extort a blessing from him, but received a wound to his thigh in the process.

Herman Melville

Alice Cary
1820–1871

Celebrated as a rural muse from the Ohio frontier, Alice Cary turned the subject matter of her humble upbringing into lyrics which, along with her novels and sketches, won her a national reputation. Achieving success in the "feminine fifties," Cary was among the first women to sign her verse and to gain financial security through her work. Readers today appreciate the "singing" quality of her verse and the originality of her treatment of nineteenth-century women's issues.

Born 26 April 1820 on a primitive farmstead eight miles north of Cincinnati, Cary suffered by the age of fifteen the deaths of two sisters and her mother. After her father remarried, she took charge of the home and four younger siblings. Her sister, Phoebe, also a poet, recalled that the meager list of household books included "a Bible, hymn-book, the History of the Jews, Lewis and Clark's Travels, Pope's Essays, and Charlotte Temple" (*Woman's Journal* 5 August 1871: 242). Alice's major source of inspiration was the "poet's corner" of the *Trumpet*, a Universalist publication to which her parents subscribed.

Both Phoebe and Alice began composing poetry in their teens, sometimes using candles or lard with a rag wick to write at night. Alice's poems first appeared in Cincinnati papers and magazines in 1838. When Cincinnati editor Gamaliel Bailey moved to Washington, D.C., to run the abolitionist paper the *National Era*, he began publishing Cary's work in 1847. That year, John G. Whittier favorably reviewed her poetry in the *Era*. Rufus Griswold brought further attention to Cary when he included her work, as well as Phoebe's, in his *Female Poets of America* (1849). Reviewer Edgar Allan Poe singled out Cary's poem "Pictures of Memory" as "decidedly the noblest poem in the collection," because of its "true imagination" and "power of exciting the only real poetical effect—elevation of the *soul*" (126). In 1850 the sisters published their first volume, *Poems of Alice and Phoebe Cary*. Determined to advance her career, Alice Cary moved in the same year to New York City. Phoebe and another sister, Elmina, joined her in 1851. By maintaining a relentless work pace—four volumes of her own poetry in addition to numerous prose works between 1850–70—

Alice was able to support the household. During her lifetime she published *Lyra and Other Poems* (1852), *Collected Poems* (1855), *Ballads, Lyrics, and Hymns* (1866), and *A Lover's Diary* (1868). Other poetry would appear in Mary Clemmer Ames' *A Memorial of Alice and Phoebe Cary, with Some of Their Later Poems* (1873) and in subsequent editions after Alice's death.

Cary also organized "the nearest approach to the first ideal blue-stocking reception ever reached in this country" (Ames 23). With cups of sweetened milk and water as fare, the Carys held open house at their East Twentieth Street address every Sunday evening for fifteen years. Regular visitors included Horace Greeley, William Lloyd Garrison, Sara Helen Whitman, Gail Hamilton, James T. Fields, and Whittier. A suffragist and abolitionist, Cary served as the first president of Sorosis, the first women's club in America. Alice Cary died of tuberculosis after a long illness on 12 February 1871 and was buried in Brooklyn's Greenwood Cemetery.

Like Whittier, who composed "The Singer" to honor her memory, Cary writes narratives of hearth, farm, and nature which often contain lessons in domestic piety, as in "An Order for a Picture," Cary's favorite poem. Capable of variety within traditional metric forms, as in the anapestic lilt of some lines in this poem, or in the disquieting, sing-song combination of anapests and feminine end rhymes in "The Bridal Veil," Cary's style raises her above the usual moralistic and sentimental poetry of her time.

Some of Cary's most engaging poems deal with female personae. In "Morna" she portrays with simple dignity and restraint an unmarried woman at her child's grave. While this poem reveals Cary's typically somber tone, she is also capable of speaking vibrantly and passionately in her love poetry. The speaker of "The Bridal Veil" argues forcefully for a woman's autonomy within marriage, and the older woman of "Snowed Under" compares her vitality to the roots of a rose "alive beneath the snow." In these poems, Cary successfully combines her power of empathy and her concern for a woman's integrity. Through them she affirms women like herself who stood, either by fate or by choice, outside roles dictated by nineteenth-century society.

—*Wilson Somerville*

Suggestions for Further Reading

Ames, Mary Clemmer. *A Memorial of Alice and Phoebe Cary, with Some of Their Later Poems.* New York: Hurd and Houghton, 1873.

Fetterley, Judith. Introduction. *Clovernook Sketches and Other Stories.*
By Alice Cary. New Brunswick: Rutgers UP, 1987. xi–xlii.*
Poe, Edgar Allan. Rev. of *The Female Poets of America.* Ed. Rufus W.
Griswold. *Southern Literary Messenger* 15 (1849): 126–27.

TEXTS

The Female Poets of America. Ed. Rufus W. Griswold. 1849.
Ballads, Lyrics, and Hymns. 1866.
*The Poetical Works of Alice and Phoebe Cary, with a Memorial of Their
Lives.* 1876.
Poems of Alice and Phoebe Cary. New York: Hurst, 1900.

꙼

Pictures of Memory

Among the beautiful pictures
   That hang on Memory's wall,
Is one of a dim old forest,
   That seemeth best of all:
Not for its gnarled oaks olden,
   Dark with the mistletoe;
Not for the violets golden
   That sprinkle the vale below;
Not for the milk-white lilies,
   That lead from the fragrant hedge,   10
Coquetting all day with the sunbeams,
   And stealing their golden edge;
Not for the vines on the upland
   Where the bright red berries rest,
Nor the pinks, nor the pale, sweet cowslip,
   It seemeth to me the best.

I once had a little brother,
   With eyes that were dark and deep—
In the lap of that old dim forest
   He lieth in peace asleep: 20
Light as the down of the thistle,
   Free as the winds that blow,
We roved there the beautiful summers,
   The summers of long ago:
But his feet on the hills grew weary,
   And, one of the autumn eves,
I made for my little brother
   A bed of the yellow leaves.

Sweetly his pale arms folded
  My neck in a meek embrace,
As the light of immortal beauty   30
  Silently covered his face:
And when the arrows of sunset
  Lodged in the tree-tops bright,
He fell, in his saint-like beauty,
  Asleep by the gates of light.
Therefore, of all the pictures
  That hang on Memory's wall,
The one of the dim old forest
  Seemeth the best of all.   40
                                               (1849)

An Order for a Picture

O, good painter, tell me true,
  Has your hand the cunning to draw
  Shapes of things that you never saw?
Ay? Well, here is an order for you.

Woods and cornfields, a little brown,—
  The picture must not be over-bright,—
  Yet all in the golden and gracious light
Of a cloud, when the summer sun is down.
  Alway and alway, night and morn,
  Woods upon woods, with fields of corn   10
    Lying between them, not quite sere,
And not in the full, thick, leafy bloom,
When the wind can hardly find breathing-room
    Under their tassels,—cattle near,
Biting shorter the short green grass,
And a hedge of sumach and sassafras,
With bluebirds twittering all around,—
(Ah, good painter, you can't paint sound!)—
  These, and the house where I was born,
Low and little, and black and old,   20
With children, as many as it can hold,
All at the windows, open wide,—
Heads and shoulders clear outside,
And fair young faces all ablush:
  Perhaps you may have seen, some day,
  Roses crowding the self-same way,
Out of a wilding, wayside bush.

Listen closer. When you have done
   With woods and cornfields and grazing herds,
  A lady, the loveliest ever the sun   30
Looked down upon you must paint for me:
Oh, if I could only make you see
  The clear blue eyes, the tender smile,
The sovereign sweetness, the gentle grace,
The woman's soul, and the angel's face
  That are beaming on me all the while,
    I need not speak these foolish words:
    Yet one word tells you all I would say,—
She is my mother: you will agree
  That all the rest may be thrown away.   40

Two little urchins at her knee
You must paint, sir: one like me,—
  The other with a clearer brow,
  And the light of his adventurous eyes
  Flashing with boldest enterprise:
At ten years old he went to sea,—
    God knoweth if he be living now,—
  He sailed in the good ship "Commodore,"—
Nobody ever crossed her track
To bring us news, and she never came back,   50
  Ah, 'tis twenty long years and more
Since that old ship went out of the bay
  With my great-hearted brother on her deck:
  I watched him till he shrank to a speck,
And his face was toward me all the way.
Bright his hair was, a golden brown,
  The time we stood at our mother's knee:
That beauteous head, if it did go down,
  Carried sunshine into the sea!

Out in the fields one summer night   60
  We were together, half afraid
  Of the corn-leaves' rustling, and of the shade
    Of the high hills, stretching so still and far,—
Loitering till after the low little light
  Of the candle shown through the open door,
And over the hay-stack's pointed top,
All of a tremble and ready to drop,
    The first half-hour, the great yellow star,
    That we, with staring, ignorant eyes,
Had often and often watched to see   70
  Propped and held in its place in the skies
By the fork of a tall red mulberry-tree,

Which close in the edge of our flax-field grew,—
Dead at the top,—just one branch full
Of leaves, notched round, and lined with wool,
    From which it tenderly shook the dew
Over our heads, when we came to play
In its handbreadth of shadow, day after day.
    Afraid to go home, Sir: for one of us bore
A nest full of speckled and thin-shelled eggs,—   80
The other, a bird, held fast by the legs,
Not so big as a straw of wheat:
The berries we gave her she wouldn't eat,
But cried and cried, till we held her bill,
So slim and shining to keep her still.
At last we stood at our mother's knee.
    Do you think, Sir, if you try,
    You can paint the look of a lie?
    If you can, pray have the grace
    To put it solely in the face   90
Of the urchin that is likest me:
    I think 'twas solely mine, indeed:
    But that's no matter,—paint it so;
    The eyes of our mother—(take good heed)—
Looking not on the nest-full of eggs,
Nor the fluttering bird, held so fast by the legs,
But straight through our faces down to our lies,
And, oh, with such injured, reproachful surprise!
    I felt my heart bleed where that glance went, as though
    A sharp blade struck through it.   100
              You, Sir, know
That you on the canvas are to repeat
Things that are fairest, things most sweet,—
Woods and cornfields and mulberry-tree,—
The mother,—the lads, with their bird, at her knee:
    But, oh, that look of reproachful woe!
High as the heavens your name I'll shout,
If you paint me the picture, and leave that out.

                                                         (1866)

The Bridal Veil

We're married, they say, and you think you have won me,—
Well, take this white veil from my head, and look on me:
Here's matter to vex you, and matter to grieve you,

Here's doubt to distrust you, and faith to believe you,—
I am all as you see, common earth, common dew;
Be wary, and mould me to roses, not rue!

Ah! shake out the filmy thing, fold after fold,
And see if you have me to keep and to hold,—
Look close on my heart—see the worst of its sinning—
It is not yours to-day for the yesterday's winning—   10
The past is not mine—I am too proud to borrow—
You must grow to new heights if I love you to-morrow.

We're married! I'm plighted to hold up your praises,
As the turf at your feet does its handful of daisies;
That way lies my honor,—my pathway of pride,
But, mark you, if greener grass grow either side,
I shall know it, and keeping in body with you,
Shall walk in my spirit with feet on the dew!

We're married! Oh, pray that our love do not fail!
I have wings flattened down and hid under my veil: 20
They are subtle as light—you can never undo them,
And swift in their flight—you can never pursue them,
And spite of all clasping, and spite of all bands,
I can slip like a shadow, a dream, from your hands.

Nay, call me not cruel, and fear not to take me,
I am yours for my lifetime, to be what you make me,—
To wear my white veil for a sign, or a cover,
As you shall be proven my lord, or my lover;
A cover for peace that is dead, or a token
Of bliss that can never be written or spoken.   30

(1866)

Snowed Under

Come let us talk together,
 While the sunset fades and dies,
And, darling, look into my heart,
 And not into my eyes.

Let us sit and talk together
 In the old, familiar place,
But look deep down into my heart,
 Not up into my face.

And with tender pity shield me—
    I am just a withered bough—   10
I was used to have your praises,
    And you cannot praise me now.

You would nip the blushing roses;
    They were blighted long ago,
But the precious roots, my darling,
    Are alive beneath the snow.

And in the coming spring-time
    They will all to beauty start—
Oh, look not in my face, beloved,
    But only in my heart!   20

You will not find the little buds,
    So tender and so bright;
They are snowed so deeply under,
    They will never come to light.

So look, I pray you, in my heart,
    And not into my face,
And think about that coming spring
    Of greenness and of grace,

When from the winter-laden bough
    The weight of snow shall drop away,   30
And give it strength to spring into
    The life of endless May.

                                                          (1876)

Morna

Alas! 'tis many a weary day
    Since, on a pleasant eve of May,
I first beheld her; slight and fair
    With simple violets in her hair,
And a pale brow of thought beneath,
    That never wore a prouder wreath;
And roses hanging on her arm,
    Fresh gathered from the mountain side;
And wherefore, by her mien and form
    She is not mother, wife, nor bride?   10

Surely the hopes of childish years
    Still freshly on her girlhood rise;
But no, her cheek is wet with tears—
    What do they in those heavenly eyes?
The mournful truth they will belie;
    The roses, and the child-like form,
I know thee, by that look and sigh,
    A pale, sweet blossom of the storm.
And see! she pauses now, and stands
    Where step save hers has scarcely trod,   20
And softly, with her milk-white hands,
    Lays down her blossoms in the sod.
There is no marble slab to tell
    Who lies so peacefully asleep;
'Tis written on the heart as well,
    Of her who lingers there to weep.
One evening in the accustomed vale
    I missed the blossoms from the turf,
For Morna's lovely brow was pale,
    And cold as ocean's beaten surf.   30
That night I learned, beside her bier,
    The story of her grief in part.—
For much, that mortal might not hear,
    Lay hidden in her broken heart.
She was the child of poverty,
    And knew from birth its friendless ills;
But never blossom fair as she
    Grew up among her native hills.
Sweet child! she early learned to sigh;
    The roses on her cheek grew pale;   40
It matters not to tell thee why—
    Who is there will not guess the tale?
He was the haughty child of pride—
    The angel of delusive dreams;
And therefore was she not a bride
    Who slumbers by her native streams.
The weeds of desolate years o'erspread
    The pathway where so oft she trod;
No mourner lingers o'er her bed,
    Or bears fresh blossoms to the sod.   50
                                                    (1900)[1]

---

1. The dating of this poem is uncertain; it appears in *Poems of Alice and Phoebe Cary* (New York: Hurst, 1900).

Frederick Goddard Tuckerman
1821–1873

Critical assessment of Frederick Goddard Tuckerman's poetic accomplishment is still evolving. Admirers argue that his sonnets and his ode, "The Cricket," rank among the greatest achievements of American poetry, but the prevailing judgment has ranked him as a minor talent who composed two or three exceptional works. One reason critics have failed to agree is that Tuckerman's work is at the same time both traditional and experimental. His fondness for the sonnet and ode implies a conventional poetic practice that is often at odds with the harsh, alienated voices of his speakers. The intensely private nature of Tuckerman's writing situates him apart from Whitman's omnivorous "I," but suggests some similarity with Dickinson's more intimate and select society.

Born 14 February 1821, Frederick Goddard Tuckerman was the third son of a prosperous Boston family. While a student at Harvard, he studied under the poet Jones Very, whose influence was more theological than poetical. One of his classmates, T. W. Higginson, later recollected that Tuckerman was a "refined and gentlemanly fellow" but "not . . . a poet" (qtd. in Golden 25). By the time he completed his legal studies, married Hannah Lucinda Jones and moved to Greenfield, Massachusetts, in 1847, he had written several poems but published nothing.

Tuckerman made two trips to England, the first in 1851 and the second in 1855. During his second visit, he spent three days discussing poetry with Tennyson (England 227). This encounter stimulated his further study of Tennyson's work and contributed to Tuckerman's interest in the refinement of poetic ability. His extensive notes on Tennyson's verse reveal his conviction that the poet must serve an apprenticeship mastering traditional verse forms.

Perhaps the most profound event in Tuckerman's life was his wife's unexpected death in 1857 of complications resulting from childbirth. Her death, along with the earlier loss of a daughter in 1848, aggravated Tuckerman's predilection for melancholy and provoked his withdrawal from community life. The two sonnet sequences published during his life and the three posthumous sequences, together with "The Cricket," explore the possibility that knowledge can accommodate death. The high point of Tuckerman's literary career came with the publication of *Poems* in 1860, but even this event did little to retard his growing seclusion. He died of heart disease on 9 May 1873 and was buried in Greenfield.

Tuckerman's poems received little critical attention until Walter Prichard Eaton wrote an article entitled "A Forgotten American Poet" for the *Forum* (January 1909). This article attracted the attention of Witter Bynner and Yvor Winters. Bynner's subsequent publication of all five sonnet sequences in *The Sonnets of Frederick Goddard Tuckerman* (1931) further sparked critical interest. N. Scott Momaday's edition, *The Complete Poems of Frederick Goddard Tuckerman* (1965), included all of Tuckerman's poems plus an appreciative introduction. Denis Donaghue's treatment of Tuckerman as a major American voice in *Connoisseurs of Chaos* (1964), a 1966 Twayne volume devoted to Tuckerman, numerous journal articles, and at least one doctoral dissertation testify to the growing interest in Tuckerman. Controversy over the relative merits of specific poems will no doubt continue, but the importance of Tuckerman's works for scholarly research seems assured. Comments made by Roland Hagenbuchle in 1984 mark Tuckerman's coming of age: "There is no need anymore at this stage to insist on the quality and originality of his work" (70).

—*Paul Crumbley*

Suggestions for Further Reading

Donaghue, Denis. *Connoisseurs of Chaos: Ideas of Order in Modern American Poetry*. 2nd ed. New York: Columbia UP, 1964. 52–75.
England, Eugene. "Tuckerman and Tennyson: 'Two Friends . . . on Either Side of the Atlantic.' " *New England Quarterly* 52 (June 1984): 225–39.
Golden, Samuel A. *Frederick Goddard Tuckerman*. New York: Twayne, 1966.*
Hagenbuchle, Roland. "Abstraction and Desire: Dissolving Contours in the Poetry of Frederick Goddard Tuckerman." *American Poetry Between Tradition and Modernism 1865–1914*. Ed. Roland Hagenbuchle. Regensberg: Pustet, 1984.
Winters, Yvor. Forward. *The Complete Poems of Frederick Goddard Tuckerman*. By Frederick Goddard Tuckerman. New York: Oxford UP, 1965.

TEXT
The Complete Poems of Frederick Goddard Tuckerman. Ed. N. Scott Momaday. New York: Oxford UP, 1965.

from The First Sonnet Sequence

III

And borne with theirs, my proudest thoughts do seem
Bald at the best and dim: a barren gleam
Among the immortal stars, and faint and brief
As northlight flitting in the dreary north.
What have thy dreams, a vague prospective worth?
An import imminent? or dost thou deem
Thy life so fair that thou wouldst set it forth
Before the day? or art thou wise in grief,
Has fruitful sorrow swept thee with her wing?
Today I heard a sweet voice carolling
In the woodlot paths, with laugh and careless cry   10
Leading her happy mates: apart I stepped,
And while the laugh and song went lightly by,
In the wild bushes I sat down and wept.

(1860)

IV

Now looks that backward life so bare to me,
My later youth, and ways I've wandered through,
But touched with innocent grace, the purring bee
O'er the maple log, the white-heaped cherry tree
That hummed all day in the sun, the April blue;
Yet hardly now one ray the Forward hath
To show where sorrow rests and rest begins,
Although I check my feet nor walk to wrath
Through days of crime, and grosser shadowings
Of evil done in the dark, but fearfully   10
Mid unfulfilled yet unrelinquished sins
That hedge me in and press about my path
Like purple-poison flowers of stramony
With their dull opiate breath and dragon wings.

(1860)

V

And so the day drops by, the horizon draws
The fading sun and we stand struck in grief,
Failing to find our haven of relief,
Wide of the way, nor sure to turn or pause,

And weep to view how fast the splendor wanes
And scarcely heed that yet some share remains
Of the red afterlight, some time to mark,
Some space between the sundown and the dark;
But not for him whose golden calms succeed
Who while the day is high and glory reigns   10
Sees it go by, as the dim pampas plain,
Hoary with salt and gray with bitter weed,
Sees the vault blacken, feels the dark wind strain,
Hears the dry thunder roll, and knows no rain.

                                                    (1860)

from The Second Sonnet Sequence

XXXI

My Anna! when for thee my head was bowed,
The circle of the world, sky, mountain, main,
Drew inward to one spot: and now again
Wide Nature narrows to the shell and shroud.
In the late dawn they will not be forgot,
And evenings early-dark, when the low rain
Begins at nightfall, though no tempests rave,
I know the rain is falling on her grave.
The morning views it, and the sunset cloud
Points with a finger to that lonely spot: 10
The crops that up the valley rolling go
Ever towards her slumber bow and blow.
I look on the sweeping corn and the surging rye,
And with every gust of wind my heart goes by.

                                                    (1860)

XXXII

O for the face and footstep! woods and shores
That looked upon us in life's happiest flush,
That saw our figures breaking from the brush;
That heard our voices calling through the bowers,
How are ye darkened! Deepest tears upgush
From the heart's heart, gathering more and more
Blindness and strangling tears, as now before
Your shades I stand and find ye still so fair.
And thou, sad mountain stream, thy stretches steal

Through fern and flag as when we gathered flowers   10
Along thy reeds and shallows cold, or where—
Over the red reef with a rolling roar—
The woods through glimmering gaps of green reveal,
Sideward, the river turning like a wheel.

(1860)

XXXIII

One still dark night I sat alone and wrote:
So still it was that distant Chanticleer
Seemed to cry out his warning at my ear,
Save for the brooding echo in his throat.
Sullen I sat, when like the nightwind's note
A voice said, "Wherefore doth he weep and fear?
Doth he not know no cry to God is dumb?"
Another spoke: "His heart is dimmed and drowned
With grief." I knew the shape that bended then
To kiss me, when suddenly I once again   10
Across the watches of the starless gloom
Heard the cock scream and pause: the morning bell
Into the gulfs of night dropped One! The vision fell
And left me listening to the sinking sound.

(1860)

XXXIV

My Anna, though thine earthly steps are done,
Nor in the garden nor beside the door
Shall I behold thee standing any more
I would not hide my face from light, nor shun
The full completion of this worldly day.
What though beside my feet no other one
May set her own to walk the forward way,
I will not fear to take the path alone,
Loving for thy sake things that cheer and bless,
Kind words, pure deeds, and gentlest charities.   10
Nor will I cease to hold a hope and aim
But, prophet-like, of these will make my bread
And feed my soul at peace, as Esdras[1] fed
On flowers, until the vision and the glory came.

(1860)

---

1. Mention of Esdras feeding on flowers refers to 2 Esdras, 9:29. At this point in the prophet's account, he has gone to a field of flowers and eaten only flowers for seven days while awaiting his fourth vision. The vision arrives at the appointed time.

from The Fifth Sonnet Sequence

V

Where will the ladder land? Who knows?—who knows?
He who would seize the planet zone by zone
As on a battlemarch, for use alone,
Nor stops for visionary wants and woes
But like the Bruce's,[2] on, his heart he throws
And leaves behind the dreamer and the drone?
Great is his work indeed, his service great,
Who seeks for Nature but to subjugate,
Break and bereave, build upward and create
And, hampering her, to carry heave and drag   10
Points to results,—towns, cables, cars and ships.
Whilst I in dim green meadows lean and lag,
He counts his course in truth by vigorous steps,
By steps of stairs; but I add crag to crag.

(1931)

The Cricket

I

The humming bee purrs softly o'er his flower;
   From lawn and thicket
The dogday locust singeth in the sun
   From hour to hour:
Each has his bard, and thou, ere day be done,
   Shalt have no wrong.
So bright that murmur mid the insect crowd,
Muffled and lost in bottom-grass, or loud
   By pale and picket:
Shall I not take to help me in my song   10
   A little cooing cricket?

II

The afternoon is sleepy; let us lie
Beneath these branches whilst the burdened brook,
Muttering and moaning to himself, goes by;

---

2. Robert Bruce, Scottish hero and king of Scotland from 1306 until his death
in 1329.

And mark our minstrel's carol whilst we look
Toward the faint horizon swooning blue.
Or in a garden bower,
Trellised and trammeled with deep drapery
Of hanging green,
Light glimmering through—   20
There let the dull hop be,
Let bloom, with poppy's dark refreshing flower:
Let the dead fragrance round our temples beat,
Stunning the sense to slumber, whilst between
The falling water and the fluttering wind
Mingle and meet,
Murmur and mix,
No few faint pipings from the glades behind,
Or alder-thicks:
But louder as the day declines,   30
From tingling tassel, blade, and sheath,
Rising from nets of river vines,
Winroes and ricks,
Above, beneath,
At every breath,
At hand, around, illimitably
Rising and falling like the sea,
Acres of cricks!

III

Dear to the child who hears thy rustling voice
Cease at his footstep, though he hears thee still,   40
Cease and resume with vibrance crisp and shrill,
Thou sittest in the sunshine to rejoice.
Night lover too; bringer of all things dark
And rest and silence; yet thou bringest to me
Always that burthen of the unresting Sea,
The moaning cliffs, the low rocks blackly stark;
These upland inland fields no more I view,
But the long flat seaside beach, the wild seamew,
And the overturning wave!
Thou bringest too, dim accents from the grave   50
To him who walketh when the day is dim,
Dreaming of those who dream no more of him,
With edged remembrances of joy and pain;
And heyday looks and laughter come again:
Forms that in happy sunshine lie and leap,
With faces where but now a gap must be,

Renunciations, and partitions deep
And perfect tears, and crowning vacancy!
And to thy poet at the twilight's hush,
No chirping touch of lips with laugh and blush,   60
But wringing arms, hearts wild with love and woe,
Closed eyes, and kisses that would not let go!

IV

So wert thou loved in that old graceful time
    When Greece was fair,
While god and hero hearkened to thy chime;
    Softly astir
Where the long grasses fringed Cayster's[3] lip;
Long-drawn, with glimmering sails of swan and ship,
    And ship and swan;
    Or where   70
Reedy Eurotas[4] ran.
Did that low warble teach thy tender flute
    Xenaphyle?[5]
Its breathings mild? say! did the grasshopper
Sit golden in thy purple hair
    O Psammethe?[6]
    Or wert thou mute,
Grieving for Pan amid the alders there?
And by the water and along the hill
That thirstly tinkle in the herbage still,   80
Though the lost forest wailed to horns of Arcady?

V

Like the Enchanter old—
Who sought mid the dead water's weeds and scum
For evil growths beneath the moonbeam cold,
    Or mandrake or dorcynium;
And touched the leaf that opened both his ears,

---

3. A body of water referred to in classic mythology as a favorite gathering place for swans.

4. Eurotas was a king of Laconia who was well known for building a canal that drained the Laconian plain. His name was given to the principle Laconian river.

5. Xenaphyle is probably a name made up by Tuckerman. The Greek roots combine notions of both guest and host with those of flourishing or trumpeting sounds and fertility.

6. Psammethe or Psamethe was a wife of Apollo who was associated with the fruit of the vineyard.

So that articulate voices now he hears
In cry of beast, or bird, or insect's hum,—
Might I but find thy knowledge in thy song!
    That twittering tongue   90
Ancient as light, returning like the years.
    So might I be,
Unwise to sing, thy true interpreter
Through denser stillness and in sounder dark,
Than ere thy notes have pierced to harrow me.
    So might I stir
     The world to hark
     To thee my lord and lawgiver,
     And cease my quest:
Content to bring thy wisdom to the world;   100
Content to gain at last some low applause,
    Now low, now lost
Like thine from mossy stone, amid the stems and straws,
    Or garden gravemound tricked and dressed—
    Powdered and pearled
    By stealing frost—
In dusky rainbow beauty of euphorbias!
For larger would be less indeed, and like
The ceaseless simmer in the summer grass
To him who toileth in the windy field,   110
Or where the sunbeams strike,
Naught in innumerable numerousness.
    So might I much possess,
    So much must yield;
But failing this, the dell and grassy dike,
The water and the waste shall still be dear,
And all the pleasant plots and places
    Where thou hast sung, and I have hung
    To ignorantly hear.
Then Cricket, sing thy song! or answer mine!   120
Thine whispers blame, but mine has naught but praises.
It matters not. Behold! the autumn goes,
    The shadow grows,
The moments take hold of eternity;
Even while we stop to wrangle or repine
    Our lives are gone—
    Like thinnest mist,
Like yon escaping color in the tree;
Rejoice! rejoice! whilst yet the hours exist—
Rejoice or mourn, and let the world swing on   130
Unmoved by cricket songs of thee or me.

             (1950)

Thomas Buchanan Read
1822–1872

Thomas Buchanan Read's con-
temporaries knew him as both a poet and a landscape and portrait
painter. Read circulated through literary and artistic societies of
Boston, Philadelphia, and New York and established himself as
part of artists' colonies in Florence and Rome. Because of this
Italian influence, his painting often reflects a traditional aesthetic
interest in Classical art and mythology. But for poetic inspira-
tion, Read consistently turned to America in his thematic use of
American scenery and history and in his eye for native details,
embellishing his poetry with indigenous species of birds and
flowers.

Thomas Buchanan Read was born in Chester, Pennsylvania,
on 12 March 1822. He moved to Cincinnati at age fourteen as an
apprentice to Shobal Clevinger, the sculptor. Read began his ar-
tistic career as a sign painter and a portrait painter. In 1840, he
moved to Boston, married, and set up a successful studio for por-
trait painting, with Longfellow as one of his clients. Read moved
to Philadelphia in 1846. In 1847, Read published *Poems*, which he
later enlarged in the 1853 and 1865 editions.

In 1861, Read became a Union propagandist on the staff of
General Lew Wallace during the Civil War. He wrote war poems,
among them the popular "Sheridan's Ride," celebrating General
Philip Sheridan's twenty-mile ride from Winchester to Cedar
Creek, Virginia, in the Battle of Cedar Creek, October, 1864
(Soria 256). This dramatic poem became a favorite of platform
readers. After the war, Read lectured in America and then settled
in Rome with his second wife (1866). He returned to New York
a week before his death on 11 May 1872. He was buried in Laurel
Hill Cemetery, Philadelphia.

Read's use of emotional subject matter will strike the reader
today as superficial sentiment. However, in "The Closing Scene,"
his skillful rendering of details (the rusting swords in line 60)
and movement (the seasonal colors and wildlife activity) suggest
careful thought and a painter's eye, while his attention to Ameri-
can species of plants and animals ("the jay, within the elm's tall
crest" in line 25) gives concreteness to his poetry. "L'Envoi," the

closing poem of *Rural Poems*, celebrates the simple beauty of a common American wildflower, and Read's longer narrative poems ("Sheridan's Ride") rely on the appeal of their American themes. His contemporaries, however, praised Read's poetic fancy. Poe admired the "subdued passion" of his poetry, and Hawthorne enjoyed "the vividness of picture" and "ethereal life" (Allibone 1753). Read enjoyed a solid popularity with both American and English audiences as an imaginative poet.

—*Taimi Olsen*

Suggestions for Further Reading

Allibone, Austin. *A Critical Dictionary of English Literature and British and American Authors.* Vol. 2. Detroit: Gale, 1965. 3 vols.*
Soria, Regina. *Dictionary of Nineteenth-Century American Artists in Italy, 1760–1914.* Rutherford: Fairleigh Dickinson UP, 1982.
Tait, John R. "Reminiscences of a Poet-Painter." *Lippincott's Magazine of Popular Literature and Science* 19 (1877): 307–21.

TEXTS
Rural Poems. 1857.
The Poetical Works of Thomas Buchanan Read. 3 vols. Philadelphia: Lippincott, 1903.

꿎

The Closing Scene

Within his sober realm of leafless trees
    The russet year inhaled the dreamy air;
Like some tanned reaper in his hour of ease,
    When all the fields are lying brown and bare.

The gray barns looking from their hazy hills
    O'er the dim waters widening in the vales,
Sent down the air a greeting to the mills,
    On the dull thunder of alternate flails.

All sights were mellowed and all sounds subdued,
    The hills seemed farther and the streams sang low,   10
As in a dream the distant woodman hewed
    His winter log with many a muffled blow.

The embattled forests, erewhile armed in gold,
    Their banners bright with every martial hue,

Now stood, like some sad beaten host of old,
  Withdrawn afar in Time's remotest blue.

On slumbrous wings the vulture held his flight;
  The dove scarce heard his sighing mate's complaint,
And like a star slow drowning in the light,
  The village church-vane seemed to pale and faint.   20

The sentinel-cock upon the hill-side crew—
  Crew thrice, and all was stiller than before,—
Silent till some replying warder blew
  His alien horn, and then was heard no more.

Where erst the jay, within the elm's tall crest,
  Made garrulous trouble round her unfledged young,
And where the oriole hung her swaying nest,
  By every light wind like a censer swung:—

Where sang the noisy masons of the eaves,
  The busy swallows, circling ever near,   30
Foreboding, as the rustic mind believes,
  An early harvest and a plenteous year;—

Where every bird which charmed the vernal feast,
  Shook the sweet slumber from its wings at morn,
To warn the reaper of the rosy east,—
  All now was songless, empty, and forlorn.

Alone from out the stubble piped the quail,
  And croaked the crow through all the dreamy gloom;
Alone the pheasant, drumming in the vale,
  Made echo to the distant cottage loom.   40

There was no bud, no bloom upon the bowers;
  The spiders wove their thin shrouds night by night;
The thistle-down, the only ghost of flowers,
  Sailed slowly by, passed noiseless out of sight.

Amid all this, in this most cheerless air,
  And where the woodbine shed upon the porch
Its crimson leaves, as if the Year stood there
  Firing the floor with his inverted torch;—

Amid all this, the centre of the scene,
  The white-haired matron, with monotonous tread,   50
Plied the swift wheel, and with her joyless mien,
  Sat, like a Fate, and watched the flying thread.

Thomas Buchanan Read   221

She had known Sorrow,—he had walked with her,
  Oft supped and broke the bitter ashen crust;
And in the dead leaves still she heard the stir
  Of his black mantle trailing in the dust.

While yet her cheek was bright with summer bloom,
  Her country summoned and she gave her all;
And twice War bowed to her his sable plume—
  Regave the swords to rust upon her wall.   60

Regave the swords,—but not the hand that drew
  And struck for Liberty its dying blow,
Nor him who, to his sire and country true,
  Fell 'mid the ranks of the invading foe.

Long, but not loud, the droning wheel went on,
  Like the low murmur of a hive at noon;
Long, but not loud, the memory of the gone
  Breathed through her lips a sad and tremulous tune.

At last the thread was snapped—her head was bowed;
  Life dropped the distaff through his hands serene,—   70
And loving neighbours smoothed her careful shroud,
  While Death and Winter closed the autumn scene.

                                        (1852, 1903)

L'Envoi[1]

I bring the flower you asked of me,
  A simple bloom, nor bright nor rare,
But like a star its light will be
  Within the darkness of your hair.

It grew not in those guarded bowers
  Where rustling fountains sift their spray,
But gladly drank the common showers
  Of dew beside the dusty way.

It may be in its humble sphere
  It cheered the pilgrim of the road,   10
And shed as blest an alms as e'er
  The generous hand of wealth bestowed.

---

1. Envoy: message; concluding stanza of a poem or book.

Or though, save mine, it met no eye,
   But secretly looked up and grew,
And from the loving air and sky
   Its little store of beauty drew,

And though it breathed its small perfumes
   So low they did not woo the bee,
Exalted, how it shines and blooms
   Above all flowers, since worn by thee!   20

And thus the song you bade me sing
   May be a rude and artless lay,
And yet it grew a sacred thing
   To bless me on Life's dusty way.

And unto this, my humble strain,
   How much of beauty shall belong,
If thou wilt in thy memory deign
   To wear my simple flower of song!

                                                            (1857)

Sheridan's Ride

Up from the South at break of day,
Bringing to Winchester fresh dismay,
The affrighted air with a shudder bore,
Like a herald in haste, to the chieftain's door,
The terrible grumble, and rumble, and roar,
Telling the battle was on once more,
And Sheridan twenty miles away.

And wider still those billows of war,
Thundered along the horizon's bar;
And louder yet into Winchester rolled   10
The roar of that red sea uncontrolled,
Making the blood of the listener cold,
As he thought of the stake in that fiery fray,
And Sheridan twenty miles away.

But there is a road from Winchester town,
A good broad highway leading down;
And there, through the flush of the morning light,
A steed as black as the steeds of night,

Was seen to pass, as with eagle flight,
As if he knew the terrible need;   20
He stretched away with his utmost speed;
Hills rose and fell; but his heart was gay,
With Sheridan fifteen miles away.

Still sprung from those swift hoofs, thundering South,
The dust, like smoke from the cannon's mouth;
Or the trail of a comet, sweeping faster and faster,
Foreboding to traitors the doom of disaster.
The heart of the steed, and the heart of the master
Were beating like prisoners assaulting their walls,
Impatient to be where the battle-field calls;   30
Every nerve of the charger was strained to full play,
With Sheridan only ten miles away.

Under his spurning feet the road
Like an arrowy Alpine river flowed,
And the landscape sped away behind
Like an ocean flying before the wind,
And the steed, like a bark fed with furnace ire,
Swept on, with his wild eye full of fire.
But lo! he is nearing his heart's desire;
He is snuffing the smoke of the roaring fray,   40
With Sheridan only five miles away.

The first that the general saw were the groups
Of stragglers, and then the retreating troops,
What was done? what to do? a glance told him both,
Then striking his spurs, with a terrible oath,
He dashed down the line, 'mid a storm of huzzas,
And the wave of retreat checked its course there, because
The sight of the master compelled it to pause.
With foam and with dust, the black charger was gray;
By the flash of his eye, and the red nostril's play,   50
He seemed to the whole great army to say,
"I have brought you Sheridan all the way
From Winchester, down to save the day!"

Hurrah! hurrah for Sheridan!
Hurrah! hurrah for horse and man!
And when their statues are placed on high,
Under the dome of the Union sky,
The American soldiers' Temple of Fame;
There with the glorious general's name,

Be it said, in letters both bold and bright,   60
   "Here is the steed that saved the day,
By carrying Sheridan into the fight,
   From Winchester, twenty miles away!"

(1865, 1903)

Phoebe Cary

1824–1871

Like her sister Alice, Phoebe Cary wrote poems inspired by the frontier life of her Ohio childhood. Praised for lyrics which offer hope in the face of death, Phoebe Cary also delighted readers with her parodies of popular works. Her refreshingly ironic poems about a woman's status in nineteenth-century society contrast the merits of a single life with ideals of motherhood and marriage.

Phoebe Cary was born 4 September 1824 in a farmhouse eight miles north of Cincinnati. The basis of her education was the Bible, a few sentimental novels, and the *Trumpet*, a Universalist publication. By 1835, tuberculosis had claimed her mother and two sisters. Despite the demands of farm work and a stepmother's disapproval, Phoebe began publishing poetry along with her sister Alice in 1838. Her readership widened from Cincinnati papers and magazines to a national audience when Rufus Griswold included her work and Alice's in *The Female Poets of America* (1849). The *Poems of Alice and Phoebe Cary*, their first volume, followed in 1850.

Phoebe moved to New York City in 1851 to live with Alice and eventually published two volumes of her own, *Poems and Parodies* (1854) and *Poems of Faith, Hope, and Love* (1868). Privately an advocate of temperance, human rights, and women's issues, Cary rarely sought a public forum, serving only a few months as assistant editor for the *Republic*, Susan B. Anthony's suffrage paper.

Biographer Mary Clemmer Ames states that Alice "placed the highest estimate on Phoebe's brilliant wit" and her potential as a writer (232). But it fell to the more disciplined older sister to generate most of the income since Phoebe did not publish consistently, once going eight years without writing a line. Clearly, the sisters were interdependent; Phoebe, unable to work alone after Alice's death, died only five months later on 31 July 1871. She was buried beside Alice and another sister, Elmina, in Brooklyn's Greenwood Cemetery. Subsequently, Ames published *A Memorial of Alice and Phoebe Cary, with Some of Their Later Poems* (1873).

Cary's poetry espouses a standard piety; her conventional "Death Scene" contrasts with Dickinson's more original "The

Last Night that She Lived" (No. 1100). But Cary was capable of forceful imagery as in the "the awful chrism" of her most famous hymn, "Nearer Home" (line 20). Competent in such forms as ballads, hymns, and lyrics, including children's verse, Cary also made lighthearted fun of such favorite works as Longfellow's "The Day is Done" and Poe's "Annabel Lee." These parodies remind us that not everyone took the nation's quest for literary greatness with equal earnestness.

Other poems challenge traditional attitudes towards the single woman. In "The Christian Woman," a "self-sustained" persona goes proudly and almost defiantly "Down to Death's chamber, and his bridal bed!" (line 42). An older, single woman in "A Woman's Conclusions" reflects that her past life was "the best" of any she could have wanted. Through that speaker's claim of "I am what I am," Cary validates a type of woman's experience that is independent of prescribed duties of wife and mother.

—*Wilson Somerville*

Suggestions for Further Reading

Ames, Mary Clemmer. *A Memorial of Alice and Phoebe Cary, with Some of Their Later Poems.* New York: Hurd and Houghton, 1873.
Fetterley, Judith. Introduction. *Clovernook Sketches and Other Stories.* By Alice Cary. New Brunswick: Rutgers UP, 1987. xi–xlii.

TEXTS
The Female Poets of America. Ed. Rufus W. Griswold. 1849.
Poems and Parodies. 1854.
Poems of Faith, Hope, and Love. 1868.

꣠꣠

The Christian Woman

Oh, beautiful as morning in those hours,
    When, as her pathway lies along the hills,
Her golden fingers wake the dewy flowers,
    And softly touch the waters of the rills,
Was she who walked more faintly day by day,
Till silently she perished by the way.

It was not hers to know that perfect heaven
    Of passionate love returned by love as deep;
Not hers to sing the cradle-song at even,

Watching the beauty of her babes asleep;   10
"Mother and brethren"—these she had not known,
Save such as do the Father's will alone.

Yet found she something still for which to live—
    Hearths desolate, where angel-like she came,
And "little ones" to whom her hand could give
    A cup of water in her Master's name;
And breaking hearts to bind away from death,
With the soft hand of pitying love and faith.

She never won the voice of popular praise,
    But, counting earthly triumph as but dross,   20
Seeking to keep her Saviour's perfect ways,
    Bearing in the still path his blessed cross,
She made her life, while with us here she trod,
    A consecration to the will of God!

And she hath lived and labored not in vain:
    Through the deep prison cells her accents thrill,
And the sad slave leans idly on his chain,
    And hears the music of her singing still;
While little children, with their innocent praise,
Keep freshly in men's hearts her Christian ways.   30

And what a beautiful lesson she made known—
    The whiteness of her soul sin could not dim;
Ready to lay down on God's altar stone
    The dearest treasure of her life for him.
Her flame of sacrifice never, never waned,
How could she live and die so self-sustained?

For friends supported not her parting soul,
    And whispered words of comfort, kind and sweet,
When treading onward to that final goal,
    Where the still bridegroom waited for her feet;   40
Alone she walked, yet with a fearless tread,
Down to Death's chamber, and his bridal bed!

                                                    (1849)

Death Scene

Dying, still slowly dying,
    As the hours of night rode by,

She had lain since the light of sunset
  Was red on the evening sky:
Till after the middle watches,
  As we softly near her trod,
When her soul from its prison fetters
  Was loosed by the hand of God.

One moment her pale lips trembled
  With the triumph she might not tell,   10
As the sight of the life immortal
  On her spirit's vision fell;
Then the look of rapture faded,
  And the beautiful smile was faint,
As that in some convent picture,
  On the face of a dying saint.

And we felt in the lonesome midnight,
  As we sat by the silent dead,
What a light on the path going downward
  The feet of the righteous shed;   20
When we thought how with faith unshrinking
  She came to the Jordan's tide,
And taking the hand of the Savior,
  Went up on the heavenly side.

                                        (1849)

Nearer Home[1]

One sweetly solemn thought
  Comes to me o'er and o'er
I am nearer home to-day
  Than I have ever been before;

Nearer my Father's house,
  Where the many mansions be;
Nearer the great white throne,
  Nearer the crystal sea;

Nearer the bound of life,
  Where we lay our burdens down;   10
Nearer leaving the cross,
  Nearer gaining the crown!

---

1. The text of this poem, somewhat revised from the 1854 version, comes
from *Poems of Faith, Hope, and Love* (1868).

But lying darkly between,
   Winding down through the night,
Is the silent, unknown stream,
   That leads at last to the light.

Closer and closer my steps
   Come to the dread abysm:
Closer Death to my lips
   Presses the awful chrism.   20

Oh, if my mortal feet
   Have almost gained the brink;
If it be I am nearer home
   Even to-day than I think;

Father, perfect my trust;
   Let my spirit feel in death,
That her feet are firmly set
   On the rock of a living faith!

                              (written 1852, 1854)

Samuel Brown[2]

It was many and many a year ago,
   In a dwelling down in town,
That a fellow there lived whom you may know,
   By the name of Samuel Brown;
And this fellow he lived with no other thought
   Than to our house to come down.

I was a child, and he was a child,
   In that dwelling down in town,
But we loved with a love that was more than love,
   I and my Samuel Brown,—   10
With a love that the ladies coveted,
   Me and Samuel Brown.

And this was the reason that, long ago,
   To that dwelling down in town,

---

2. A parody of Edgar Allan Poe's "Annabel Lee." The following two poems
are parodies as well, one of Longfellow's "The Day Is Done," the other of
Wordsworth's "She Dwelt among the Untrodden Ways."

Phoebe Cary

A girl came out of her carriage, courting
    My beautiful Samuel Brown;
So that her high-bred kinsman came
    And bore away Samuel Brown,
And shut him up in a dwelling house,
    In a street quite up in town.   20

The ladies not half so happy up there,
    Went envying me and Brown;
Yes! that was the reason (as all men know,
    In this dwelling down in town),
That the girl came out of the carriage by night,
    Coquetting and getting my Samuel Brown.

But our love is more artful by far than the love
    Of those who are older than we,—
    Of many far wiser than we,—
And neither the girls that are living above,   30
    Nor the girls that are down in town,
Can ever dissever my soul from the soul
    Of the beautiful Samuel Brown.

For the morn never shines without bringing me lines
    From my beautiful Samuel Brown;
And the night's never dark, but I sit in the park
    With my beautiful Samuel Brown.
And often by day, I walk down in Broadway,
With my darling, my darling, my life and my stay,
    To our dwelling down in town,
    To our house in the street down town.

                                                        (1854)

The Day Is Done

The day is done, and darkness
    From the wing of night is loosed,
As a feather is wafted downward
    From a chicken going to roost.

I see the lights of the baker,
    Gleam through the rain and mist,
And a feeling of sadness comes o'er me,
    That I cannot well resist.

A feeling of sadness and *longing*,
    That is not like being sick,   10
And resembles sorrow only
    As a brick-bat resembles a brick.

Come, get for me some supper,—
    A good and regular meal,
That shall soothe this restless feeling,
    And banish the pain I feel.

Not from the pastry baker's,
    Not from the shops for cake,
I wouldn't give a farthing
    For all that they can make.   20

For, like the supper at dinner,
    Such things would but suggest
Some dishes more substantial,
    And to-night I want the best.

Go to some honest butcher,
    Whose beef is fresh and nice
As any they have in the city,
    And get a liberal slice.

Such things through days of labor,
    And nights devoid of ease,   30
For sad and desperate feelings
    Are wonderful remedies.

They have an astonishing power
    To aid and reinforce,
And come like the "Finally, brethren,"
    That follows a long discourse.

Then get me a tender sirloin
    From off the bench or hook,
And lend to its sterling goodness
    The science of the cook.   40

And the night shall be filled with comfort,
    And the cares with which it begun
Shall fold up their blankets like Indians,
    And silently cut and run.

                                                            (1854)

Jacob

He dwelt among apartments let,
    About five stories high;
A man I thought that none would get,
    And very few would try.

A boulder, by a larger stone
    Half hidden in the mud,
Fair as a man when only one
    Is in the neighborhood.

He lived unknown, and few could tell
    When Jacob was not free;   10
But he has got a wife,—and O!
    The differences to me!

                (1854)

A Woman's Conclusions

I said, if I might go back again
    To the very hour and place of my birth;
Might have my life whatever I chose,
    And live it in any part of the earth;

Put perfect sunshine into my sky,
    Banish the shadow of sorrow and doubt;
Have all my happiness multipled,
    And all my suffering stricken out;

If I could have known in the years now gone,
    The best that a woman comes to know;   10
Could have had whatever will make her blest,
    Or whatever she thinks will make her so;

Have found the highest and purest bliss
    That the bridal-wreath and ring inclose;
And gained the one out of all the world,
    That my heart as well as my reason chose;

And if this had been, and I stood tonight
    By my children, lying asleep in their beds

And could count in my prayers, for a rosary,
    The shining row of their golden heads;   20

Yea! I said, if a miracle such as this
    Could be wrought for me, at my bidding, still
I would choose to have my past as it is,
    And to let my future come as it will!

I would not make the path I have trod
    More pleasant or even, more straight or wide;
Nor change my course the breadth of a hair,
    This way or that way, to either side.

My past is mine, and I take it all;
    Its weakness—its folly, if you please;   30
Nay, even my sins, if you come to that,
    May have been my helps, not hindrances!

If I saved my body from the flames
    Because that once I had burned my hand;
Or kept myself from a greater sin
    By doing a less—you will understand;

It was better I suffered a little pain,
    Better I sinned for a little time,
If the smarting warned me back from death,
    And the sting of sin withheld from crime.   40

Who knows its strength, by trial, will know
    What strength must be set against a sin;
And how temptation is overcome
    He has learned, who has felt its power within!

And who knows how a life at the last may show?
    Why, look at the moon from where we stand!
Opaque, uneven, you say; yet it shines,
    A luminous sphere, complete and grand!

So let my past stand, just as it stands,
    And let me now, as I may, grow old;   50
I am what I am, and my life for me
    Is the best—or it had not been, I hold.

                                                    (1868)

Bayard Taylor
1825–1878

Bayard Taylor was one of the nineteenth century's most popular poets, esteemed both by the general public and by other poets and critics. A well-traveled, educated, intelligent, emotional man, Taylor wrote an enormous body of poetry glorifying the exotic and drawing from his wide travels. He also wrote many travel books. His poems gave those less traveled a fantasy glimpse of other lands and people. Sometimes, they gave a warm look at rural American life.

Taylor was born 11 January 1825 in Kennett Square, Chester County, Pennsylvania, the fourth child of Joseph and Rebecca Way Taylor, and the first to survive infancy. His family was mostly English Quaker. When Taylor was four years old, the family moved to a farm near Kennett Square, where they lived until he was twelve, at which time the family moved to West Chester. At fifteen, Taylor published his first essay in the *West Chester Register*. A year later, he published his first poem in the *Saturday Evening Post* (1841).

Unable to afford college, he was apprenticed at age seventeen to a printer. He worked there only one year; publication of his first volume of poems and commitments for travel letters allowed him to buy out his apprenticeship and to travel in Europe for two years. After this enterprising beginning, Taylor returned from abroad to publish, at age twenty-one, a best-selling collection of travel essays, *Views A-Foot* (1846). He also published two volumes of verse: *Ximmena: or, The Battle of the Sierra Morena and Other Poems* (1844) and *Rhymes of Travel, Ballads, and Poems* (1849). Soon thereafter, a more successful effort, *A Book of Romances, Lyrics and Songs* (1851), "gave the first measure of his lyrical powers" (Stedman 404).

Taylor married Mary Agnew on 24 October 1850; she died two months later. Partly to expiate his grief, Taylor embarked on a tour of Africa that resulted in *Poems of the Orient* (1854), his best-selling book of poetry, and two books of travel. On 27 October 1857, Taylor married Marie Hansen, a German woman; their daughter was born in 1858.

To support his plush lifestyle, Taylor wrote popular fiction and travel pieces for magazines and newspapers; he also hobnobbed-with wealthy and famous publishers and writers and gave numerous lectures and readings across the country. E. C. Stedman remembers him as a magnanimous, loyal friend whose delight in some of his own works led some to wrongly deem him an egotist (410).

In all, Taylor published twelve volumes of poetry, plus travel books, novels, short story collections, and translations (most notably one of *Faust*). He died in Berlin on 22 December 1878 at the age of fifty-three, having just been named minister to Germany. He is buried at the Hicksite burial ground, Longwood, Pennsylvania.

Taylor's popularity as a poet was in large part due to the social and literary climate of nineteenth-century America. His poetry reflects his commitment to what George Santayana called the "genteel tradition," which was characterized by idealized, universalized visions of people and events. Taylor's style, following this tradition, was often abstract and high-toned, presumably because such language seemed to represent a more refined aesthetic than a plainer style. Although he occasionally wrote poems about rural Quaker and domestic life, such as his ballad "The Quaker Widow," Taylor preferred more conventional poetic forms and themes. His poems were often long lyrics which retold classical myths. Many of his poems depict a paradisic East of lush gardens, rich hues, and idealized natives.

A Book of Romances, Lyrics and Songs contains several well-wrought "romances" that deal with mythical and exotic themes and are reminiscent of Shelley. Stedman and other critics of the time especially admired "Hylas," a long, blank verse version of the Narcissus tale. Stedman noted in 1890, "Nor do I know one of our elder or younger poets who might not be glad to have composed such an idyl as 'Hylas' " (404). This piece is notable for its explicit (for the time) description of the nude young god and for its rich imagery.

Taylor's most popular book of poems, *Poems of the Orient* (1854), included "The Temptation of Hassan Ben Kaled," an eleven-stanza tale about a Cairo street singer who succumbs to the temptation of rich food and beautiful women. He awakens in the street, still poor, but with a moral tale to tell. In this poem, Taylor's language is richly imagistic; he avoids the abstractions he sometimes falls into.

Many critics find Taylor's poetry easier to respect than to admire. As Alfred Kreymborg notes, "Though he was a man of rare personal character, popular with distinguished men, as well as with the public, he left too little of himself in his poetry for a better judgment of his claim on posterity" (238). Though today his poems seem sentimental and derivative, Taylor was a highly respected, ambitious, and popular artist of his time.

—*Lisa Carl*

Suggestions for Further Reading

Kreymborg, Alfred, ed. *An Anthology of American Poetry*. New York: Tudor Publishing, 1935.

Smyth, Albert H. *Bayard Taylor*. Boston: Houghton, 1896.

Stedman, E. C. *Poets of America*. Boston: Houghton, 1890.

Taylor, Bayard. *The Story of Kennett*. 1866. Ed. C. W. LaSalle. New Haven, CT: College and UP, 1973.

Wermuth, Paul C. *Bayard Taylor*. New York: Twayne, 1973.*

TEXT
The Poetical Works of Bayard Taylor. 1879.

꙳

from Hylas[1]

Storm-wearied Argo slept upon the water.
No cloud was seen; on blue and craggy Ida[2]
The hot noon lay, and on the plain's enamel;
Cool, in his bed, alone, the swift Scamander.[3]
"Why should I haste?" said young and rosy Hylas:
"The seas were rough, and long the way from Colchis.[4]
Beneath the snow-white awning slumbers Jason,
Pillowed upon his tame Thessalian panther;
The shields are piled, the listless oars suspended
On the black thwarts, and all the hairy bondsmen   10
Doze on the benches. They may wait for water,
Till I have bathed in mountain-born Scamander."

---

1. In Greek mythology, Hylas figures in "The Quest of the Golden Fleece." Hylas was Hercules' armor-bearer, who was drawn under water "by a water nymph who saw the rosy flush of his beauty and wished to kiss him. She threw her arms around his neck and drew him down to the depths and he was seen no more. Hercules sought him madly everywhere, shouting his name and plunging deeper and deeper into the forest away from the sea. He had forgotten the [Golden] Fleece and the [ship the] *Argo* and his comrades: everything except Hylas. He did not come back, and finally the ship had to sail without him." [Edith Hamilton, *Mythology* (Boston: Little, 1942), 163–64]

2. Mount Ida, one of two mountains in Greece where the Muses dwell.

3. The river which runs through Troy. Also known as Xanthus.

4. Ancient region in Asia.

So said, unfilleting his purple chlamys,[5]
And putting down his urn, he stood a moment,
Breathing the faint, warm odor of the blossoms
That spangled thick the lovely Dardan meadows.
. . . .
His back was like a god's; his loins were moulded
As if some pulse of power began to waken;
The springy fulness of his thighs, outswerving,
Sloped to his knee, and, lightly dropping downward,
Drew the curved lines that breathe, in rest, of motion.

He saw his glorious limbs reversely mirrored   20
In the still wave, and stretched his foot to press it
On the smooth sole that answered at the surface:
Alas! the shape dissolved in glimmering fragments.
Then, timidly at first, he dipped, and catching
Quick breath, with tingling shudder, as the waters
Swirled round his thighs, and deeper, slowly deeper,
Till on his breast the River's cheek was pillowed,
And deeper still, till every shoreward ripple
Talked in his ear, and like a cygnet's bosom
His white, round shoulder shed a dripping crystal.   30
There, as he floated, with a rapturous motion,
The lucid coolness folding close around him,
The lily-cradling ripples murmured, "Hylas!"
He shook from off his ears the hyacinthine
Curls, that had lain unwet upon the water,
And still the ripples murmured, "Hylas! Hylas!"
He thought: "The voices are but earborn music.
Pan dwells not here, and Echo still is calling
From some high cliff that tops a Thracian valley:
So long mine ears, on tumbling Hellespontus,   40
Have heard the sea waves hammer Argo's forehead,
That I misdeem the fluting of this current
For some lost nymph—" Again the murmur, "Hylas!"
And with the sound a cold, smooth arm around him
Slid like a wave, and down the clear, green darkness
Glimmered, uprising slow; and ever closer
Wound the cold arms, till, climbing to his shoulders,
Their cheeks lay nestled, while the purple tangles
Their loose hair made, in silken mesh enwound him.
Their eyes of clear, pale emerald then uplifting,   50
They kissed his neck with lips of humid coral,
And once again there came a murmur, "Hylas!
Oh, come with us! Oh, follow where we wander

---

5. Cloak.

Deep down beneath the green, translucent ceiling,—
Where on the sandy bed of old Scamander
With cool white buds we braid our purple tresses,
Lulled by the bubbling waves around us stealing!
Thou fair Greek boy, Oh, come with us! Oh, follow
Where thou no more shalt hear Propontis riot,
But by our arms be lapped in endless quiet,   60
Within the glimmering caves of Ocean hollow!
We have no love; alone, of all the Immortals,
We have no love. Oh, love us, we who press thee
With faithful arms, though cold,—whose lips caress thee,—
Who hold thy beauty prisoned! Love us, Hylas!"

The boy grew chill to feel their twining pressure
Lock round his limbs, and bear him, vainly striving,
Down from the noonday brightness. "Leave me, Naiads!
Leave me!" he cried; "the day to me is dearer
Than all your caves deep-sphered in Ocean's quiet.   70
I am but mortal, seek but mortal pleasure:
I would not change this flexile, warm existence,
Though swept by storms, and shocked by Jove's dread
          thunder,
To be a king beneath the dark-green waters."
. . . .
But still with unrelenting arms they bound him,
And still, accordant, flowed their watery voices:
"We have thee now,—we hold thy beauty prisoned;
Oh, come with us beneath the emerald waters!   80
We have no love: we have thee, rosy Hylas.
Oh, love us, whose milky arms will be thy cradle
Far down on the untroubled sands of ocean,
Where now we bear thee, clasped in our embraces."
And slowly, slowly sank the amorous Naiads;
The boy's blue eyes, upturned, looked through the water,
Pleading for help; but Heaven's immortal Archer
Was swathed in cloud. The ripples hid his forehead,
And last, the thick, bright curls a moment floated,
So warm and silky that the stream upbore them,   90
Closing reluctant, as he sank forever.

The sunset died behind the crags of Imbros.
Argo was tugging at her chain; for freshly
Blew the swift breeze, and leaped the restless billows.
The voice of Jason roused the dozing sailors,
And up the mast was heaved the snowy canvas.
But mighty Heracles, the Jove-begotten,
Unmindful stood, beside the cool Scamander,

Leaning upon his club. A purple chlamys
Tossed o'er an urn was all that lay before him: 100
And when he called, expectant, "Hylas! Hylas!"
The empty echoes made him answer,—"Hylas!"

(1850, 1851)

from The Temptation of Hassan Ben Kaled

VI

The guests were near a fountain. As I came
They rose in welcome, wedding to my name
Titles of honor, linked in choicest phrase,
For Poets' ears are ever quick to Praise,
The 'Open Sesame!' whose magic art
Forces the guarded entrance of the heart.
. . . .
There came a troop of swarthy slaves, who bore
Ewars and pitchers all of silver ore,
Wherein we washed our hands; then, tables placed,
And brought us meats of every sumptuous taste   10
That makes the blood rich—pheasants stuffed with spice;
Young lambs, whose entrails were of cloves and rice;
Ducks bursting with pistachio nuts, and fish
That in a bed of parsley swam. Each dish,
Cooked with such art, seemed better than the last,
And our indulgence in the rich repast
Brought on the darkness ere we missed the day.

IX

"I swear it, that from him the morning drew
Its freshness, and the moon her silvery hue,
The sun its brightness, and the stars their fire,   20
And musk and camphor all their odorous breath:
And if he answer not my love's desire
Day will be night to me, and Life be Death!"

X

Scarce had she ceased, when, overcome, I fell
Upon her bosom, where the lute no more
That night was cradled; song was silenced well

With kisses, each one sweeter than before,
Until their fiery dew so long was quaffed,
I drank delirium in the infectious draught.
The guests departed, but the sound they made   30
I heard not; in the fountain-haunted shade
The lamps burned out; the moon rode far above,
But the trees chased her from our nest of love.
Dizzy with passion, in mine ears the blood
Tingled and hummed in a tumultuous flood,
Until from deep to deep I seeemed to fall,
Like him, who from El Sirat's hair-drawn wall
Plunges to endless gulfs.

(1854)

Bedouin Song

From the Desert I come to thee
On a stallion shod with fire;
And the winds are left behind
In the speed of my desire.
Under thy window I stand,
And the midnight hears my cry:
I love thee, I love but thee,
With a love that shall not die
        Till the sun grows cold,
        And the stars are old,   10
        And the leaves of the Judgment
            Book unfold!

Look from thy window and see
My passion and my pain;
I lie on the sands below,
And I faint in thy disdain.

Let the night-winds touch thy brow
With the heat of my burning sigh,
And melt thee to hear the vow
Of a love that shall not die   20
        Till the sun grows cold,
        And the stars are old,
        And the leaves of the Judgment
            Book unfold!

My steps are nightly driven,
By the fever in my breast,
To hear from thy lattice breathed
The word that shall give me rest.
Open the door of thy heart,
And open thy chamber door,   30
And my kisses shall teach thy lips
The love that shall fade no more
        Till the sun grows cold,
        And the stars are old,
        And the leaves of the Judgment
        Book unfold!

                       (written 29 October 1853, 1855)

Sonnet

The soul goes forth and finds no resting place
      On the wide breast of Life's unquiet sea
      But in the heart of Man. The blazonry
Of Wealth and Power fades out, and leaves no trace;
Renown's fresh laurels for awhile may grace
      The brow that wears them, but the dazzling tree
      Has canker in its heart; philosophy
Is not Content, and Art's immortal face
      Is trenched with weary furrow: but the heart
Hoards in its cells the satisfying dew   10
      Which all our thirst is powerless to exhaust.
Let Life's uncertain dignities depart,
And if one single manly heart be true,
      My own, contented, counts them cheaply lost.

                       (1855)

from The Quaker Widow

I

Thee finds me in the garden, Hannah,—come in! 'Tis kind
    of thee
To wait until the Friends were gone, who came to comfort
    me.
The still and quiet company a peace may give, indeed,
But blessed is the single heart that comes to us at need.

II

Come, sit thee down! Here is the bench where Benjamin
   would sit
On the First-day[6] afternoons in spring, and watch the
   swallows flit;
He loved to smell the sprouting box, and hear the pleasant
   bees
Go humming round the lilacs and through the apple trees.

III

I think he loved the spring: not that he cared for flowers;
   most men
Think such things foolishness,—but we were first ac-
   quainted then,   10
One spring: the next he spoke his mind; the third I was his
   wife,
And in the spring (it happen'd so) our children enter'd life.

IV

He was but seventy-five: I did not think to lay him yet
In Kennett[7] graveyard, where at Monthly Meeting first we
   met.
The Father's mercy shows in this: 'tis better I should be
Picked out to bear the heavy cross—alone in age—than he.

V

We've lived together fifty years: it seems but one long day,
One quiet Sabbath of the heart, till he was called away;
And as we bring from Meeting-time a sweet contentment
   home,
So, Hannah, I have store of peace for all the days to come. 20

VI

I mind (for I can tell thee now) how hard it was to know
If I had heard the Spirit right, that told me I should go;[8]
For Father had a deep concern upon his mind that day,
But mother spoke for Benjamin,—she knew what best to say.

---

6. Sunday, to the Quakers.
7. Taylor's birthplace, a village in Chester County, Pennsylvania.
8. To marry.

VII

Then she was still: they sat a while: at last she spoke again,
"The Lord incline thee to the right!" and "Thou shalt have
      him, Jane!"
My father said. I cried. Indeed, 'twas not the least of shocks,
For Benjamin was Hicksite,[9] and father Orthodox.

VIII

I thought of this ten years ago, when daughter Ruth we lost:
Her husband's of the world, and yet I could not see her
      cross'd.   30
She wears, thee knows, the gayest gowns,[10] she hears a
      hireling priest—
Ah, dear! the cross was ours: her life's a happy one, at least.

IX

Perhaps she'll wear a plainer dress when she's as old as I,—
Would thee believe it, Hannah? once *I* felt temptation nigh!
My wedding-gown was ashen silk, too simple for my taste:
I wanted lace around the neck, and a ribbon at the waist.

X

How strange it seem'd to sit with him upon the women's side!
I did not dare to lift my eyes: I felt more fear than pride,
Till, "in the presence of the Lord," he said, and then there
      came   40
A holy strength upon my heart, and I could say the same.

XV

Eusebius never cared to farm,—'twas not his call, in truth,
And I must rent the dear old place, and go to daughter Ruth.
Thee'll say her ways are not like mine,— young people now-
      a-days
Have fallen sadly off, I think, from all the good old ways. 50

---

9. A liberal branch of Quakers, after Elias Hicks, an American Quaker
minister.

10. Quaker rules stipulate that Friends wear simple, plain-colored dress as a
sign of humility.

XVI

But Ruth is still a Friend at heart; she keeps the simple
    tongue,
The cheerful, kindly nature we loved when she was young;
And it was brought upon my mind, remembering her, of
    late,
That we on dress and outward things perhaps lay too much
    weight.

XVII

I once heard Jesse Kersey say, a spirit clothed with grace,
And pure, almost, as angels are, may have a homely face.
And dress may be of less account: the Lord will look within:
The soul it is that testifies of righteousness or sin.

XVIII

Thee mustn't be too hard on Ruth: she's anxious I should go,
And she will do her duty as a daughter should, I know.   60
'Tis hard to change so late in life, but we must be resign'd:
The Lord looks down contentedly upon a willing mind.

                                                    (1875)

Richard Henry Stoddard

1825–1903

Although Richard Henry Stoddard produced several volumes of sentimental verse, he made his most significant contribution to American poetry as a learned and uncompromising critic. His reviews helped shape the reputations of many young poets. Host of one of New York's major literary salons, Stoddard also influenced the careers of a new generation of writers—Bayard Taylor, George Henry Boker, Edmund Clarence Stedman, Paul Hamilton Hayne, Thomas Buchanan Read, Herman Melville, and William Dean Howells—by bringing them together with established authors such as Hawthorne, Lowell, Longfellow, and Bryant.

Stoddard was born into a seafaring family in Hingham, Massachusetts, on 2 July 1825. Seven years after his father died at sea in 1828, Stoddard's mother settled in New York. Poverty forced Stoddard to leave school at fifteen to work at odd jobs. At eighteen, he became an apprentice in an iron foundry. Despite his lack of formal education, Stoddard aspired to a literary career and befriended many writers and publishers, including Poe and Hawthorne. From his literary friendships and his assiduous study of the English masters after his daily work at the foundry, Stoddard learned the history and forms of English poetry. After 1845, his own poetry appeared in such periodicals as the *Rover*, the *Southern Literary Messenger*, the *Knickerbocker Magazine*, and the *Home Journal*.

Stoddard privately published his first volume of poetry, *Foot-Prints*, in 1849, but immediately recognized its amateurishness and destroyed all but one copy. In 1852, he published *Poems*, which won favorable reviews. Hawthorne got him a job as a customs inspector in New York in 1853 so that Stoddard might support himself and his wife, novelist Elizabeth Drew Barstow, while still pursuing a literary career. He held this post for seventeen years; from 1860 to 1870 he also wrote literary reviews for the New York *World*. He served as literary editor of the *Mail and Express* from 1880 until 1903, produced several books of children's verse, and published more volumes of poetry (*Songs of Summer*, 1857; *The King's Bell*, 1863; *The Book of the East*, 1871; *The Poems of Richard Henry Stoddard*, 1880; *The Lion's Cub*, 1890) in addition to editing anthologies and writing his memoirs. When he died in New York on 12 May 1903, Stoddard had achieved wide recognition and popularity as a man of letters.

Had Stoddard not been a famous critic, his poetry might not have received the attention it did. Many of his poems, such as "The Flight of Youth," weakly imitate the great English masters, particularly Keats, Wordsworth, and Tennyson. One of the earlier devotees of the "orientalizing" craze, Stoddard also wrote poetry that supposedly captured oriental themes and style. His oriental verse caught the public's fancy less than his poetic tributes to famous men and women ("Adsum," for example), or his lyric poetry about love, loss, writing, and the inadequacy of language. Stoddard attempted a wide range of poetic forms and genres, including verse fables and children's poems, and wrote on themes ranging from the lofty to the mundane, the predictable to the surprising (see "A Woman's Poem" for the latter). His lyricism and homely but sincere expressions of sentiment appealed to a popular contemporary audience, but Stoddard lacked the originality and technical skill to establish his place as a poet for subsequent generations.

—*Ellen Giduʒ*

Suggestions for Further Reading

Harvey, Robert D. "Richard Henry Stoddard." *American Literary Critics and Scholars, 1850–1880*. Vol. 64 of *Dictionary of Literary Biography*. Ed. John W. Rathbun and Monica M. Grecu. Detroit: Gale, 1988. 230–35.

Macdonough, August Rodney. "Stoddard's Poems." *Scribner's Monthly* 20 (1880): 686–94.

Stoddard, Richard Henry. *Recollections, Personal and Literary*. Ed. Ripley Hitchcock. New York: A. S. Barnes, 1903.

TEXT
The Poems of Richard Henry Stoddard. 1880.

ꙮ

Silent Songs

If I could ever sing the songs
　　Within me day and night,
The only fit accompaniment
　　Would be a lute of light!

A thousand dreamy melodies,
   Begot with pleasant pain,
Like incantations float around
   The chambers of my brain!

But when I strive to utter one,
   It mocks my feeble art,   10
And leaves me silent, with the thorns
   Of Music in my heart!

                    (1852)

The Flight of Youth[1]

There are gains for all our losses,
   There are balms for all our pain:
But when youth, the dream, departs,
It takes something from our hearts,
   And it never comes again.

We are stronger, and are better,
   Under manhood's sterner reign:
Still we feel that something sweet
Followed youth, with flying feet,
   And will never come again.   10

Something beautiful is vanished,
   And we sigh for it in vain:
We behold it everywhere,
On the earth, and in the air,
   But it never comes again.

                    (1857)

Adsum[2]
(December 23–24, 1863)

I

The Angel came by night,
   (Such angels still come down,)
And like a winter cloud

---

1. Originally entitled "There Are Gains for All Our Losses."
2. Latin for "I am here."

Passed over London town;
Along its lonesome streets,
　　Where Want had ceased to weep,
Until it reached a house
　　Where a great man[3] lay asleep:
The man of all his time
　　Who knew the most of men,　　　　　　　　　　10
The soundest head and heart,
　　The sharpest, kindest pen.
It paused beside his bed,
　　And whispered in his ear;
He never turned his head,
　　But answered, "I am here."

II

Into the night they went.
　　At morning, side by side,
They gained the sacred Place
　　Where the greatest Dead abide.　　　　　　　　20
Where grand, old Homer sits
　　In godlike state benign;
Where broods in endless thought
　　The awful Florentine;[4]
Where sweet Cervantes walks,
　　A smile on his grave face;
Where gossips quaint Montaigne,
　　The wisest of his race;
Where Goethe looks through all
　　With that calm eye of his;　　　　　　　　　　30
Where—little seen but Light—
　　The only Shakespeare is!
When the new Spirit came,
　　They asked him, drawing near,
"Art thou become like us?"
　　He answered, "I am here."

　　　　　　　　　　　　　　(written 1863, 1871)

A Woman's Poem

You say you love me and you lay
　　Your hand and fortune at my feet:

---

3. William Makepeace Thackeray (1811–1863).
4. Dante Alighieri (1265–1321).

I thank you, sir, with all my heart,
　　For love is sweet.

It is but little to you men,
　　To whom the doors of Life stand wide;
But much, how much to woman! She
　　Has naught beside.

You make the worlds wherein you move,
　　You rule your tastes, or coarse, or fine;　　10
Dine, hunt, or fish, or waste your gold
　　At dice and wine.

Our world (alas, you make that, too!)
　　Is narrower, shut in four blank walls:
Know you, or care, what light is there?
　　What shadow falls?

We read the last new novel out,
　　And live in dream-land till it ends:
We write romantic school-girl notes,
　　That bore our friends.　　20

We learn to trill Italian songs,
　　And thrum for hours the tortured keys:
We think it pleases you, and we
　　But live to please.

We feed our birds, we tend our flowers,
　　(Poor in-door things of sickly bloom,)
Or play the housewife in our gloves,
　　And dust the room.

But some of us have hearts and minds,
　　So much the worse for us and you;　　30
For grant we seek a better life,
　　What can we do?

We cannot build and sail your ships,
　　Or drive your engines; we are weak,
And ignorant of the tricks of Trade.
　　To think, and speak,

Or write some earnest, stammering words
　　Alone is ours, and that you hate;
So forced within ourselves again
　　We sigh and wait.　　40

Ah, who can tell the bitter hours,
    The dreary days, that women spend?
Their thoughts unshared, their lives unknown,
        Without a friend!

Without a friend? And what is he,
    Who, like a shadow, day and night,
Follows the woman he prefers—
        Lives in her sight?

Her lover, he: a gallant man,
    Devoted to her every whim;   50
He vows to die for her, so she
        Must live for him!

We should be very grateful, sir,
    That, when you've nothing else to do,
You waste your idle hours on us—
        So kind of you!

Profuse in studied compliments,
    Your manners like your clothes are fine,
Though both at times are somewhat strong
        Of smoke and wine.   60

What can we hope to know of you?
    Or you of us? We act our parts:
We love in jest: it is the play
        Of hands, not hearts!

You grant my bitter words are true
    Of others, not of you and me;
Your love is steady as a star:
        But we shall see.

You say you love me: have you thought
    How much those little words contain?   70
Alas, a world of happiness,
        And worlds of pain!

You know, or should, your nature now,
    Its needs and passions. Can I be
What you desire me? Do you find
        Your all in me?

You do. But have you thought that I
    May have my ways and fancies, too?

You love me; well, but have you thought
    If I love you?   80

But think again. You know me not:
    I, too, may be a butterfly,
A costly parlor doll on show
    For you to buy.

You trust me wholly? One word more.
    You see me young: they call me fair:
I think I have a pleasant face,
    And pretty hair.

But by and by my face will fade,
    It must with time, it may with care: 90
What say you to a wrinkled wife,
    With thin, gray hair?

You care not, you: in youth, or age,
    Your heart is mine, while life endures.
Is it so? Then, Arthur, here's my hand,
    My heart is yours.

              (1871)

An Old Song Reversed

"There are gains for all our losses."
    So I said when I was young.
If I sang that song again,
'Twould not be with that refrain,
    Which but suits an idle tongue.

Youth has gone, and hope gone with it,
    Gone the strong desire for fame.
Laurels are not for the old.
Take them, lads. Give Senex gold.
    What's an everlasting name?   10

When my life was in its summer
    One fair woman liked my looks:
Now that Time has driven his plough
In deep furrows on my brow,
    I'm no more in her good books.

"There are gains for all our losses?"
    Grave beside the wintry sea,
Where my child is, and my heart,
For they would not live apart,
    What has been your gain to me?   20

No, the words I sang were idle,
    And will ever so remain:
Death, and Age, and vanished Youth,
All declare this bitter truth,
    There's a loss for every gain!

                                    (1880)

Frances Ellen Watkins Harper
1825–1911

By some accounts, Frances Ellen Watkins Harper "was the leading black poet in nineteenth-century America prior to Paul Laurence Dunbar" (Ammons 61). For most of her life, Harper wrote lyric and narrative poetry linked to her political and social crusades. Her poetry, which addresses the central concerns of nineteenth-century black Americans, is significant as an artistic record of an oppressed people's reaction to a troubled age.

Frances Ellen Watkins was born to free black parents in Baltimore, Maryland, on 24 September 1825. At the age of three, Watkins was orphaned; her aunt and uncle, Mr. and Mrs. William J. Watkins, took her in. Frances Ellen studied at William Watkins' school for free blacks until, at age fourteen, she took a job as a domestic in the home of a Baltimore bookshop owner. Watkins read widely in her employer's library, and in the 1840s she began writing poetry and prose for publication in the Baltimore newspapers. In 1845, she published a volume entitled "*Forest Leaves* (also on occasion cited as *Autumn Leaves*), of which no copy is known to have survived" (Ammons 61).

In 1850, Watkins moved to Ohio. She taught sewing at Union Seminary, a school later absorbed by Wilberforce University. She moved to Little York, Pennsylvania, in 1853, taught school, and became involved in the anti-slavery movement. In 1854 she gave her first anti-slavery speech, and from 1854 until 1860, when she married Fenton Harper, Watkins traveled the country making abolitionist speeches. When Fenton died in 1864, Harper returned to the lecture circuit, speaking "to black and mixed audiences on the themes of black education, civil rights, temperance, domestic reform, and an end to lynching." She subsidized her career by selling her lectures and poems (Ammons 62). Harper died on 20 February 1911 in Philadelphia.

Harper generally favored the ballad stanza for her poetry. The major exception is *Moses: A Story of the Nile*, a book-length narrative poem in blank verse. Her themes reflect the content of her lectures. Harper wrote seven volumes of poetry: *Poems on Miscellaneous Subjects* (1854), *Moses: A Story of the Nile* (1869), *Poems* (1871),

Sketches of Southern Life (1872), *Sparrow's Fall* (1890?), *Light Beyond Darkness* (n.d.), and *The Martyr of Alabama and Other Poems* (1894). In addition, she also wrote the first published short story by a black American, "The Two Offers" (1859), and the novel *Iola Leroy* (1892).

Harper's politics shaped her art. Her poems address the evils of slavery, the treatment of blacks after the Civil War, the poet's theory of art, and moral themes. Some of Harper's best poetry, including "The Slave Mother, a Tale of the Ohio" and "Bury Me in a Free Land," deals with the horrors of slavery. After the Civil War, Harper addressed the issues of lynching and equal rights in poems like "The Martyr of Alabama" and "Learning to Read." In "A Double Standard," Harper voiced the problems that all women face in a male-dominated society. She was a crusader who used art as a weapon for the elevation of her race.

—William R. Nash

Suggestions for Further Reading

Ammons, Elizabeth. "*Legacy* Profile: Frances Ellen Watkins Harper (1825–1911)." *Legacy: A Journal of Nineteenth-Century American Women Writers* 2.2 (Fall 1985): 61–66.

Gates, Henry Louis. *The Signifying Monkey: A Theory of Afro-American Literary Criticism*. New York: Oxford UP, 1988.

Hill, Patricia Liggins. " 'Let Me Make Songs for the People': A Study of Frances Ellen Watkins Harper's Poetry." *Black American Literature Forum* 15.2 (Summer 1981): 60–65.

Rubin, Louis D., Jr. "The Search for a Language, 1746–1923." *Black Poetry in America*. Ed. Louis D. Rubin Jr. and Blyden Jackson. Baton Rouge: Lousiana State UP, 1974. 1–36.

Sherman, Joan R. *Invisible Poets: Afro-Americans of the Nineteenth Century*. Urbana: U of Illinois P, 1979.

TEXT

Complete Poems of Frances Ellen Watkins Harper. Ed. Maryanne Graham. New York: Oxford UP, 1988.

ᘏᗷᘏ

The Slave Mother, a Tale of the Ohio

I have but four, the treasures of my soul,
    They lay like doves around my heart;
I tremble lest some cruel hand
    Should tear my household wreaths apart.

My baby girl, with childish glance,
Looks curious in my anxious eye,
She little knows that for her sake
Deep shadows round my spirit lie.

My playful boys could I forget,
My home might seem a joyous spot,   10
But with their sunshine mirth I blend
The darkness of their future lot.

And thou my babe, my darling one,
My last, my loved, my precious child,
Oh! when I think upon thy doom
My heart grows faint and then throbs wild.

The Ohio's bridged and spanned with ice,
The northern star is shining bright,
I'll take the nestlings of my heart
And search for freedom by its light.   20

Winter and night were on the earth,
And feebly moaned the shivering trees,
A sigh of winter seemed to run
Through every murmur of the breeze.

She fled, and with her children all,
She reached the stream and crossed it o'er,
Bright visions of deliverance came
Like dreams of plenty to the poor.

Dreams! vain dreams, heroic mother,
Give all thy hopes and struggles o'er,   30
The pursuer is on thy track,
And the hunter at thy door.

Judea's refuge cities had power
To shelter, shield and save,
E'en Rome had altars, 'neath whose shade
Might crouch the wan and weary slave.

But Ohio had no sacred fane,
To human rights so consecrated,
Where thou may'st shield thy hapless ones
From their darkly gathering fate.   40

Then, said the mournful mother,
If Ohio cannot save,

I will do a deed for freedom,
  Shalt find each child a grave.

I will save my precious children
  From their darkly threatened doom,
I will hew their path to freedom
  Through the portals of the tomb.

A moment in the sunlight,
  She held a glimmering knife,   50
The next moment she had bathed it
  In the crimson fount of life.

They snatched away the fatal knife,
  Her boys shrieked wild with dread;
The baby girl was pale and cold,
  They raised it up, the child was dead.

Sends this deed of fearful daring
  Through my country's heart no thrill,
Do the icy hands of slavery
  Every pure emotion chill?   60

Oh! if there is any honor,
  Truth or justice in the land,
Will ye not, us men and Christians,
  On the side of freedom stand?

                                                   (1854)

Bury Me in a Free Land

Make me a grave where'er you will,
In a lowly plain, or a lofty hill,
Make it among earth's humblest graves,
But not in a land where men are slaves.

I could not rest if around my grave
I heard the steps of a trembling slave:
His shadow above my silent tomb
Would make it a place of fearful gloom.

I could not rest if I heard the tread
Of a coffle gang to the shambles led,   10
And the mother's shriek of wild despair
Rise like a curse on the trembling air.

I could not sleep if I saw the lash
Drinking her blood at each fearful gash,
And I saw her babes torn from her breast,
Like trembling doves from their parent nest.

I'd shudder and start if I heard the bay
Of blood-hounds seizing their human prey,
And I heard the captive plead in vain
As they bound afresh his galling chain.   20

If I saw young girls from their mother's arms
Bartered and sold for their youthful charms,
My eye would flash with a mournful flame,
My death-paled cheek grow red with shame.

I would sleep, dear friends, where bloated might
Can rob no man of his dearest right;
My rest shall be calm in any grave
Where none can call his brother a slave.

I ask no monument, proud and high
To arrest the gaze of the passers-by;   30
All that my yearning spirit craves,
Is bury me not in a land of slaves.

                                        (1864, 1866)

Learning to Read

Very soon the Yankee teachers
    Came down and set up school;
But, oh! how the Rebs did hate it,—
    It was agin' their rule.

Our masters always tried to hide
    Book learning from our eyes;
Knowledge didn't agree with slavery—
    'Twould make us all too wise.

But some of us would try to steal
    A little from the book,   10
And put the words together,
    And learn by hook or crook.

I remember Uncle Caldwell,
    Who took pot liquor fat

And greased the pages of his book,
    And hid it in his hat.

And had his master ever seen
    The leaves upon his head,
He'd have thought them greasy papers,
    But nothing to be read.   20

And there was Mr. Turner's Ben,
    Who heard the children spell,
And picked the words right up by heart,
    And learned to read 'em well.

Well, the Northern folks kept sending
    The Yankee teachers down;
And they stood right up and helped us,
    Though Rebs did sneer and frown.

And I longed to read my Bible,
    For precious words it said;   30
But when I begun to learn it,
    Folks just shook their heads.

And said there is no use trying,
    Oh! Chloe, you're too late;
But as I was rising sixty,
    I had no time to wait.

So I got a pair of glasses,
    And straight to work I went,
And never stopped till I could read
    The hymns and Testament.   40

Then I got a little cabin
    A place to call my own—
And I felt as independent
    As the queen upon her throne.

               (1872)

A Double Standard

Do you blame me that I loved him?
    If when standing all alone
I cried for bread a careless world
    Pressed to my lips a stone.

Do you blame me that I loved him,
    That my heart beat glad and free,
When he told me in the sweetest tones
    He loved but only me?

Can you blame me that I did not see
    Beneath his burning kiss   10
The serpent's wiles, nor even hear
    The deadly adder hiss?

Can you blame me that my heart grew cold
    That the tempted, tempter turned;
When he was feted and caressed
    And I was coldly spurned?

Would you blame him, when you draw from me
    Your dainty robes aside.
If he with gilded baits should claim
    Your fairest as his bride?   20

Would you blame the world if it should press
    On him a civic crown;
And see me struggling in the depth
    Then harshly press me down?

Crime has no sex and yet to-day
    I wear the brand of shame;
Whilst he amid the gay and proud
    Still bears an honored name.

Can you blame me if I've learned to think
    Your hate of vice a sham,   30
When you so coldly crushed me down
    And then excused the man?

Would you blame me if to-morrow
    The coroner should say,
A wretched girl, outcast, forlorn,
    Has thrown her life away?

Yes, blame me for my downward course,
    But oh! remember well,
Within your homes you press the hand
    That led me down to hell.   40

I'm glad God's ways are not our ways,
    He does not see as man,

Within His love I know there's room
　　For those whom others ban.

I think before His great white throne,
　　His throne of spotless light,
That whited sepulchres shall wear
　　The hue of endless night.

That I who fell, and he who sinned,
　　Shall reap as we have sown;　　　　　　　　　　　　　　50
That each the burden of his loss
　　Must bear and bear alone.

No golden weights can turn the scale
　　Of justice in His sight;
And what is wrong in woman's life
　　In man's cannot be right.

　　　　　　　　　　　　　　　　　　　　　　　　　　(1890)

The Martyr of Alabama

> The following news item appeared in the newspapers
> throughout the country, issue of December 27, 1894:
> "Tim Thompson, a little negro boy, was asked to dance for
> the amusement of some white toughs. He refused, saying he
> was a church member. One of the men knocked him down
> with a club and then danced upon his prostrate form. He
> then shot the boy in the hip. The boy is dead; his murderer is
> still at large."

He lifted up his pleading eyes,
　　And scanned each cruel face,
Where cold and brutal cowardice
　　Had left its evil trace.

It was when tender memories
　　Round Beth'lem's manger lay,
And mothers told their little ones
　　Of Jesu's natal day.

And of the Magi from the East
　　Who came their gifts to bring,　　　　　　　　　　　　10
And bow in rev'rence at the feet
　　Of Salem's new-born King.

And how the herald angels sang
  The choral song of peace,
That war should close his wrathful lips,
  And strife and carnage cease.

At such an hour men well may hush
  Their discord and their strife,
And o'er that manger clasp their hands
  With gifts to brighten life.   20

Alas! that in our favored land,
  That cruelty and crime
Should cast their shadows o'er a day,
  The fairest pearl of time.

A dark-browed boy had drawn anear
  A band of savage men,
Just as a hapless lamb might stray
  Into a tiger's den.

Cruel and dull, they saw in him
  For sport an evil chance,   30
And then demanded of the child
  To give to them a dance.

"Come dance for us" the rough men said;
  "I can't," the child replied,
"I cannot for the dear Lord's sake,
  Who for my sins once died."

Tho they were strong and he was weak,
  He wouldn't his Lord deny,
His life lay in their cruel hands,
  But he for Christ could die.   40

Heard they aright? Did that brave child
  Their mandates dare resist?
Did he against their stern commands
  Have courage to resist?

Then recklessly a man(?) arose,
  And dealt a fearful blow.
He crushed the portals of that life,
  And laid the brave child low.

And trampled on his prostrate form,
  As on a broken toy;   50

Then danced with careless, brutal feet,
   Upon the murdered boy.

Christians! behold that martyred child!
   His blood cries from the ground;
Before the sleepless eye of God,
   He shows each gaping wound.

Oh! Church of Christ arise! arise!
   Let crimson stain thy hand,
When God shall inquisition make
   For blood shed in the land.   60

Take sackcloth of the darkest hue,
   And shroud the pulpit round;
Servants of him who cannot lie
   Sit mourning on the ground.

Let holy horror blanch each brow,
   Pale every cheek with fears,
And rocks and stones, if ye could speak,
   Ye well might melt to tears.

Through every fane set forth a cry,
   Of sorrow and regret,   70
Nor in an hour of careless ease
   Thy brother's wrongs forget.

Veil not thine eyes, nor close thy lips,
   Nor speak with bated breath;
This evil shall not always last,—
   The end of it is death.

Avert the doom that crime must bring
   Upon a guilty land;
Strong in the strength that God supplies,
   For truth and justice stand.   80

For Christless men, with reckless hands,
   Are sowing around thy path
The tempests wild that yet shall break
   In whirlwinds of God's wrath.

          (1894)

John Townsend Trowbridge
1827–1916

John Townsend Trowbridge began his literary career writing verse but soon turned to popular fiction to earn a living. He wrote over forty books, mostly adventure stories for boys, such as *Cudjo's Cave* (1863), but considered his poetry his most thoughtful work. Though readers spurned his long, metaphysical lyrics and didactic poems, Trowbridge's narrative poems enjoyed popular success.

Born 10 September 1827 on a farm in Ogden Township, New York, John Townsend Trowbridge attended a local common school and a Lockport school. Poor eyesight hindered his formal education, and he was largely self-taught. In 1847, Trowbridge arrived in New York City and offered his poetry to Major Noah, the prominent editor of the *Sunday Times*. Advised that only prose would sell, Trowbridge began writing humorous short stories, putting his verse aside for years. He became the youngest regular contributor to the new *Atlantic Monthly* in 1857, publishing there both verse and prose, including the popular favorite "Midsummer." He accepted the editorship of *Our Young Folks* in 1860 and moved to Arlington, Massachusetts. In 1903, he published both his autobiography, *My Own Story, with Recollections of Noted Persons* and *The Poetical Works of John Townsend Trowbridge*. The latter, reprinted in 1972, represents five books of verse, plus his latest poems in a section entitled "Newly Gathered Leaves." Trowbridge remained in Arlington until his death on 12 February 1916.

The Vagabonds and Other Poems (1869) contains Trowbridge's most successful poetry; "The Vagabonds" was popular with platform readers. Contemporary readers must have found the poem convincing, for his oldest sister commented, "I cannot help feeling that it was written by a person who has gone through some such terrible experience of intemperance and misery as he describes" (*My Own Story* 253). *The Book of Gold and Other Poems* (1877) featured "The Book of Gold," a long narration of a despairing young man. *A Home Idyl and Other Poems* (1881) contained a sentimental eulogy of boyhood, "The Boy I Love." His final collection, *The Lost Earl and Other Poems*, was published in 1888.

In his narrative poems, Trowbridge celebrates the home,

marriage, friendships, and children. His poetic structures include the dramatic monologue, as in "The Vagabonds," or a combination of poetic narration and monologue, as in "Darius Green and His Flying-Machine." Trowbridge's lyrics usually concentrate on natural scenes or events exhibiting pathos and drama.

The popularity of "The Vagabonds" as a platform piece must stem from its mixture of various contemporary styles. In creating a humorous portrait of a man and his dog, Trowbridge draws upon traditions of humor and realism, sentimentality, and temperance literature of the times. He fuses sentimentality (as when the man idealizes the sole love of his youth) with social criticism: "What do you care for a beggar's story? / Is it amusing?" (lines 91–92). The poem also provides a temperance lesson through its speaker, a homeless drinking man.

In praising Walt Whitman's poetry, Trowbridge commented, "I get to prefer the original, strong, poetic spirit, even expressed in crude words, to any fluency. Fluency is apt to run away with a man. The want of it results in condensation and point" (Colfman 483). Unlike Whitman, Trowbridge consistently follows traditional forms, using iambic rhythms and rhymed stanzas (either couplets, triplets, or quatrains). Trowbridge also avoids the richer sound combinations found in Whitman, preferring instead to convey the experience of common speech.

—*Taimi Olsen*

Suggestions for Further Reading

Colfman, Rufus. "Trowbridge and Whitman." *PMLA* 63.1 (1948): 262–73.
———. "Two Meetings with Emerson." *Modern Language Notes* 65 (1950): 482–84.
Trowbridge, John Townsend. *My Own Story, with Recollections of Noted Persons*. Boston: Riverside Press, 1903.

TEXT
The Poetical Works of John Townsend Trowbridge. New York: Arno Press, 1972.

The Vagabonds

We are two travellers, Roger and I.
   Roger's my dog.—Come here, you scamp!

Jump for the gentlemen,—mind your eye!
　　Over the table,—look out for the lamp!—
The rogue is growing a little old;
　　Five years we've tramped through wind and weather,
And slept out-doors when nights were cold,
　　And eaten and drank—and starved—together.

We've learned what comfort is, I tell you!　　　　　10
　　A bed on the floor, a bit of rosin,
A fire to thaw our thumbs (poor fellow!
　　The paw he holds up there's been frozen),
Plenty of catgut for my fiddle
　　(This out-door business is bad for strings),
Then a few nice buckwheats hot from the griddle,
　　And Roger and I set up for kings!

No, thank ye, Sir,—I never drink;
　　Roger and I are exceedingly moral,—
Aren't we, Roger?—See him wink!—
　　Well, something hot, then,—we won't quarrel.　　20
He's thirsty, too,—see him nod his head?
　　What a pity, Sir, that dogs can't talk!
He understands every word that's said,—
　　And he knows good milk from water-and-chalk.

The truth is, Sir, now I reflect,
　　I've been so sadly given to grog,
I wonder I've not lost the respect
　　(Here's to you, Sir!) even of my dog.
But he sticks by, through thick and thin;
　　And this old coat, with its empty pockets,　　　30
And rags that smell of tobacco and gin,
　　He'll follow while he has eyes in his sockets.

There isn't another creature living
　　Would do it, and prove, through every disaster,
So fond, so faithful, and so forgiving,
　　To such a miserable, thankless master!
No, Sir!—see him wag his tail and grin!
　　By George! it makes my old eyes water!
That is, there's something in this gin
　　That chokes a fellow. But no matter!　　　　　40

We'll have some music, if you're willing,
　　And Roger here (what a plague a cough is, Sir!)
Shall march a little—Start, you villain!

Paws up! Eyes front! Salute your officer!
'Bout face! Attention! Take your rifle!
    (Some dogs have arms, you see!) Now hold your
Cap while the gentlemen give a trifle,
    To aid a poor old patriot soldier!

March! Halt! Now show how the rebel shakes
    When he stands up to hear his sentence.   50
Now tell us how many drams it takes
    To honor a jolly new acquaintance.
Five yelps,—that's five; he's mighty knowing!
    The night's before us, fill the glasses!—
Quick, Sir! I'm ill,—my brain is going!—
    Some brandy,—thank you,—there!—it passes!

Why not reform? That's easily said;
    But I've gone through such wretched treatment,
Sometimes forgetting the taste of bread,
    And scarce remembering what meat meant,   60
That my poor stomach's past reform;
    And there are times when, mad with thinking,
I'd sell out heaven for something warm
    To prop a horrible inward sinking.

Is there a way to forget to think?
    At your age, Sir, home, fortune, friends,
A dear girl's love,—but I took to drink;—
    The same old story; you know how it ends.
If you could have seen these classic features,—
    You needn't laugh, Sir; they were not then   70
Such a burning libel on God's creatures:
    I was one of your handsome men!

If you had seen HER, so fair and young,
    Whose head was happy on this breast!
If you could have heard the songs I sung
    When the wine went round, you wouldn't have guessed
That ever I, Sir, should be straying
    From door to door, with fiddle and dog,
Ragged and penniless, and playing
    To you to-night for a glass of grog!   80

She's married since,—a parson's wife:
    'Twas better for her that we should part,—
Better the soberest, prosiest life
    Than a blasted home and a broken heart.

I have seen her? Once: I was weak and spent
  On the dusty road: a carriage stopped:
But little she dreamed, as on she went,
  Who kissed the coin that her fingers dropped!

You've set me talking, Sir; I'm sorry;
  It makes me wild to think of the change!   90
What do you care for a beggar's story?
  Is it amusing? you find it strange?
I had a mother so proud of me!
  'Twas well she died before—Do you know
If the happy spirits in heaven can see
  The ruin and wretchedness here below?

Another glass, and strong, to deaden
  This pain; then Roger and I will start.
I wonder, has he such a lumpish, leaden,
  Aching thing in place of a heart?   100
He is sad sometimes, and would weep, if he could,
  No doubt, remembering things that were,—
A virtuous kennel, with plenty of food,
  And himself a sober, respectable cur.

I'm better now; that glass was warming.—
  You rascal! limber your lazy feet!
We must be fiddling and performing
  For supper and bed, or starve in the street.—
Not a very gay life to lead, you think?
  But soon we shall go where lodgings are free,   110
And the sleepers need neither victuals nor drink;—
  The sooner, the better for Roger and me!

                                                        (1869)

from Darius Green and His Flying-Machine

If ever there lived a Yankee lad,
Wise or otherwise, good or bad,
Who, seeing birds fly, didn't jump
With flapping arms from stake or stump,
    Or, spreading the tail
    Of his coat for a sail,
Take a soaring leap from post or rail,

And wonder why
He couldn't fly,
And flap and flutter and wish and try,—   10
If ever you knew a country dunce
Who didn't try that as often as once,
All I can say is, that's a sign
He never would do for a hero of mine.

An aspiring genius was D. Green:
The son of a farmer,—age fourteen;
His body was long and lank and lean,—
Just right for flying, as will be seen;
He had two eyes, each bright as a bean,
And a freckled nose that grew between,   20
A little awry,—for I must mention
That he had riveted his attention
Upon his wonderful invention,
Twisting his tongue as he twisted the strings,
Working his face as he worked the wings,
And with every turn of gimlet and screw
Turning and screwing his mouth round too.
    Till his nose seemed bent
    To catch the scent,
Around some corner, of new-baked pies,   30
And his wrinkled cheeks and his squinting eyes
Grew puckered into a queer grimace,
That made him look very droll in the face,
    And also very wise.

And wise he must have been, to do more
Than ever a genius did before,
Excepting Daedalus of yore
And his son Icarus, who wore
    Upon their backs
    Those wings of wax   40
He had read of in the old almanacs.
Darius was clearly of the opinion,
That the air is also man's dominion,
And that, with paddle or fin or pinion,
    We soon or late
    Shall navigate
The azure as now we sail the sea.
    The thing looks simple enough to me;
    And if you doubt it,
Hear how Darius reasoned about it.   50

"Birds can fly,
An' why can't I?
Must we give in,"
Says he with a grin,
    " 'T the bluebird an' phoebe
    Are smarter 'n we be?
Jest fold our hands an' see the swaller
An' blackbird an' catbird beat us holler?
Doos the leetle chatterin', sassy wren,
No bigger 'n my thumb, know more than men?   60
    Jest show me that!
    Er prove 't the bat
Hez got more brains than's in my hat,
An' I'll back down, an' not till then!"

He argued further: "Ner I can't see
What's th' use o' wings to a bumble-bee,
Fer to git a livin' with, more 'n to me;—
    Ain't my business
    Important's his'n is?

    "That Icarus   70
    Was a silly cuss,—
Him an' his daddy Daedalus.
They might 'a' knowed wings made o' wax
Wouldn't stan' sun-heat an' hard whacks.
    I'll make mine o' luther,
    Er suthin' er other."

And he said to himself, as he tinkered and planned:
"But I ain't goin' to show my hand
To nummies that never can understand
The fust idee that's big an' grand.   80
    They'd 'a' laft an' made fun
O' Creation itself afore 'twas done!"
So he kept his secret from all the rest,
Safely buttoned within his vest;
And in the loft above the shed
Himself he locks, with thimble and thread
And wax and hammer and buckles and screws,
And all such things as geniuses use;—
Two bats for patterns, curious fellows!
A charcoal-pot and a pair of bellows;   90
An old hoop-skirt or two, as well as
Some wire, and several old umbrellas;
A carriage-cover, for tail and wings;

A piece of harness; and straps and strings;
    And a big strong box,
    In which he locks
These and a hundred other things.
. . . .
    So day after day
He stitched and tinkered and hammered away,
    Till at last 'twas done,—   100
The greatest invention under the sun!
"An' now," says Darius, "hooray fer some fun!"

    'Twas the Fourth of July,
    And the weather was dry,
And not a cloud was on all the sky,
Save a few light fleeces, which here and there,
    Half mist, half air,
Like foam on the ocean went floating by:
Just as lovely a morning as ever was seen
For a nice little trip in a flying-machine.   110

Thought cunning Darius: "Now I shan't go
Along 'ith the fellers to see the show.
I'll say I've got sich a terrible cough!
An' then, when the folks 'ave all gone off,
    I'll hev full swing
    Fer to try the thing,
An' practyse a leetle on the wing."
"Ain't goin' to see the celebration?"
Says Brother Nate. "No; botheration!
I've got sich a cold—a toothache—I—   120
My gracious!—feel's though I should fly!"
. . . .
    He crept from his bed;
    And, seeing the others were gone, he said,
    "I'm a gittin' over the cold 'n my head."
    And away he sped,
    To open the wonderful box in the shed.

His brothers had walked but a little way
When Jotham to Nathan chanced to say,
"What on airth is he up to, hey?"
"Don'o',—the' 's suthin' er other to pay,   130
Er he wouldn't 'a' stayed to hum to-day."
Says Burke, "His toothache's all 'n his eye!
He never 'd miss a Fo'th-o'-July,
Ef he hedn't got some machine to try."

Then Sol, the little one, spoke: "By darn!
Le's hurry back an' hide 'n the barn,
An' pay him fer tellin' us that yarn!"
"Agreed!" Through the orchard they creep back,
Along by the fences, behind the stack,
And one by one, through a hole in the wall,   140
In under the dusty barn they crawl,
Dressed in thelr Sunday garments all;
And a very astonishing sight was that,
When each in his cobwebbed coat and hat
Came up through the floor like an ancient rat.
        And there they hid;
        And Reuben slid
The fastenings back, and the door undid.
        "Keep dark!" said he,
"While I squint an' see what the' is to see."   150
. . . .
        "Hush!" Reuben said,
        "He's up in the shed!
He's opened the winder,—I see his head!
He stretches it out, an' pokes it about,
Lookin' to see 'f the coast is clear,
        An' nobody near;—
Guess he don'o' who's hid in here!
He's riggin' a spring-board over the sill!
Stop laffin', Solomon! Burke, keep still!
He's climbin' out now—Of all the things!   160
What's he got on? I van, it's wings!
An' that 't other thing? I vum, it's a tail!
An' there he sets like a hawk on a rail!
Steppin' careful, he travels the length
Of his spring-board, and teeters to try its strength.
Now he stretches his wings, like a monstrous bat;
Peeks over his shoulder, this way an' that,
Fer to see 'f the' 's any one passin' by;
But the' 's on'y a ca'f an' a goslin' nigh.
They turn up at him a wonderin' eye,   170
To see—The dragon! he's goin' to fly!
Away he goes! Jimminy! what a jump!
        Flop—flop—an' plump
        To the ground with a thump!
Flutt'rin' an' flound'rin', all 'n a lump!"

As a demon is hurled by an angel's spear,
Heels over head, to his proper sphere,—
Heels over head, and head over heels,

Dizzily down the abyss he wheels,—
So fell Darius. Upon his crown,   180
In the midst of the barnyard, he came down,
In a wonderful whirl of tangled strings,
Broken tail and broken wings,
Shooting-stars, and various things!
Away with a bellow fled the calf,
And what was that? Did the gosling laugh?
          'Tis a merry roar
          From the old barn-door,
And he hears the voice of Jotham crying,
"Say, D'rius! how de yeou like flyin'?"   190

Slowly, ruefully, where he lay,
Darius just turned and looked that way,
As he stanched his sorrowful nose with his cuff.
"Wal, I like flyin' well enough,"
He said; "but the' ain't sich a thunderin' sight
O' fun in't when ye come to light."

MORAL

I just have room for the moral here:
And this is the moral,—Stick to your sphere.
Or if you insist, as you have the right,   200
On spreading your wings for a loftier flight,
The moral is,—Take care how you light.

                                                                    (1869)

Henry Timrod

1828–1867

The tag, "Poet Laureate of the Confederacy," has clung to Henry Timrod's name since his death in 1867. In many ways this appellation is apt. Louis D. Rubin, Jr. has written that "of all the poets North and South who penned lyrics having to do with the American Civil War, only three produced work that has survived its immediate occasion—Walt Whitman, Herman Melville, and Henry Timrod" (*Literary South* 195). Few would argue that Timrod was the most distinguished poet of the Confederacy. But Timrod deserves the title of laureate because of *his* history as well as that of the South. In the public turmoil of the war, Timrod "found the subject that could deepen his insight and extend the range of his sensibilities" (Rubin, *Literary South* 195).

Henry Timrod was born on 8 December 1828 in Charleston, South Carolina. By the age of twelve he matriculated to a classical school run by Christopher Cotes, where he met Paul Hamilton Hayne, who would become his lifelong friend, fellow poet and, after Timrod's death, his editor. After several failed efforts to train himself for a career in law and academics, he tutored at various lowland plantations, teaching off and on from 1850 until the beginning of the war. Timrod probably began writing serious poetry while still in school, and by 1846 his poems began to appear in Charleston newspapers.

During the 1850s, as he continued to tutor and write, Timrod joined the Russell's Bookshop Group in Charleston: an informal coterie of amateur (except for William Gilmore Simms) writers and academics who met regularly to discuss literature. The older, well-established Simms was the guiding spirit, and both Timrod and Hayne became important figures as well. In 1857, the group founded *Russell's Magazine* with Hayne as editor. The magazine was a godsend for Timrod; he published in it several important essays and numerous poems. This productive period culminated in the 1859 publication of Timrod's *Poems* by Ticknor and Fields, the only collection to appear in his lifetime.

The bombardment of Fort Sumter in Charleston Harbor on

12 April 1861 signaled a hectic and ultimately tragic period in the history of these Charleston literati as well as that of the South. Between 1860 and his death, Timrod tried twice to enlist in the Confederate army, was engaged to and married Kate Goodwin, saw the birth and death of his only child, served as a war correspondent and editor, suffered horribly from tuberculosis, and wrote his greatest poems.

Though Timrod wrote his best poetry during the Civil War, his earlier correspondence and essays prove that he was at the center of the literary life of his city and region. He wrote three important essays—"What Is Poetry?" "Theory of Poetry" (a reply to Poe's "Poetic Principle"), and "Literature in the South"—between 1857 and 1863. In "Literature in the South," he condemns the indifference with which the antebellum South treated its writers, labeling "the Southern author the Pariah of modern literature" (*Essays* 83).

Timrod's prewar poetry is softly sentimental. His two consistent concerns were nature and love, with an occasional venture into poetic theory in verse. Timrod apparently wrote poems to almost every woman who caught his eye. The early sonnet "Most Men Know Love" reveals his prewar obsession with romantic love and with the sonnet form.

Timrod's "Spring" (1863) marks the culmination of his second lifelong interest: nature. It took the war to both inspire Timrod's romantic melancholy and provide for it a dramatic public background. In "Spring," "I Know Not Why," "Ethnogenesis," and "The Unknown Dead," written between 1861 and 1866, he expressed in personal, concrete terms the tension of a new nation facing a violent and uncertain future. As in Whitman's *Drum-Taps*, the patriotism of Timrod's early war poems is eventually lost in the more somber tone of his last poems. The final outcome of the war deepens the pathos of personal lyrics like "I Know Not Why" and "The Unknown Dead." While Timrod's prewar poems are more abstract, more likely to contain rhetorical filler, the poems written after 1860 convey a desperate urgency and a sense of intense personal engagement that is missing from the earlier verse.

And that, ultimately, is what made Timrod's public poetry from the war years so compelling—the degree to which his personal fate mirrored that of the Confederacy. He died in Columbia, South Carolina, on 7 October 1867 and was buried there in the Trinity Churchyard.

Inspired by Timrod's personal tragedies as well as his verse, friend and poet Paul Hamilton Hayne found a publisher for and edited an 1873 collection of Timrod's poems. This last act of friendship proved significant as this edition saved many lesser-known poems for twentieth-century readers, readers who have re-affirmed Timrod's reputation as the "laureate of the Confederacy."

— *Terry Roberts*

Suggestions for Further Reading

DeBellis, Jack. "Henry Timrod." *Fifty Southern Writers Before 1900.* Ed. Robert Bain and Joseph M. Flora. New York: Greenwood, 1987. 464–72.*

Green, Claude B. "Henry Timrod and the South." *South Carolina Review* 2 (1970): 27–33.

Murphey, Christina. "The Artistic Design of Societal Commitment: Shakespeare and the Poetry of Henry Timrod." *Shakespeare and Southern Writers: A Study in Influence.* Jackson: UP of Mississippi, 1985. 29–47.

Parks, Edd Winfield. *Henry Timrod.* New York: Twayne, 1964.

Rubin, Louis D., Jr., ed. *The Literary South.* Baton Rouge: Louisiana State UP, 1986.

Rubin, Louis D., Jr. "The Poet Laureate of the Confederacy." *The Edge of the Swamp.* Baton Rouge: Louisiana State UP, 1989. 190–225.

Timrod, Henry. *The Essays of Henry Timrod.* Athens: U of Georgia P, 1942.

TEXT
The Collected Poems of Henry Timrod. Athens: U of Georgia P, 1965.

꧁꧂

Most Men Know Love

Most men know love but as a part of life;
They hide it in some corner of the breast,
Even from themselves; and only when they rest
In the brief pauses of that daily strife,
Wherewith the world might else be not so rife,
They draw it forth (as one draws forth a toy
To soothe some ardent, kiss-exacting boy)
And hold it up to sister, child, or wife.
Ah me! why may not love and life be one?
Why walk we thus alone, when by our side,   10
Love, like a visible God, might be our guide?

How would the marts grow noble! and the street,
Worn like a dungeon-floor by weary feet,
Seem then a golden court-way of the Sun!

(1859)

Ethnogenesis
*Written During the Meeting of the First Southern Congress,
at Montgomery, February, 1861*

I

Hath not the morning dawned with added light?
And shall not evening call another star
Out of the infinite regions of the night,
To mark this day in Heaven? At last, we are
A nation among nations; and the world
Shall soon behold in many a distant port
      Another flag unfurled!
Now, come what may, whose favor need we court?
And, under God, whose thunder need we fear?
     Thank Him who placed us here   10
Beneath so kind a sky—the very sun
Takes part with us; and on our errands run
All breezes of the ocean; dew and rain
Do noiseless battle for us; and the Year,
And all the gentle daughters in her train,
March in our ranks, and in our service wield
      Long spears of golden grain!
A yellow blossom as her fairy shield,
June flings her azure banner to the wind,
     While in the order of their birth   20
Her sisters pass, and many an ample field
Grows white beneath their steps, till now, behold
     Its endless sheets unfold
THE SNOW OF SOUTHERN SUMMERS! Let the earth
Rejoice! beneath those fleeces soft and warm
     Our happy land shall sleep
     In a repose as deep
As if we lay intrenched behind
Whole leagues of Russian ice and Arctic storm!

II

And what if, mad with wrongs themselves have wrought,   30
                In their own treachery caught,
                By their own fears made bold,
                And leagued with him of old,
Who long since in the limits of the North
Set up his evil throne, and warred with God—
What if, both mad and blinded in their rage,
Our foes should fling us down their mortal gage,
And with a hostile step profane our sod!
We shall not shrink, my brothers, but go forth
To meet them, marshaled by the Lord of Hosts,   40
And overshadowed by the mighty ghosts
    Of Moultrie and of Eutaw[1]—who shall foil
Auxiliars such as these? Nor these alone,
                But every stock and stone
                Shall help us; but the very soil,
And all the generous wealth it gives to toil,
And all for which we love our noble land,
Shall fight beside, and through us, sea and strand,
                The heart of woman, and her hand,
Tree, fruit, and flower, and every influence,   50
                Gentle, or grave, or grand;
                The winds in our defence
Shall seem to blow; to us the hills shall lend
                Their firmness and their calm;
And in our stiffened sinews we shall blend
                The strength of pine and palm!

III

Nor would we shun the battle-ground,
                Though weak as we are strong;
Call up the clashing elements around,
                And test the right and wrong!   60
On one side, creeds that dare to teach
What Christ and Paul refrained to preach;
Codes built upon a broken pledge,
And Charity that whets a poniard's edge;
Fair schemes that leave the neighboring poor
To starve and shiver at the schemer's door,

---

1. Revolutionary War battles at Fort Moultrie and Eutaw Springs in which
Southern Americans repelled the British.

While in the world's most liberal ranks enrolled,
He turns some vast philanthropy to gold;
Religion, taking every mortal form
But that a pure and Christian faith makes warm,   70
Where not to vile fanatic passion urged,
Or not in vague philosophies submerged,
Repulsive with all Pharisaic leaven,
And making laws to stay the laws of Heaven!
And on the other, scorn of sordid gain,
Unblemished honor, truth without a stain,
Faith, justice, reverence, charitable wealth,
And, for the poor and humble, laws which give,
Not the mean right to buy the right to live,
                But life, and home, and health!   80
To doubt the end were want of trust in God,
                Who, if he has decreed
        That we must pass a redder sea
Than that which rang to Miriam's holy glee,[2]
                Will surely raise at need
                A Moses with his rod!

IV

But let our fears—if fears we have—be still,
And turn us to the future! Could we climb
Some mighty Alp, and view the coming time,
                The rapturous sight would fill   90
                Our eyes with happy tears!
Not for the glories which a hundred years
Shall bring us; not for lands from sea to sea,
And wealth, and power, and peace, though these shall be;
But for the distant people we shall bless,
And the hushed murmurs of a world's distress:
        For, to give labor to the poor,
                The whole sad planet o'er,
And save from want and crime the humblest door,
Is one among the many ends for which   100
                God makes us great and rich!
The hour perchance is not yet wholly ripe
When all shall own it, but the type
Whereby we shall be known in every land
Is that vast gulf which laves our Southern strand,

---

2. Miriam, prophetess and sister of Moses, who led the children of Israel
through the Red Sea, Exodus 14.

And through the cold, untempered ocean pours
Its genial streams, that far off arctic shores
May sometimes catch upon the softened breeze
Strange tropic warmth and hints of summer seas!

(1861, 1873)

The Cotton Boll

While I recline
At ease beneath
This immemorial pine,
Small sphere!
(By dusky fingers brought this morning here
And shown with boastful smiles),
I turn thy cloven sheath,
Through which the soft white fibres peer,
That, with their gossamer bands,
Unite, like love, the sea-divided lands,   10
And slowly, thread by thread,
Draw forth the folded strands,
Than which the trembling line,
By whose frail help yon startled spider fled
Down the tall spear-grass from his swinging bed,
Is scarce more fine;
And as the tangled skein
Unravels in my hands,
Betwixt me and the noonday light,
A veil seems lifted, and for miles and miles   20
The landscape broadens on my sight,
As, in the little boll, there lurked a spell
Like that which, in the ocean shell,
With mystic sound,
Breaks down the narrow walls that hem us round,
And turns some city lane
Into the restless main,
With all his capes and isles!

Yonder bird,
Which floats, as if at rest,   30
In those blue tracts above the thunder, where
No vapors cloud the stainless air,
And never sound is heard,
Unless at such rare time

When, from the City of the Blest,
Rings down some golden chime,
Sees not from his high place
So vast a cirque of summer space
As widens round me in one mighty field,
Which, rimmed by seas and sands,   40
Doth hail its earliest daylight in the beams
Of gray Atlantic dawns;
And, broad as realms made up of many lands
Is lost afar
Behind the crimson hills and purple lawns
Of sunset, among plains which roll their streams
Against the Evening Star!
And lo!
To the remotest point of sight,
Although I gaze upon no waste of snow,   50
The endless field is white;
And the whole landscape glows,
For many a shining league away,
With such accumulated light
As Polar lands would flash beneath a tropic day!
Nor lack there (for the vision grows,
And the small charm within my hands—
More potent even than the fabled one,
Which oped whatever golden mystery
Lay hid in fairy wood or magic vale,   60
The curious ointment of the Arabian tale—[3]
Beyond all mortal sense
Doth stretch my sight's horizon, and I see,
Beneath its simple influence,
As if with Uriel's crown,[4]
I stood in some great temple of the Sun,
And looked, as Uriel, down!)
Nor lack there pastures rich and fields all green
With all the common gifts of God,
For temperate airs and torrid sheen   70
Weave Edens of the sod;
Through lands which look one sea of billowy gold
Broad rivers wind their devious ways;
A hundred isles in their embraces fold
A hundred luminous bays;
And through yon purple haze
Vast mountains lift their plumed peaks cloud-crowned;

---

3. Magic ointment which, when rubbed on the eyes, produced supernatural
eyesight.
    4. Uriel, guardian of the sun in *Paradise Lost*, Book 3.

Henry Timrod   281

And, save where up their sides the ploughman creeps,
An unhewn forest girds them grandly round,
In whose dark shades a future navy sleeps!   80
Ye Stars, which, though unseen, yet with me gaze
Upon this loveliest fragment of the earth!
Thou Sun, that kindlest all thy gentlest rays
Above it, as to light a favorite hearth!
Ye Clouds, that in your temples in the West
See nothing brighter than its humblest flowers!
And you, ye Winds, that on the ocean's breast
Are kissed to coolness ere ye reach its bowers!
Bear witness with me in my song of praise,
And tell the world that, since the world began,   90
No fairer land hath fired a poet's lays,
Or given a home to man!

But these are charms already widely blown!
His be the meed whose pencil's trace
Hath touched our very swamps with grace,
And round whose tuneful way
All Southern laurels bloom;
The Poet of "The Woodlands,"[5] unto whom
Alike are known
The flute's low breathing and the trumpet's tone,   100
And the soft west wind's sighs;
But who shall utter all the debt,
O Land wherein all powers are met
That bind a people's heart,
The world doth owe thee at this day,
And which it never can repay,
Yet scarcely deigns to own!
Where sleeps the poet who shall fitly sing
The source wherefrom doth spring
That mighty commerce which, confined   110
To the mean channels of no selfish mart,
Goes out to every shore
Of this broad earth, and throngs the sea with ships
That bear no thunders; hushes hungry lips
In alien lands;
Joins with a delicate web remotest strands;
And gladdening rich and poor,
Doth gild Parisian domes,

---

5. William Gilmore Simms, Southern poet and friend of Timrod's.
References are to his poem "The Edge of the Swamp" and his plantation "The
Woodlands."

Or feed the cottage-smoke of English homes,
And only bounds its blessings by mankind!   120
In offices like these, thy mission lies,
My Country! and it shall not end
As long as rain shall fall and Heaven bend
In blue above thee; though thy foes be hard
And cruel as their weapons, it shall guard
Thy hearth-stones as a bulwark; make thee great
In white and bloodless state;
And haply, as the years increase—
Still working through its humbler reach
With that large wisdom which the ages teach—   130
Revive the half-dead dream of universal peace!
As men who labor in that mine
Of Cornwall, hollowed out beneath the bed
Of ocean, when a storm rolls overhead,
Hear the dull booming of the world of brine
Above them, and a mighty muffled roar
Of winds and waters, yet toil calmly on,
And split the rock, and pile the massive ore,
Or carve a niche, or shape the arched roof;
So I, as calmly, weave my woof   140
Of song, chanting the days to come,
Unsilenced, though the quiet summer air
Stirs with the bruit of battles, and each dawn
Wakes from its starry silence to the hum
Of many gathering armies. Still,
In that we sometimes hear,
Upon the Northern winds, the voice of woe
Not wholly drowned in triumph, though I know
The end must crown us, and a few brief years
Dry all our tears,   150
I may not sing too gladly. To Thy will
Resigned, O Lord! we cannot all forget
That there is much even Victory must regret.
And, therefore, not too long
From the great burthen of our country's wrong
Delay our just release!
And, if it may be, save
These sacred fields of peace
From stain of patriot or of hostile blood!
Oh, help us, Lord! to roll the crimson flood   160
Back on its course, and, while our banners wing
Northward, strike with us! till the Goth shall cling
To his own blasted altar-stones, and crave

Mercy; and we shall grant it, and dictate
The lenient future of his fate
There, where some rotting ships and crumbling quays
Shall one day mark the Port which ruled the Western seas.[6]

(1861, 1873)

I Know Not Why

I know not why, but all this weary day,
Suggested by no definite grief or pain,
Sad fancies have been flitting through my brain:
Now it has been a vessel losing way
Rounding a stormy headland; now a gray
Dull waste of clouds above a wintry main;
And then a banner drooping in the rain,
And meadows beaten into bloody clay.
Strolling at random with this shadowy woe
At heart, I chanced to wander hither! Lo!   10
A league of desolate marsh-land, with its lush,
Hot grasses in a noisome, tide-left bed,
And faint, warm airs, that rustle in the hush
Like whispers round the body of the dead!

(1861, 1873)

Spring

Spring, with that nameless pathos in the air
Which dwells with all things fair,
Spring, with her golden suns and silver rain,
Is with us once again.

Out in the lonely woods the jasmine burns
Its fragrant lamps, and turns
Into a royal court with green festoons
The banks of dark lagoons.

In the deep heart of every forest tree
The blood is all aglee,   10

---

6. The "Port," New York harbor.

And there's a look about the leafless bowers
As if they dreamed of flowers.

Yet still on every side we trace the hand
Of Winter in the land,
Save where the maple reddens on the lawn,
Flushed by the season's dawn;

Or where, like those strange semblances we find
That age to childhood bind,
The elm puts on, as if in Nature's scorn,
The brown of Autumn corn.   20

As yet the turf is dark, although you know
That, not a span below,
A thousand germs are groping through the gloom,
And soon will burst their tomb.

Already, here and there, on frailest stems
Appear some azure gems,
Small as might deck, upon a gala day,
The forehead of a fay.

In gardens you may see, amid the dearth,
The crocus breaking earth;   30
And near the snowdrop's tender white and green,
The violet in its screen.

But many gleams and shadows need must pass
Along the budding grass,
And weeks go by, before the enamored South
Shall kiss the rose's mouth.

Still there's a sense of blossoms yet unborn
In the sweet airs of morn;
One almost looks to find the very street
Grow purple at his feet.   40

At times a fragrant breeze comes floating by,
And brings, you know not why,
A feeling as when eager crowds await
Before a palace gate

Some wondrous pageant; and you scarce would start,
If from a beech's heart

A blue-eyed Dryad, stepping forth, should say,
"Behold me! I am May!"

Ah! who would couple thoughts of war and crime
With such a blessed time!   50
Who in the west-wind's aromatic breath
Could hear the call of Death!

Yet not more surely shall the Spring awake
The voice of wood and brake
Than she shall rouse, for all her tranquil charms,
A million men to arms.

There shall be deeper hues upon her plains
Than all her sunlit rains,
And every gladdening influence around,
Can summon from the ground.   60

Oh! standing on this desecrated mould,
Methinks that I behold,
Lifting her bloody daisies up to God,
Spring kneeling on the sod,

And calling with the voice of all her rills
Upon the ancient hills,
To fall and crush the tyrants and the slaves
Who turn her meads to graves.

                                        (1863, 1873)

The Unknown Dead[7]

The rain is plashing on my sill,
But all the winds of Heaven are still;
And so it falls with that dull sound
Which thrills us in the church-yard ground,
When the first spadeful drops like lead
Upon the coffin of the dead.

---

7. Ironically, "The Unknown Dead" was first published in the *Southern Illustrated News* on 4 July 1863, the day of Lee's retreat from Gettysburg, the Confederate military disaster in which Lee's army suffered an estimated 20,000 casualties. The poem was not written in response to that particular battle, but rather out of the growing pessimism Timrod felt by this point in the war.

Beyond my streaming window-pane,
I cannot see the neighboring vane,
Yet from its old familiar tower
The bell comes, muffled, through the shower.   10
What strange and unsuspected link
Of feeling touched, has made me think—
While with a vacant soul and eye
I watch that gray and stony sky—
Of nameless graves on battle-plains
Washed by a single winter's rains,
Where, some beneath Virginian hills,
And some by green Atlantic rills,
Some by the waters of the West,
A myriad unknown heroes rest.   20
Ah! not the chiefs who, dying, see
Their flags in front of victory,
Or, at their life-blood's noble cost
Pay for a battle nobly lost,
Claim from their monumental beds
The bitterest tears a nation sheds.
Beneath yon lonely mound—the spot
By all save some fond few forgot—
Lie the true martyrs of the fight,
Which strikes for freedom and for right.   30
Of them, their patriot zeal and pride,
The lofty faith that with them died,
No grateful page shall farther tell
Than that so many bravely fell;
And we can only dimly guess
What worlds of all this world's distress,
What utter woe, despair, and dearth,
Their fate has brought to many a hearth.
Just such a sky as this should weep
Above them, always, where they sleep;   40
Yet, haply, at this very hour,
Their graves are like a lover's bower;
And Nature's self, with eyes unwet,
Oblivious of the crimson debt
To which she owes her April grace,
Laughs gaily o'er their burial place.

(1863, 1873)

Ode

*Sung on the Occasion of Decorating the Graves of the
Confederate Dead, at Magnolia Cemetery, Charleston, S.C., 1866*

Sleep sweetly in your humble graves,
    Sleep, martyrs of a fallen cause!—
Though yet no marble column craves
    The pilgrim here to pause.

In seeds of laurels in the earth,
    The garlands of your fame are sown;
And, somewhere, waiting for its birth,
    The shaft is in the stone.

Meanwhile, your sisters for the years
    Which hold in trust your storied tombs,   10
Bring all they now can give you—tears,
    And these memorial blooms.

Small tributes, but your shades will smile
    As proudly on these wreaths to-day,
As when some cannon-moulded pile
    Shall overlook this Bay.

Stoop, angels, hither from the skies!
    There is no holier spot of ground,
Than where defeated valor lies
    By mourning beauty crowned.   20

(1866, 1873)

Paul Hamilton Hayne
1830–1886

Although his health and fi-
nances were destroyed by the Civil War, Paul Hamilton Hayne
became the best known of postwar Southern poets. His adept
self-promotion from 1865 until his death in 1886 paid off in
national publication and recognition despite sectional preju-
dice.

Hayne was remarkable for his resiliency. He was born on New
Year's Day in 1830 to a distinguished Charleston family. A South-
ern patrician, he was devoted to the antebellum order and found
it difficult late in life to reconcile himself to the South's having
lost the war. Unlike other Southern writers, he was finally able to
recover from the ravages of that loss. Through his tireless corre-
spondence with Northern as well as Southern contemporaries—
Whittier, Longfellow, Holmes, Simms, Timrod, Thompson—he
managed to promote and publish his poetry for a national audi-
ence in an age wracked by regional strife. Despite losing home
and health during the war, he was able to move his family in 1866
to a pinewoods farm near Augusta, Georgia, that he named
Copse Hill. There, he and his family barely survived on his earn-
ings as a poet for twenty more years. Not only did he publish
three postwar collections of his own verse, including the col-
lected *Poems* in 1882, but he was also able to use his influence to
edit and publish the *Poems of Henry Timrod* in 1873. When he died
on 6 July 1886 after years of declining health, he was honored
with an elaborate public burial in the Magnolia Cemetery in
Augusta.

Hayne and his family suffered tremendous privation during
the postwar years at Copse Hill. His correspondence, which is as
significant as his poetry, records years of poverty and illness
shared with a devoted wife and son. It is perhaps because of
these difficulties that Hayne's poetry suffers from a lack of objec-
tivity. At its worst, it is self-absorbed and tritely romantic. As
Rayburn S. Moore described them, many of the poems "smack
of the lamp rather than of life" (*Hayne* 167). Despite this, his
collected *Poems* is an important book because it captures in its

very bulk the amount of competent verse that Hayne wrote during his life.

Hayne divided this large collection into sections that suggest his lifelong interests. He was fascinated, for example, with the sonnet. "Death's Self" (an unusually dramatic lyric) and "Of all the woodland flowers of spring" are poems representative of this interest. "Aspects of the Pines" and "The Mockingbird" were written at Copse Hill and bear the stamp of this pastoral postwar period of Hayne's life. It seems likely that Hayne intended the few natural elements in these poems—the jasmine, the mockingbird, the long-leaf pines—to identify this landscape as Southern. In addition to his nature poetry, Hayne wrote a number of "Dramatic Sketches" and "Poems of the War," most of which have not stood the test of time.

Though he is often dismissed by modern scholars, Hayne was not an entirely derivative poet. There is evidence that he was willing to experiment with form and rhyme, if only within traditional parameters. He often shows the influence of Poe as well as the Fireside poets. The startlingly modern "Fire Pictures" proves that Hayne cannot be uniformly dismissed. Here Hayne's attention to sound and use of the refrain are hauntingly Poe-esque, and his series of sensuous vignettes anticipates the imagists. Unfortunately, the power of "Fire-Pictures" is the exception rather than the rule for Hayne.

Despite the attention Hayne received in the postwar years, he was a holdover from an earlier era. As distasteful as he found Whitman, Whitman represented the future. By 1882, the year of Hayne's *Poems*, Whitman's *Leaves of Grass* had gone through seven editions and was approaching the form that would bury Hayne and so many of his contemporaries. For the majority of modern readers, Hayne's letters are more significant than his poems. He did, however, produce several lyrics of undeniable power. His "Fire-Pictures," for example, burns just as vividly today as it did in 1872.

—*Terry Roberts*

Suggestions For Further Reading

Hayne, Paul Hamilton. *A Man of Letters in the Nineteenth-Century South: Selected Letters of Paul Hamilton Hayne.* Ed. Rayburn S. Moore. Baton Rouge: Louisiana State UP, 1982.

Moore, Rayburn S. "Paul Hamilton Hayne." *Fifty Southern Writers Before 1900.* Ed. Robert Bain and Joseph M. Flora. New York: Greenwood, 1987. 240–49.*

———. *Paul Hamilton Hayne.* New York: Twayne, 1972.

Young, Thomas Daniel. "How Time Has Served Two Southern Poets: Paul Hamilton Hayne and Sidney Lanier." *Southern Literary Journal* 6 (Fall 1973): 101–10.

TEXT
Poems. 1882.

ᓄᐩᕊ

By the Grave of Henry Timrod[1]

When last we parted—thy frail hand in mine—
    Above us smiled September's passionless sky,
And touched by fragrant airs, the hillside pine
    Thrilled in the mellow sunshine tenderly;
        So rich the robe on nature's slow decay,
We scarce could deem the winter tide was near,
    Or lurking death, masked in imperial grace;
        Alas! that autumn day
Drew not more close to winter's empire drear
    Than thou, my heart! to meet grief face to face!   10

I clasped thy tremulous hand, nor marked how weak
    Its answering grasp; and if thine eyes did swim
In unshed tears, and on thy fading cheek
    Rested a nameless shadow, gaunt and dim,—
        My soul was blind; fear had not touched her
            sight
To awful vision; so, I bade thee go,
    Careless, and tranquil as that treacherous morn;
        Nor dreamed how soon the blight
Of long-implanted seeds of care would throw
    Their nightshade flowers above the springing corn. 20

Since then, full many a year hath risen and set,
    With spring-tide showers, and autumn pomps
    unfurled
O'er gorgeous woods, and mountain walls of jet—
    While love and loss, alternate, ruled the world;
        Till now once more we meet—my friend
        and I—

---

1. Hayne's friend and fellow poet Timrod died in Columbia on 7 October 1867 and was buried there in the Trinity Churchyard. Hayne apparently wrote the poem in January of 1874 after visiting Timrod's grave. In the opening lines, Hayne recalls their last visit at Copse Hill in September 1867.

Once more, once more—and thus, alas! we meet—
    Above, a rayless heaven; beneath, a grave;
        Oh, Christ! and dost thou lie
Neglected here, in thy worn burial-sheet?
    Friend! were there none to shield thee, none to
        save?   30

Ask of the winter winds—scarce colder they
    Than that strange land—thy birth-place and thy
    tomb:
Ask of the sombre cloud-wracks trooping gray,
    And grim as hooded ghosts at stroke of doom;
        At least, the winds, though chill, with gentler
        sweep
Seem circling round and o'er thy place of rest,
    While the sad clouds, as clothed in tenderer guise,
        Do lowly bend, and weep
O'er the dead poet, in whose living breast
    Dumb nature found a voice, how sweet and wise!   40

Once more we meet, once more—my friend and I—
    But ah! his hand is dust, his eyes are dark;
Thy merciless weight, thou dread mortality,
    From out his heart hath crushed the latest spark
        Of that warm life, benignly bright and
        strong;
Yet no; we have *not* met—my friend and I—
    Ashes to ashes in this earthly prison!
        Are these, O child of song,
Thy glorious self, heir of the stars and sky?
    Thou are not here, not *here*, for thou hast risen!   50

Death gave thee wings, and lo! thou hast soared above
    All human utterance and all finite thought;
Pain may not hound thee through that realm of love,
    Nor grief, wherewith thy mortal days were fraught,
        Load thee again—nor vulture want, that fed
Even on thy heart's blood, wound thee; idle, then,
    Our bitter sorrowing; what though bleak and wild
        Rests thine uncrowned head?
Known art thou now to angels and to men—
    Heaven's saint and earth's brave singer undefiled.   60

Even as I spake in broken under-breath
    The winds drooped lifeless; faintly struggling
    through

The heaven-bound pall, which seemed a pall of death,
          One cordial sunbeam cleft the opening blue;
                    Swiftly it glanced, and settling, softly shone
O'er the grave's head; in that same instant came
          From the near copse a bird-song half divine;
                    "Heart," said I, "hush thy moan,
List the bird's singing, mark the heaven-born flame,
          God-given are these—an omen and a sign!"   70

In the bird's song an omen *his* must live!
          In the warm glittering of that golden beam,
A sign his soul's majestic hopes survive,
          Raised to fruition o'er life's weary dream.
                    So now I leave him, low, yet, restful here;
So now I leave him, high-exalted, far
          Beyond all memory of earth's guilt or guile;
                    Hark! tis his voice of cheer,
Dropping, methinks, from some mysterious star;
          His face I see, and on his face—a smile!   80

                                                (1874, 1875)

Fire-Pictures[2]

          O! The rolling, rushing fire!
                    O! the fire!
          How it rages, wilder, higher,
          Like a hot heart's fierce desire,
          Thrilled with passion that appalls us,
          Half appalls, and yet enthralls us,
                    O! the madly mounting fire!

Up it sweepeth,—wave and quiver,—
Roaring like an angry river,—
                    O! the fire!   10
Which an earthquake backward turneth,
Backward o'er its riven courses,
Backward to its mountain sources,
While the blood-red sunset burneth,
Like a God's face grand with ire,
                    O! the bursting, billowy fire!
Now the sombre smoke-clouds thicken

---

2. Rayburn S. Moore argues that this poem serves as evidence of "Poe's influence on his younger contemporaries."

To a dim Plutonian night;—
　　　O! the fire!
How its flickering glories sicken,　　　　　　　　20
Sicken at the blight!
Pales the flame, and spreads the vapor,
Till scarce larger than a taper,
Flares the waning, struggling light:
O! thou wan, faint-hearted fire,
　　　　　Sadly darkling,
　　　　　Weakly sparkling,
　　　Rise! assert thy might!
　　　Aspire! aspire!

At the word, a vivid lightning,　　　　　　　　　30
Threatening, swaying, darting, brightening,
Where the loftiest yule-log towers,—
　　　　　Bursts once more,
Sudden bursts the awakened fire;
　　　　　Hear it roar!
Roar, and mount high, high, and higher,
　　　　　Till beneath,
Only here and there a wreath
Of the passing smoke-cloud lowers,—
　　　Ha! the glad, victorious fire!　　　　　　　40

　　　O! the fire!
　　　How it changes,
　　　Changes, ranges
Through all phases fancy-wrought,
Changes like a wizard thought;
See Vesuvian lavas rushing
'Twixt the rocks! the ground asunder
Shivers at the earthquake's thunder;
And the glare of Hell is flushing
Startled hill-top, quaking town;　　　　　　　　50
Temples, statues, towers go down,
While beyond that lava flood,
Dark-red like blood,
I behold the children fleeting
Clasped by many a frenzied hand;
What a flight, and what a meeting,
On the ruined strand!

　　　　O! the fire!
Eddying higher, higher, higher
From the vast volcanic cones;　　　　　　　　　60

O! the agony, the groans
Of those thousands stifling there!
"Fancy," say you? but how near
Seem the anguish and the fear!
Swelling, turbulent, pitiless fire:
'Tis a mad northeastern breeze
Raving o'er the prairie seas;
How, like living things, the grasses
Tremble as the storm-breath passes,
Ere the flames' devouring magic   70
Coils about their golden splendor,
   And the tender
Glory of the mellowing fields
To the wild destroyer yields;
Dreadful waste for flowering blooms,
Desolate darkness, like the tomb's,
Over which there broods the while,
Instead of daylight's happy smile,
A pall malign and tragic!

   Marvellous fire!   80
   Changing, ranging
Through all phases fancy-wrought,
Changing like a charmed thought;
A stir, a murmur deep,
Like airs that rustle over jungle-reeds,
Where the gaunt tiger breathes but half asleep;
   A bodeful stir,—
And then the victim of his own pure deeds,
   I mark the mighty fire
Clasps in its cruel palms a martyr-saint,   90
   Christ's faithful worshipper;
One mortal cry affronts the pitying day,
One ghastly arm uplifts itself to heaven—
When the swart smoke is riven,—
Ere the last sob of anguish dies away,
The worn limbs droop and faint,
And o'er those reverend hairs, silvery and hoary,
Settles the semblance of a crown of glory.

   Tireless fire!
   Changing, ranging   100
Through all phases fancy-wrought,
Changing like a Protean thought;
Here's a glowing, warm interior,
A Dutch tavern, rich and rosy

With deep color,—sill and floor
Dazzling as the white seashore,
Where within his armchair cozy
Sits a toper, stout and yellow,
Blinking o'er his steamy bowl;
           Hugely drinking,   110
           Slyly winking,
As the pot-house Hebe passes,
With a clink and clang of glasses;
Ha! 'tis plain, the stout old fellow—
As his wont is—waxes mellow,
Nodding 'twixt each dreamy leer,
Swaying in his elbow chair,
Next to one,—a portly peasant,—
Pipe in hand, whose swelling cheek,
Jolly, rubicund, and sleek,   120
Puffs above the blazing coal;
While his heavy, half-shut, eyes
Watch the smoke-wreaths evanescent,
Eddying lightly as they rise,
Eddying lightly and aloof
Toward the great, black, oaken roof!

Dreaming still, from out the fire
Faces grinning and grotesque,
Flash an eery glance upon me;
Or, once more, methinks I sun me   130
On the breadths of happy plain
Sloping towards the southern main,
Where the inmost soul of shadow
           Wins a golden heat,
And the hill-side and the meadow
(Where the vines and clover meet,
Twining round the virgins' feet,
While the natural arabesque
Of the foliage grouped above them
Droops, as if the leaves did love them,   140
Over brow, and lips, and eyes)
Gleam with hints of paradise!

          Ah! the fire!
          Gently glowing,
          Fairly flowing,
Like a rivulet rippling deep
Through the meadow-lands of sleep,
Bordered where its music swells,

By the languid lotos-bells,
And the twilight asphodels;   150
Mingled with a richer boon
Of queen-lilies, each a moon,
Orbed into white completeness;
O! the perfume! the rare sweetness
Of those grouped and fairy flowers,
Over which the love-lorn hours
Linger,—not alone for them,
Though the lotos swings its stem
With a lulling stir of leaves,—
Though the lady-lily waves,   160
And a silvery undertune
From some mystic wind-song grieves
Dainty sweet amid the bells
Of the twilight asphodels;
But because a charm more rare
Glorifies the mellow air,
In the gleam of lifted eyes,
In the tranquil ecstasies
Of two lovers, leaf-embowered,
             Lingering there,   170
Each of whose fair lives hath flowered,
Like the lily-petals finely,
Like the asphodel divinely.

          Titan arches!
          Titan spires!
Pillars whose vast capitals
Towe toward Cyclopean halls,
And whose unknown bases pierce
Down the nether universe;
Countless coruscations glimmer,   180
Glow and darken, wane and shimmer,
'Twixt majestic standards, swooping,—
Like the wings of some strange bird
By mysterious currents stirred
Of great winds,—or darkly drooping,
In a hush sublime as death,
When the conflict's quivering breath
Sobs its gory life away,
At the close of fateful marches,
On an empire's natal day: 190
Countless coruscations glimmer,
Glow and darken, wane and shimmer,
Round the shafts, and round the walls,

Whence an ebon splendor falls
On the scar-seamed, angel bands,—
             (Desolate bands!)
Grasping in their ghostly hands
Weapons of an antique rage,
From some lost, celestial age,
When the serried throngs were hurled   200
Blasted to the under world:
Shattered spear-heads, broken brands,
And the mammoth, moonlike shields,
Blazoned on their lurid fields,
With uncouth, malignant forms,
             Glowering, wild,
Like the huge cloud-masses piled
Up a Heaven of storms!
             * * * * *

Ah, the faint and flickering fire!
             Ah, the fire!   210
Like a young man's transient ire,
Like an old man's last desire,
Lo! it falters, dies!
Still, through weary, half-closed lashes,
             Still I see,
       But brokenly, but mistily,
             Fall and rise,
             Rise and fall,
       Ghosts of shifting fantasy;
Now the embers, smouldered all,   220
Send to ruin; sadder dreams
Follow on their vanished gleams;
Wailingly the spirits call,
Spirits on the night-winds solemn,
Wraiths of happy Hopes that left me;
(Cruel! why did ye depart?)
Hopes that sleep, their youthful riot
Merged in an awful quiet,
With the heavy grief-moulds pressed
On each pallid, pulseless breast,   230
In that graveyard called THE HEART,
             Stern and lone.
       Needing no memorial stone,
       And no blazoned column:
             Let them rest!
             Let them rest!
Yes, 'tis useless to remember
May-morn in the mirk December;

Still, O Hopes! because ye were
Beautiful, and strong, and fair,   240
Nobly brave, and sweetly bright,
            Who shall dare
Scorn me, if through moistened lashes,
Musing by my hearthstone blighted,
Weary, desolate, benighted,—
I, because those sweet Hopes left me,
I, because my fate bereft me,
            Mourn my dead,
            Mourn,—and shed
    Hot tears in the ashes?   250
                                                        (1871, 1872)

Sonnet

Of all the woodland flowers of earlier spring,
These golden jasmines, each an air-hung bower,
Meet for the Queen of Fairies' tiring hour,
Seem loveliest and most fair in blossoming;
How yonder mock-bird thrills his fervid wing
And long, lithe throat, where twinkling flower on flower
Rains the globed dewdrops down, a diamond shower,
O'er his brown head poised as in act to sing;
Lo! the swift sunshine floods the flowery urns,
Girding their delicate gold with matchless light,   10
Till the blent life of bough, leaf, blossom, burns;
Then, then outbursts the mock-bird clear and loud,
Half-drunk with perfume, veiled by radiance bright,
A star of music in a fiery cloud!
                                                        (1871, 1872)

Aspects of the Pines

Tall, sombre, grim, against the morning sky
            They rise, scarce touched by melancholy airs,
Which stir the fadeless foliage dreamfully,
            As if from realms of mystical despairs.

Tall, sombre, grim, they stand with dusky gleams
            Brightening to gold within the woodland's core,

Beneath the gracious noontide's tranquil beams—
　　But the weird winds of morning sigh no more.

A stillness, strange, divine, ineffable,
　　Broods round and o'er them in the wind's surcease, 10
And on each tinted copse and shimmering dell
　　Rests the mute rapture of deep hearted peace.

Last, sunset comes—the solemn joy and might
　　Borne from the West when cloudless day declines—
Low, flutelike breezes sweep the waves of light,
　　And lifting dark green tresses of the pines.

Till every lock is luminous—gently float,
　　Fraught with hale odors up the heavens afar
To faint when twilight on her virginal throat
　　Wears for a gem the tremulous vesper star.　　20

(1872, 1875)

The Mocking-Bird at Night

A golden pallor of voluptuous light
Filled the warm southern night:
The moon, clear orbed, above the sylvan scene
Moved like a stately queen,
So rife with conscious beauty all the while,
What could she do but smile
At her own perfect loveliness below,
Glassed in the tranquil flow
Of crystal fountains and unruffled streams?
Half lost in waking dreams,　　　　　　　　　　10
As down the loneliest forest dell I strayed,
Lo! from a neighboring glade,
Flashed through the drifts of moonshine, swiftly came
A fairy shape of flame.
It rose in dazzling spirals overhead,
Whence to wild sweetness wed,
Poured marvellous melodies, silvery trill on trill;
The very leaves grew still
On the charmed trees to hearken; while for me,
Heart-trilled to ecstasy,　　　　　　　　　　　20
I followed—followed the bright shape that flew,
Still circling up the blue,

Till as a fountain that has reached its height,
Falls back in sprays of light
Slowly dissolved, so that enrapturing lay,
Divinely melts away
Through tremulous spaces to a music-mist,
Soon by the fitful breeze
    How gently kissed
Into remote and tender silences.   30
                                            (1882)

Death's Self

The thought of death walks ever by my side,
    It walks in sunshine, and it walks in shade,
    A thing protean, by strange fancies made
Lovely or loathsome, dark or glorified.
But past such fantasies Death's self must hide,
    While his dread hour to smite is still delayed,
    Like a masked Presence in a cypress glade,
By all save heaven's keen vision undescried.
For me what final aspect shalt thou take,
    O Death? Or shalt thou take no shape at all,   10
    But viewless, soundless, on my spirit fall,
    Soft as the sleep-balm of a summer's night,
From which the flower-like soul, new-born, shall wake
    In God's fair gardens on the hills of light?
                                  (1885, 1972)

Helen Hunt Jackson
1830–1885

Helen Hunt Jackson is probably most famous today for her novel *Ramona* (1884), a sentimental local-color romance that championed Native American rights. Modern readers may also know Jackson as a friend of Emily Dickinson. Thomas Wentworth Higginson considered Jackson the best American woman poet of her time, with Dickinson her only rival. Ralph Waldo Emerson thought her better than most male poets, a rare compliment. Emerson wrote that Jackson's poem's "have rare merit of thought and expression, and will reward the reader for the careful attention which they require" (*Parnassus*, qtd. in Higginson). Despite these encomiums, Jackson's poetry languished in obscurity soon after her death.

Jackson's personal life was tainted by misfortune. Helen Maria Fiske (her maiden name) was born in Amherst, Massachusetts, on 14 October 1830 to minister, college professor, and writer Nathan Welby Fiske and Deborah Vinal Fiske, a religious, well-educated woman. Both parents died of tuberculosis while Helen was a teenager. At twenty-two, she married Captain (afterwards Major) Edward Bissell Hunt and had two sons, one of whom died in infancy. Hunt was killed in 1863 while testing a torpedo he had invented. Two years later, Helen's son Rennie died of diptheria, and she began writing poetry to express her despair. Her early poems express a grief common in an age plagued by tuberculosis and other diseases.

Jackson's first published adult poem, "A Key to the Casket," was signed "Marah" and published in the *New York Evening Post* 9 June 1865. Her next published poem, "Lifted Over" (*Nation* 20 July 1865), also concerned the death of her son. Both poems brought her recognition. She followed these with several more poems, most of which dealt with sorrow and loss, in *Nation* and the New York *Independent*. Although she paid to have *Verses*, her first book of poems published (1870), four years later Roberts Brothers issued a well-received enlarged version.

In 1875, Jackson married William Sharpless Jackson, a Quaker businessman, in Colorado Springs, Colorado, where she lived and wrote until her death. Writing as "Saxe Holm," Jackson published two story collections, and as "No Name," two novels:

Mercy Philbrick's Choice (1876) and *Hetty's Strange History* (1877). She also wrote three children's books during this time. Jackson spent her later years protesting the ill treatment of Native Americans by the U.S. Government.

Jackson died of cancer on 12 August 1885. She is buried in the Evergreen Cemetery in Colorado Springs. Shortly after Jackson's death, Emily Dickinson appears to have written Jackson's husband this note: "Helen of Troy will die, but Helen of Colorado, never. Dear friend, can you walk, were the last words I wrote her. Dear friend, I can fly—her immortal (soaring) reply" (Johnson 325). Besides her collection of verse, three novels featuring powerful female characters appeared posthumously.

Jackson's best poems exude the homely appeal of Whitman, a sprightly tone and attention to natural detail reminiscent of Dickinson, and a refreshing lack of the intellectual pretension in which the more scholarly poets indulged. Such poems as "A Woman's Death Wound" display anger and hurt honestly. Jackson often struggles to break out of a singsong rhythm. The first five sestets of "My Legacy" have a regular, exact rhyme with consistently alternating iambic pentameter and iambic trimeter rhythm. Jackson alters the last stanza's meter in an admirable, if somewhat awkward, attempt to emphasize her final idea. Her sonnet "Thought," Emerson's favorite of all her poems, has consistently patterned, exact rhyme. One pair of rhymes, "mockery" and "prophecy," resonates especially well because their opposing ideas contrast with their similar sounds. Sound and sense clash; the reader pauses. More interesting than her triumph over an ironclad poetic framework in "Thought" is Jackson's success at expressing abstraction in concrete terms. Her language, while formal and old fashioned, contrasts strikingly with her expression of a common human experience: frustration at the mind's inability to call up thoughts at will.

E. C. Stedman wrote of Jackson shortly after her death that her poems, although well-received, "lack the variety of mood which betokens an inborn and always dominant poetic faculty" (445). Soon after her death, Jackson's poetry was going out of style; today, much of her poetry is far too sentimental to be considered modern. Nonetheless, modern readers will discover in Jackson's poetry a refreshing clarity and simplicity.

—*Lisa Carl*

Suggestions for Further Reading

Banning, Evelyn I. *Helen Hunt Jackson*. New York: Vanguard Press, 1973.*

Higginson, Thomas Wentworth. *Contemporaries*. Boston: Houghton, 1899. 142–67.

Johnson, Thomas H., ed. *Emily Dickinson: Selected Letters*. Cambridge: Harvard UP, 1958.

Stedman, E. C. *Poets of America*. Boston: Houghton, 1890.

Whitaker, Rosemary. *Helen Hunt Jackson*. Boise: Boise State U, 1987.*

TEXTS
Verses by H. H. 1874.
Sonnets and Lyrics. 1886.

꒐ꉈ

Thought

O Messenger, art thou the king, or I?
Thou dalliest outside the palace gate
Till on thine idle armor lie the late
And heavy dews: the morn's bright, scornful eye
Reminds thee; then in subtle mockery,
Thou smilest at the window where I wait,
Who bade thee ride for life. In empty state
My days go on, while false hours prophecy
Thy quick return; at last, in sad despair,
I cease to bid thee, leave thee free as air;   10
When lo, thou stand'st before me glad and fleet,
And lay'st undreamed-of treasures at my feet.
Ah! messenger, thy royal blood to buy,
I am too poor. Thou art the king, not I.

(1874)

Spinning

Like a blind spinner in the sun,
    I tread my days;
I know that all the threads will run
    Appointed ways;
I know each day will bring its task,
    And, being blind, no more I ask.

I do not know the use or name
    Of that I spin:
I only know that some one came,
    And laid within   10

My hand the thread, and said, "Since you
Are blind, but one thing you can do."

Sometimes the threads so rough and fast
    And tangled fly,
I know wild storms are sweeping past,
    And fear that I
Shall fall; but dare not try to find
A safer place, since I am blind.

I know not why, but I am sure
    That tint and place,   20
In some great fabric to endure
    Past time and race,
My threads will have; so from the first,
Though blind, I never felt accurst.

I think, perhaps, this trust has sprung
    From one short word
Said over me when I was young,—
    So young, I heard
It, knowing not that God's name signed
My brow, and sealed me His, though blind.   30

But whether this be seal or sign
    Within, without,
It matters not. The bond divine
    I never doubt.
I know he set me here, and still,
And glad, and blind, I wait His will;

But listen, listen, day by day,
    To hear their tread
Who bear the finished web away,
    And cut the thread,   40
And bring God's message in the sun,
"Thou poor blind spinner, work is done."

                                              (1874)

Gondolieds

I. Yesterday

Dear Yesterday, glide not so fast;
    O, let me cling

To thy white garments floating past;
Even to shadows which they cast
    I cling, I cling.
    Show me thy face
Just once, once more; a single night
Cannot have brought a loss, a blight
    Upon its grace.

Nor are they dead whom thou dost bear,   10
    Robed for the grave.
See what a smile their red lips wear;
To lay them living wilt thou dare
    Into a grave?
    I know, I know,
I left thee first; now I repent;
I listen now; I never meant
        To have thee go.

Just once, once more, tell me the word
    Thou hadst for me!   20
Alas! although my heart was stirred,
I never fully knew or heard
    It was for me.
    O yesterday,
My yesterday, thy sorest pain,
Were joy couldst thou but come again,—
    Sweet yesterday.
                        (written 26 May 1874, 1874)

II. To-morrow

All red with joy the waiting west,
    O little swallow,
Couldst thou tell me which road is best?   30
Cleaving high air with thy soft breast
    For keel, O swallow,
    Thou must o'erlook
My seas and know if I mistake;
I would not the same harbour make
    Which yesterday forsook.

I hear the swift blades dip and plash
    Of unseen rowers;
On unknown land the waters dash;
Who knows how it be wise or rash   40

To meet the rowers!
    Premi! Premi!
Venetia's boatmen lean and cry;
With voiceless lips, I drift and lie
Upon the twilight sea.

The swallow sleeps. Her last low call
    Had sound of warning.
Sweet little one, whate'er befall,
Thou wilt not know that it was all
    In vain thy warning.   50
    I may not borrow
A hope, a help. I close my eyes;
Cold wind blows from the Bridge of Sighs;
Kneeling I wait to-morrow.

                (written 30 May 1874, 1874)

Ariadne's Farewell

The daughter of a king, how should I know
That there were tinsels wearing face of gold,
And worthless glass, which in the sunlight's hold
Could shameless answer back my diamond's glow
With cheat of kindred fire? The currents slow,
And deep, and strong, and stainless, which had rolled
Through royal veins for ages, what had told
To them that hasty heat and lie could show
As quick and warm a red as theirs? Go free!   10
The sun is breaking on the sea's blue shield
Its golden lances; by their gleam I see
Thy ship's white sails. Go free, if scorn can yield
Thee freedom!
Then, alone, my love and I,—
We both are royal; we know how to die.

                    (1874)

Coronation

At the king's gate the subtle noon
    Wove filmy yellow nets of sun;

Into the drowsy snare too soon
  The guards fell one by one.

Through the king's gate, unquestioned then,
  A beggar went, and laughed, "This brings
Me chance, at last, to see if men
  Fare better, being kings."

The king sat bowed beneath his crown,
  Propping his face with listless hand;   10
Watching the hour-glass sifting down
  Too slow its shining sand.

"Poor man, what wouldst thou have of me?"
  The beggar turned, and pitying,
Replied, like one in dream, "Of thee,
  Nothing. I want the king."

Uprose the king, and from his head
  Shook off the crown, and threw it by.
"O man, thou must have known," he said,
  "A greater king than I."   20

Through all the gates, unquestioned then,
  Went king and beggar hand in hand.
Whispered the king, "Shall I know when
  Before *his* throne I stand?"

The beggar laughed. Free winds in haste
  Were wiping from the king's hot brow
The crimson lines the crown had traced.
  "This is his presence now."

At the king's gate, the crafty noon
  Unwove its yellow nets of sun;   30
Out of their sleep in terror soon
  The guards waked one by one.

"Ho here! Ho there! Has no man seen
  The king?" The cry ran to and fro;
Beggar and king, they laughed, I ween,
  The laugh that free men know.

On the king's gate the moss grew gray;
  The king came not. They called him dead;

And made his eldest son one day
    Slave in his father's stead.   40

(1874)

My Legacy

They told me I was heir, I turned in haste,
    And ran to seek my treasure,
And wondered as I ran, how it was placed,—
    If I should find a measure
Of gold, or if the titles of fair lands
And houses would be laid within my hands.

I journeyed many roads; I knocked at gates;
    I spoke to each wayfarer
I met, and said, "A heritage awaits
    Me. Art not thou the bearer   10
Of news? Some message sent to me whereby
I learn which way my new possessions lie?"

Some asked me in; naught lay beyond their door;
    Some smiled and would not tarry,
But said that men were just behind who bore
    More gold than I could carry;
And so the morn, the noon, the day were spent,
While empty handed up and down I went.

At last one cried, whose face I could not see,
    As through the mists he hasted;   20
"Poor child, what evil ones have hindered thee,
    Till this whole day is wasted?
Hath no man told thee that thou art joint heir
With one named Christ, who waits the goods to share?"

This one named Christ I sought for many days,
    In many places vainly;
I heard men name his name in many ways;
    I saw his temples plainly;
But they who named him most gave me no sign
To find him by, or prove the heirship mine.   30

And when at last I stood before his face,
    I knew him by no token

Save subtle air of joy which filled the place;
    Our greeting was not spoken;
In solemn silence I received my share,
Kneeling before my brother and "joint heir."

My share! To-day men call it grief and death;
    I see the joy and life to-morrow;
I thank our Father with my every breath,
    For this sweet legacy of sorrow;   40
And through my tears I call to each, "Joint heir
With Christ, make haste to ask him for thy share."

                                              (1874)

The Gods Said Love Is Blind

The gods said Love is blind. The earth was young
With foolish, youthful laughter when it heard;
It caught and spoke the letter of the words,
And from that time till now hath said and sung,
"Oh, Love is blind! The falsest face and tongue
Can cheat him, once his passion's thrill is stirred:
He is so blind, poor Love!"
                    Strange none demurred
At this, nor saw how hollow false it rang,
When all men know that sightless men can tell   10
Unnumbered things which vision cannot find.
Powers of the air are leagued to guide them well;
And things invisible weave clew and spell
By which all labyrinths they safely wind.
Ah, we were lost, if Love had not been blind!

                                              (1886)

A Woman's Death Wound

It left upon her tender flesh no trace.
The murderer is safe. As swift as light
The weapon fell, and, in the summer night,
Did scarce the silent, dewy air displace;
'Twas but a word. A blow had been less base.
Like dumb beast branded by an iron white
With heat, she turned in blind and helpless flight,

But then remembered, and with piteous face
Came back.
Since then, the world has nothing missed   10
In her, in voice or smile. But she—each day
She counts until her dying be complete.
One moan she makes, and ever doth repeat:
"O lips that I have loved and kissed and kissed,
Did I deserve to die this bitterest way?"

(1886)

Semitones

Ah me, the subtle boundary between
What pleases and what pains! The difference
Between the word that thrills our every sense
With joy and one which hurts, although it mean
No hurt! It is the things that are unseen,
Invisible, not things of violence,
For which the mightiest are without defence.
On kine most fair to see one may grow lean
With hunger. Many a snowy bread is doled
Which is far harder than the hardest stones.   10
'Tis but a narrow line that divides the zones
Where suns are warm from those where suns are cold.
'Twixt harmonies divine as chords can hold
And torturing discords, lie but semitones!

(1886)

Edmund Clarence Stedman

1833–1908

Edmund Clarence Stedman, New York poet and critic, spent his life defining and defending American poetry. He coined the phrase "twilight period" to describe the late-nineteenth-century literary scene during which realistic and naturalistic fiction usurped poetry as America's innovative art form. For Stedman, poetry was the more important art, and he sought to revive the faltering form through his criticism, his support of other poets, and his own writing. He became the "unofficial poet laureate" of the United States with his popular occasional and dedicatory poems. He advocated a more scientific criticism that separated a writer's life and morality from his aesthetic achievement, and in doing so, introduced Poe and Whitman into the American canon. While Stedman himself never reached the poetic excellence of Poe, Dickinson, or Whitman, his efforts on behalf of American literature paved the way for later poets.

E. C. Stedman, born in Hartford, Connecticut, on 8 October 1833, was raised by his Calvinist great-uncle. Entering Yale at fifteen, he was expelled two years later for misconduct. He then studied classics and literature on his own while working as journalist for Horace Greeley's *New York Tribune*, as a war correspondent during the Civil War, and finally as businessman on Wall Street. Once settled in New York, Stedman juggled a business and a literary career. He wrote or edited numerous critical works such as *Poets of America* (1885) and *A Library of American Literature* (1888–90), both influential works on American literature and criticism. Stedman also kept an open house for poets and friends, among them Bayard Taylor, Lizette Woodworth Reese, Emma Lazarus, E. A. Robinson, and Harriet Monroe. Stedman died 18 January 1908, remembered by writers and readers as one of America's important men-of-letters.

Stedman's own works aspire to his belief that "good poetry" represented truth and beauty, demonstrated a spontaneity within traditional poetic structures, and renounced didacticism. He wrote sonnets, lyrics, long narratives, occasional poems, and satirical verse in attempt to achieve his belief. Two of his popular, long, satiric poems include "Pan in Wall Street" and "The Diamond Wedding." Yet in most of his work Stedman allowed his

love for lofty themes, elevated language, and conventional struc-
ture to defeat his purpose. Had he cultivated his strengths—light
verse, descriptive lyrics—had he, as Whitman urged him, let
himself go (Scholnick 120), his poetry might have exhibited
more energy and a truer voice. Indeed, his regional poems about
New England ("Witchcraft") and the Caribbean ("Sargasso
Weed," "Panama") reveal a talent for conveying a vivid, evoca-
tive atmosphere not found in most of his other verse.

While Stedman's occasional and satirical poems earned him
praise and popularity in his day, it is his constructive criticism and
defense of American poetry that has won him recognition as an
influential shaper of the American literary canon today.

—*Mary K. Edmonds*

Suggestions for Further Reading

Scholnick, Robert J. *Edmund Clarence Stedman*. Boston: Twayne, 1977.
Stedman, Laura, and George M. Gould. *Life and Letters of Edmund
    Clarence Stedman*. 2 vols. New York: Moffat, Yard, 1910.*

TEXT
The Poems. Boston: Houghton, 1908.

꩜

Witchcraft[1]

I
A.D. 1692

Soe, Mistress Anne,[2] faire neighbour myne,
How rides a witche when nighte-winds blowe?
Folk saye that you are none too goode
To joyne the crewe in Salem woode,
When one you wot[3] of gives the signe:
Righte well, methinks, the pathe you knowe.

In Meetinge-time I watched you well,
Whiles godly Master Parris[4] prayed:

---

1. From "Poems of New England," this poem refers to the infamous Salem
witch trials.
2. Most likely Ann Pudeator, hanged for witchcraft in September 1692.
3. Know.
4. Samuel Parris, minister to Salem Village, sat in judgment of the accused
witches.

Your folded hands laye on your booke;
But Richard answered to a looke   10
That fain would tempt him unto hell,
Where, Mistress Anne, your place is made.

You looke into my Richard's eyes
With evill glances shameless growne;
I found about his wriste a hair,[5]
And guesse what fingers tyed it there:
He shall not lightly be your prize—
Your Master firste shall take his owne.

'Tis not in nature he should be
(Who loved me soe when Springe was greene)   20
A childe, to hange upon your gowne!
He loved me well in Salem Towne
Until this wanton witcherie
His hearte and myne crept dark betweene.

Last Sabbath nighte, the gossips saye,
Your goodman missed you from his side.
He had no strength to move, untill
Agen, as if in slumber still,
Beside him at the dawne you laye.
Tell, nowe, what meanwhile did betide.   30

Dame Anne, mye hate goe with you fleete
As driftes the Bay fogg overhead—
Or over yonder hill-topp, where
There is a tree ripe fruite shall bear
When, neighbour myne, your wicked feet
The stones of Gallowes Hill[6] shall tread.

                                                      (1884, 1897)

W. W.[7]

Good-bye, Walt!
Good-bye, from all you loved of earth—
Rock, tree, dumb creature, man and woman—
To you, their comrade human.

---

5. Superstition. The Devil's mark.
6. The site where the bodies of those executed were interred.
7. Lines sent to Walt Whitman's funeral, 30 March 1892.

The last assault
Ends now; and now in some great world has birth
A minstrel, whose strong soul finds broader wings,
    More brave imaginings.
Stars crown the hilltop where your dust shall lie,
Even as we say good-bye,   10
    Good-bye, old Walt!

                      (1892, 1908)

Sargasso Weed

Out from the seething Stream
    To the steadfast trade-wind's courses,
Over the bright vast swirl
    Of a tide from evil free,—
Where the ship has a level beam,
    And the storm has spent his forces,
And the sky is a hollow pearl
    Curved over a sapphire sea.

Here it floats as of old,
    Beaded with gold and amber,   10
Sea-frond buoyed with fruit,
    Sere as the yellow oak,
Long since carven and scrolled,
    Of some blue-ceiled Gothic chamber
Used to the viol and lute
    And the ancient belfry's stroke.

Eddying far and still
    In the drift that never ceases,
The dun Sargasso weed
    Slips from before our prow,   20
And in its sight makes strong our will,
    As of old the Genoese's,[8]
When he stood in his hour of need
    On the Santa Maria's bow.

Ay, and the winds at play
    Toy with these peopled islands,
Each of itself as well
    Naught but a brave New World,

---

8. Christopher Columbus was a native of Genoa, Italy.

Where the crab and sea-slug stay
    In the lochs of its tiny highlands,   30
And the nautilus moors his shell
    With his sail and streamers furled.

Each floats ever and on
    As the round green Earth is floating
Out through the sea of space
    Bearing our mortal kind,
Parasites soon to be gone,
    Whom others be sure are noting,
While to their astral race
    We in our turn are blind.   40
                (1897, 1908)

Panama

Two towers the old Cathedral lifts
    Above the sea-walled town,—
The wild pine bristles from their rifts,
    The runners dangle down;
In either turret, staves in hand,
All day the mongrel ringers stand
And sound, far over bay and land,
    The Bells of Panama.

Loudly the cracked bells, overhead,
    Of San Francisco ding,   10
With Santa Ana, La Merced,
    Felipe, answering;
Banged all at once, and four times four,
Morn, noon, and night, the more and more
Clatter and clang with huge uproar
    The Bells of Panama.

From out their roosts the bellmen see
    The red-tiled roofs below,—
The Plaza folk that lazily
    To mass and cockpit go,—
Then pound afresh, with clamor fell,
Each ancient, broken, thrice-blest bell,
    The Bells of Panama.

The Cordillera[9] guards the main   20
    As when Pedrarias[10] bore
The cross, the castled flag of Spain,
    To the Pacific shore;
The tide still ebbs a league from quay,
The buzzards scour the emptied Bay:
"There's a heretic to singe to-day,—
Come out! Come Out!"—still strive to say
    The Bells of Panama.

                                        (1897, 1908)

---

9. A mountain chain or ridge. Applied by the Spaniards to the Andes in South America.

10. A Spanish explorer.

John James Piatt
1835–1917

John James Piatt earned his reputation as a bard of the region then considered the American West (now the Midwest, primarily Ohio and Illinois). Readers and critics detected a "Western" freshness and vigor even in poems on topics unrelated to region, but it was Piatt's poems of the West that most fired his readers' imaginations and, apparently, his own.

Piatt was born on 1 March 1835 in James' Mills, Indiana, and moved as a boy to Ohio, home to many members of his family. He attended Capital University and Kenyon College, but served a more important apprenticeship at the *Ohio State Journal*, where he met the young William Dean Howells. He published poems as early as 1857 in the *Louisville Journal* (of which he subsequently became an editor), and in 1860 he and Howells collaborated on *Poems of Two Friends*. In the following year, he married fellow poet and *Louisville Journal* contributor Sarah Morgan Bryan. For the next twenty years, he divided his time between Ohio, where he edited and contributed to various periodicals, and Washington, D.C., where he held several government clerkships, including a six-year appointment as librarian to the House of Representatives. During the Civil War he became friendly with Whitman, who was then in Washington on his informal nursing mission to wounded soldiers. From 1882 to 1893 he was a United States consul in Ireland; afterwards he returned to Ohio, contributing frequently to periodicals until his death on 16 February 1917.

Piatt published steadily throughout his life, producing fifteen volumes of poetry, including the collaboration with Howells and two with Sarah Piatt. *Landmarks, and Other Poems* (1872), *Idyls and Lyrics of the Ohio Valley* (1881), and *Little New World Idyls* (1893) combine new verse with previously published selections; they contain most of Piatt's best work.

Despite obvious pride in his region and his pioneering ancestors, Piatt's poems about the West strike a surprisingly pensive note. While the adherents of manifest destiny looked ever forward, Piatt turned repeatedly to the past. Though the Anglo-

American settlement of Ohio had only been thoroughly accomplished for about three generations, this short history evoked for Piatt intimations of lost opportunity and faded promise like those Wordsworth found in the ruined cottages and abandoned sheepfolds of England's lake country. This preoccupation appears in "The Lost Farm" and "The Lost Hunting Ground." Such poems of bittersweet recollection metaphorically captured the mood of the nation in the post–Civil War years. Piatt was noted for his Civil War poems; one of these, "The Mower in Ohio," may be his best.

Piatt's poems are often more subtly crafted than their conventional appearance suggests. "Half-Lives," for instance, employs a complex irregular rhyme scheme. "To Walt Whitman, the Man," tells of Whitman's ministrations to hospitalized soldiers who "keep the memory of your form and feel / A light forerun your face where'er it comes" (lines 7–8). Here "feel" associates with "form"—the soldiers recall Whitman's touch as well as his look—while the oxymoronic "feel a light" suggests the disordered perceptions of the wounded.

Piatt liked and admired Whitman, but considered his work "so-called poetry" and declared that his influence on younger writers had "certainly been bad." Despite this opinion, Piatt's poetry owes some of its "freshness" to Whitman's influence, evident in its use of exclamation, parenthesis and colloquialism. Overtones of Whitman—and of Wordsworth—notwithstanding, Piatt is still a distinctly individual voice, one of the country's talented minor poets.

—Harry Crockett

Suggestions for Further Reading

Barrus, Clara. *Whitman and Burroughs, Comrades.* Boston: Houghton, 1931.
Bowerman, Sarah G. "John James Piatt" and "Sarah Morgan Bryan Piatt." *Dictionary of American Biography*, Vol. 14. Ed. Dumas Malone. New York: Scribner's, 1934. 556–58.

TEXTS
Idyls and Lyrics of the Ohio Valley. 1881.
Little New World Idyls. 1893.

᠁

The Mower in Ohio
June, MDCCCLXIV

The bees in the clover are making honey, and I am making
    my hay:
The air is fresh, I seem to draw a young man's breath to-day.

The bees and I are alone in the grass: the air is so very still
I hear the dam, so loud, that shines beyond the sullen mill.

Yes, the air is so still that I hear almost the sounds I can not
    hear—
That, when no other sound is plain, ring in my empty ear:

The chime of striking scythes, the fall of the heavy swaths
    they sweep—
They ring about me, resting, when I waver half asleep;

So still, I am not sure if a cloud, low down, unseen there be,
Or if something brings a rumor home of the cannon so far
    from me: 10

Far away in Virginia, where Joseph and Grant, I know,
Will tell them what I meant when first I had my mowers go!

Joseph, he is my eldest one, the only boy of my three
Whose shadow can darken my door again, and lighten my
    heart for me.

Joseph, he is my eldest—how his scythe was striking ahead!
William was better at shorter heats, but Jo in the long-run
    led.

William, he was my youngest; John, between them, I some
    how see,
When my eyes are shut, with a little board at his head in
    Tennessee.

But William came home one morning early, from
    Gettysburg, last July,
(The mowing was over already, although the only mower
    was I:)   20

William, my captain, came home for good to his mother;
    and I'll be bound

We were proud and cried to see the flag that wrapt his coffin
    around;

For a company from the town came up ten miles with music
    and gun:
It seemed his country claimed him then—as well as his
    mother—her son.

But Joseph is yonder with Grant to-day, a thousand miles or
    near,
And only the bees are abroad at work with me in the clover
    here.

Was it a murmur of thunder I heard that hummed again in
    the air?
Yet, may be, the cannon are sounding now their Onward to
    Richmond there.

But under the beech by the orchard, at noon, I sat an hour it
    would seem—
It may be I slept a minute, too, or wavered into a dream.   30

For I saw my boys, across the field, by the flashes as they
    went,
Tramping a steady tramp as of old, with the strength in
    their arms unspent;

Tramping a steady tramp, they moved like soldiers that
    march to the beat
Of music that seems, a part of themselves, to rise and fall
    with their feet;

Tramping a steady tramp, they came with flashes of silver
    that shone,
Every step, from their scythes that rang as if they needed
    the stone—

(The field is wide and heavy with grass)—and, coming
    toward me, they beamed
With a shine of light in their faces at once, and—surely I
    must have dreamed!

For I sat alone in the clover-field, the bees were working
    ahead.
There were three in my vision—remember, old man: and
    what if my Joseph were dead!   40

But I hope that he and Grant (the flag above them both, to
    boot,)
Will go to Richmond together, no matter which is ahead or
    afoot!

Meantime, alone at the mowing here—an old man somewhat
    gray—
I must stay at home as long as I can, making, myself, the
    hay.

And so another round—the quail in the orchard whistles
    blithe;—
But first I'll drink at the spring below, and whet again my
    scythe.

                                   (1868)

The Lost Farm
The Schoolmaster's Story

When my strong fathers came into the West,
They chose a tract of land which seemed the best,
Near a swift river, in whose constant flow
Peacefully earth and heaven were one below;
Gigantic wardens, on the horizon, stood
Far-circling hills, rough to their tops with wood.

They came, a long and dangerous journey then,
Through paths that had not known of civil men;
With wives and children looking back, and still
Returning long in dreams confusing will,   10
They came, and in the panther-startled shade
The deep foundations of a State were laid.
The axe, in stalwart hands, with steadfast stroke,
The savage echoes of the forest woke,
And, one-by-one, breaking the world-old spell,
The hardy trees, long-crashing, with thunder fell.
The log-house rose, within the solitude,
And civilized the tenants of the wood.
It was not long before the shadow'd mold
Open'd to take the sunshine's gift of gold;   20
In the dark furrow dropp'd the trusted seed,
And the first harvest bless'd the sower's need.

Oh, dear the memory of their simpler wealth,
Whose hardship nursed the iron flower of health;
Oh, sweet the record of the lives they spent,

Whose breath was peace, whose benison content;
Unenvied now by us, their delicate sons,
The dangers which they braved, those heartier ones!
The Indian's midnight coming, long ago,
And the wolf's howl in nights that shone with snow,
These are but dreams to us (who would but dream),
Pictured far off, heard as lost sounds that seem: 30
They knew the terror, seventy years gone by,
Of the realities we may not try,
Who left the farm on which my new-born eyes
Saw the great miracle of earth and skies.

The fields were clear'd; the farm-house, girt around
With meadow-lands and orchards, held its ground;
The goodly place had wavering uplands, sweet
With cattle-pastures, hot with ripening wheat.
The house look'd Westward, where the river lay
Shimmering o'er level lands at close of day,   40
Or, many-twinkling through the autumnal morn,
In the hazy heat rustled the languid corn.

Not far were neighbors—heirs of acres wide,
Or the small farms in which the old divide.
By the close pike, a half-mile off to the north,
The tavern, with old-fashion'd sign thrust forth,
Show'd Washington, a little faded then,
(Too faded now, among new-famous men!)
And, close beside, the blacksmith-shop was found,
In August noons obtrusive with its sound,   50
Or late in winter eves, a welcome sight,
Burning and brightening through with bursting light!

Such was the farm—how dear to my regret!—
Whose fresh life runs into my bosom yet.
My dreams may bear me thither even now.
Again, with eager heart and sunburnt brow,
Homesick at times, I take a noiseless train,
Wandering, breath-like, to my home again;
See my glad brothers, in the June-sweet air,
Toss the green hay, the hot sheaves of harvest bear;   60
The fireside warms into my heart—how plain!
And my lost mother takes her boy again;
My sisters steal around me tenderly—
And all that can not be yet seems to be!

In thirty years what changes there have been!—
How disappear the landmarks that were seen!

If I should go to seek my boyhood's place,
What chart would show the way, what guide would trace?

New people came. Around the tavern grew
New dwellings and new manners—all things new.   70
The impetus of something in the land
(Some gold, unseen, diviners understand),
Some mystic loadstone of the earth or air,
Drew all the nimble spirits of action there.
The village, not without a conscious pride,
Grew fast and gather'd in the country-side,
Then took the style of town. And now, behold,
A wild, strange rumor through the country roll'd!—
A railroad was projected, East and West,
Which would not slight us, so the shrewd ones guess'd.   80
Strange men with chain and compass came at last
Among the hills, across the valley pass'd;
Through field and woodland, pasture, orchard, they
Turn'd not aside, but kept straight on their way.
Old farmers threaten'd, but it did no good—
The quick conservatives of the neighborhood.
"We do not want it!" many said, and one,
"Through field of mine I swear it shall not run!"
And paced his boundary-line with loaded gun.
Others replied (wise, weather-sighted, they!)   90
"You'll think a little different, friend, some day.
The wheels of progress will you block—good speed!
(Cut off your nose to spite your face, indeed!)
'Twill make the land worth double, where you walk."
"Stuff! stuff!" the old fogies answer'd—"how you talk!"

The road was open'd. Soon another, down
Northward and Southward, cut across the town:
Both pass'd through meadows where my boyhood stray'd:
One through the barn within whose mow I play'd.
And then a newer force of circumstance   100
Took hold and pull'd the place in quick advance:
The lovely river—swift, and deep, and strong—
Upon whose shore I fish'd and idled long,
(The still companion of my dreaming hour,)
Had great advantages of water-power.
Saw-mills and grist-mills, factories builded there,
Cover'd the banks and jarr'd the quiet air.
The river could not sleep nor dream its old
Beautiful dream, in morn or evening gold,

Or as a fallen soul had fitful glance 110
At its divine and lost inheritance.

The town became a city—growing still,
And growing ever, with a giant's will
Gathering and grasping, changing all it took.
A city sewer was my school-boy brook.
The farm remain'd, but only in the name;
The old associations lived the same.
The approaching city drew its arm around,
And threaten'd more and more the invaded ground;
Near and more near its noises humm'd and groan'd, 120
(Higher and higher priced the land we own'd!)
My father held his ground, and would not sell.
The stiff wiseacres praised his wisdom well.

At last I came from home. At college long
Absent, at home something, meanwhile, went wrong.
I need not tell the fact. What house is proof,
With jealous threshold and protected roof,
Against the subtle foes that every-where
Stand waiting to attack in safest air—
The insidious foes of Fortune or of Fate, 130
Who plan our ruin while we estimate
Our sum of new success? My father died—
(My mother soon was buried by his side;)
The farm pass'd into speculative hands,
Who turn'd to sudden profit all its lands.
The greedy city seized upon them fast,
And the dear home was swept into the Past.
Across its quiet meadows streets were laid,
White-hot, the dusty thoroughfares of trade.
Where the gray farm-house had its sacred hearth 140
Sprang buildings hiding heaven and crowding earth.

A score of years were pass'd. Return'd by chance
(A railway accident the circumstance)
To that strange city only known by name,
Unwilling visitor by night I came;
And, sleeping there within some great hotel,
There rose a dream that fills my heart to tell.
I came, a boy—it seem'd not long away—
Close to my father's house at shut of day.
I cross'd the pasture and the orchard where 150
Glimmer'd the cider-mill in golden air;

The faint, soft tremor of the wandering bell
Of cattle mingled with the old clover-smell.
I leap'd the brook that twinkled darkly bright,
And saw the farm-house dusk'd in mellow light.
The river, painted with the Western gleam,
Show'd through the leaves a Paradisal dream.
By the side-door my father met me then,
My mother kiss'd me in the porch again—
A moment all that was not was! I 'woke   160
And through my window saw the morning smoke
Of the loud city. And my dream, behold,
Was on the spot of the dear hearth of old!
A man's vain tears hung vague within my eyes.

The Lost Farm underneath the city lies.

(1872)

Half-Lives

I

Two were they, two;—but one
They might have been. Each knew
The other's spirit fittest mate, apart.
Ah, hapless! though once jealous Fortune drew
Them almost heart to heart,
In a brief-lighted sun!

II

So near they came, and then—they are
So far!
They seemed like two who pass,
Each on a world-long journey opposite,   10
Their two trains hurrying dark
With far-drawn roar through the dread deeps of night,
(Oh, faces close—they almost touched, alas!
Oh, hands that might have thrilled with meeting spark!
Oh, lips that might have kissed!
Oh, eyes with folded sight,
Dreaming some vision bright!)
In mystery and in mist.

(1885)

To Walt Whitman, the Man
Washington, May, MDCCCLXIII

Homeward, last midnight, in the car we met,
While the long street streamed by us in the dark
With scattered lights in blurs of misty rain;
Then, while you spoke to me of hospitals
That know your visits, and of wounded men
(From those dread battles yonder in the South)
Who keep the memory of your form and feel
A light forerun your face where'er it comes,
In places hushed with fever, thrilled with pain,
I thought of Charity, and self-communed: 10
"Not only a slight girl, as poets dream,
With gentle footsteps stealing forth alone,
Veiling her hand from her soft timid eyes
Lest they should see her self-forgetful alms,
Or moving, lamp in hand, through glimmering wards
With her nun's coif or nurse's sacred garb:
Not only this,—but oft a sunburnt man,
Grey-garmented, grey-bearded, gigantesque,
Walking the highway with a cheerful stride,
And, like that Good Samaritan (rather say   20
This Good American!), forgetting not
To lift the hurt one as a little child
And make the weakest strong with manly cheer,
On Red-Cross errands of Good-Comradeship."

                                                        (1893)

An Idyl of Illinois
September, MDCCCXL—

They waken in the dewy-fragrant space
New-mown at sunset for their camping-ground—
Island-like 'mid the horizon-girdled grass—
With tented wagons, tethered teams a-graze
Beside them, near their smouldering bivouac fire.
. . . What ruddy lights are flitting through the sky,
Brightening the dusky distance far away?
The flames! the flames! the dreadful prairie flames!—
Across the horizon hastening weirdly still,
Now with quick-shooting spires, now bounding wild   10
Like maddened wolves in battle each with all,

(The shadows leaping black amid the blaze,)
In the shrewd wind that breathes a furnace-blast.
. . . No time to give away to last hour's dream!
They fire the grass about them. Soon, behold,
Safe-breathing in the gleaming solitude,
All gaze in wonder at the advancing tide—
The tide of flame—that breaks in vain around.
The fiery deluge leaves their ark secure;
Then dreams reopen eastern gates of Time.   20

(1893)

The Lost Hunting Ground in Illinois

To these Atlantic fields the bee
(An earlier emigrant was he)[1]
          Came in far years, and found
(O careless gardens! fenceless soil!
Unscarred by plough, untouched by toil!)
          The red man's Hunting Ground.

From some old world of song and strife,
From hives o'erfull with restless life,
          The glowing flight began,
And, journeying with the journeying sun,   10
He came, his busy empire won,
          Before the white-faced man.

Lord of the flower-land, jealously
The Indian watched the moving bee
          Steer his long Westward way;
Or, deep in fragrant-wooded dells,
Building ambrosial waxen cells,
          Toil through the sultry day.

He saw (what flying omen gleams
O'er tribal mounds, o'er haunted streams,   20
          O'er fields a boundless flower!)
His Hunting Ground—it is the Past!—
Roofed with far-murmuring cities vast,
          Splendent with spire and tower!

---

1. The honeybee, it is said, preceded the white settler in western North America.

What workers these? He heard, he saw
Those other swarms (by partial law
    Denied their right of birth),
Who claim, where they new States may build,
Division of his lands untilled—
    Earth's children's share of earth!   30

They come!—They came! . . . In dream I hear,
O phantom chaser of the deer,
    Thy cry, a ghost of sound—
When noisy hives of men are still,
And the night-mist hides vale and hill—
    In thy lost Hunting Ground!

                (1893)

Thomas Bailey Aldrich

1836–1907

Thomas Bailey Aldrich said of himself, "Though I am not genuine Boston, I am Boston-plated" (Greenslet 78). The influence of Lowell, Holmes, Emerson, and especially Longfellow on Aldrich's work provided his "Boston-plating." Aldrich wrote his ballads, lyrics, and sonnets to amuse or uplift by creating a sentimental or exotic mood and by skillfully manipulating standard poetic devices and diction. When he collected his poems, he omitted his early, lighthearted society verse and included only those poems he considered his best work, altering their arrangement from edition to edition. As twentieth-century poetry moved on to new themes and forms, his work, tied to the poetic past, went into eclipse.

Thomas Bailey Aldrich was born 11 November 1836 at his grandfather's home in Portsmouth, New Hampshire. Aldrich and his parents, Elias and Sarah Aldrich, lived first in New York and then in New Orleans, but young Tom spent summers in Portsmouth and returned there for school in 1849. Dismal family finances after his father's death later that year ended plans for Aldrich's higher education.

Aldrich used his Portsmouth boyhood as a source for his best-known work, a novel entitled *The Story of a Bad Boy*. At the time of its publication in 1869, stories for children typically taught moral lessons or indulged in extreme sentimentality. Aldrich treated his story realistically, calling his hero "bad" to differentiate him from what he called "that unwholesome and altogether improbable little prig which had hitherto been held up as an example to the young" (Samuels 83).

Aldrich moved to New York in 1852 to work as a clerk in his uncle's brokerage house. In his free time, he wrote and eventually published poetry; L. C. Derby published Aldrich's first volume of poetry, *The Bells: A Collection of Chimes* (1855), which sold fairly well. In that year Aldrich also published "The Ballad of Babie Bell." One of the best of many contemporary poems on a child's death, it brought Aldrich national recognition and his first job as an editor.

Aldrich moved in two very different literary circles in New York: R. H. Stoddard's genteel set and the bohemians of Pfaff's beer cellar. His Portsmouth background made him too conservative to be completely at ease with the bohemians, and except for lasting friendships with Bayard Taylor, Launt Thompson, and Edwin Booth, Aldrich drifted away from the writers and artists surrounding Stoddard.

In 1865, Aldrich went to work for Boston publisher James Osgood. The new position enabled him to marry Lillian Woodman. The same year, Ticknor and Fields published Aldrich's poems in their Blue and Gold Series, a sign of his arrival as an established American poet. When William Dean Howells retired as editor of the *Altantic*, Aldrich succeeded him and held that position from 1881 to 1890. Aldrich traveled and wrote after retiring as the *Atlantic*'s editor; he died on 19 March 1907.

When he published *Poems* in 1863, Aldrich selected poems from his three previous volumes to include with his new poems. He followed the same pattern in his subsequent collections for more than thirty years, so that each new volume comprised his work to date. Houghton Mifflin published *The Poems of Thomas Bailey Aldrich: Revised Complete Household Edition* in 1897. Successive editions in 1898, 1904, and 1907 added one poem each, and the final edition included all the poems Aldrich wished to acknowledge.

Aldrich's most successful poems defend his view of art. "Realism" rails against those writers Aldrich believed offensive and unattractive. Even in *The Story of a Bad Boy*, Aldrich concentrated on pleasant memories, and he opposed the growing emphasis on ugly and brutal reality. In "At the Funeral of a Minor Poet," he refers to the "Zolaistic movement," as "a miasmic breath / Blown from the slums" (lines 27–28). Other poems praise craftsmanship in service to art or encourage the artist to pursue a personal vision of beauty.

Aldrich's reputation could not survive the changing poetic tastes of the twentieth century. He accepted forms and conventions as given, leaving experiments to others. Aldrich wrote his best poems to say something specific. The poems about the value of art have fewer archaic or "poetic" words and less complicated word order, but what they lose in decoration, they gain in clarity. Aldrich wrote in the style of an earlier time. He remains a follower of the New England poets: "not genuine Boston, but Boston-plated."

—*Susan Bales*

Suggestions for Further Reading

Greenslet, Ferris. *Thomas Bailey Aldrich*. Boston: Houghton, 1908.
Samuels, Charles E. *Thomas Bailey Aldrich*. New York: Twayne, 1965.*

TEXTS

The Bells: A Collection of Chimes. 1855.
The Ballad of Babie Bell, and Other Poems. 1859.
Flower and Thorn, Later Poems. 1877.
Mercedes, and Later Lyrics. 1884.
The Sisters' Tragedy, with Other Poems, Lyrical and Dramatic. 1891.
Unguarded Gates, and Other Poems. 1895.
The Poems of Thomas Bailey Aldrich. New York: Houghton, 1907.

Fannie

Fannie has the sweetest foot
Ever in a gaiter boot!
And the hoyden knows it,
And, of course, she shows it,—
Not the knowledge, but the foot,—
Yet with such a modest grace,
Never seems it out of place,
    Ah, there are not many
      Half so sly, or sad, or mad,
    Or wickeder than Fannie.   10

Fannie has the blackest hair
  Of any of the village girls;
It does not shower on her neck
  In silken or coquettish curls.
It droops in folds around her brow,
  As clouds, at night, around the moon,
Looped with lilies here and there,
  In many a dangerous festoon.
And Fannie wears a gipsy hat,
Saucily—yes, all of that!   20
    Ah, there are not many
      Half so sly, or sad, or mad,
    Or wickeder than Fannie.

Fannie wears an open dress—
  Ah! the charming chemisette!
Half concealing, half revealing
  Something far more charming yet.
Fannie drapes her breast with lace,
As one would drape a costly vase
To keep away mischievous flies;   30

But lace can't keep away one's eyes,
For every time her bosom heaves,
   Ah, it peepeth through it;
Yet Fannie looks the while as if
   Never once she knew it.
      Ah, there are not many
         Half so sly, or sad, or mad,
      Or wickeder than Fannie.

Fannie lays her hand in mine;
   Fannie speaks with *naivete*,   40
Fannie kisses me, she does!
   In her own coquettish way.
Then softly speaks and deeply sighs,
With angels nestled in her eyes.
In the merrie month of May,
   Fannie swears sincerely
She will be my own, my wife,
   And love me dearly, dearly
Ever after all her life.
      Ah, there are not many   50
         Half so sly, or sad, or mad,
      As my true-hearted Fannie.

                                 (1855)

Baby Bell[1]

I

Have you not heard the poets tell
How came the dainty Baby Bell
Into this world of ours?
The gates of heaven were left ajar:
With folded hands and dreamy eyes,
Wandering out of Paradise,
She saw this planet, like a star,
Hung in the glistening depths of even—
Its bridges, running to and fro,
O'er which the white-winged Angels go,   10
Bearing the holy Dead to heaven.
She touched a bridge of flowers—those feet,
So lightly they did not bend the bells

---

1. Aldrich used the spelling "Babie Bell" until 1874.

Of the celestial asphodels,
They fell like dew upon the flowers:
Then all the air grew strangely sweet.
And thus came dainty Baby Bell
Into this world of ours.

II

She came and brought delicious May;
The swallows built beneath the eaves;   20
Like sunlight, in and out the leaves
The robins went, the livelong day;
The lily swung its noiseless bell;
And on the porch the slender vine
Held out its cups of fairy wine.
How tenderly the twilights fell!
Oh, earth was full of singing-birds
And opening springtide flowers,
When the dainty Baby Bell
Came to this world of ours.   30

III

O Baby, dainty Baby Bell,
How fair she grew from day to day!
What woman-nature filled her eyes,
What poetry within them lay—
Those deep and tender twilight eyes,
So full of meaning, pure and bright
As if she yet stood in the light
Of those oped gates of Paradise.
And so we loved her more and more:
Ah, never in our hearts before   40
Was love so lovely born.
We felt we had a link between
This real world and that unseen—
The land beyond the morn;
And for the love of those dear eyes,
For love of her whom God led forth,
(The mother's being ceased on earth
When Baby came from Paradise,)—
For love of Him who smote our lives,
And woke the chords of joy and pain,   50
We said, *Dear Christ!*—our hearts bowed down
Like violets after rain.

IV

And now the orchards, which were white
And pink with blossoms when she came,
Were rich in autumn's mellow prime;
The clustered apples burnt like flame,
The folded chestnut burst its shell,
The grapes hung purpling, range on range:
And time wrought just as rich a change
In little Baby Bell.   60
Her lissome form more perfect grew,
And in her features we could trace,
In softened curves, her mother's face.
Her angel-nature ripened too:
We thought her lovely when she came,
But she was holy, saintly now . . .
Around her pale angelic brow
We saw a slender ring of flame.

V

God's hand had taken away the seal
That held the portals of her speech;   70
And oft she said a few strange words
Whose meaning lay beyond our reach.
She never was a child to us,
We never held her being's key;
We could not teach her holy things
Who was Christ's self in purity.

VI

It came upon us by degrees,
We saw its shadow ere it fell—
The knowledge that our God had sent
His messenger for Baby Bell.   80
We shuddered with unlanguaged pain,
And all our hopes were changed to fears,
And all our thoughts ran into tears
Like sunshine into rain.
We cried aloud in our belief,
"Oh, smite us gently, gently, God!
Teach us to bend and kiss the rod,
And perfect grow through grief."
Ah! how we loved her, God can tell;

Her heart was folded deep in ours.
Our hearts were broken, Baby Bell!

VII

At last he came, the messenger,
The messenger from unseen lands:
And what did dainty Baby Bell?
She only crossed her little hands,
She only looked more meek and fair!
We parted back her silken hair,
We wove the roses round her brow—
White buds, the summer's drifted snow—
Wrapt her from head to foot in flowers . . .   100
And thus went dainty Baby Bell
Out of this world of ours.

                                                    (1855, 1859)

Realism

Romance beside his unstrung lute
        Lies stricken mute.
The old-time fire, the antique grace,
You will not find them anywhere.
To-day we breathe a commonplace,
Polemic, scientific air:
We strip Illusion of her veil;
We vivisect the nightengale
To probe the secret of his note.
The Muse in alien ways remote   10
        Goes wandering.

                                                    (1884)

At the Funeral of a Minor Poet

One of the Bearers Soliloquises:

. . . Room in your heart for him, O Mother Earth,[2]
Who loved each flower and leaf that made you fair,

---

2. Aldrich rarely begins a poem in mid-sentence. Here he uses the ellipsis to
break in on the thoughts of the Bearer.

And sang your praise in verses manifold
And delicate, with here and there a line
From end to end in blossom like a bough
The May breathes on, so rich it was. Some thought
The workmanship more costly than the thing
Moulded or carved as in those ornaments
Found at Mycenae.[3] And yet Nature's self
Works in this wise; upon a blade of grass,   10
Or what small note she lends the woodland thrush,
Lavishing endless patience. He was born
Artist, not artisan, which some few saw
And many dreamed not. As he wrote no odes
When Croesus wedded or Maecenas[4] died,
And gave no breath to civic feasts and shows,
He missed the glare that gilds more facile men—
A twilight poet, groping quite alone,
Belated, in a sphere where every nest
Is emptied of its music and its wings.   20
Not great his gift; yet we can poorly spare
Even his slight perfection in an age
Of limping triolets and tame rondeaux.
He had at least ideals, though unreached,
And heard, far off, immortal harmonies,
Such as fall coldly on our ear to-day.
The mighty Zolasitic[5] Movement now
Engrosses us—a miasmatic breath
Blown from the slums. We paint life as it is,
The hideous side of it, with careful pains,
Making a god of the dull Commonplace.   30
For have we not the old gods overthrown
And set up strangest idols? We would clip
Imagination's wing and kill delight,
Our sole art being to leave nothing out
That renders art offensive. Not for us
Madonnas leaning from their starry thrones
Ineffable, nor any heaven-wrought dream
Of sculptor or of poet; we prefer
Such nightmare visions as in morbid brains
Take form and substance, thoughts that taint the air   40
And make all life unlovely. Will it last?
Beauty alone endures from age to age,
From age to age endures, handmaid of God.
Poets who walk with her on earth go hence
Bearing a talisman. You bury one,

3. A center of ancient Greek culture.
4. Typical names of patrons in classical poetry.
5. Emile Zola, nineteeth-century French writer, a founder of naturalism.

With his hushed music, in some Potter's Field;
The snows and rains blot out his very name,
As he from life seems blotted: through Time's glass
Slip the invisible and silent sands
That mark the century, then falls a day   50
The world is suddenly conscious of a flower,
Imperishable, ever to be prized,
Sprung from the mould of a forgotten grave.
'Tis said the seeds wrapped up among the balms
And hieroglyphics of Egyptian kings
Hold strange vitality, and, planted, grow
After the lapse of thrice a thousand years.
Some day, perchance, some unregarded note
Of this dead Singer—some sweet minor chord
That failed to lure our more accustomed ear—   60
Shall wake to life, like those long buried seeds,
And witch the fancy of an unborn age.
Meanwhile he sleeps, with scantiest laurel won
And little of our Nineteenth Century gold.
So, take him, Earth, and this his mortal part,
With that shrewd alchemy thou hast, transmute
To flower and leaf in thine unending Springs!

                                                           (1891)

Art

"Let art be all in all," one time I said,
And straightway stirred the hypercritic gall.
I said not, "Let technique be all in all,"
But art—a wider meaning. Worthless, dead—
The shell without its pearl, the corpse of thing—
Mere words are, till the spirit lend them wings.
The poet who wakes no soul within his lute
Falls short of art: 'twere better he were mute.

The workmanship wherewith the gold is wrought
Adds yet a richness to the richest gold;   10
Who lacks the art to shape his thought, I hold,
Were little poorer if he lacked the thought.
The statue's slumber were unbroken still
In the dull marble, had the hand no skill.
Disparage not the magic touch that gives
The formless thought the grace whereby it lives!

                                                           (1895)

Fireflies

See where at intervals the firefly's spark
Glimmers, and melts into the fragrant dark;
Gilds a leaf's edge one happy instant, then
Leaves darkness all a mystery again!

(1895)

Longfellow
1807–1907

Above his grave the grass and snow
Their soft antiphonal strophes write:
Moonrise and daybreak come and go:
Summer by summer on the height
The thrushes find melodious breath.
Here let no vagrant winds that blow
Across the spaces of the night
        Whisper of death.

They do not die who leave their thought
    Imprinted on some deathless page.   10
Themselves may pass; the spell they wrought
    Endures on earth from age to age.
And thou, whose voice but yesterday
    Fell upon charmed listening ears,
    Thou shalt not know the touch of years;
Thou holdest time and chance at bay.
    Thou livest in thy living word
    As when its cadence first was heard.
O gracious Poet and benign,
    Beloved presence! now as then   20
    Thou standest by the hearths of men.

Their fireside joys and griefs are thine;
    Thou speakest to them of their dead,
    They listen and are comforted.
They break the bread and pour the wine
Of life with thee, as in those days
    Men saw thee passing on the street
    Beneath the elms—O reverend feet
That walk in far celestial ways!

(1907)

Thomas Bailey Aldrich

Joaquin Miller

1837–1913

Joaquin Miller's reputation as a poet has completed a curious circle, so that contemporary assessments bear a remarkable resemblance to those made by his earliest readers. In his heyday, Miller represented what the public wanted to believe about the West; his association of masculinity with the rugged contours of western landscape gained him immediate celebrity. His melodramatic accounts of male experience in such works as "The Sea of Fire" clearly establish the grandeur of nature as the ideal setting for the manly man. The closing of the American frontier in the 1890s meant that Miller was both one of the first writers to romanticize the West and one of the last writers to have encountered the land in its raw state.

Miller's life and career fall into three phases: the period from 1837 to 1870, when he first traveled through Oregon and California; the period from 1871 to 1880, when he dedicated himself to writing and achieved his greatest fame; and the period from 1880 until his death in 1913, when he settled on a ranch outside of Oakland and wrote about his early life. Critics and biographers debate the date of his birth, events of his early life, the circumstances surrounding his marriages, and even what assistance he may or may not have received with his writing.

He was born Cincinnatus Hiner Miller on a farm outside Liberty, Indiana, on 8 September 1837. In 1854, Miller left his family to try his luck in the California gold fields. From then until 1870, Miller lived with and fought with Indians, was jailed as a horse thief, acquired partial ownership in a pony-express service, edited a newspaper, married and divorced the poet Theresa Dyer (Minnie Myrtle), was elected judge of Grant County, Oregon, and published two volumes of poetry: *Specimens* (1868) and *Joaquin et al.* (1869). As early as 1859, acquaintances began to compare Miller's behavior with that of the Mexican bandit Joaquin Murietta. In 1870, he adopted Joaquin as his *nom de plume*.

Critics generally agree that during his first forty-three years Miller gathered the experience that he would expand upon in his writing. His greatest fame came during the 1870s, when he produced over half of all he ever wrote. During these years the English lionized him, and he traveled extensively through Europe and the Middle East. Miller lived his last thirty-three years in the shadow of his earlier success. Though he did cover the Klondike gold rush in 1897 and the Boxer Rebellion in 1900 for the Hearst newspapers, Miller spent most of his time at "The Hights," his ranch outside of Oakland, California. Three months after his death on 17 February 1913, Miller's ashes were transported to The Hights and ceremonially placed on a funeral pyre he had constructed years earlier.

Commenting on Miller's skill as a poet, O. W. Frost observes that there is little evidence of clear reasoning: "He simply narrates, describes, affirms, and reaffirms" (85). Such a heavy dependence on the force of delivery suggests some similarity with Whitman, but Miller does not fare well in the comparison. Where Whitman experimented with form and challenged conventional knowledge, Miller strained to preserve his iambs and his regular rhymes, reiterating picturesque descriptions rather than drawing new insights from his material. Of the thirty-seven poetic, fictional, and dramatic works Miller wrote, the following represent the best known: *Pacific Poems* (1871); *Songs of the Sierras* (1871); *Songs of the Sunlands* (1873); *Life Among the Modocs: Unwritten History* (1873); *The Ship in the Desert* (1875); *The Baronness of New York* (1877); *Songs of Far-Away Lands* (1878); *Shadows of Shasta* (1881); *The Danites in the Sierras* (1882); *In Classic Shades and Other Poems* (1890); *The Complete Poetical Works of Joaquin Miller* (1897) and *Joaquin Miller's Poems*, in six volumes (1909–10).

As the circle of criticism on Miller continues to close, readers begin to value once again the exotic appeal that his vision of the West first afforded the nineteenth-century public. Readers interested in more fully accounting for the growth of western archetypes and myths will find *Songs of the Sierras* and *Songs of the Sunlands* especially useful.

—*Paul Crumbley*

Suggestions for Further Reading

Frost, O. W. *Joaquin Miller*. New York: Twayne, 1967.*
Lawson, Benjamin S. *Joaquin Miller*. Boise: Boise State U Western Writers Series, 1980.
Longtin, Ray C. *The Writers of the Far West: A Reference Guide*. Boston: Hall, 1980.*

TEXT
The Complete Poetical Works of Joaquin Miller. New York: Arno Press, 1972.

꧁꧂

Kit Carson's Ride

Room! room to turn around in, to breathe and be free,
To grow to be giant, to sail as at sea
With the speed of the wind on a steed with his mane
To the wind, without pathway or route or a rein.
Room! room to be free where the white-border'd sea
Blows a kiss to a brother as boundless as he;
Where the buffalo come like a cloud on the plain,
Pouring on like the tide of a storm driven main,
And the lodge of the hunter to friend or to foe
Offers rest; and unquestioned you come or you go.   10
My plains of America! Seas of wild lands!
From a land in the seas in a raiment of foam,
That has reached to a stranger the welcome of home,
I turn to you, lean to you, lift you my hands.
    London 1871.

Run? Run? See this flank, sir, and I do love him so!
But he's blind as a badger. Whoa, Pache, boy, whoa.
No, you wouldn't believe it to look at his eyes,
But he's blind, badger blind, and it happened this wise:

    "We lay in the grass and the sunburnt clover
That spread on the ground like a great brown cover   20
Northward and southward, and west and away
To the Brazos, where our lodges lay,
One broad and unbroken level of brown.
We were waiting the curtains of night to come down
To cover us trio and conceal our flight
With my brown bride, won from an Indian town
That lay in the rear the full ride of a night.

    "We lounged in the grass—her eyes were in mine,
And her hands on my knee, and her hair was as wine
In its wealth and its flood, pouring on and all over   30
Her bosom wine red, and press'd never by one.
Her touch was as warm as the tinge of the clover
Burnt brown as it reach'd to the kiss of the sun.
Her words they were low as the lute-throated dove,
And as laden with love as the heart when it beats
In its hot, eager answer to earliest love,
Or the bee hurried home by its burden of sweets.

    "We lay low in the grass on the broad plain levels,
Old Revels and I, and my stolen brown bride;

'Forty full miles if a foot to ride!   40
Forty full miles if a foot, and the devils
Of red Comanches are hot on the track
When once they strike it. Let the sun go down
Soon, very soon,' muttered bearded old Revels
As he peer'd at the sun, lying low on his back,
Holding fast to his lasso. Then he jerk'd at his steed
And he sprang to his feet, and glanced swiftly around,
And then dropp'd, as if shot, with an ear to the ground;
Then again to his feet, and to me, to my bride,
While his eyes were like flame, his face like a shroud,   50
His form like a king, and his beard like a cloud,
And his voice loud and shrill, as both trumpet and reed,—
'Pull, pull in your lassoes, and bridle to steed,
And speed you if ever for life you would speed.
Aye, ride for your lives, for your lives you must ride!
For the plain is aflame, the prairie on fire,
And the feet of wild horses hard flying before
I hear like a sea breaking high on the shore,
While the buffalo come like a surge of the sea,
Driven far by the flame, driving fast on us three   60
As a hurricane comes, crushing palms in his ire.'

     "We drew in the lassoes, seized saddle and rein,
Threw them on, cinched them on, cinched them over again,
And again drew the girth; and spring was to horse,
With head to the Brazos, with a sound in the air
Like the surge of a sea, with a flash in the eye,
From that red wall of flame reaching up to the sky;
A red wall of flame and a black rolling sea
Rushing fast upon us, as the wind sweeping free
And afar from the desert blown hollow and hoarse.   70

     "Not a word, not a wail from a lip was let fall,
We broke not a whisper, we breathed not a prayer,
There was work to be done, there was death in the air,
And the chance was as one to a thousand for all.

     "Twenty miles! . . . thirty miles! . . . a dim distant speck. . . .
Then a long reaching line, and the Brazos in sight!
And I rose in my seat with a shout of delight.
I stood in my stirrup and look'd to my right—
But Revels was gone; I glanced by my shoulder
And saw his horse stagger; I saw his head drooping   80
Hard down on his breast, and his naked breast stooping
Low down to the mane, as so swifter and bolder
Ran reaching out for us the red-footed fire.

He rode neck to neck with a buffalo bull,
That made the earth shake where he came in his course,
The monarch of millions, with a shaggy mane full
Of smoke and of dust, and it shook with desire
Of battle, with rage and with bellowings hoarse.
His keen, crooked horns, through the storm of his mane,
Like black lances lifted and lifted again;   90
And I looked but this once, for the fire licked through,
And Revels was gone, as we rode two and two.

"I look'd to my left then—and nose, neck, and shoulder
Sank slowly, sank surely, till back to my thighs,
And up through the black blowing veil of her hair
Did beam full in mine her two marvelous eyes,
With a longing and love yet a look of despair,
And of pity for me, as she felt the smoke fold her,
And flames leaping far for her glorious hair.
Her sinking horse falter'd, plunged, fell and was gone   100
As I reach'd through the flame and I bore her still on.
On! into the Brazos, she, Pache and I—
Poor, burnt, blinded Pache. I love him..That's why.

(1871)

from The Sea of Fire[1]

XXXVII

Encompassed, lorn, the lovers stood,
Abandoned there, death in the air!
That beetling steep, that blazing wood—
Red flame! red flame, and everywhere!
Yet he was born to strive, to bear
The front of battle. He would die
In noble effort, and defy
The grizzled visage of despair.

He threw his two strong arms full length
As if to surely test their strength;   10

---

1. In this excerpt, a white man in love with a beautiful Indian maiden chooses
to die with her rather than live in a world that would separate the two races. The
fire that closes in around the lovers is a figure for the corrupt influence of
civilization. The "manliest man" achieves a tragic victory as he sacrifices all for
the purity of true love.

Then tore his vestments, textile things
That could but tempt the demon wings
Of flame that girt them round about,
Then threw his garments to the air
As one that laughed at death, at doubt,
And like a god stood thewed and bare.

   She did not hesitate; she knew
The need of action; swift she threw
Her burning vestments by, and bound
Her wondrous wealth of hair that fell   20
An all-concealing cloud around
Her glorious presence, as he came
To seize and bear her through the flame,—
An Orpheus out of burning hell!

   He leaned above her, wound his arm
About her splendor, while the noon
Of flood tide, manhood, flushed his face,
And high flames leapt the high headland!—
They stood as twin-hewn statues stand,
High lifted in some storied place.   30

   He clasped her close, he spoke of death,—
Of death and love in the same breath.
Like ship safe anchored in some bay,
Where never rage or rack of main
Might even shake her anchor chain.

XXXVIII

   The flames! They could not stand or stay;
Beyond, the beetling steep, the sea!
But at his feet a narrow way,
A short steep path, pitched suddenly
Safe open to the river's beach,   40
Where lay a small white isle in reach,—
A small, white, rippled isle of sand
Where yet the two might safely land.

   And there, through smoke and flame, behold
The priest stood safe, yet all appalled!
He reached the cross; he cried, he called;
He waved his high-held cross of gold.

He called and called, he bade them fly
Through flames to him, nor bide and die!

Her lover saw; he saw, and knew   50
His giant strength could bear her through.
And yet he would not start or stir.
He clasped her close as death can hold,
Or dying miser clasp his gold,—
His hold became a part of her.

He would not give her up! He would
Not bear her waveward though he could!
That height was heaven; the wave was hell.
He clasped her close,—what else had done
The manliest man beneath the sun?   60
Was it not well? was it not well?

O man, be glad! be grandly glad,
And king-like walk thy ways of death!
For more than years of bliss you had
That one brief time you breathed her breath,
Yea, more than years upon a throne
That one brief time you held her fast,
Soul surged to soul, vehement, vast,—
True breast to breast, and all your own.

Live me one day, one narrow night,   70
One second of supreme delight
Like that, and I will blow like chaff
The hollow years aside, and laugh
A loud triumphant laugh, and I,
King-like and crowned, will gladly die.

Oh, but to wrap my love with flame!
With flame within, with flame without!
Oh, but to die like this, nor doubt—
To die and know her still the same!
To know that down the ghostly shore   80
Snow-white she walks for ever more!

XXXIX

He poised her, held her high in air,—
His great strong limbs, his great arm's length!—
Then turned his knotted shoulders bare
As birth-time in his splended strength,

And strode with lordly, kingly stride
To where the high and wood-hung edge
Looked down, far down upon the molten tide.
The flames leaped with him to the ledge,
The flames leapt leering at his side.   90

XL

He leaned above the ledge. Below
He saw the black ship grope and cruise,—
A midge below, a mile below.
His limbs were knotted as the thews
Of Hercules in his death-throe.

The flame! the flame! the envious flame!
She wound her arms, she wound her hair
About his tall form, grand and bare,
To stay the fierce flame where it came.

The black ship, like some moonlit wreck,   100
Below along the burning sea
Groped on and on all silently,
With silent pigmies on her deck.

That midge-like ship, far, far below;
That mirage lifting from the hill!
His flame-lit form began to grow,—
To glow and grow more grandly still.
The ship so small, that form so tall,
It grew to tower over all.

A tall Colossus, bronze and gold,   110
As if that flame-lit form were he
Who once bestrode the Rhodian sea,
And ruled the watery world of old:
As if the lost Colossus stood
Above that burning sea of wood.

And she! that shapely form upheld,
Held high as if to touch the sky,
What airy shape, how shapely high,—
What goddess of the seas of eld!

Her hand upheld, her high right hand,   120
As if she would forget the land;
As if to gather stars, and heap

The stars like torches there to light
Her hero's path across the deep
To some far isle that fearful night.

XLI

The envious flame, one moment leapt
Enraged to see such majesty,
Such scorn of death; such kingly scorn . . .
Then like some lightning-riven tree
They sank down in that flame—and slept   130
Then all was hushed above that steep
So still that they might sleep and sleep,
As when a Summer's day is born.

At last! from out the embers leapt
Two shafts of light above the night—
Two wings of flame that lifting swept
In steady, calm, and upward flight;
Two wings of flame against the white
Far-lifting, tranquil, snowy cone;
Two wings of love, two wings of light,   140
Far, far above that troubled night,
As mounting, mounting to God's throne.

XLII

And all night long that upward light
Lit up the sea-cow's bed below:
The far sea-cows still calling so
It seemed as they must call all night.
All night! there was no night. Nay, nay,
There was no night. The night that lay
Between that awful eve and day,—
That nameless night was burned away.   150
(1877)

The Heroes of America

O perfect heroes of the earth,
That conquer'd forests, harvest set!
O sires, mothers of my West!

How shall we count your proud bequest?
But yesterday ye gave us birth;
We eat your hard-earn'd bread to-day,
Nor toil nor spin nor make regret,
But praise our petty selves and say
How great we are. We all forget
The still endurance of the rude   10
Unpolish'd sons of solitude.

    What strong, uncommon men were these,
These settlers hewing to the seas!
Great horny-handed men and tan;
Men blown from many a barren land
Beyond the sea; men red of hand,
And men in love, and men in debt,
Like David's men in battle set;
And men whose very hearts had died,
Who only sought these woods to hide   20
Their wretchedness, held in the van;
Yet every man among them stood
Alone, along that sounding wood,
And every man somehow a man.
They push'd the mailed wood aside,
They toss'd the forest like a toy,
That grand forgotten race of men—
The boldest band that yet has been
Together since the siege of troy.
    San Francisco, 1871.

                                                   (1878)

Grant at Shiloh

    The blue and the gray! Their work was well done!
They lay as to listen to the water's flow.
Some lay with their faces upturned to the sun,
As seeking to know what the gods might know.
Their work was well done, each soldier was true.
But what is the question that comes to you?

    For all that men do, for all that men dare,
That river still runs with its stateliest flow.
The sun and the moon I scarcely think care
A fig for the fallen, of friend or of foe.   10

But the moss-mantled cypress, the old soldiers say,
Still mantles in smoke of that battle day!

These men in the dust! These pitiful dead!
The gray and the blue, the blue and the gray,
The headless trunk and the trunkless head;
The image of God in the gory clay!
And who was the bravest? Say, can you tell
If Death throws dice with a loaded shell?

(1890)

John Hay
1838–1905

Best known for his frontier ballads, John Hay was a popular poet in his time. "Jim Bludso of the Prairie Bell" was a best-selling poem in pamphlet form in late 1870 and early 1871 before its inclusion in *Pike County Ballads* (1871).

Born 8 October 1838 in Salem, Indiana, Hay attended Brown University where he was class poet and earned a master's degree in 1858. He then read law at his uncle's Springfield, Illinois, office and passed the bar in February 1861. From 1861 through 1870 Hay served first as President Lincoln's assistant private secretary and then as a diplomat in Vienna, Poland, Turkey, and Madrid.

Returning from Spain, Hay worked as an editor for the New York *Tribune* and published *Pike County Ballads* (1871) and *Castilian Days* (1871). He married on 4 February 1874, and in June 1875 settled with his wife, Clara Louise Stone, in Cleveland, Ohio. Recalled to public life in November 1879, he returned to Washington to become assistant secretary of state. After editing the New York *Tribune* from April to October, 1881, he published *The Bread-Winners* (1884), a novel.

In 1885, Hay began work with John G. Nicolay on their biography of Lincoln. The work appeared serially from 1886 until 1890, at which time the authors brought out their complete ten-volume *Abraham Lincoln: A History*. From March 1867 until his death, Hay was active in politics, serving first as ambassador to England, then as secretary of state. Three treaties and one convention carry his name and bear witness to his tireless public service. Hay died 1 July 1905 at Lake Sunapee, New Hampshire, and was buried in Lake View cemetery.

Hay numbered among his friends such prominent literary figures as Henry Adams, Mark Twain, William Dean Howells, Henry James, and Walt Whitman. Hay and Whitman probably met in the early 1860s when both were in Washington (Rosenfeld 94), and the friendship continued until Whitman's death. Whitman spoke of Hay: "[H]e was a very handsome fellow: good body, open face, easy manners. . . . Hay married a millionairess. . . . [H]e has, however, remained simple, himself, unaffected—

and is still my friend" (Traubel 4:31–32). On several occasions Hay did favors for Whitman and was always generous toward him in times of need. Hay received one of the fifty copies of the Deathbed Edition of *Leaves of Grass* done up in gray paper for Whitman's closest friends (Rosenfeld 98–99).

In his lifetime, Hay published two poetry volumes: *Pike County Ballads* (1871) and *Poems* (1890). The dialect pieces in *Pike County Ballads* portray country life and encourage traditional values; they often concentrate on one of his favorite themes, the heroism of ordinary individuals in aid or defense of the helpless. *Poems* includes the Pike County poems, and three new sections. In the "Wanderlieder," one of the new sections, Hay deals often with love, as in "A Woman's Love," or with European history and politics. The forty-six poems of "New and Old," another new section, focus on love, religion, philosophy, war, and nature.

Though John Hay's literary reputation declined immediately after his death, Kelly Thurman in 1974 praised Hay's original subject matter, natural expression, experimentation with various stanza forms, and skillful use of humor (34, 36, 61–63), while candidly acknowledging his significant technical shortcomings. Robert Gale judged Hay's verse "[l]ogical, suspenseful and surprising, [and] sincere," but he criticized Hay's "cloying didacticism, his generalized and otherwise inadequate passion, his insufficient attention to detail, and his unwillingness to experiment with new forms and new topics" (67).

—*E. Frances Frame*

Suggestions for Further Reading

Gale, Robert. *John Hay*. Boston: Twayne, 1978.
Howells, William Dean. "John Hay in Literature." *North American Review* 181 (1905): 345–51.
Monteiro, George. *Henry James and John Hay: The Record of a Friendship*. Providence: Brown UP, 1965.
Rosenfeld, Alvin. "Whitman and the Providence Literati." *Books at Brown* 24 (1971): 82–103.
Thurman, Kelly. *John Hay as a Man of Letters*. Reseda, CA: Mojave Books, 1974.
Traubel, Horace. *With Walt Whitman in Camden*. Ed. Sculley Bradley. 6 vols. Philadelphia: U of Pennsylvania P, 1953.

TEXT
The Complete Poetical Works of John Hay. Boston: Houghton, 1917.

೨ುಲಿ

Jim Bludso of the *Prairie Belle*

Wall, no! I can't tell whar he lives,
　　Because he don't live, you see;
Leastways, he's got out of the habit
　　Of livin' like you and me.
Whar have you been for the last three year
　　That you haven't heard folks tell
How Jimmy Bludso passed in his checks
　　The night of the Prairie Belle?

He weren't no saint,—them engineers
　　Is all pretty much alike,—　　　　　　　　10
One wife in Natchez-under-the-Hill
　　And another one here, in Pike;
A keerless man in his talk was Jim,
　　And an awkward hand in a row,
But he never flunked, and he never lied,—
　　I recken he never knowed how.

And this was all the religion he had,—
　　To treat his engine well;
Never to be passed on the river;
　　To mind the pilot's bell;　　　　　　　　20
And if ever the Prairie Belle took fire,—
　　A thousand times he swore,
He'd hold her nozzle agin the bank
　　Till the last soul got ashore.

All boats has their day on the Mississip,
　　And her day come at last,—
The Movastar was a better boat,
　　But the Belle she *wouldn't* be passed.
And so she come tearin' along that night—
　　The oldest craft on the line—　　　　　　30
With a nigger squat on her safety valve,
　　And her furnace crammed, rosin and pine.

The fire burst out as she clared the bar,
　　And burnt a hole in the night,
And quick as a flash she turned, and made
　　For that willer-bank on the right.
There was runnin' and cursin', but Jim yelled out,
　　Over all the infernal roar,
"I'll hold her nozzle agin the bank
　　Till the last galoot's ashore."　　　　　　40

Through the hot, black breath of the burnin' boat
    Jim Bludso's voice was heard,
And they all had trust in his cussedness,
    And knowed he would keep his word.
And, sure's you're born, they all got off
    Afore the smokestacks fell,—
And Bludso's ghost went up alone
    In the smoke of the Prairie Belle.

He weren't no saint,—but at jedgment
    I'd run my chance with Jim,   50
'Longside of some pious gentlemen
    That wouldn't shake hands with him.
He seen his duty, a dead-sure thing,—
    And went for it thar and then;
And Christ ain't a-going to be too hard
    On a man that died for men.

                                        (6 January 1871, 1871)

A Woman's Love

A sentinel angel sitting high in glory
    Heard this shrill wail ring out from Purgatory:
"Have mercy, mighty angel, hear my story!

"I loved,—and, blind with passionate love, I fell.
Love brought me down to death, and death to Hell.
For God is just, and death for sin is well.

"I do not rage against his high decree,
Nor for myself do ask that grace shall be;
But for my love on earth who mourns for me.

"Great Spirit! Let me see my love again   10
And comfort him one hour, and I were fain
To pay a thousand years of fire and pain."

Then said the pitying angel, "Nay, repent
That wild vow! Look, the dial-finger's bent
Down to the last hour of thy punishment!"

But still she wailed, "I pray thee, let me go!
I cannot rise to peace and leave him so.
Oh, let me soothe him in his bitter woe!"

The brazen gates ground sullenly ajar,
And upward, joyous, like a rising star,   20
She rose and vanished in the ether far.

But soon adown the dying sunset sailing,
And like a wounded bird her pinions trailing,
She fluttered back, with broken-hearted wailing.

She sobbed, "I found him by the summer sea
Reclined, his head upon a maiden's knee,—
She curled his hair and kissed him. Woe is me!"

She wept, "Now let my punishment begin!
I have been fond and foolish. Let me in
To expiate my sorrow and my sin."   30

The angel answered, "Nay, sad soul, go higher!
To be deceived in your true heart's desire
Was bitterer than a thousand years of fire!"

                                    (20 May 1871, 1871)

The Prairie

The skies are blue above my head,
    The prairie green below,
And flickering o'er the tufted grass
    The shifting shadows go,
Vague-sailing, where the feathery clouds
    Fleck white the tranquil skies,
Black javelins darting where aloft
    The whirring pheasant flies.

A glimmering plain in drowsy trance
    The dim horizon bounds,   10
Where all the air is resonant
    With sleepy summer sounds,—
The life that sings among the flowers,
    The lisping of the breeze,
The hot cicala's sultry cry,
    The murmurous dream of bees.

The butterfly—a flying flower—
    Wheels swift in flashing rings,
And flutters round his quiet kin,

With brave flame-mottled wings.   20
The wild Pinks burst in crimson fire,
   The Phlox' bright clusters shine,
And Prairie-Cups are swinging free
   To spill their airy wine.

And lavishly beneath the sun,
   In liberal splendor rolled,
The Fennel fills the dipping plain
   With floods of flowery gold;
And widely weaves the Iron-Weed
   A woof of purple dyes   30
Where Autumn's royal feet may tread
   When bankrupt Summer flies.

In verdurous tumult far away
   The prairie-billows gleam,
Upon their crests in blessing rests
   The noontide's gracious beam.
Low quivering vapors steaming dim
   The level splendors break
Where languid Lilies deck the rim
   Of some land-circled lake.   40

Far in the East like low-hung clouds
   The waving woodlands lie;
Far in the West the glowing plain
   Melts warmly in the sky.
No accent wounds the reverent air,
   No footprint dints the sod,—
Lone in the light the prairie lies,
   Rapt in a dream of God.

                                                        (1871)

Religion and Doctrine

He stood before the Sanhedrin;[1]
The scowling rabbis gazed at him.
He recked not of their praise or blame;
There was no fear, there was no shame,
For one upon whose dazzled eyes

---

1. Sanhedrin were members of the highest judicial and ecclesiastical council of the ancient Jewish nation. That council was composed of from seventy to seventy-two members.

The whole world poured its vast surprise.
The oped heaven was far too near,
His first day's light too sweet and clear,
To let him waste his new-gained ken
On the hate-clouded face of men.   10

   But still they questioned, Who art thou?
What hast thou been? What art thou now?
Thou art not he who yesterday
Sat here and begged beside the way;
For he was blind.
                    —*And I am he;*
For I was blind, but now I see.

   He told the story o'er and o'er;
It was his full heart's only lore:
A prophet on the Sabbath-day
Had touched his sightless eyes with clay,   20
And made him see who had been blind.
Their words passed by him like the wind,
Which raves and howls, but cannot shock
The hundred-fathom-rooted rock.

   Their threats and fury all went wide;
They could not touch his Hebrew pride.
Their sneers at Jesus and His band,
Nameless and homeless in the land,
Their boasts of Moses and his Lord,
All could not change him by one word.   30
I know not what this man may be,
Sinner or saint; but as for me,
One thing I know,—that I am he
Who once was blind, and now I see.

   They were all doctors of renown,
The great men of a famous town,
With deep brows, wrinkled, broad, and wise,
Beneath their wide phylacteries;
The wisdom of the East was theirs,
And honor crowned their silver hairs.   40
The man they jeered and laughed to scorn
Was unlearned, poor, and humbly born;
But he knew better far than they
What came to him that Sabbath-day;
And what the Christ had done for him
He knew, and not the Sanhedrin.

                                                          (1890)

                    John Hay

Abram Joseph Ryan

1838?–1886

For Southern readers, Father Abram Ryan popularized the "Lost Cause," a tragic and romantic view of the war. In doing so, he earned the title "Poet-Priest of the South."

Biographers date Ryan's birth between 1834 and 1840. The day, however, is known: 15 August. Abram Joseph Ryan was born to an Irish immigrant family in Hagerstown, Maryland. When he was a small child, the family moved to St. Louis, where he received a Catholic education. Later, he studied at Niagara University in New York and received ordination to the priesthood in 1860, a date which suggests a birth year earlier than 1840. Father Ryan taught in New York and Missouri until the Civil War. An ardent Southern partisan, he accompanied Confederate troops as a free-lance chaplain, conducted himself bravely in battlefield ministry, and at times reportedly fought as a soldier. In 1863, he volunteered to minister in New Orleans's Gratiot prison during a smallpox quarantine. After the war, Ryan served as priest in various Southern parishes and edited periodicals, including the *Banner of the South* in Augusta, Georgia. During his last years, he lectured for charitable causes and began writing a life of Christ that was never finished. He died at a Franciscan monastary in Louisville, Kentucky, on 23 April 1886.

Father Ryan's poems were appearing in periodicals by 1868, and he published *Father Ryan's Poems* in 1879. The 1880 and 1888 editions, called *Poems: Patriotic, Religious, and Miscellaneous*, included a few more poems, but the first edition contained the ones that made his reputation. "The Conquered Banner" and "The Sword of Robert Lee" were printed and reprinted, illustrated, and set to music throughout the South. Into the early twentieth century, books on Southern literature gave Ryan attention comparable to that bestowed on Lanier, Timrod, and Hayne.

Strong, regular rhythm and the use of rhyme, alliteration, and assonance mark Father Ryan's work. Critics have generally praised the intense feeling of his verse, not his technical skill. Many use "The Conquered Banner" as an example of his excesses, but in 1973, Gordon Weaver defended Ryan's prosody in that poem as subtle and varied (xii). Ryan's own preface declares that the verses "were written at random.—off and on,—here,—there,—anywhere,—just when the mood came, with little of study and less of art,—and always in a hurry" (*Father Ryan's Poems* 5).

Ryan's patriotic Confederate poems have received much more attention than his religious verse. Although critics single out for mention "Song of the Mystic" and one or two others, they dismiss the majority with only general comment. The generation for whom the Civil War was a pivotal experience treasured Father Ryan's poetry; he gave Southerners grieving the losses of the war words as from their own hearts.

—*Susan Bales*

Suggestions for Further Reading

Moran, John. "Memoir of Father Ryan." *Poems: Patriotic, Religious, Miscellaneous*. By Abram J. Ryan. 12th ed. Baltimore, 1888.
Weaver, Gordon. Introduction. *Selected Poems of Father Ryan*. By Abram J. Ryan. Ed. Gordon Weaver. Jackson: UP of Mississippi, 1973.

TEXTS
Father Ryan's Poems. 1879.
Poems: Patriotic, Religious, and Miscellaneous. 1880.

ɘӿϵ

The Conquered Banner

Furl that Banner, for 'tis weary;
Round its staff 'tis drooping dreary;
    Furl it, fold it, it is best;
For there's not a man to wave it,
And there's not a sword to save it,
And there's not one left to lave it
In the blood which heroes gave it;
And its foes now scorn and brave it;
    Furl it, hide it—let it rest!

Take that Banner down! 'tis tattered;   10
Broken is its staff and shattered;
And the valiant hosts are scattered
    Over whom it floated high.

Oh! 'tis hard for us to fold it;
Hard to think there's none to hold it;
Hard that those who once unrolled it
    Now must furl it with a sigh.

Furl that Banner! furl it sadly!
Once ten thousands hailed it gladly,
And ten thousands wildly, madly,   20
    Swore it should forever wave;
Swore that foeman's sword should never
Hearts like theirs entwined dissever,
Till that flag should float forever
    O'er their freedom or their grave!

Furl it! for the hands that grasped it,
And the hearts that fondly clasped it,
    Cold and dead are lying low;
And that Banner—it is trailing!
While around it sounds the wailing   30
    Of its people in their woe.

For, though conquered, they adore it!
Love the cold, dead hands that bore it!
Weep for those who fell before it!
Pardon those who trailed and tore it!
But, oh! wildly they deplore it,
    Now who furl and fold it so.

Furl that Banner! True, 'tis gory,
Yet 'tis wreathed around with glory,
And 'twill live in song and story,   40
    Though its folds are in the dust:
For its fame on brightest pages,
Penned by poets and by sages,
Shall go sounding down the ages—
    Furl its folds though now we must.

Furl that Banner, softly, slowly!
Treat it gently—it is holy—
    For it droops above the dead.
Touch it not—unfold it never,
Let it droop there, furled forever,   50
    For its people's hopes are dead!

                                        (1866, 1879)

The Sword of Robert Lee

Forth from its scabbard, pure and bright,
　　Flashed the sword of Lee!
Far in the front of the deadly fight,
High o'er the brave in the cause of Right,
Its stainless sheen, like a beacon light,
　　Led us to Victory.

Out of its scabbard, where, full long,
　　It slumbered peacefully,
Roused from its rest by the battle's song,
Shielding the feeble, smiting the strong,　　　　　　10
Guarding the right, avenging the wrong,
　　Gleamed the sword of Lee.

Forth from its scabbard, high in air
　　Beneath Virginia's sky—
And they who saw it gleaming there,
And know who bore it, knelt to swear
That where that sword led they would dare
　　To follow—and to die.

Out of its scabbard! Never hand
　　Waved sword from stain as free,　　　　　　　　20
Nor purer sword led braver band,
Nor braver bled for a brighter land,
Nor brighter land had a cause so grand,
　　Nor cause a chief like Lee!

Forth from its scabbard! How we prayed
　　That sword might victor be;
And when our triumph was delayed,
And many a heart grew sore afraid,
We still hoped on while gleamed the blade
　　Of noble Robert Lee.　　　　　　　　　　　　30

Forth from its scabbard all in vain
　　Bright flashed the sword of Lee;
'Tis shrouded now in its sheath again,
It sleeps the sleep of our noble slain,
Defeated, yet without a stain,
　　Proudly and peacefully.

　　　　　　　　　　　　　　　　　　(1868, 1879)

Abram Joseph Ryan　　　　　　　　　　　　*361*

Song of the Mystic

I walk down the Valley of Silence—
    Down the dim, voiceless valley—alone!
And I hear not the fall of a footstep
    Around me, save God's and my own;
And the hush of my heart is as holy
    As hovers where angels have flown!

Long ago was I weary of voices
    Whose music my heart could not win;
Long ago was I weary of noises
    That fretted my soul with their din;   10
Long ago was I weary of places
    Where I met but the human—and sin.

I walked in the world with the worldly;
    I craved what the world never gave;
And I said: "In the world each Ideal,
    That shines like a star on life's wave,
Is wrecked on the shores of the Real,
    And sleeps like a dream in a grave."

And still did I pine for the Perfect,
    And still found the False with the True: 20
I sought 'mid the Human for Heaven,
    But caught a mere glimpse of its Blue:
And I wept when the clouds of the Mortal
    Veiled even that glimpse from my view.

And I toiled on, heart-tired of the Human;
    And I moaned 'mid the mazes of men;
Till I knelt, long ago, at an altar
    And I heard a voice call me:—since then
I walk down the Valley of Silence
    That lies far beyond mortal ken.   30

Do you ask what I found in the Valley?
    'Tis my Trysting Place with the Divine.
And I fell at the feet of the Holy,
    And above me a voice said: "Be mine."
And there arose from the depths of my spirit
    An echo—"My heart shall be thine."

Do you ask how I live in the Valley?
    I weep—and I dream—and I pray.

But my tears are as sweet as the dewdrops
     That fall on the roses in May;   40
And my prayer, like a perfume from Censers,
     Ascendeth to God night and day.

In the hush of the Valley of Silence
     I dream all the songs that I sing;
And the music floats down the dim Valley,
     Till each finds a word for a wing,
That to hearts, like the Dove of the Deluge,
     A message of Peace they may bring.

But far on the deep there are billows
     That never shall break on the beach;   50
And I have heard songs in the Silence,
     That never shall float into speech;
And I have had dreams in the Valley,
     Too lofty for language to reach.

And I have seen Thought in the Valley—
     Ah! me, how my spirit was stirred!
And they wear holy veils on their faces,
     Their footsteps can scarcely be heard:
They pass through the Valley like Virgins,
     Too pure for the touch of a word!   60

Do you ask me the place of the Valley,
     Ye hearts that are harrowed by Care?
It lieth afar between mountains,
     And God and His angels are there:
And one is the dark mount of Sorrow,
     And one the bright mountain of Prayer!

                                              (1879)

Bret Harte

1839–1902

Remembered mostly for his local color stories about gold rush era California, Bret Harte was also a popular poet in his time. Writing on the Civil War, race relations, California, and romance, Harte spoke to his public's interests. While all of his subject matter is now dated, Harte's poems are nonetheless important as part of the popular literary history of his era.

Francis Bret Harte was born 25 August 1839 in Albany, New York, to Henry Harte, an educator with aspirations for his son, and Elizabeth Ostrander Harte, who permitted Frank to "run pretty wild, most of the time out of doors" (O'Connor 12). At the age of eleven, Harte published his first poem, "Autumn Musings," in the New York *Sunday Atlas*. Harte went to school in New York until he was thirteen, studying sciences, languages, philosophy, and reading Dickens, Fenimore Cooper, the *Arabian Nights*, and *Gulliver's Travels* (O'Connor 21). His father's death necessitated Bret's finding work, first at a law office and then in a counting house. His fortunes changed in 1853 when Mrs. Harte married Colonel Andrew Williams and the family moved to California.

Life in California was difficult for Harte. Often broke and hungry, he wandered from place to place, working what jobs he could find. Between 1854 and 1860, Harte labored "as a schoolteacher, miner, printer, and perhaps a few other things" (O'Connor 21). He also collected memories and experiences that he would draw on for the rest of his literary career.

In 1858, Harte began newspaper work with Colonel S. G. Whipple on the *Northern Californian*, setting type, printing, and reporting the news. He subsequently got involved in a controversy over the rights of Native Americans, criticizing white citizens who had murdered a group of Indians near Eureka. His community's response to his statement was so violent that Harte moved to San Francisco, where he entered into the Abolitionist movement and Republican politics. When the Civil War broke out, Harte began writing propaganda poetry and became the most popular of the patriot-poets (O'Connor 62). When the war ended, Harte turned to other sources for his creations.

In 1868, Harte became editor of the *Overland Monthly* and published "The Luck of Roaring Camp," the story that made him famous (Erskine 334). Soon after he caught the public's eye with his tale of the California mining camps, he published a poem that further enhanced his reputation: "Plain Language from Truthful James," commonly known as "The Heathen Chinee." The poem, like its author's earlier patriotic prose, inspired people to battle. "Hawked on street corners and endlessly reprinted in cheap illustrated editions, the poem became a rallying cry for a powerful anti-Chinese movement." The poem was meant to be ironic, but the nation missed the point (Morrow, *Bret Harte* 26). Nevertheless, Bret Harte's reputation was secure, so he moved East to join the American literary elite.

When Harte returned to the East, he found that the public wanted western stories. At first, he easily turned out pieces like "The Luck" and rested on his laurels. Increasingly, however, he gained the reputation of being a deadbeat with a drinking problem. Harte also made a series of unwise career decisions, not the least of which was his collaboration with Mark Twain on a play. *Ah Sin*, the result, was a dramatic disaster and the beginning of the end of the Twain-Harte friendship.

After this, Harte's career suffered a steady decline. Receiving an appointment as a consular aide, he moved first to Crefeld, Germany, and later to Glasgow, Scotland. In 1884, Harte moved to England, where he died on 5 May 1902 of throat cancer. In his later years, his work descended into formulaic repetition of his early popular works.

Although known mainly for his prose, Harte deserves recognition for his poetry as well. His verse is extremely regular, both rhythmically and metrically. He used iambic tetrameter and an *ababb* rhyme scheme, giving his poems a sing-song pattern. Modern critics denigrate Harte's verse for its sentimentality, but that viewpoint neglects the popular standards of the time. What makes Harte's poetry interesting is the content, which changed dramatically throughout his career. The poems included here fall into three categories: patriotic poetry ("John Burns of Gettysburg"), dialect poems ("Plain Language from Truthful James"), and parodies ("The Ballad of the Emeu").

—*William R. Nash*

Suggestions for Further Reading

Erskine, John. "Bret Harte." *Leading American Novelists*. New York: Holt, 1910.

Morrow, Patrick D. *Bret Harte*. Boise: Boise State U Western Writers
Series, 1972.
————. *Bret Harte, Literary Critic*. Bowling Green: Bowling Green
State U Popular Press, 1979.
O'Connor, Richard. *Bret Harte: A Biography*. Boston: Little, 1966.

TEXT
The Complete Poetical Works of Bret Harte. 1870.

꧁꧂

Plain Language from Truthful James
Table Mountain, 1870

Which I wish to remark,
    And my language is plain,
That for ways that are dark
    And for tricks that are vain,
The heathen Chinee is peculiar,
    Which the same I would rise to explain.

Ah Sin was his name;
    And I shall not deny,
In regard to the same,
    What that name might imply;   10
But his smile it was pensive and childlike,
    As I frequently remarked to Bill Nye.

It was August the third,
    And quite soft was the skies;
Which it might be inferred
    That Ah Sin was likewise;
Yet he played in that day upon William
    And me in a way I despise.

Which we had a small game,
    And Ah Sin took a hand: 20
It was Euchre. The same
    He did not understand;
But he smiled as he sat by the table,
    With the smile that was childlike and bland.

Yet the cards they were stocked
    In a way that I grieve,
And my feelings were shocked
    At the state of Nye's sleeve,

Which was stuffed full of aces and bowers,
　And the same with intent to deceive.　　　　　　　　30

But the hands that were played
　By that heathen Chinee,
And the points that he made,
　Were quite frightful to see,—
Till at last he put down a right bower,
　Which the same Nye had dealt unto me.

Then I looked up at Nye,
　And he gazed upon me;
And he rose with a sigh,
　And said, "Can this be?　　　　　　　　　　　　40
We are ruined by cheap Chinese labor,"—
　And he went for that heathen Chinee.

In the scene that ensued
　I did not take a hand,
But the floor it was strewed
　Like the leaves on the strand
With the cards that Ah Sin had been hiding,
　In the game "he did not understand."

In his sleeves, which were long,
　He had twenty-four jacks,—　　　　　　　　　　50
Which was coming it strong,
　Yet I state but the facts;
And we found on his nails, which were taper,
　What is frequent in tapers,—that's wax.

Which is why I remark,
　And my language is plain,
That for ways that are dark
　And for tricks that are vain,
The heathen Chinee is peculiar,—
　Which the same I am free to maintain.　　　　　　60
　　　　　　　　　　　　　　　　　　　(1870, 1871)

John Burns of Gettysburg

Have you heard the story that gossips tell
Of Burns of Gettysburg?—No? Ah, well:
Brief is the glory that hero earns,

Briefer the story of poor John Burns.
He was the fellow who won renown,—
The only man who didn't back down
When the rebels rode through his native town;
But held his own in the fight next day,
When all his townsfolk ran away.
That was in July sixty-three,   10
The very day that General Lee,
Flower of Southern chivalry,
Baffled and beaten, backward reeled
From a stubborn Meade and a barren field.

I might tell how but the day before
John Burns stood at his cottage door,
Looking down the village street,
Where, in the shade of his peaceful vine,
He heard the low of his gathered kine,
And felt their breath with incense sweet;   20
Or I might say, when the sunset burned
The old farm gable, he thought it turned
The milk that fell like a babbling flood
Into the milk-pail red as blood!
Or how he fancied the hum of bees
Were bullets buzzing among the trees.
But all such fanciful thoughts as these
Were strange to a practical man like Burns,
Who minded only his own concerns,
Troubled no more by fancies fine   30
Than one of his calm-eyed, long-tailed kine,—
Quite old-fashioned and matter-of-fact,
Slow to argue, but quick to act.
That was the reason, as some folk say,
He fought so well on that terrible day.

And it was terrible. On the right
Raged for hours the heady fight,
Thundered the battery's double bass,—
Difficult music for men to face;
While on the left—where now the graves   40
Undulate like the living waves
That all that day unceasing swept
Up to the pits the rebels kept—
Round shot ploughed the upland glades,
Sown with bullets, reaped with blades;
Shattered fences here and there
Tossed their splinters in the air;

The very trees were stripped and bare;
The barns that once held yellow grain
Were heaped with harvests of the slain;   50
The cattle bellowed on the plain,
The turkeys screamed with might and main,
And brooding barn-fowl left their rest
With strange shells bursting in each nest.

Just where the tide of battle turns,
Erect and lonely stood old John Burns.
How do you think the man was dressed?
He wore an ancient long buff vest,
Yellow as saffron,—but his best;
And buttoned over his manly breast   60
Was a bright blue coat, with a rolling collar,
And large gilt buttons,—size of a dollar,—
With tails that the country-folk called "swaller."
He wore a broad-brimmed, bell-crowned hat,
White as the locks on which it sat.
Never had such a sight been seen
For forty years on the village green,
Since old John Burns was a country beau,
And went to the "quiltings" long ago.

Close at his elbows all that day,   70
Veterans of the Peninsula,
Sunburnt and bearded, charged away;
And striplings, downy of lip and chin,—
Clerks that the Home Guard mustered in,—
Glanced, as they passed, at the hat he wore,
Then at the rifle his right hand bore,
And hailed him, from out their youthful lore,
With scraps of a slangy *répertoire*:
"How are you, White Hat?" "Put her through!"
"Your head's level!" and "Bully for you!"   80
Called him "Daddy,"—begged he'd disclose
The name of the tailor who made his clothes,
And what was the value he set on those;
While Burns, unmindful of jeer and scoff,
Stood there picking the rebels off,—
With his long brown rifle and bell-crown hat,
And the swallow-tails they were laughing at.

'Twas but a moment, for that respect
Which clothes all courage their voices checked;
And something the wildest could understand   90

Spake in the old man's strong right hand,
And his corded throat, and the lurking frown
Of his eyebrows under his old bell-crown;
Until, as they gazed, there crept an awe
Through the ranks in whispers, and some men saw,
In the antique vestments and long white hair,
The Past of the Nation in battle there;
And some of the soldiers since declare
That the gleam of his old white hat afar,
Like the crested plume of the brave Navarre,[1]   100
That day was their oriflamme of war.

So raged the battle. You know the rest:
How the rebels, beaten and backward pressed,
Broke at the final charge and ran.
At which John Burns—a practical man—
Shouldered his rifle, unbent his brows,
And then went back to his bees and cows.

That is the story of old John Burns;
This is the moral the reader learns:
In fighting the battle, the question's whether   110
You'll show a hat that's white, or a feather!

(1871?)

The Ballad of the Emeu

Oh, say, have you seen at the Willows so green—
  So charming and rurally true—
A singular bird, with a manner absurd,
  Which they call the Australian Emeu?
               Have you
Ever seen this Australian Emeu?

It trots all around with its head on the ground,
  Or erects it quite out of your view;
And the ladies all cry, when its figure they spy,
  "Oh! what a sweet pretty Emeu!
               Oh! do
Just look at that lovely Emeu!"   10

1. Perhaps a reference to Pedro Navarro (1460–1528), a Spanish general who
repeatedly distinguished himself in military engagements.

One day to this spot, when the weather was hot,
 Came Matilda Hortense Fortescue;
And beside her there came a youth of high name,—
 Augustus Florell Montague
     The two
Both loved that wild, foreign Emeu.

With two loaves of bread then they fed it, instead
 Of the flesh of the white Cockatoo,
Which once was its food in that wild neighborhood
 Where ranges the sweet Kangaroo,
     That too
Is game for the famous Emeu!   20

Old saws and gimlets but its appetite whets,
 Like the world-famous bark of Peru;
There's nothing so hard that the bird will discard,
 And nothing its taste will eschew
     That you
Can give that long-legged Emeu!

The time slipped away in this innocent play,
 When up jumped the bold Montague:
"Where's that specimen pin that I gayly did win
 In raffle, and gave unto you,
     Fortescue?"
No word spoke the guilty Emeu!   30

"Quick! tell me his name whom thou gavest that same,
 Ere these hands in thy blood I imbrue!"
"Nay, dearest," she cried, as she clung to his side,
 "I'm as innocent as that Emeu!"
     "Adieu!"
He replied, "Miss M. H. Fortescue!"

Down she dropped at his feet, all as white as a sheet,
 As wildly he fled from her view;
He thought 'twas her sin,—for he knew not the pin
 Had been gobbled up by the Emeu;
     All through
The voracity of that Emeu!   40
        (1871)

Edward Rowland Sill

1841–1887

Edward Rowland Sill was esteemed in his day for the high moral tone exemplified by "The Fool's Prayer," far and away his most popular poem. Like Tennyson, his poetic touchstone, he sought to wed religious vision, intellectual rigor, and poetic beauty while exploring the questions of his age. Though his simpler affirmative statements earned the most acclaim, he continued to write searching poems throughout his career.

Born in Windsor, Connecticut, on 29 April 1841 to an old New England family, Sill was orphaned at age twelve and lived with relatives in Ohio until he entered Yale in 1857. After graduating, he spent six years in California, making abortive attempts at various occupations before returning to Ohio and eventually determining to be a schoolteacher. He taught first in several Ohio towns, then in Oakland, California. In 1874, he joined the faculty of the University of California, where he remained until poor health forced his return to Ohio. He died in Cleveland on 27 February 1887.

Sill wrote poetry from his Yale years on, though only two volumes appeared during his lifetime: *The Hermitage and Other Poems* (1868) and *The Venus of Milo and Other Poems* (1883), a privately printed collection. He published considerably in periodicals, often under pseudonyms.

Sill's work bears the mark of a questioner. He felt deep religious impulses but remained skeptical of orthodox creeds; he pondered the spiritual implications of contemporary scientific discoveries (he appears to have penned the country's earliest poetic response to Darwin's theories); and he wondered endlessly about what makes a good and useful life. His poems reflect these concerns, sometimes posing questions and at other times answering them according to his latest views.

Technically, Sill's verse is always competent and sometimes even better. Occasional lines, phrases and images are strikingly apt, such as the transcendentalist's bubble in "Five Lives," so insubstantial it can be "pricked by the air" (line 26). He also uses a wide variety of forms successfully.

Nevertheless, the high value he placed on intellectual substance produced a marked tendency toward abstraction, and sometimes toward sententiousness. Fortunately, Sill leavened his earnestness with a well-developed ironic sense of human limitations, evident in poems such as "Strange," and "Five Lives." These ethical and ironic visions converge on a more personal level in Sill's best work—later poems, for the most part, such as "Tempted" and "Her Explanation."

Since the publication of a collected edition in 1906, Sill's poetry has received little attention. In the 1930s, Newton Arvin, who admired Sill's probing intellect and sense of irony, condemned Sill with extravagant praise, declaring him one of the three important post-Civil War poets (the other two were Emily Dickinson and Sidney Lanier), yet a failure for not making fuller use of those attributes. Time has not borne out the former assertion, though Sill deserves credit for a score of truly fine poems, and for rejecting sentimentalism and easy piety.

—*Harry Crockett*

Suggestions for Further Reading

Arvin, Newton. "The Failure of E. R. Sill." *Bookman* 62 (Feb. 1931): 581–89.
Ferguson, Alfred Riggs. *Edward Rowland Sill: The Twilight Poet.* The Hague: Martinus Nijhoff, 1955.*

TEXTS
The Hermitage and Other Poems. 1868.
The Venus of Milo and Other Poems. 1883.
The Poetical Works of Edward Rowland Sill. Ed. William Belmont Parker. Boston: Houghton, 1906.

૭ᚷᏉ

Five Lives

Five mites of monads dwelt in a round drop
That twinkled on a leaf by a pool in the sun.
To the naked eye they lived invisible;
Specks, for a world of whom the empty shell
Of a mustard seed had been a hollow sky.

One was a meditative monad, called a sage;
And, shrinking all his mind within, he thought:
"Tradition, handed down for hours and hours,

Tells that our globe, this quivering crystal world,
Is slowly dying. What if, seconds hence,   10
When I am very old, yon shimmering dome
Come drawing down and down, till all things end?"
Then with a weazen smirk he proudly felt
No other mote of God had ever gained
Such giant grasp of universal truth.

One was a transcendental monad; thin
And long and slim in the mind; and thus he mused:
"Oh, vast, unfathomable monad-souls!
Made in the image"—a hoarse frog croaks from the pool—
"Hark! 'twas some god, voicing his glorious thought   20
In thunder music! Yea, we hear their voice,
And we may guess their minds from ours, their work.
Some taste they have like ours, some tendency
To wriggle about, and munch a trace of scum."
He floated up on a pin-point bubble of gas
That burst, pricked by the air, and he was gone.

One was a barren-minded monad, called
A positivist; and he knew positively:
"There is no world beyond this certain drop.
Prove me another! Let the dreamers dream   30
Of their faint dreams, and noises from without,
And higher and lower; life is life enough."
Then swaggering half a hair's breadth, hungrily
He seized upon an atom of bug, and fed.

One was a tattered monad, called a poet;
And with shrill voice ecstatic thus he sang:
"Oh the little female monad's lips!
Oh, the little female monad's eyes:
Ah, the little, little, female, female monad!"

The last was a strong-minded monadess,   40
Who dashed amid the infusoria,
Danced high and low, and wildly spun and dove
Till the dizzy others held their breath to see.

But while they led their wondrous little lives
Aeonian moments had gone wheeling by.
The burning drop had shrunk with fearful speed;
A glistening film—'twas gone; the leaf was dry.
The little ghost of an inaudible squeak
Was lost to the frog that goggled from his stone;

Who, at the huge, slow tread of a thoughtful ox   50
Coming to drink, stirred sideways fatly, plunged,
Launched backward twice, and all the pool was still.

(1870, 1883)

The Fool's Prayer

The royal feast was done; the King
    Sought some new sport to banish care,
And to his jester cried: "Sir Fool,
    Kneel now, and make for us a prayer!"

The jester doffed his cap and bells,
    And stood the mocking court before;
They could not see the bitter smile
    Behind the painted grin he wore.

He bowed his head, and bent his knee
    Upon the monarch's silken stool;   10
His pleading voice arose: "O Lord,
    Be merciful to me, a fool!

"No pity, Lord, could change the heart
    From red with wrong to white as wool;
The rod must heal the sin: but, Lord,
    Be merciful to me, a fool!

" 'Tis not by guilt the onward sweep
    Of truth and right, O Lord, we stay;
'Tis by our follies that so long
    We hold the earth from heaven away.   20

"These clumsy feet, still in the mire,
    Go crushing blossoms without end;
These hard, well-meaning hands we thrust
    Among the heart-strings of a friend.

"The ill-timed truth we might have kept—
    Who knows how sharp it pierced and stung?
The word we had not sense to say—
    Who knows how grandly it had rung?

"Our faults no tenderness should ask,
    The chastening stripes must cleanse them all;   30

Edward Rowland Sill   375

But for our blunders—oh, in shame
    Before the eyes of heaven we fall.

"Earth bears no balsam for mistakes;
    Men crown the knave, and scourge the tool
That did his will; but Thou, O Lord,
    Be merciful to me, a fool!"

The room was hushed; in silence rose
    The King, and sought his gardens cool,
And walked apart, and murmured low,
    "Be merciful to me, a fool!"

(1879, 1883)

Opportunity

This I beheld, or dreamed it in a dream:—
There spread a cloud of dust along a plain;
And underneath the cloud, or in it, raged
A furious battle, and men yelled, and swords
Shocked upon swords and shields. A prince's banner
Wavered, then staggered backward, hemmed by foes.
A craven hung along the battle's edge,
And thought, "Had I a sword of keener steel—
That blue blade that the king's son bears,—but this
Blunt thing—!" he snapt and flung it from his hand,   10
And lowering crept away and left the field.
Then came the king's son, wounded, sore bestead,
And weaponless, and saw the broken sword,
Hilt-buried in the dry and trodden sand,
And ran and snatched it, and with battle-shout
Lifted afresh he hewed his enemy down,
And saved a great cause that heroic day.

(1880, 1906)

Strange

He died at night. Next day they came
To weep and praise him: sudden fame
These suddenly warm comrades gave.
They called him pure, they called him brave;

One praised his heart, and one his brain;
All said, You'd seek his like in vain,—
Gentle, and strong, and good: none saw
In all his character a flaw.

At noon he wakened from his trance,
Mended, was well! They looked askance;   10
Took his hand coldly; loved him not,
Though they had wept him; quite forgot
His virtues; lent an easy ear
To slanderous tongues; professed a fear
He was not what he seemed to be;
Thanked God they were not such as he;
Gave to his hunger stones for bread;
And made him, living, wish him dead.

(1885, 1906)

Her Explanation

So you have wondered at me,—guessed in vain
What the real woman is you know so well?
   I am a lost illusion. Some strange spell
Once made your friend there, with his fine disdain
Of fact, conceive me perfect. He would fain
   (But could not) see me always, as befell
   His dream to see me, plucking asphodel,
In saffron robes, on some celestial plain.
All that I was he marred and flung away
   In quest of what I was not, could not be,—   10
   Lilith, or Helen, or Antigone.
Still he may search; but I have had my day,
   And now the Past is all the part for me
That this world's empty stage has left to play.

(1885, 1906)

Tempted

Yes, I know what you say:
   Since it cannot be soul to soul,
Be it flesh to flesh, as it may;
   But is Earth the whole?

Edward Rowland Sill   377

Shall a man betray the Past
    For all Earth gives?
"But the Past is dead?" At last,
    It is all that lives.

Which were the nobler goal—
    To snatch at the moment's bliss,   10
Or to swear I will keep my soul
    Clean for her kiss?

(1885, 1906)

On Second Thought

The end's so near,
    It is all one
What track I steer,
    What work's begun.
    It is all one
    If *nothing's* done,
The end's so near!

The end's so near,
    It is all one
What track thou steer,   10
    What work's begun—
    Some deed, *some* plan,
    As thou'rt a man!
The end's so near!

(1887, 1906)

Sidney Lanier
1842–1881

Sidney Lanier tried to write his way out of the sentimental legacy of the Old South. Some critics say he never sufficiently distanced his idea of a poet-prophet from the chivalric code of the Confederacy. His readers responded to his noble character and moral earnestness, but his diffuse metaphors, luxuriant tonality, and increasingly irregular rhythms confused many. Lanier, nevertheless, devised a unique musicality that has earned him a significant place among nineteenth-century poets. For the success of a handful of his later poems, and for his exacting analysis of prosody in musical terms, critics value him today.

Born into a prosperous Macon, Georgia, family on 3 February 1842, Lanier showed early interests in music and philosophy, graduating from Ogelthorpe College with highest honors in 1860. Enlisting in the Macon Volunteers in 1861, he contracted tuberculosis while imprisoned at Point Lookout, Maryland, in 1864. Lanier completed some poetry and a novel, *Tiger-Lilies* (1876), after the war, but poor health and the impact of Reconstruction forced him to take up the practice of law in 1868. On a recuperative trip to Texas in 1872, he decided to devote the remainder of his life to the arts, and landed the position of first flutist with the Peabody Orchestra in Baltimore the following year. Lanier planned to spend more time on poetry while holding this position, but interrupted his efforts to write a travel book on Florida (1876), and to lecture, first, on Shakespeare at the Peabody Institute (1878), and then on English verse at Johns Hopkins University (1879). He began to achieve a national reputation during this period, beginning with the publication of "Corn" in *Lippincott's* in 1875. The next year he wrote a cantata, the *Centennial Meditation of Columbia*, at the request of the U.S. Centennial Commission, and in 1877, he published a small volume of ten poems.

Lanier wrote his best poetry during these years, but faced with declining health, he retired from his Johns Hopkins lectureship in 1880. Lanier died 7 September 1881. From his poem "Sunrise" comes the line on his gravestone in Baltimore: "I am lit with the sun." His wife, Mary Day Lanier, subsequently edited one hundred of his poems, many of which had appeared in magazines, for *Poems of Sidney Lanier* (1884).

Lanier's subject matter, even through the Civil War, was not his own experience. He disdained what he called "the drunken, rude barbarity" of the war (line 10 of "To J. L." in *Centennial Edition*, 1:8). Inspired by his reading of Thomas Carlyle, Phillip James Bailey, Elizabeth Barrett and Robert Browning, and Alfred, Lord Tennyson while a scout on the James River, Lanier created in his early poems a heroic persona who asserts the primacy of feeling over intellect. Not until Reconstruction did he write dialect poems or poems such as "The Ship of Earth," which allude to actual conditions in the South. In "Corn," Lanier identifies the South's regeneration with a crop to be distinguished from "coquette Cotton."

"Corn" reveals Lanier's growing experimentation with form, as well as a greater rhythmic variation than earlier poems built on iambic pentameter or ballad meters. Lanier continued this exploration with "The Symphony" in 1875, a poem reflecting his new interest in the program music of such composers as Berlioz.

While convalescing in Florida in 1877, Lanier wrote friends that he had found in Emerson a new vision of the artist as seer, an inspiration reflected in such a poem as "Tampa Robins." The poet as priest of nature appears in "The Marshes of Glynn," a poem that displays Lanier's technical innovations. Discovering Whitman's *Leaves of Grass* in 1878, a work he called "a real refreshment to me—like rude salt spray in your face" (letter to Bayard Taylor, 3 February 1878, in *Centennial Edition* 10: 18), Lanier took encouragement from the similarity between Whitman's experiments and his own interest in "symphonic sound."

The Science of English Verse (1880) represents Lanier's effort to crystallize his thoughts about prosody. His poem "Opposition" reflects a main tenet of this volume, namely that a poet expresses within the rhythmic tension of a line the tension within his own moral view. With scientific precision, Lanier explored in this volume the musical properties of verse, especially the use of dactyls, an important component, curiously, of some of Whitman's "free" verse. Doing work well in advance of twentieth-century poets' concerns for variable speech patterns, Lanier triggered little critical response at the time.

Influenced early on by Poe, Lanier later turned his back on him, because Poe "did not *know* enough . . . to be a great poet." Acutely aware of his own limited education, Lanier strove to go beyond a knowledge of standard musical effects. If Poe attained a mastery of conventions, Lanier aimed further. Through his systematic study of prosody, Lanier sought a release of the full rhythmic potential of a line. This theoretical emphasis and the hauntingly original lines of his last poems continue to interest readers.

—*Wilson Somerville*

Suggestions for Further Reading

De Bellis, Jack. *Sidney Lanier*. New York: Twayne, 1972.

————. *Sidney Lanier, Henry Timrod, and Paul Hamilton Hayne: A Reference Guide*. Boston: Hall, 1978.*

Gabin, Jane S. *A Living Minstrelsy: The Poetry and Music of Sidney Lanier*. Macon: Mercer UP, 1985.

————. "Sidney Lanier." *Fifty Southern Writers Before 1900*. Ed. Robert Bain and Joseph Flora. New York: Greenwood, 1987. 303–11.*

Rubin, Louis D., Jr. "The Passion of Sidney Lanier." *William Elliott Shoots a Bear: Essays on the Southern Literary Imagination*. Baton Rouge: Louisiana State UP, 1976. 107–44.

TEXT

The Centennial Edition of the Works of Sidney Lanier. Ed. Charles R. Anderson. 10 vols. Baltimore: Johns Hopkins UP, 1945.

◦◦◦

The Ship of Earth

Thou Ship of Earth, with Death, and Birth, and Life, and
    Sex aboard,
  And fires of Desires burning hotly in the hold,
I fear thee, O! I fear thee, for I hear the tongue and sword
  At battle on the deck, and the wild mutineers are bold!
The dewdrop morn may fall from off the petal of the sky,
  But all the deck is wet with blood and stains the crystal
    red.
A pilot, God, a pilot! for the helm is left awry,
  And the best sailors in the ship lie there among the dead!

                        (written 1868, 1884)

Corn

To-day the woods are trembling through and through
With shimmering forms, that flash before my view,

Then melt in green as dawn-stars melt in blue.
The leaves that wave against my cheek caress
Like women's hands; the embracing boughs express
A subtlety of mighty tenderness;
The copse-depths into little noises start,
That sound anon like beatings of a heart,
Anon like talk 'twixt lips not far apart.
The beech dreams balm, as a dreamer hums a song;   10
Through that vague wafture, expirations strong
Throb from young hickories breathing deep and long
With stress and urgence bold of prisoned spring
And ecstasy of burgeoning.
Now, since the dew-plashed road of morn is dry,
Forth venture odors of more quality
And heavenlier giving. Like Jove's locks awry,
Long muscadines
Rich-wreathe the spacious foreheads of great pines,
And breathe ambrosial passion from their vines.   20
I pray with mosses, ferns and flowers shy
That hide like gentle nuns from human eye
To life adoring perfumes to the sky.
I hear faint bridal-sighs of brown and green
Dying to silent hints of kisses keen
As far lights fringe into a pleasant sheen.
I start at fragmentary whispers, blown
From undertalks of leafy souls unknown,
Vague purports sweet, of inarticulate tone.

Dreaming of gods, men, nuns and brides, between   30
Old companies of oaks that inward lean
To join their radiant amplitudes of green
I slowly move, with ranging looks that pass
Up from the matted miracles of grass
Into yon veiled complex of space
Where sky and leafage interlace
So close, the heaven of blue is seen
Inwoven with a heaven of green.

I wander to the zigzag-cornered fence
Where sassafras, intrenched in brambles dense,   40
Contests with stolid vehemence
The march of culture, setting limb and thorn
As pikes against the army of the corn.
There, while I pause, my fieldward-faring eyes
Take harvests, where the stately corn-ranks rise,
Of inward dignities

And large benignities and insights wise,
    Graces and modest majesties.
Thus, without theft, I reap another's field;
Thus, without tilth, I house a wondrous yield,   50
And heap my heart with quintuple crops concealed.

Look, out of line one tall corn-captain stands
Advanced beyond the foremost of his bands,
    And waves his blades upon the very edge
    And hottest thicket of the battling hedge.
Thou lustrous stalk, that ne'er mayst walk nor talk,
    Still shalt thou type the poet-soul sublime
    That leads the vanward of his timid time
    And sings up cowards with commanding rhyme—

Soul calm, like thee, yet fain, like thee, to grow   60
By double increment, above, below;
    Soul homely, as thou art, yet rich in grace like thee,
    Teaching the yeoman selfless chivalry
    That moves in gentle curves of courtesy;
Soul filled like thy long veins with sweetness tense,
    By every godlike sense
Transmuted from the four wild elements.
    Drawn to high plans,
    Thou lift'st more stature than a mortal man's,
Yet ever piercest downward in the mould   70
    And keepest hold
    Upon the reverend and steadfast earth
    That gave thee birth;
    Yea, standest smiling in thy future grave,
    Serene and brave,
    With unremitting breath
    Inhaling life from death,
Thine epitaph writ fair in fruitage eloquent,
    Thyself thy monument.

    As poets should,   80
Thou hast built up thy hardihood
With universal food,
    Drawn in select proportion fair
    From honest mould and vagabond air;
From darkness of the dreadful night,
    And joyful light;
    From antique ashes, whose departed flame
    In thee has finer life and longer fame;
From wounds and balms,

From storms and calms,   90
From potsherds and dry bones
        And ruin-stones.
Into thy vigorous substance thou hast wrought
Whate'er the hand of Circumstance hath brought;
    Yea, into cool solacing green hast spun
    White radiance hot from out the sun.
So thou dost mutually leaven
Strength of earth with grace of heaven;
    So thou dost marry new and old
    Into a one of higher mold;   100
    So thou dost reconcile the hot and cold,
        The dark and bright,
And many a heart-perplexing opposite,
        And so,
    Akin by blood to high and low,
Fitly thou playest out thy poet's part,
Richly expending thy much-bruised heart
    In equal care to nourish lord in hall
        Or beast in stall:
Thou took'st from all that thou might'st give to all.   110

O steadfast dweller on the selfsame spot
Where thou was born, that still repinest not—
Type of the home-fond heart, the happy lot!—
    Deeply thy mild content rebukes the land
    Whose flimsy homes, built on the shifting sand
Of trade, for ever rise and fall
With alternation whimsical,
    Enduring scarce a day,
    Then swept away
By swift engulfments of incaculable tides   120
Whereon capricious Commerce rides.

Look, thou substantial spirit of content!
Across this little vale, thy continent,
    To where, beyond the mouldering mill,
    Yon old deserted Georgian hill
Bares to the sun his piteous aged crest
        And seamy breast,
    By restless-hearted children left to lie
Untended there beneath the heedless sky,
As barbarous folk expose their old to die.   130

Upon that generous-rounding side,
        With gullies scarified

Where keen Neglect his lash hath plied,
Dwelt one I knew of old, who played at toil,
And gave to coquette Cotton soul and soil.
  Scorning the slow reward of patient grain,
  He sowed his heart with hopes of swifter gain,
  Then sat him down and waited for the rain.
He sailed in borrowed ships of usury—
A foolish Jason on a treacherous sea,   140
Seeking the Fleece and finding misery.[1]
  Lulled by smooth-rippling loans, in idle trance
  He lay, content that unthrift Circumstance
  Should plough for him the stony field of Chance.
Yea, gathering crops whose worth no man might tell,
He staked his life on games of Buy-and-Sell,
And turned each field into a gambler's hell.
  Aye, as each year began,
  My farmer to the neighboring city ran;
Passed with a mournful anxious face   150
Into the banker's inner place;
Parleyed, excused, pleaded for longer grace;
  Railed at the drought, the worm, the rust, the grass;
  Protested ne'er again 'twould come to pass;
  With many an *oh* and *if* and *but alas*
Parried or swallowed searching questions rude,
And kissed the dust to soften Dives's mood.[2]
At last, small loans by pledges great renewed,
  He issues smiling from the fatal door,
  And buys with lavish hand his yearly store   160
  Till his small borrowings will yield no more.
Aye, as each year declined,
With bitter heart and ever-brooding mind
He mourned his fate unkind.
  In dust, in rain, with might and main,
  He nursed his cotton, cursed his grain,
  Fretted for news that made him fret again,
Snatched at each telegram of Future Sale,
And thrilled with Bulls' or Bears' alternate wail—
In hope or fear alike for ever pale.   170
  And thus from year to year, through hope and fear,
  With many a curse and many a secret tear,
  Striving in vain his cloud of debt to clear,
        At last
He woke to find his foolish dreaming past,

---

1. Jason was the leader of the Argonauts in the quest for the Golden Fleece.
2. The Latin word *Dives* means "rich man" and occurs in the Vulgate version
of the parable of Lazarus (Luke 16).

And all his best-of-life the easy prey
Of squandering scamps and quacks that lined his way
   With vile array,
From rascal statesman down to petty knave;
Himself, at best, for all his bragging brave.   180
A gamester's catspaw and a banker's slave.
  Then, worn and gray, and sick with deep unrest,
  He fled away into the oblivious West,
    Unmourned, unblest.

Old hill! old hill! thou gashed and hairy Lear
Whom the divine Cordelia of the year,
E'en pitying Spring, will vainly strive to cheer—
  King, that no subject man nor beast may own,
  Discrowned, undaughtered and alone—
Yet shall the great God turn thy fate,   190
And bring thee back into thy monarch state
    And majesty immaculate.
Lo, through hot waverings of thy August morn,
  Thou givest from thy vasty sides forlorn
  Visions of golden treasuries of corn—
Ripe largesse lingering for some bolder heart
That manfully shall take thy part,
    And tend thee,
    And defend thee,
With antique sinew and with modern art.   200
                (written 1874, 1877)

Evening Song

Look off, dear Love, across the sallow sands,
  And mark yon meeting of the sun and sea;
How long they kiss, in sight of all the lands!
    Ah longer, longer, we.

Now in the sea's red vintage melts the sun,
  As Egypt's pearl dissolved in rosy wine,
And Cleopatra Night drinks all. 'Tis done!
    Love, lay thine hand in mine.

Come forth, sweet stars, and comfort Heaven's heart;
  Glimmer, ye waves, round else unlighted sands;   10

O Night, divorce our sun and sky apart—
Never our lips, our hands.

(written 1876, 1884)

Tampa Robins

The robin laughed in the orange-tree:
"Ho, windy North, a fig for thee:
While breasts are red and wings are bold
And green trees wave us globes of gold,
Time's scythe shall reap but bliss for me
—Sunlight, song, and the orange-tree.

"Burn, golden globes in leafy sky,
My orange-planets: crimson, I
Will shine and shoot among the spheres
(Blithe meteor that no mortal fears)   10
And thrid the heavenly orange-tree
With orbits bright of minstrelsy.

"If that I hate wild winter's spite—
The gibbet trees, the world in white,
The sky but gray wind over a grave—
Why should I ache, the season's slave?
I'll sing from the top of the orange-tree
Gramercy, winter's tyranny.

"I'll south with the sun, and keep my clime;
My wing is king of the summer-time;   20
My breast to the sun his torch shall hold;
And I'll call down through the green and gold
Time, take thy scythe, reap bliss for me,
Bestir thee under the orange-tree."

(written 1877, 1884)

The Marshes of Glynn

Glooms of the live-oaks, beautiful-braided and woven
With intricate shades of the vines that myriad-cloven
Clamber the forks of the multiform boughs,—

Sidney Lanier   387

Emerald twilights,—
Virginal shy lights,
Wrought of the leaves to allure to the whisper of vows,
When lovers pace timidly down through the green
colonnades
Of the dim sweet woods, of the dear dark woods,
Of the heavenly woods and glades,
That run to the radiant marginal sand-beach within   10
The wide sea-marshes of Glynn;—

Beautiful glooms, soft dusks in the noon-day fire,—
Wildwood privacies, closets of lone desire,
Chamber from chamber parted with wavering arras of
leaves,—
Cells for the passionate pleasure of prayer to the soul that
grieves,
Pure with a sense of the passing of saints through the
wood,
Cool for the dutiful weighing of ill with good;—

O braided dusks of the oak and woven shades of the vine,
While the riotous noon-day sun of the June-day long did
shine,
Ye held me fast in your heart and I held you fast in mine;   20
But now when the noon is no more, and riot is rest,
And the sun is a-wait at the ponderous gate of the West,
And the slant yellow beam down the wood-aisle doth
seem
Like a lane into heaven that leads from a dream,—
Ay, now, when my soul all day hath drunken the soul of the
oak,
And my heart is at ease from men, and the wearisome sound
of the stroke
Of the scythe of time and the trowel of trade is low,
And belief overmasters doubt, and I know that I know
And my spirit is grown to a lordly great compass within,
That the length and the breadth and the sweep of the
marshes of Glynn   30
Will work no fear like the fear they have wrought me of
yore
When length was fatigue, and when breadth was but
bitterness sore,
And when terror and shrinking and dreary unnamable
pain
Drew over me out of the merciless miles of the plain,—
Oh, now, unafraid, I am fain to face

The vast visage of space.
To the edge of the wood I am drawn, I am drawn,
Where the gray beach glimmering runs, as a belt of the
    dawn,
        For a mete and a mark
        To the forest-dark:—   40
            So:
Affable live-oak, leaning low,—
Thus—with your favor—soft, with a reverent hand,
(Not lightly touching your person, Lord of the land!)
Bending your beauty aside, with a step I stand
        On the firm-packed sand,
            Free
By a world of marsh that borders a world of sea.
Sinuous southward and sinuous northward the shimmering
    band
Of the sand-beach fastens the fringe of the marsh to the
    folds of the land.   50
Inward and outward to northward and southward the beach-
    lines linger and curl
As a silver-wrought garment that clings to and follows the
    firm sweet limbs of a girl.
Vanishing, swerving, evermore curving again into sight,
Softly the sand-beach wavers away to a dim gray looping
    of light.
And what if behind me to westward the wall of the
    woods stands high?
The world lies east: how ample, the marsh and the sea and
    the sky!
A league and a league of marsh-grass, waist-high, broad
    in the blade,
Green, and all of a height, and unflecked with a light or a
    shade,
        Stretch leisurely off, in a pleasant plain,
        To the terminal blue of the main.   60

    Oh, what is abroad in the marsh and the terminal sea?
        Somehow my soul seems suddenly free
    From the weighing of fate and the sad discussion of sin,
    By the length and the breadth and the sweep of the
        marshes of Glynn.
Ye marshes, how candid and simple and nothing-withhold-
    ing and free
Ye publish yourselves to the sky and offer yourselves to the
    sea!
Tolerant plains, that suffer the sea and the rains and the sun,

Ye spread and span like the catholic man who hath mightily
   won
      God out of knowledge and good out of infinite pain
      And sight out of blindness and purity out of a stain. 70

      As the marsh-hen secretly builds on the watery sod,
      Behold I will build me a nest on the greatness of God:
      I will fly in the greatness of God as the marsh-hen flies
      In the freedom that fills all the space 'twixt the marsh
         and the skies:
      By so many roots as the marsh-grass sends in the sod
      I will heartily lay me a-hold on the greatness of God:
      Oh, like to the greatness of God is the greatness within
      The range of the marshes, the liberal marshes of
         Glynn.

And the sea lends large, as the marsh: lo, out of his plenty
   the sea
      Pours fast: full soon the time of the flood-tide must
         be: 80
         Look how the grace of the sea doth go
      About and about through the intricate channels that
         flow
               Here and there,
               Everywhere,
Till his waters have flooded the utermost creeks and the low-
   lying lanes,
         And the marsh is meshed with a million veins,
         That like as with rosy and silvery essences flow
            In the rose-and-silver evening glow.
            Farewell, my lord Sun!
         The creeks overflow, a thousand rivulets run   90
         'Twixt the roots of the sod; the blades of the marsh-
            grass stir;
Passeth a hurrying sound of wings that westward whirr;
Passeth, and all is still; and the currents cease to run;
            And the sea and the marsh are one.
         How still the plains of the waters be!
         The tide is in his ecstasy.
         The tide is at his highest height:
            And it is night.
      And now from the Vast of the Lord will the waters of
         sleep
            Roll in on the souls of men,   100
         But who will reveal to our waking ken
         The forms that swim and the shapes that creep

Under the waters of sleep?
And I would I could know what swimmeth below when the
  tide comes in
  On the length and the breadth of the marvellous
  marshes of Glynn.

(written 1878, 1884)

Opposition

Of fret, of dark, of thorn, of chill,
  Complain no more; for these, O heart,
Direct the random of the will
  As rhymes direct the rage of art.

The lute's fixt fret, that runs athwart
  The strain and purpose of the string,
For governance and nice consort
  Doth bar his wilful wavering.

The dark hath many dear avails;
  The dark distills divinest dews;   10
The dark is rich with nightingales,
  With dreams, and with the heavenly Muse.

Bleeding with thorns of petty strife,
  I'll ease (as lovers do) my smart
With sonnets to my lady Life
  Writ red in issues from the heart.

What grace may lie within the chill
  Of favor frozen fast in scorn!
When Good's a freeze, we call it Ill!
  This rosy Time is glacier-born.   20

Of fret, of dark, of thorn, of chill,
  Complain thou not, O heart; for these
Bank-in the current of the will
  To uses, arts, and charities.

(written 1879, 1884)

A Ballad of Trees and the Master

Into the woods my Master went,
    Clean forspent, forspent.
Into the woods my Master came,
    Forspent with love and shame.
But the olives they were not blind to Him,
The little gray leaves were kind to Him:
The thorn-tree had a mind to Him
    When into the woods He came.

Out of the woods my Master went,
    And He was well content.   10
Out of the woods my Master came,
    Content with death and shame.
When Death and Shame would woo Him last,
From under the trees they drew Him last:
'Twas on a tree they slew Him—last
    When out of the woods He came.

(written 1880, 1884)

John Banister Tabb

1845–1909

John Banister Tabb is best known for his experiments in short, lyric verse and his use of nature to communicate spiritual experience. His most productive years were the 1890s, and some early readers compared Tabb with Emily Dickinson as an innovator. Few critics subscribe to this notion today. Though Tabb wrote over nine hundred poems, his range of subject and his prosody appear limited next to Dickinson's. Current scholarship has emphasized Tabb's lifelong devotion to the South and his conversion to Catholicism as central influences on his writing.

On 22 March 1845, John Banister Tabb was born at "The Forest," the Tabb family plantation located in Amelia County, Virginia. He lived at The Forest until the summer of 1862, when he became a blockade-runner for the Confederacy. Captured by Union forces in June 1864, Tabb spent seven months at Bull Pen Prison, Point Lookout, Maryland, where he befriended Sidney Lanier. That friendship inspired a number of poems, notably "At Lanier's Grave" and "The Captives."

After the war, Tabb traveled to Baltimore, where he hoped to make a career as a pianist. When these plans failed, he taught briefly at St. Paul's School for Boys before being called home to attend his sick sister Hallie and help his family avoid financial ruin. Contrary to his family's wishes, Tabb converted from Episcopalianism to Catholicism, and in November 1872, he entered St. Charles College in Maryland with the aim of becoming a priest. Tabb was ordained in 1884, after completing his studies at St. Mary's Seminary in Baltimore. He then returned to St. Charles where he remained until his death on 19 November 1909. Tabb was buried at Hollywood Cemetery in Richmond, Virginia.

Tabb published his first poem, "The Cloud," in *Harper's Monthly* in July 1877. Giles Henry Zimmer points out that before 1892 Tabb wrote fewer than a hundred poems (78). Then, in 1892, Tabb composed over three hundred poems and began to write the short, highly crafted lyrics that mark his highest achievement. Thomas Wentworth Higginson observed of Tabb's second volume, *Poems* (1894), that both Tabb and Dickinson possessed "the same fine, shy, recluse observations of nature and men, and the same terse brevity of utterance" (402). Prior to *Poems* (1894), Tabb had published *An Octave to Mary* in 1893. After 1894, he published seven books of poetry: *Lyrics* (1897), *Child Verse* (1899), *Two Lyrics* (1900), *Later Lyrics* (1902), *The Rosary in Rhyme* (1904), *Quips and Quiddits* (1907), and *Later Poems* (1910).

Most of Tabb's best work takes the form of quatrains built of iambs in alternating six- and eight-syllable lines. This dependency on common ballad meter, together with Tabb's use of ellipses, establishes the most pronounced formal link with Dickinson. Thematic parallels have more to do with the way both poets saw nature as a vehicle for spiritual commentary than with any common understanding of spiritual life. While Tabb writes frequently about death, as in "Evolution" and "The Tollmen," his view is religiously orthodox. He also wrote extensively about nature, as in "The Humming-Bird," "A Sunset," and "My Captive." Late in life, as his eyesight began to fail, Tabb became more concerned with blindness ("Going Blind"). Also during these last years, he composed one of his few poems on politics; in "Variety Is the Spice of Life," Tabb condemns Theodore Roosevelt for inviting Booker T. Washington to the White House. In this poem, Tabb betrays his racial prejudice by suggesting Roosevelt's impropriety for bringing a black man into the presence of white women.

Few modern critics have assessed Tabb's work. Thomas H. Johnson's comments in 1950 on the "arresting" similarities between Tabb and Dickinson kept alive the comparison, but added little of substance to what Higginson and others had noted earlier. Critics see Tabb as a minor poet whose verse experiments parallel those of Dickinson, but whose poetry is finally conventional and undistinguished. As scholars continue to discover cross-currents that inform regional identity, Tabb may acquire significance as a post–Civil War Southern Catholic poet.

—*Paul Crumbley*

Suggestions for Further Reading

Higginson, Thomas W. "Recent American Poetry." *Nation* 60 (May 23, 1895): 402.
Johnson, Thomas H., ed. *John Banister Tabb on Emily Dickinson*. New York: Seven Gables Bookshop, 1950.
Litz, Francis A., ed. *The Best Poems of John Banister Tabb*. Westminster, MD: Newman P, 1957.*
Williams, John Joseph. *A Critical Study of the Poetry of John Banister Tabb*. Diss. U of Georgia, 1966.*

Zimmer, Giles Henry. *A Poet's Progress: The Achievement of John Banister Tabb*. Diss. U of Arkansas, 1982.*

TEXT
The Poetry of Father Tabb. New York: Dodd, 1928.

꧅

At Lanier's Grave

I stand beside a comrade tree
That guards the spot where thou art laid;
For since thy light is lost to me
    I loiter in the shade.
I lean upon the rugged stone
As on the breast from whence I came,
To learn 'tis not my heart alone
    That bears thy sacred name.

(1892)

The Debtor Christ

What, woman, is my debt to thee
    That I should not deny
The boon thou dost demand of me?
    "I gave thee power to die."

(1892)

Narcissus

The god enamoured never knew
The shadow that beguiled his view,
Nor deemed it less divinely true
    Than Life and Love.

And so the poet, while he wrought
His image in the tide of thought,
Deemed it a glimpse in darkness caught
    Of light above.

(1894)

The Humming-Bird

A flash of harmless lightning,
    A mist of rainbow dyes
The burnished sunbeams brightening,
    From flower to flower he flies;

While wakes the nodding blossom,
    But just too late to see
What lip hath touched her bosom
    And drained her nectary.

(1894)

Poetry

A gleam of heaven; the passion of a star
    Held captive in the clasp of harmony;
A silence, shell-like breathing from afar
    The rapture of the deep—eternity.

(1894)

The Captives[1]

Apart forever dwelt the twain,
Save for one oft-repeated strain
Wherein what love alone could say
They learned and lavished day by day.

Strangers in all but misery
And music's hope-sustaining tie,
They lived and loved and died apart,
But soul to soul and heart to heart.

(1894)

---

1. "Suggested by a Point Lookout experience, where I first heard Lanier's flute, before I met the player." [Tabb's note]

Evolution

Out of the dusk a shadow,
    Then a spark;
Out of the cloud a silence,
    Then a lark;
Out of the heart a rapture,
    Then a pain;
Out of the dead, cold ashes,
    Life again.

        (1894)

Beethoven and Angelo[2]

One made the Surging sea of tone
    Subservient to his rod;
One from the sterile womb of stone
    Raised children unto God.

        (1894)

The Tollmen

    Lo, Silence, Sleep, and Death
    Await us on the way
To take of each the tribute breath
    That God himself did pay.

    Nor Solomon's as great
    Nor Caesar's strong control,
As his who sits beside his gate
    To take of each the toll.

        (1897)

2. Ludwig van Beethoven, German composer (1770–1827); Michaelangelo, Italian sculptor and painter (1475–1564).

Deus Absconditus[3]

My God has hid himself from me
Behind whatever else I see;
Myself—the nearest mystery—
As far beyond my grasp as He.

And yet, in darkest night, I know,
While lives a doubt-discerning glow,
That larger lights above it throw
These shadows in the vale below.

(1897)

A Sunset

What means it, Lord? No Daniel
In Nature's banquet-hall
Appears, thy messenger, to spell
The writing on the wall.

Is it the Babylonian doom—
A kingdom passed away—
A midnight monarch to assume
The majesty of Day?

(1900?)

Variety Is the Spice of Life

Contrasts are striking, Teddy knows;
And so, for a variety,
The Black man to the White House goes,
Rough-riding o'er society.
We wonder how "the spice of life"
Impressed the *daughter* and the *wife*.

(1902?)

---

3. *Deus absconditus* is Latin for "God concealed, hidden, secret."

John Banister Tabb

My Captive

I brought a blossom home with me
    Beneath my roof to stay;
But timorous and frail was she,
    And died before the day:
    She missed the measureless expanse
    Of heaven, and heaven her countenance.

(1902)

The Coronation of Mary

Thee, Mother-Queen of Heaven, He crowned,
    And not for love alone;
For in thy bosom first He found
    The life-spring of his own.

(1904)

The Grave-Digger

Here underneath the sod,
    Where night till now hath been,
With every lifted clod
    I let the sunshine in.

How dark soe'er the gloom
    Of death's approaching shade,
The first within the tomb
    Is light that cannot fade.

And from the deepest grave
    I banish it in vain;   10
For, like a tidal wave,
    Anon 'twill come again.

(1907)

Going Blind

Back to the primal gloom
  Where life began,
As to my mother's womb
    Must I a man
      Return:
Not to be born again,
    But to remain;
And in the School of Darkness learn
    What mean
      "The things unseen."

(1908)

John Banister Tabb

Emma Lazarus

1849–1887

Emma Lazarus held a unique
position as a writer in nineteenth-cenury America; a wealthy, un-
married woman, she knew German, Hebrew, the classics, and fine
arts; A Jew, she dealt publicly with what she herself described as
the "Jewish problem" (the lack of a national homeland) in both
her poetry and in an 1883 *Century* magazine essay entitled "The
Jewish Problem." Her ancestry sensitized her to the problems of
immigrants struggling to make a new life in America. Lazarus's
poetry embraced a variety of issues, including Transcendental-
ism, the place of the woman and artist in American society, the
Jewish culture, and immigration. She also translated the verse of
the German-Jewish poet Heinrich Heine along with many medie-
val rabbinical hymns. Her work earned praise from Emerson,
E. C. Stedman, Henry James, Robert Browning, William Morris,
and readers in America and across the Atlantic.

Emma Lazarus, daughter of Moses and Esther Lazarus, was
born in New York City on 22 July 1849, of Portuguese Jewish
descent. Privately tutored, she began writing at age fourteen and
at seventeen printed and circulated her *Poems and Translations*
(1867). Emerson read this work and appointed himself her men-
tor, encouraging her to look to nature. Her poems "Links" and
"On a Tuft of Grass" indicate that she followed his advice. She
gratefully dedicated *Admetus and Other Poems* (1871) to him.
Lazarus ceased to rely on Emerson's poetic judgment when he
failed to include her work in *Parnassus*, his poetry anthology. Af-
ter this disappointment, Lazarus contributed often to *Lippincott's*,
Century, and *American Hebrew*.

The Russian pogroms of 1879–1883 led Lazarus to denounce
the oppressors in essays and poetry. E. C. Stedman published
"The Crowing of the Red Cock," "The Banner of the Jew," and
"The New Ezekial" in his influential *American Anthology, 1787–
1900*. Lazarus reasserted her Jewish heritage in *Songs of a Semite*
(1882), a volume dedicated to George Eliot whose *Daniel Deronda*,
as Dan Vogel notes, sympathetically portrays the Jewish desire
for both social acceptance and a national homeland (141). Lazarus

closed her career with a poem addressed to all people searching for freedom, a homeland, and acceptance: "The New Colossus," the poem chosen in 1886 to adorn the Statue of Liberty's pedestal. When Lazarus died on 18 January 1887, she left behind a treasury of poems, essays, and translations along with an example of what a poet, facing social restrictions of both sex and religion, could accomplish.

Lazarus's poetic forms include the sonnet and narrative. The elevated language of her early verse gives, as Louis Harap observes, an effect of "remoteness from living reality" (287). Yet as Lazarus matured, her poetry became more alive. "Assurance" is reminiscent of Whitman, whom she admired. "Echoes" and "How Long" reflect Lazarus's status as a female, American poet writing in a patriarchal society still influenced by British writers. Her interest in Hebraic and Hellenic art appears in "Venus of the Louvre" and "The Cranes of Ibycus."

Though Lazarus's name today has largely disappeared from the roll of American poets, her words still ring familiarly: "Give me your tired, your poor, / Your huddled masses yearning to breathe free."

—Mary K. Edmonds

Suggestions for Further Reading

Harap, Louis. "Emma Lazarus." *The Image of the Jew in American Literature*. Philadelphia: The Jewish Publication Society of America, 1974.

Lichtenstein, Diane. "Words and Worlds: Emma Lazarus's Conflicting Citizenships." *Tulsa Studies in Women's Literature* 6.2 (Fall 1987): 247–63.

Schappes, Morris U., ed. *Emma Lazarus: Selections from Her Poetry and Prose*. New York: Emma Lazarus Foundation of Jewish Women's Clubs, 1982.

Vogel, Dan. *Emma Lazarus*. Boston: Twayne, 1980.*

TEXTS
Songs of a Semite: The Dance to Death and Other Poems. 1882.
"The Jewish Problem." *Century* 25 (Feb. 1883):602–11.
The Poems of Emma Lazarus. 1888.
Admetus and Other Poems. Upper Saddle River, NJ: Literature House, 1970.

꧁꧂

Links

The little and the great are joined in one
By God's great force. The wondrous golden sun
    Is linked unto the glow-worm's tiny spark;
The eagle soars to heaven in his flight;
And in those realms of space, all bathed in light,
    Soar none except the eagle and the lark.

(1865, 1888)

On a Tuft of Grass

Weak, slender blades of tender green,
With little fragrance, little sheen,
    What maketh ye so dear to all?
Nor bud, nor flower, nor fruit have ye,
So tiny, it can only be
    'Mongst fairies ye are counted tall.

No beauty is in this,—ah, yea,
E'en as I gaze on you to-day,
    Your hue and fragrance bear me back
Into the green, wide fields of old,
With clear, blue air, and manifold
    Bright buds and flowers in blossoming track.   10

All bent one way like flickering flame,
Each blade caught sunlight as it came,
    Then rising, saddened into shade;
A changeful, wavy, harmless sea,
Whose billows none could bitterly
    Reproach with wrecks that they had made.

No gold ever was buried there
More rich, more precious, or more fair
    Than buttercups with yellow gloss.
No ships of mighty forest trees
E'er foundered in these guiltless seas
    Of grassy waves and tender moss.   20

Ah, no! ah, no! not guiltless still,
Green waves on meadow and on hill,
    Not wholly innocent are ye;

For what dead hopes and loves, what graves,
Lie underneath your placid waves,
        While breezes kiss them lovingly!
Calm sleepers with sealed eyes lie there;
They see not, neither feel nor care
        If over them the grass be green.
And some sleep here who ne'er knew rest,
Until the grass grew o'er their breast,
        And stilled the aching pain within.   30

Not all the sorrow man hath known,
Not all the evil he hath done,
        Have ever cast thereon a stain.
It groweth green and fresh and light,
As in the olden garden bright,
        Beneath the feet of Eve and Cain.

It flutters, bows, and bends, and quivers,
And creeps through forests and by rivers,
        Each blade with dewy brightness wet,
So soft, so quiet, and so fair,
We almost dream of sleeping there,
        Without or sorrow or regret.   40

                                                        (1867, 1871)

In the Jewish Synagogue at Newport[1]

Here, where the noises of the busy town,
        The ocean's plunge and roar can enter not,
We stand and gaze around with tearful awe,
        And muse upon the consecrated spot.

No signs of life are here: the very prayers
        Inscribed around are in a language dead;
The light of the "perpetual lamp" is spent
        That an undying radiance was to shed.

What prayers were in this temple offered up,
        Wrung from sad hearts that knew no joy on earth,   10
By these lone exiles of a thousand years,
        From the fair sunrise land that gave them birth!

---

1. Written in response to Longfellow's poem, "The Jewish Cemetery at
Newport." Lazarus's congregation helped finance the construction of the Touro
Synagogue at Newport.

Now as we gaze, in this new world of light,
    Upon this relic of the days of old,
The present vanishes, and tropic bloom
    And Eastern towns and temples we behold.

Again we see the patriarch with his flocks,
    The purple seas, the hot blue sky o'erhead,
The slaves of Egypt,—omens, mysteries,—
    Dark fleeing hosts by flaming angels led.   20

A wondrous light upon a sky-kissed mount,
    A man who reads Jehovah's written law,
'Midst blinding glory and effulgence rare,
    Unto a people prone with reverent awe.

The pride of luxury's barbaric pomp,
    In the rich court of royal Solomon—
Alas! we wake: one scene alone remains,—
    The exiles by the streams of Babylon.

Our softened voices send us back again
    But mournful echoes through the empty hall;   30
Our footsteps have a strange unnatural sound,
    And with unwonted gentleness they fall.

The weary ones, the sad, the suffering,
    All found their comfort in the holy place,
And children's gladness and men's gratitude
    Took voice and mingled in the chant of praise.

The funeral and the marriage, now, alas!
    We know not which is sadder to recall;
For youth and happiness have followed age,
    And green grass lieth gently over all.   40

Nathless the sacred shrine is holy yet,
    With this lone floors where reverent feet once trod.
Take off your shoes as by the burning bush,
    Before the mystery of death and God.

                                        (1867, 1871)

How Long

    How long, and yet how long,
Our leaders will we hail from over seas,

Masters and kings from feudal monarchies,
    And mock their ancient song
With echoes weak of foreign melodies?

    That distant isle mist-wreathed,
Mantled in unimaginable green,
Too long hath been our mistress and our queen.
    Our fathers have bequeathed
Too deep a love for her our hearts within.   10

    She made the whole world ring
With the brave exploits of her children strong,
And with the matchless music of her song.
    Too late, too late we cling
To alien legends, and their strains prolong.

    This fresh young world I see,
With heroes, cities, legends of her own;
With a new race of men, and overblown
    By winds from sea to sea,
Decked with the majesty of every zone.   20

    I see the glittering tops
Of snow-peaked mounts, the wid'ning vale's expanse
Large prairies where free herds of horses prance,
    Exhaustless wealth of crops,
In vast, magnificent extravagance.

    These grand, exuberant plains,
These stately rivers, each with many a mouth,
The exquisite beauty of the soft-aired south,
    The boundless seas of grains,
Luxuriant forests' lush and splendid growth.   30

    The distant siren-song
Of the green island in the eastern sea,
Is not the lay for this new chivalry.
    It is not free and strong
To chant on prairies 'neath this brilliant sky.

    The echo faints and fails;
It suiteth not, upon this western plain,
Our voice or spirit; we should stir again
    The wilderness, and make the plain
Resound unto a yet unheard-of strain.   40
                                            (1871)

Echoes

Late-born and woman-souled I dare not hope,
The freshness of the elder lays, the might
Of manly, modern passion shall alight
Upon my Muse's lips, nor may I cope
(Who veiled and screened by womanhood must grope)
With the world's strong-armed warriors and recite
The dangers, wounds, and triumphs of the fight;
Twanging the full-stringed lyre through all its scope.
But if thou ever in some lake-floored cave
O'erbrowed by rocks, a wild voice wooed and heard,   10
Answering at once from heaven and earth and wave,
Lending elf-music to thy harshest word,
Misprize thou not these echoes that belong
To one in love with solitude and song.

(1880, 1888)

The Crowing of the Red Cock[2]

Across the Eastern sky has glowed
    The flicker of a blood-red dawn,
Once more the clarion cock has crowed,
    Once more the sword of Christ is drawn.
A million burning rooftrees light
The world-wide path of Israel's flight.

Where is the Hebrew's fatherland?
    The folk of Christ is sore bestead;
The Son of Man is bruised and banned,
    Nor finds whereon to lay his head.   10
His cup is gall, his meat is tears,
His passion lasts a thousand years.

Each crime that wakes in man the beast,
    Is visited upon his kind.
The lust of mobs, the greed of priest,
    The tyranny of kings, combined
To root his seed from earth again,
His record is one cry of pain.

---

2. The red cock acted as the Russian Jewish code-image for the anti-Jewish pogroms in Russia.

When the long roll of Christian guilt
    Against his sires and kin is known,
The flood of tears, the life-blood spilt,   20
    The agony of ages shown,
What oceans can the stain remove,
From Christian law and Christian love?

Nay, close the book; not now, not here,
    The hideous tale of sin narrate,
Reechoing in the martyr's ear,
    Even he might nurse revengeful hate,
Even he might turn in wrath sublime,
With blood for blood and crime for crime.

Coward? Not he, who faces death,
    Who singly against worlds has fought,   30
For what? A name he may not breathe,
    For liberty of prayer and thought.
The angry sword he will not whet,
His nobler task is—to forget.

                                    (1882)

The New Colossus[3]

Not like the brazen giant of Greek fame,
With conquering limbs astride from land to land;
Here at our sea-washed, sunset gates shall stand
A mighty woman with a torch, whose flame
Is the imprisoned lightning, and her name
Mother of Exiles. From her beacon-hand
Glows world-wide welcome; her mild eyes command
The air-bridged harbor that twin cities frame.
"Keep, ancient lands, your storied pomp!" cries she
With silent lips. "Give me your tired, your poor,   10
Your huddled masses yearning to breathe free,
The wretched refuse of your teeming shore.
Send these, the homeless, tempest-tost to me,
I lift my lamp beside the golden door!"

                             (1883, 1888)

---

   3. Refers to the Colossus of Rhodes, the bronze statue of Helios reputed to stand astride the waterway of Rhodes' harbor. The statue, overthrown by an earthquake, was one of the seven wonders of the world.

The Cranes of Ibycus[4]

There was a man who watched the river flow
Past the huge town, one gray November day.
Round him in narrow high-piled streets at play
The boys made merry as they saw him go,
Murmuring half-loud, with eyes upon the stream,
The immortal screed[5] he held within his hand.
For he was walking in an April land
With Faust and Helen.[6] Shadowy as a dream
Was the prose-world, the river and the town.
Wild joy possessed him; through enchanted skies   10
He saw the cranes of Ibycus swoop down.
He closed the page, he lifted up his eyes,
Lo—a black line of birds in wavering thread
Bore him the greetings of the deathless dead!

(1888)

Venus of the Louvre[7]

Down the long hall she glistens like a star,
The foam-born mother of Love, transfixed to stone,
Yet none the less immortal, breathing on.
Time's brutal hand hath maimed but could not mar.
When first the enthralled enchantress from afar
Dazzled mine eyes, I saw not her alone,
Serenely poised on her world-worshipped throne,
As when she guided once her dove-drawn car,—
But at her feet a pale, death-stricken Jew,
Her life adorer, sobbed farewell to love.   10
Here **Heine**[8] wept! Here still he weeps anew,

---

4. From a myth in which a flock of cranes, representative of freedom, imagination, and justice, avenge a poet ambushed by robbers.

5. A fragment of a piece of writing.

6. Faust and Helen are characters from Christopher Marlowe's *Dr. Faustus* (c. 1588) and from Johann Wolfgang Goethe's *Faust* (1808). Faust represents the search for knowledge and experience; he sells his soul to the devil for experience, knowledge, and power. Helen, of Troy legend, represents beauty and appears to Faust in a vision.

7. Armless, marble statue of Venus de Milo, goddess of love and daughter of the sea, orginally found on the island of Melos (Milo) and later placed in the Louvre.

8. Heinrich Heine (1797–1856), a German, self-named "the last Romantic poet." Lazarus felt an affinity to Heine and translated much of his work.

Nor ever shall his shadow lift or move,
While mourns one ardent heart, one poet-brain,
For vanished Hellas and Hebraic pain.

(1888)

Assurance

Last night I slept, and when I woke her kiss
Still floated on my lips. For we had strayed
Together in my dream, through some dim glade,
Where the shy moonbeams scarce dared light our bliss.
The air was dank with dew, between the trees,
The hidden glow-worms kindled and were spent.
Cheek pressed to cheek, the cool, the hot night-breeze
Mingled our hair, our breath, and came and went,
As sporting with our passion. Low and deep
Spake in mine ear her voice: "And didst thou dream,   10
This could be thrall to death! Nay, whatso seem,
Have faith, dear heart; this is the thing that is!"
Thereon I woke, and on my lips her kiss.

(1980)

James Whitcomb Riley
1849–1916

Immensely popular in his day for both dialect and nondialect verse, James Whitcomb Riley reaffirmed traditional values in his poetry and provided an escape from reality by romanticizing it. He was generally successful in reproducing actual speech, conveying nuances of character compactly, and creating suspense (Revell 32). Though academic critics of his time did not hold Riley in high esteem, William Dean Howells, Mark Twain, Rudyard Kipling, John Hay, James Russell Lowell, Joel Chandler Harris, and Hamlin Garland all praised his work. Riley's great talent for dramatic reading, especially from his own work, also helped to spread his fame.

Riley was born 7 October 1849 in Greenfield, Indiana. His education was scattered, and he did not attend college. "The Same Old Story Told Again," Riley's first published poem, appeared in the *Greenfield Official*, 7 September 1870. He performed his first solo recitation in the summer of 1874 at Monrovia, Indiana, and toured central Indiana alone the next year. From April to August 1877, he was assistant to the editor of the *Anderson Democrat* and contributed poetry, humorous sketches, and parodies to this and other newspapers.

The Redpath Lyceum Bureau signed Riley on the circuit in 1881, and he appeared successfully almost every year from 1882 to 1903. Riley published *The Old Swimmin'-Hole, and 'Leven More Poems* (1883) and *Afterwhiles* (1887), both of which are collections of pieces previously published in magazines and newspapers. Many of the over ninety titles Riley published by 1914 were old material reorganized. Publication of *Poems Here at Home* (1893) by a New York firm and the appearance of "The Name of Old Glory" in the December 1898 *Atlantic Monthly* were important milestones marking the Eastern establishment's gradual acceptance of Riley as a poet of national stature. He received several honorary degrees between 1902 and 1907, and both the National Institute of Arts and Letters (1908) and the American Academy of Arts and Letters (1911) elected him to membership. Riley died 22 July 1916 in Indianapolis and was buried there at Crown Hill cemetery.

Riley wrote mostly sentimental and pastoral verse dealing

with love, family life, parting, the passage of time, and death, among other topics. He emphasized the brotherhood of humanity and encouraged readers to care for the poor and helpless ("Little Orphant Annie"). His work teaches morality and holds up a traditional picture of the good life as the goal for all. Favorite Riley characters are the rustic philosopher, the unlearned believer, the coward who ultimately triumphs, the hard-working, long-suffering woman, and the faithfully loving young girl. In his dialect verse Riley attempted to convey the "natural forms and rhythms of Hoosier speech" that he hoped his work would preserve (Revell 37, 91). His portrayal of farm life influenced later writers such as Edgar Lee Masters, Sinclair Lewis, and Thornton Wilder, who inherited Riley's version of the small-town myth, and rejected it or changed it to meet their own needs (Revell 25). Riley's popularity plummeted after his death, but his poems for children are still anthologized.

—*E. Frances Frame*

Suggestions for Further Reading

Crowder, Richard. *Those Innocent Years: The Legacy and Inheritance of a Hero of the Victorian Era, James Whitcomb Riley*. Indianapolis: Bobbs, 1957.
Revell, Peter. *James Whitcomb Riley*. New York: Twayne, 1970.

TEXT
The Complete Poetical Works of James Whitcomb Riley. New York: Grosset, 1937.

۞

The Old Swimmin'-Hole

Oh! the old swimmin'-hole! whare the crick so still and deep
Looked like a baby-river that was laying half asleep,
And the gurgle of the worter round the drift jest below
Sounded like the laugh of something we onc't ust to know
Before we could remember anything but the eyes
Of the angels lookin' out as we left Paradise;
But the merry days of youth is beyond our controle,
And it's hard to part ferever with the old swimmin'-hole.

Oh! the old swimmin'-hole! In the happy days of yore,
When I ust to lean above it on the old sickamore,   10
Oh! it showed me a face in its warm sunny tide

That gazed back at me so gay and glorified,
It made me love myself, as I leaped to caress
My shadder smilin' up at me with such tenderness.
But them days is past and gone, and old Time's tuck his toll
From the old man come back to the old swimmin'-hole.

Oh! the old swimmin'-hole! In the long, lazy days
When the humdrum of school made so many run-a-ways,
How pleasant was the jurney down the old dusty lane,
Whare the tracks of our bare feet was all printed so plane 20
You could tell by the dent of the heel and the sole
They was lots o' fun on hands at the old swimmin'-hole.
But the lost joys is past! Let your tears in sorrow roll
Like the rain that ust to dapple up the old swimmin'-hole.

Thare the bullrushes growed, and the cattails so tall,
And the sunshine and shadder fell over it all;
And it mottled the worter with amber and gold
Tel the glad lilies rocked in the ripples that rolled;
And the snake-feeder's four gauzy wings fluttered by
Like the ghost of a daisy dropped out of the sky,   30
Or a wownded apple-blossom in the breeze's controle
As it cut acrost some orchurd to'rds the old swimmin'-hole.

Oh! the old swimmin'-hole! When I last saw the place,
The scenes was all changed, like the change in my face;
The bridge of the railroad now crosses the spot
Whare the old divin'-log lays sunk and fergot.
And I stray down the banks whare the trees ust to be—
But never again will theyr shade shelter me!
And I wish in my sorrow I could strip to the soul,
And dive off in my grave like the old swimmin'-hole.   40
(17 June 1882, 1883)

Little Orphant Annie
Inscribed with All Faith and Affection

To all the little children:—The happy ones; and sad ones;
The sober and the silent ones; the boisterous and glad ones;
The good ones—Yes, the good ones, too; and all the lovely
bad ones.

Little Orphant Annie's come to our house to stay,
An' wash the cups an' saucers up, an' brush the crumbs away,
An' shoo the chickens off the porch, an' dust the hearth, an'
sweep,

An' make the fire, an' bake the bread, an' earn her board-an'-
    keep;
An' all us other childern, when the supper-things is done,
We set around the kitchen fire an' has the mostest fun
A-list'nin to the witch-tales 'at Annie tells about,
An' the Gobble-uns 'at gits you
            Ef you
                Don't   10
                    Watch
                        Out!

Wunst they wuz a little boy wouldn't say his prayers,—
An' when he went to bed at night, away up-stairs,
His Mammy heerd him holler, an' his Daddy heerd him
    bawl,
An' when they turn't the kivvers down, he wuzn't there at
    all!
An' they seeked him in the rafter-room, an' cubby-hole, an'
    press,
An' seeked him up the chimbly-flue, an' ever'-wheres, I
    guess;
But all they ever found wuz thist his pants an' roundabout:—
An' the Gobble-uns 'll git you   20
            Ef you
                Don't
                    Watch
                        Out!

An' one time a little girl 'ud allus laugh an' grin,
An' make fun of ever' one, an' all her blood-an'-kin;
An' wunst, when they was "company," an' ole folks wuz
    there,
She mocked 'em an' shocked 'em, an' said she didn't care!
An' thist as she kicked her heels, an' turn't to run an' hide,
They wuz two great big Black Things a-standin' by her
    side,   30
An' they snatched her through the ceilin' 'fore she knowed
    what she's about!
An' the Gobble-uns 'll git you
            Ef you
                Don't
                    Watch
                        Out!

An' little Orphant Annie says, when the blaze is blue,
An' the lamp-wick sputters, an' the wind goes *woo-oo!*

An' you hear the crickets quit, an' the moon is gray,
An' the lightnin'-bugs in dew is all squenched away,—   40
You better mind yer parunts, an' yer teachers fond an' dear,
An' churish them 'at loves you, an' dry the orphant's tear,
An' he'p the pore an' needy ones 'at clusters all about,
Er the Gobble-uns 'll git you
   Ef you
    Don't
     Watch
      Out!
      (15 November 1885, 1885)

Craqueodoom

The Crankadox leaned o'er the edge of the moon
 And wistfully gazed on the sea
Where the Gryxabodill madly whistled a tune
 To the air of "Ti-fol-de-ding-dee."
The quavering shriek of the Fly-up-the-creek
 Was fitfully wafted afar
To the Queen of the Wunks as she powdered her cheek
 With the pulverized rays of a star.

The Gool closed his ear on the voice of the Grig,
 And his heart it grew heavy as lead   10
As he marked the Baldekin adjusting his wing
 On the opposite side of his head,
And the air it grew chill as the Gryxabodill
 Raised his dank, dripping fins to the skies,
And plead with the Plunk for the use of her bill
 To pick the tears out of his eyes.

The ghost of the Zhack flitted by in a trance,
 And the Squidjum hid under a tub
As he heard the loud hooves of the Hooken advance
 With a rub-a-dub—dub-a-dub—dub!   20
And the Crankadox cried, as he lay down and died,
 "My fate there is none to bewail,"
While the Queen of the Wunks drifted over the tide
 With a long piece of crape to her tail.
      (1 June 1877, 1888)

Our Hired Girl

Our hired girl, she's Lizabuth Ann;
  An' she can cook best things to eat!
She ist puts dough in our pie-pan,
  An' pours in somepin' 'at's good an' sweet;
An' nen she salts it all on top
With cinnamon; an' nen she'll stop
An' stoop an' slide it, ist as slow,
In th' old cook-stove, so's 'twn't slop
An' git all spilled; nen bakes it, so
  It's custard-pie, first thing you know!   10
     An' nen she'll say,
     "Clear out o' my way!
They's time fer work, an' time fer play!
Take yer dough, an' run, child, run!
Er I cain't git no cookin' done!"

When our hired girl 'tends like she's mad,
  An' says folks got to walk the chalk
When *she's* around, ar wisht they had!
  I play out on our porch an' talk
To Th' Raggedy Man 'at mows our lawn;   20
An' he says, *"Whew!"* an nen leans on
  His crook-scythe, and blinks his eyes,
An' sniffs all 'round an' says, "I swawn!
Ef my old nose don't tell me lies,
  It 'pears like I smell custard-pies!"
     An' nen *he'll* say,
     "Clear out o' my way!
They's time fer work, an' time fer play!
Take yer dough, an' run, child, run!
Er she can't git no cookin' done!"   30

Wunst our hired girl, when she
  Got the supper, an' we all et,
An' it wuz night, an' Ma an' me
  An' Pa went wher' the "Social" met,—
An' nen when we come home, an' see
A light in the kitchen door, an' we
Heerd a maccordeum, Pa says,
"Lan'-O'-Gracious! who can her beau be?"
  An' I marched in, an' Lizabuth Ann
  Wuz parchin' corn fer The Raggedy Man!   40
     Better say,

"Clear out o' the way!
They's time fer work, an' time fer play!
Take the hint, an' run, child, run!
Er we cain't git no courtin' done!"

(December 1890, 1890)

Eugene Field

1850–1895

Eugene Field's children's poetry earned him the title "Poet Laureate of Childhood," and a popularity that overshadowed his other writings. His works include prose fiction, dialect poems, political satire, translations, newspaper columns, and privately circulated bawdy verse.

Eugene Field was born on 2 or 3 September 1850 in St. Louis, Missouri, to Roswell Martin Field and Frances Reed Field. After his mother's death in 1856, Field's father sent him to live with his cousin, Mary Field French, in Amherst, Massachusetts. Leaving school in 1872, Field financed a European trip with an inheritance from his father, returning only when the money ran out. Lack of money would be a lifelong problem.

Field married Julia Sutherland Comstock on 16 October 1873, and they established a home fostering the strong family ties Field missed in his own youth. The Fields had eight children and lost three in childhood. Field's "Little Boy Blue" (1888), which expressed a parental grief too common in the nineteenth century, soon became popular and made Field's poetic reputation.

Field supported his family by writing for various newspapers. *Western and Other Verse*, written during his editorship of the Denver *Tribune*, reflects the city's frontier flavor and gold rush past. Field moved eastward in 1883, recruited as a columnist for the Chicago *Morning News*. The poetry in his "Sharps and Flats" column ranged from political satire to poems on childhood. After his death on 4 November 1895, Field's wife and journalist friends championed his reputation, extolling him as the sentimental father figure of his verse.

Field's lullabies and nonsense verse do not moralize, but entertain, unlike most nineteenth-century poetry for children. However, many poems appeal to adults; "Little Boy Blue" addresses readers who understand death and loss. In his comic western verse, Field created childlike characters, uncivilized but essentially innocent. Field's political poetry was more adult, ridiculing government officials and the upper classes. Living in Chicago during early union strikes, he risked his reputation by publicly supporting labor leaders.

Field read avidly, calling himself and his fellow book lovers "bibliomaniacs" (*Sharps and Flats* 2:6). He paraphrased poems of Horace in *Echoes from a Sabine Farm*, attempting to show the liveliness and irreverence lost in literal translation. He translated many poems on drinking and pursuit of women, unlikely subjects for a genteel children's poet. Field recited original bawdy verse at men's club parties and circulated it among male friends. Field's friends suppressed these poems after his death, even though they are more humorous than erotic.

Today, Eugene Field does not hold the national reputation he did in the late nineteenth century. "Little Boy Blue," "The Duel," and "Jest 'Fore Christmas" are still anthologized, and "Wynken, Blynken, and Nod" is a favorite of children's book illustrators. Since his death, the poetry for children has overshadowed his other work.

—Susan Bales

Suggestions for Further Reading

Conrow, Robert. *Field Days: The Life, Times & Reputation of Eugene Field*. New York: Scribners, 1974.*
Dennis, Charles H. *Eugene Field's Creative Years*. Garden City: Doubleday, 1924.
Thompson, Slason. *Eugene Field: A Study in Heredity and Contradictions*. New York: Scribners, 1901, 1924.

TEXTS
Love-Songs of Childhood. 1894.
Second Book of Verse. 1896.
Sharps and Flats. 2 vols. New York: Scribner's, 1900.
The Poems of Eugene Field. New York: Scribner's, 1910.

ꙮ

An Ohio Ditty

Mary had a little lamb,
   Down in Ohio state,
And ere it grew to be a ram,
   Most dismal was its fate.

Its fleece was long and white and full,
   And Mary loved to shear
Her lamb for the amount of wool
   It brought her twice a year.

But once, upon a summer's day,
   She learned, to her dejection.   10
Her wool investment didn't pay—
   And so she craved protection.

And then, with many a pleading word
   And copious flow of tears,
She flew to genial Mr. Hurd[1]
   To set at rest her fears.

But Mr. Hurd in scorn did hold
   Poor Mary and her kid,
And when their tale of woe was told
   No kindly act he did.   20

In vain for help the maiden cried
   Upon her bended knees.
"No tariff, girl," the man replied;
   "Go serve your lamb with peas!"

So Mary slew her little lamb—
   As might have been expected,
For little lambs aren't worth a d——
   When they are not protected.

                                (1884, 1900)

Little Boy Blue

The little toy dog is covered with dust,
   But sturdy and stanch he stands;
And the little toy soldier is red with rust,
   And his musket moulds in his hands.
Time was when the little toy dog was new,
   And the soldier was passing fair;
And that was the time when our Little Boy Blue
   Kissed them and put them there.

"Now don't you go till I come," he said,
   "And don't you make any noise!"   10
So, toddling off to his trundle-bed,

---

1. Frank Hunt Hurd, Democrat from Ohio, served in the U.S. House of Representatives at a time when the use of protective tariffs was an important issue.

He dreamt of the pretty toys;
And, as he was dreaming, an angel song
    Awakened our Little Boy Blue—
Oh! the years are many, the years are long,
    But the little toy friends are true!

Ay, faithful to Little Boy Blue they stand,
    Each in the same old place—
Awaiting the touch of a little hand,
    The smile of a little face;   20
And they wonder, as waiting the long years through
    In the dust of that little chair,
What had become of our Little Boy Blue,
    Since he kissed them and put them there.

                                                    (1888, 1892)

To Chloe[2]

I

Why do you shun me, Chloe, like the fawn,
    That, fearful of the breezes and the wood,
Has sought her timorous mother since the dawn,
    And on the pathless mountain tops has stood?

Her trembling heart a thousand fears invites,
    Her sinking knees with nameless terrors shake,—
    Whether the rustling leaf of spring affrights,
Or the green lizards stir the slumbering brake.

I do not follow with tigerish thought,
    Or with the fierce Gaetulian[3] lion's quest;   10
So, quickly leave your mother, as you ought,
    Full ripe to nestle on a husband's breast.

II

Chloe, you shun me like a hind
    That, seeking vainly for her mother

---

2. From *Echoes from a Sabine Farm*.
3. From northwest Africa, now Morocco.

Hears danger in each breath of wind,
    And wildly darts this way and t'other;

Whether the breezes sway the wood
    Or lizards scuttle through the brambles
She starts, and off, as though pursued,
    The foolish, frightened creature scrambles.

But, Chloe, you're no infant thing
    That should esteem a man an ogre;   10
Let go your mother's apron-string,
    And pin your faith upon a toga!

III
A Paraphrase

How happens it, my cruel miss,
    You're always giving me the mitten?
You seem to have forgotten this:
    That you no longer are a kitten!

A woman that has reached the years
    Of that which people call discretion
Should put aside all childish fears
    And see in courtship no transgression.

A mother's solace may be sweet,
    But Hymen's tenderness is sweeter;   10
And though all virile love be meet,
    You'll find the poet's love is metre.

                                        (1891)

The Duel

The gingham dog and the calico cat
Side by side on the table sat;
'Twas half-past twelve, and (what do you think!)
Nor one nor t'other has slept a wink!
        The old Dutch clock and the Chinese plate
        Appeared to know as sure as fate
There was going to be a terrible spat.
            (*I wasn't there; I simply state*
            What was told to me by the Chinese plate!)

The gingham dog went "Bow-wow-wow!"   10
And the calico cat replied Mee-ow!"
The air was littered, an hour or so,
With bits of gingham and calico,
    While the old Dutch clock in the chimney-place
    Up with its hands before its face,
For it always dreaded a family row!
    (*Now mind: I'm only telling you*
    What the old Dutch clock declares is true!)

The Chinese plate looked very blue,
And wailed, "Oh, dear! what shall we do!"   20
But the gingham dog and the calico cat
Wallowed this way and tumbled that,
    Employing every tooth and claw
    In the awfullest way you ever saw
And, oh! how the gingham and calico flew!
    (*Don't fancy I exaggerate—*
    I got my news from the Chinese plate!)

Next morning, whence the two had sat
They found no trace of dog or cat;
And some folks think unto this day   30
That burglars stole that pair away!
    But the truth about the cat and pup
    Is this: they ate each other up!
Now what do you really think of that!
    (*The old Dutch clock it told me so,*
    And that is how I came to know.)

                         (1894)

Little Willie

When Willie was a little boy,
    No more than five or six,
Right constantly he did annoy
    His mother with his tricks.
Yet not a picayune cared I
    For what he did or said
Unless, as happened frequently,
    The rascal wet the bed.

Closely he cuddled up to me,
    And put his hands in mine,   10

Till all at once I seemed to be
    Afloat in seas of brine.
Sabean odors clogged the air,
    And filled my soul with dread,
Yet I could only grin and bear
    When Willie wet the bed.

'Tis many times that rascal has
    Soaked all the bedclothes through,
Whereat I'd feebly light the gas
    And wonder what to do.   20
Yet there he lay, so peaceful like;
    God bless his curly head,
I quite forgave the little tyke
    For wetting of the bed.

Ah me, those happy days have flown.
    My boy's a father, too,
And little Willies of his own
    Do what he used to do.
And I! Ah, all that's left for me
    Is dreams of pleasure fled   30
Our boys ain't what they used to be
    When Willie wet the bed.

Had I my choice no shapely dame
    Should share my couch with me,
No amorous jade of tarnished fame
    Nor wench of high degree;
But I would choose and choose again
    The little curly head
Who cuddled close beside me when
    He used to wet the bed.[4]   40
                                      (1927)

---

4. Although privately circulated in its entirety among Field's male friends, the poem appeared in Slason Thompson's 1927 revised biography without the final stanza because of the sexual references.

Ella Wheeler Wilcox

1850–1919

Ella Wheeler Wilcox, known as the "Poetess of Passion" (more because of her most famous volume's title than the content of her poetry), reached an enormous audience with her didactic sentimental verse. Shortly after her death in 1919, the London *Times* called her "the most popular poet of either sex and of any age, read by thousands who never open Shakespeare" (31 October 1919: 15).

Born on 5 November 1850 in Johnstown Center, Wisconsin, Ella Wheeler was the last of four children of Marius Hartwell Wheeler and Sarah Pratt Wheeler. Both parents encouraged her literary interests, and she grew up reading the romantic melodramas of Ouida, Mary J. Holmes, May Agnes Fleming, and Mrs. E. D. E. N. Southworth. A precocious child, she wrote at the age of ten her first "novel" and bound it in kitchen wallpaper. The New York *Mercury* accepted an essay when she was fourteen, and soon after she published poetry in the *Waverly Magazine* and *Leslie's Weekly*. She enrolled in 1867 at the University of Wisconsin where she stayed for only one term, preferring to return home to write. By the time she was eighteen, she was able to aid her impoverished family with her substantial income from publications.

Her first book, *Drops of Water*, a collection of temperance verse, appeared in 1872, followed a year later by *Shells*, a volume of the optimistic religious and moral poetry for which she would become famous. She began to attract an audience with "Maurine" (1876), a long narrative poem, but did not achieve fame until 1883, when a Chicago publisher rejected *Poems of Passion*—most of which had already appeared in newspapers and periodicals—as being immoral. Hearing of the "scandal," a Chicago newspaper denounced the "Badger Girl, Whose Verses out-Swinburne Swinburne and out-Whitman Whitman" (qtd. in Ballou 82). The volume's title, not its content, upset Victorian sensibility; one contemporary reviewer remarked that the poems could not have upset the morals of a ladybug (qtd. in Lewis 49). Another publisher soon accepted the book, and within two years, it sold over sixty thousand copies.

In 1884, Ella married Robert Wilcox, a business executive, and moved to his home in Meriden, Connecticut. The marriage was long and happy despite the death of their only child, a son; he died shortly after birth in 1887. After the couple's subsequent move to New York City, Wilcox frequented the literary salons and held, according to the November 1888 issue of *Cosmopolitan*, "a scepter and influence which compare favorably with any other American poet" (47). The Wilcoxes spent their summers in Short Beach, Connecticut, living there year-round after Robert retired in 1906. Wilcox continued to write prolifically; in addition to her poetry, she contributed to Hearst newspapers and *Cosmopolitan*.

After her husband's death in 1916, she became increasingly interested in spiritualism and theosophy. In 1918, she told a reporter, "[my husband] comes to see me every night and talks to me on the ouija board" (deFord 435). Convinced that Robert had told her to do so, she toured Allied army camps during World War I, reading her poetry and urging the American soldiers to "come back clean," a reference to venereal disease. Following a nervous breakdown in England, she returned home to Short Beach, where she died on 30 October 1919.

Wilcox was not an accomplished poet, a fact many critics of her time pointed out. She refused to innovate, preferring instead to yoke together with violence such lines as those found in "Art and Heart": "It is not the artist's skill, which into our soul comes stealing / With a joy that is almost pain, but it is the player's feeling" (lines 11–12). As these lines suggest, Wilcox was more concerned with being a "moral uplifter" than a skillful poet; in the same poem she affirms, "It is not art, but heart, which wins the wide world over" (line 16). This epigrammatic quality led one critic to label her "The High Priestess of Platitude." She wrote often of love and shared with Whitman a concern for the "common man." The size and appreciation of her audience show that if she was not a poet for all time, she was an important one for her own age.

Disparaged by the critics of her time and ignored during the era of New Criticism, Wilcox has sparked recent interest among feminists seeking to rediscover the cultural context of her day. As a leader of the so-called "Erotic School" and a woman who wrote of passion (however innocuously), she offended Victorian ideas of decorum; that she managed marriage and a career, as Cheryl Walker points out in *The Nightingale's Burden: Women Poets and American Culture Before 1900*, was an inspiration to other women. In her preeminent position as poetic moralist, Wilcox helped define the roles available for women in the arena of public discourse. If her poetry has not survived as art, it retains for the cultural historian its value as artifact.

—*Scott Romine*

Ballou, Jenny. *Period Piece: Ella Wheeler Wilcox and Her Times.* Boston: Houghton, 1940.

deFord, Miriam Allen. "Poetess of Passion." *American Mercury* 32 (Aug. 1934): 435–39.

Groben, Anne R. "Ella Wheeler Wilcox." *American Women Writers.* Vol. 2. Ed. Langdon Lynne Faust. New York: Ungar, 1983. 394–96.

Lewis, Naomi. "The Domestic Bard: Ella Wheeler Wilcox." *Harper's Magazine* (Mar. 1952): 47–53.

Walker, Cheryl. *The Nightingale's Burden: Women Poets and American Culture Before 1900.* Bloomington: Indiana UP, 1982.

TEXTS

Poems of Passion. 1883.
Poems of Pleasure. 1888.
An Erring Woman's Love. 1892.
Poems of Reflection. Chicago: M. A. Donohue, 1905.

※

Lines from "Maurine"

I'd rather have my verses win
    A place in common peoples' hearts,
Who, toiling through the strife and din
    Of life's great thoroughfares, and marts,

May read some line my hand has penned;
    Some simple verse, not fine, or grand,
    But what their hearts can understand
And hold me henceforth as a friend,—

I'd rather win *such* quiet fame
    Than by some fine thought, polished so   10
    But those of learned minds would know,
    Just what the meaning of my song,—
To have the critics sound my name
    In high-flown praises, loud and long.

I sing not for the critic's ear,
But for the masses. If they hear,
Despite the turmoil, noise and strife
Some least low note that gladdens life,
I shall be wholly satisfied,
Though critics to the end deride.   20

(1876, 1905)

Art and Heart

THOUGH critics may bow to art, and I am its own true
    lover,
It is not art, but heart, which wins the wide world over.

Though smooth may be the heartless prayer, no ear in
    Heaven will mind it,
And the finest phrase falls dead, if there is no feeling
    behind it.

Though perfect the player's touch, little if any he sways us,
Unless we feel his heart throb through the music he plays us.

Though the poet may spend his life in skillfully rounding a
    measure,
Unless he writes from a full warm heart, he gives us little
    pleasure.

So it is not the speech which tells, but the impulse which
    goes with the saying,
And it is not the words of the prayer, but the yearning back
    of the praying.   10

It is not the artist's skill, which into our soul comes stealing
With a joy that is almost pain, but it is the player's feeling.

And it is not the poet's song, though sweeter than sweet
    bells chiming,
Which thrills us through and through, but the heart which
    beats under the rhyming.

And therefore I say again, though I am art's own true lover,
That it is not art, but heart, which wins the wide world over.

                               (1883)

The Common Lot

It is a common fate—a woman's lot—
    To waste on one the riches of her soul,
Who takes the wealth she gives him, but cannot
    Repay the interest, and much less the whole.

As I look up into your eyes, and wait
        For some response to my fond gaze and touch,
It seems to me there is no sadder fate
        Than to be doomed to loving overmuch.

Are you not kind? Ah, yes, so very kind—
        So thoughtful of my comfort, and so true.   10
Yes, yes, dear heart; but I, not being blind,
        Know that I am not loved, as I love you.

One tenderer word, a little longer kiss,
        Will fill my soul with music and with song;
And if you seem abstracted, or I miss
        The heart-tone from your voice, my world goes
            wrong.

And oftentimes you think me childish—weak—
        When at some thoughtless word the tears will start;
You cannot understand how aught you speak
        Has power to stir the depths of my poor heart.   20

I cannot help it, dear—I wish I could,
        Or feign indifference where I now adore;
For if I seemed to love you less, you would,
        Manlike, I have no doubt, love me the more.

'Tis a sad gift, that much applauded thing,
        A constant heart; for fact doth daily prove
That constancy finds oft a cruel sting,
        While fickle natures win the deeper love.

                                                     (1883)

Solitude

Laugh, and the world laughs with you;
        Weep, and you weep alone,
For this sad old earth must borrow its mirth,
        But has trouble enough of its own.
Sing, and the hills will answer;
        Sigh, it is lost on the air,
The echoes bound to a joyful sound,
        But shrink from voicing care.

Rejoice, and men will seek you;
    Grieve, and they turn and go.   10
They want full measure of all your pleasure,
    But they do not need your woe.
Be glad, and your friends are many;
    Be sad, and you lose them all,—
There are none to decline your nectar'd wine,
    But alone you must drink life's gall.

Feast, and your halls are crowded;
    Fast, and the world goes by.
Succeed and give, and it helps you live,
    But no man can help you die.   20
There is room in the halls of pleasure
    For a large and lordly train,
But one by one we must all file on
    Through the narrow aisles of pain.

(1883, 1905)

The Difference

Passion is what the sun feels for the earth
When harvests ripen into golden birth.

Lust is the hot simoon whose burning breath
Sweeps o'er the fields with devastating death.

Passion is what God felt, the Holy One,
Who loved the world so, He begot his Son.

Lust is the impulse Satan peering in
To Eden had, when he taught Eve to sin.

One sprang from light, and one from darkness grew
How dim the vision that confounds the two!   10

(1888)

Artist and Man

Take thy life better than thy work. Too oft
Our artists spend their skill in rounding soft

Fair curves upon their statues, while the rough
And ragged edges of the unhewn stuff
In their own natures startle and offend
The eye of critic and the heart of friend.

If in thy too brief day thou must neglect
Thy labor or thy life, let men detect
Flaws in thy work! while their most searching gaze
Can fall on nothing which they may not praise   10
In thy well chiseled character. The Man
Should not be shadowed by the Artisan!

(1888)

The City

I own the charms of lovely Nature; still,
　　In human nature more delight I find.
Though sweet the murmuring voices of the rill,
　　I much prefer the voices of my kind.

I like the roar of cities. In the mart
　　Where busy toilers strive for place and gain,
I seem to read humanity's great heart,
　　And share its hopes, its pleasures, and its pain.

The rush of hurrying trains that cannot wait,
　　The tread of myriad feet, all say to me: 10
"You are the architect of your own fate,
　　Toil on, hope on, and dare to do and be."

I like the jangled music of the loud
　　Bold bells; the whistle's sudden shrill reply;
And there is inspiration in a crowd—
　　A magnetism flashed from eye to eye.

My sorrows all seem lightened, and my joys
　　Augmented when the comrade world walks near;
Close to mankind my soul best keeps its poise.
Give me the great town's bustle, strife, and noise   20
　　And let who will, hold nature's calm more dear.

(1888)

Woman

Give us that grand word "woman" once again,
And let's have done with "lady": one's a term
Full of fine force, strong, beautiful, and firm,
Fit for the noblest use of tongue or pen;
And one's a word for lackeys. One suggests
The Mother, Wife, and Sister! One the dame
Whose costly robe, mayhap, gives her the name.
One word upon its own strength leans and rests;
The other minces tiptoe. Who would be
The perfect woman must grow brave of heart   10
And broad of soul to play her troubled part
Well in life's drama. While each day we see
The "perfect lady" skilled in what to do
And what to say, grace in each tone and act
('Tis taught in schools, but needs some native tact),
Yet narrow in her mind as in her shoe.
Give the first place then to the nobler phrase,
And leave the lesser word for lesser praise.

(1888)

Achievement

Trust in thine own untried capacity
        As thou wouldst trust in God Himself. Thy soul
        Is but an emanation from the whole.
Thou dost not dream what forces lie in thee,
Vast and unfathomed as the grandest sea.
        Thy silent mind o'er diamond caves may roll,
        Go seek them—but let pilot will control
Those passions which thy favouring winds can be.
No man shall place a limit in thy strength;
        Such triumphs as no mortal ever gained   10
        May yet be thine if thou wilt but believe
In thy Creator and thyself. At length
        Some feet will tread all heights now unattained—
        Why not thine own? Press on; achieve! achieve!

(1888)

What Love Is

Love is the center and circumference;
    The cause and aim of all things—'tis the key
To joy and sorrow, and the recompense
    For all the ills that have been, or may be.

Love is as bitter as the dregs of sin,
    As sweet as clover-honey in its cell;
Love is the password whereby souls get in
    To heaven—the gate that leads, sometimes, to Hell.

Love is the crown that glorifies; the curse
    That brands and burdens; it is life and death.   10
It is the great law of the universe;
    And nothing can exist without its breath.

Love is the impulse which directs the world,
    And all things know it and obey its power.
Man, in the maelstrom of his passions whirled;
    The bee that takes the pollen to the flower.

The earth, uplifting her bare, pulsing breast
    To fervent kisses of the amorous sun;—
Each but obeys creative Love's behest,
    Which everywhere instinctively is done.   20

Love is the only thing which pays for birth,
    Or makes death welcome. Oh, dear God above
This beautiful but sad, perplexing earth,
    Pity the hearts that know—or know not—Love!

                              (1888)

Optimism

I'm no reformer; for I see more light
Than darkness in the world; mine eyes are quick
To catch the first dim radiance of the dawn,
And slow to note the cloud that threatens storm.
The fragrance and the beauty of the rose
Delight me so, slight thought I give its thorn;
And the sweet music of the lark's clear song
Stays longer with me than the night-hawk's cry.

And e'en in this great throe of pain called Life
I find a rapture linked with each despair,   10
Well worth the price of anguish. I detect
More good than evil in humanity.
Love lights more fires than hate extinguishes,
And men grow better as the world grows old.

(1888)

Concentration

The age is too diffusive. Time and Force
      Are frittered out and bring no satisfaction.
      The way seems lost to straight determined action.
Like shooting stars that zig-zag from their course
We wander from our orbit's pathway! spoil
      The role we're fitted for, to fail in twenty.
      Bring empty measures that were shaped for plenty,
At last as guerdon for a life of toil.
There's a lack of greatness in this generation
      Because no man centres on one thought.   10
      We know this truth and yet we heed it not,
The secret of success is Concentration.

(1892)

Life's Opera

Like an opera-house is the world I ween,
    Where the passionate lover of music is seen
        In the balcony near the roof:
While the very best seat in the first stage-box
Is filled by the person who laughs and talks
        Through the harmony's warp and woof.

(1892)

Edwin Markham
1852–1940

On his eightieth birthday, in 1932, Edwin Markham was honored with a gala celebration at Carnegie Hall (Filler 193). Markham's colleagues, President Hoover, and his public hailed him as one of the premier artists of the age. The event marked the apex of a long, important career; in his heyday, Markham set the standards for American poetry. Best known for his verses on the problems of labor, Markham also gave attention to romance, religion, and the role of the artist.

Charles Edward Anson Markham was born 23 April 1852 in Oregon City in the Oregon Territory. Shortly after "Charley's" birth, his parents divorced; young Markham stayed with his mother, Elizabeth. In 1856, Elizabeth took her children with her to California, where she bought a desolate, run-down ranch. Realizing that their mother was a tyrant, Charley's siblings gradually wandered or fled away, leaving him alone with her. He ultimately left his mother's farm, got an education, and became a teacher. In little communities like Coloma, California, Markham achieved status; because of his education, he played an active role in town life.

During the early phase of Markham's career, he encountered two of his major poetic themes. While in Coloma, Markham learned of the problems of the farm laborers; these difficulties touched him deeply. Already intent on using his art for some noble purpose, in 1877 Markham wrote to a colleague that he felt a calling to alleviate suffering. About the same time, Markham discovered the writings of Thomas Lake Harris, "a mystic, poet, and utopian communist whose influence upon Markham was complete" (Filler 39). Part of what drew Markham to Harris's *The Lord: The Two-in-One; Declared, Manifested, and Glorified* was that the latter's "religious drives mixed freely with his responses to temporal affairs" (Filler 40). From "Father" Harris, Markham drew the core of what would become his own philosophy: in many of his poems he fuses religion and pro-labor sentiment.

Although Markham was keenly interested in these two topics, he was aware that the public might not be receptive of them, so he also published more conventional verse. Although he had some success in the magazines, Markham was impatient. Intent on solidifying his reputation with a book publication, Markham offered in 1897 to pay production costs for a volume of poems and guarantee the purchase of a certain number of copies. "The Man with the Hoe," a powerful statement on American labor inspired by the François Millet woodcut of the same name, provided Markham with the title of his first volume, *The Man with the Hoe and Other Poems* (1899). In 1901, Markham published *Lincoln and Other Poems*, the title piece of which Markham read both at the Lincoln birthday dinner in 1900 and at the dedication of the Lincoln Memorial in 1922. In 1915, Markham published his third volume of poetry, *The Shoes of Happiness*; his fourth book of poems, *The Gates of Paradise*, appeared in 1920. In his later years, Markham was a respected critic and a senior statesman of American poetry. He died on 7 March 1940 in Staten Island, New York.

The chief feature of Markham's poetry is its regularity. A devotee of the rules of poetry, he concentrated on using full rhyme and regular meter. Poems included here are either rhymed couplets, very regular blank verse, or quatrains rhyming *abab*. While the poet is accomplished, there is nothing innovative about his style. Markham chose serious topics for his verse, but he wrote of suffering he never experienced. For example, although he wrote stirringly of the labor problem, Markham was not a worker. Poems like "The Man with the Hoe" stirred the sentiments of a nation ripe for reform. Today, however, the poem lacks the power necessary to make it more than a verbal portrait of individuals. Poems like "The Whirlwind Road" explain Markham's philosophy of the role of the poet as seer, but he limits the vision of the poet too strictly to the issues of his day. In much the same way, Markham's religious verses like "Song Made Flesh" reflect a spiritual approach to the same specific labor difficulties addressed in the worker poems.

Although Markham's central themes are still important, his expression of them lacks universality. Unlike Whitman and Dickinson, he cannot transcend a time period to create immortal verse. Markham is important, then, because he spoke to the nation of the need for reform. His role as the bringer of change and the recorder of society's evils at the century's end makes him a vital figure in the study of nineteenth-century American poetry.

—*William R. Nash*

Suggestions for Further Reading

Filler, Louis. *The Unknown Edwin Markham: His Mystery and Its Significance*. Yellow Springs, OH: Antioch P, 1966.

TEXTS
The Man with the Hoe and Other Poems. 1899.
Lincoln and Other Poems. New York: McClure, Phillips, 1901.

ᗖᕍᑫ

The Man with the Hoe[1]
(Written after Seeing Millet's World-Famous Painting)

> God made man in His own image,
> in the image of God made He him.
> — *Genesis*

Bowed by the weight of centuries he leans
Upon his hoe and gazes on the ground,
The emptiness of ages in his face,
And on his back the burden of the world.
Who made him dead to rapture and despair,
A thing that grieves not and that never hopes,
Stolid and stunned, a brother to the ox?
Who loosened and let down this brutal jaw?
Whose was the hand that slanted back this brow?
Whose breath blew out the light within this brain?   10

Is this the Thing the Lord God made and gave
To have dominion over sea and land;
To trace the stars and search the heavens for power;
To feel the passion of Eternity?
Is this the Dream[2] He dreamed who shaped the suns
And pillared the blue firmament with light?[3]
Down all the stretch of Hell to its last gulf[4]
There is no shape more terrible than this—
More tongued with censure of the world's blind greed—
More filled with signs and portents for the soul—   20
More fraught with menace to the universe.[5]

---

1. The copy text included here is from *The Man with the Hoe and Other Poems* (1899); the subsequent notes are included to indicate variations between this text and the version of the poem that appears in *Poems of Edwin Markham*, ed. Charles L. Wallis (New York: Harper, 1950). The first variation is the inclusion of a footnote containing Markham's description of his reaction to Millet's woodcut. Although too long for inclusion here, it is certainly interesting and useful for students of Markham's poetry.

2. "Dream" changed to "dream" in the 1950 volume.

3. In the later text, this line is replaced by "And marked their ways upon the ancient deep?"

4. "stretch" changed to "caverns"; "its" changed to "their."

5. "More fraught with menace" changed to "More packt with danger."

What gulfs between him and the seraphim!
Slave of the wheel of labor, what to him
Are Plato and the swing of Pleiades?
What are the long reaches of the peaks of song,
The rift of dawn, the reddening of the rose?
Through this dread shape the suffering ages look;
Time's tragedy is in that aching stoop;
Through this dread shape humanity betrayed,
Plundered, profaned and disinherited,   30
Cries protest to the Judges of the World,
A protest that is also prophecy.

O masters, lords and rulers in all lands,
Is this the handiwork you give to God,
This monstrous thing distorted and soul-quenched?
How will you ever straighten up this shape;
Touch it again with immortality;
Give back the upward looking and the light;
Rebuild in it the music and the dream;
Make right the immemorial infamies,   40
Perfidious wrongs, immedicable woes?

O masters, lords and rulers in all lands,
How will the Future reckon with this Man?
How answer his brute question in that hour
When whirlwinds of rebellion shake the world?[6]
How will it be with kingdoms and with kings—
With those who shaped him to the thing he is—
When this dumb Terror shall reply to God,[7]
After the silence of the centuries.

                                                    (1899)

The Whirlwind Road

The Muses wrapped in mysteries of light
Came in a rush of music on the night;
And I was lifted wildly on quick wings,
And borne away into the deep of things.
The dead doors of my being broke apart;
A wind of rapture blew across the heart;

---

6. "shake the world" changed to "shake all shores."
7. In the later text, this line is replaced by "When this dumb terror shall rise to judge the world."

The inward song of worlds rang still and clear;
I felt the Mystery the Muses fear;
Yet they went swiftening on the ways untrod,
And hurled me breathless at the feet of God.   10

I felt faint touches of the Final Truth—
Moments of trembling love, moments of youth.
A vision swept away the human wall;
Slowly I saw the meaning of it all—
Meaning of life and time and death and birth,
But can not tell it to the men of Earth.
I only point the way, and they must go
The whirlwind road of song if they would know.

                                                        (1899)

Song Made Flesh

I have no glory in these songs of mine:
    If one of them can make a brother strong,
It came down from the peaks of the divine—
    I heard it in the Heaven of Lyric Song.

The one who builds the poem into fact,
    He is the rightful owner of it all:
The pale words are with God's own power packed
    When brave souls answer to their bugle-call.

And so I ask no man to praise my song,
    But I would have him build it in his soul;   10
For that great praise would make me glad and strong,
    And build the poem to a perfect whole.

                                                        (1899)

Lincoln, the Man of the People

When the Norn-Mother saw the Whirlwind Hour,
Greatening and darkening as it hurried on,
She bent the strenuous Heavens and came down
To make a man to meet the mortal need.
She took the tried clay of the common road—
Clay warm yet with the genial heat of Earth,

Dashed through it all a strain of prophecy;
Then mixed a laughter with the serious stuff.
It was a stuff to wear for centuries,
A man that matched the mountains, and compelled   10
The stars to look our way and honor us.

The color of the ground was in him, the red earth;
The tang and odor of the primal things—
The rectitude and patience of the rocks;
The gladness of the wind that shakes the corn;
The courage of the bird that dares the sea;
The justice of the rain that loves all leaves;
The pity of the snow that hides all scars;
The loving-kindness of the wayside well;
The tolerance and equity of light   20
That gives as freely to the shrinking weed
As to the great oak flaring to the wind—
To the grave's low hill as to the Matterhorn
That shoulders out the sky.

                    And so he came.
From prairie cabin up to Capitol,
One fair Ideal led our chieftain on.
Forevermore he burned to do his deed
With the fine stroke and gesture of a king.
He built the rail-pile as he built the State,   30
Pouring his splendid strength through every blow,
The conscience of him testing every stroke,
To make his deed the measure of a man.

So came the Captain with the mighty heart:
And when the step of Earthquake shook the house,
Wrenching the rafters from their ancient hold,
He held the ridgepole up, and spiked again
The rafters of the Home. He held his place—
Held the long purpose like a growing tree—
Held on through blame and faltered not at praise.   40
And when he fell in whirlwind, he went down
As when a kingly cedar green with boughs
Goes down with a great shout upon the hills,
And leaves a lonesome place against the sky.

                                        (1900, 1901)

Henrietta Cordelia Ray
1852?–1916

Henrietta Cordelia Ray's po-
etry passionately celebrated black and abolitionist heroes. To do
this, she used formal language and forms that elevated her sub-
jects. Although her poetry and her life are unfamiliar to most
modern readers, they exemplify an important American contin-
gent: educated Northern blacks who were active not only in the
abolitionist movement, but also in other social reform and liter-
ary circles.

Henrietta Cordelia Ray, or H. Cordelia, as she preferred to be
called, was born in New York City in the early 1850s (the exact
date is not known). Her father, the Rev. Charles Ray, was active
in the Underground Railroad and in other reform organizations
and edited the *Colored American*. Her sister, Charlotte, was the
first black woman to practice law in Washington, D.C. H. Cor-
delia was also well educated. She earned her pedagogy degree in
1891 from the University of the City of New York and was re-
puted to have graduated from the Sauveneur School of Lan-
guages and to have been fluent in Greek, Latin, French, and Ger-
man. She taught school for thirty years in New York City,
after which she tutored music, mathematics, and languages and
cared for her invalid sister Florence, with whom she lived all her
life.

Ray's poems are formal and filled with literary allusions, often
dedicated to such British writers as Shakespeare and Milton. Her
goal was probably to describe blacks in the same style with which
white people and experience were described, thus elevating the
image of the race itself. One sonnet, "To My Father," describes
the hero in the conventional poetic diction of her time. Seen in
that light, the poem, although not particularly inventive in itself,
is touching and rare. Likewise, in "In Memoriam, Frederick
Douglass" she proposes, "Let his example be a shining light"
(line 5).

Besides tributes to black heroes, her poems consider nature,
love, Christianity, and literature. In "A Thought on Lake On-
tario," she observes,

The lucent lake was lit with sheen
Shining the crested waves between,
    And through the purpling air
The young birds trilled their lightsome lays,
To join the hymn of Nature's praise,
    And earth was passing fair.

(Sherman 131)

Although Ray's images are imprecise, her lines are stylistically
pleasing: the alliteration in the first line ("lucent lake") echoes
later with "lightsome lays," and occasional meter irregularities
save the verse from monotony. This example is typical of much
of Ray's poetry. She employs a variety of stanza forms and
rhyme schemes, some original, and varies her line length and me-
ter within her poems to avoid monotony.

Although stylistically rougher than her other poems, "Verses
to My Heart's Sister" contains real emotion. This poem explores
the speaker's grief over the deaths of her father, mother, and four
siblings, and her gratitude for her sister Florence's love. As Joan
R. Sherman notes, "Except for a few such personal poems, Miss
Ray's verse labors under the blessing of a fine education" (133).
Indeed, although Ray's poems display mastery of structure and
style, they do not exhibit much creative spark; many are formal
sonnets without the illuminating image or idea that makes for
memorable poetry.

—*Lisa Carl*

Suggestions for Further Reading

Jackson, Blyden. *The History of Afro-American Literature*. Baton
    Rouge: Louisiana State UP, 1989.
Sherman, Joan R. *Invisible Poets: Afro-Americans of the Nineteenth
    Century*. 2nd ed. Chicago: U of Illinois P, 1989.

TEXTS
Poems. New York: Grafton, 1910. Reprints much of *Sonnets* (1893).
*Emancipation: its course and progress from 1481 B.C. to A.D. 1875, with
    a review of President Lincoln's proclamations, the XIII amendment,
    and the progress of the freed people since emancipation; with a history
    of the emancipation monument*. 1893.
Early Black American Poets. Ed. William Henry Robinson. Dubuque,
    IA: W. C. Brown, 1969.

Lincoln[1]

To-day O martyred chief! beneath the sun
We would unveil thy form; to thee who won
The applause of nations, for thy soul sincere,
A living tribute we would offer here.
'Twas thine not worlds to conquer, but men's hearts;
To change to balm the sting of slavery's darts;
In lowly charity thy joy to find,
And open "gates of mercy on mankind,"
And so they come, the freed, with grateful gift,
From whose sad path the shadows thou didst lift.   10

Eleven years have rolled their seasons round
Since its most tragic close thy life-work found.
Yet through the vistas of the vanished days
We see thee still, responsive to our gaze
As ever to thy country's solemn needs.
Not regal coronets, but princely deeds
Were thy chaste diadem; of truer worth
Thy modest virtues than the gems of earth.
Staunch, honest, fervent in the purest cause.
Truth was thy guide; her mandates were thy laws.   20

Rare heroism; spirit purity;
The storied Spartan's stern simplicity;
Such moral strength as gleams like burnished gold
Amid the doubts of men of weaker mold
Were thine. Called in thy country's sorest hour,
When brother knew not brother—mad for power—
To guide the helm through bloody deeps of war,
While distant nations gazed in anxious awe,
Unflinching in the task, thou didst fulfill
Thy mighty mission with a deathless will.   30

Born to a destiny the most sublime,
Thou wert, O Lincoln! in the march of time.
God bade thee pause—and bid the oppressed go free—
Most glorious boon giv'n to humanity,
While Slavery ruled the land, what deeds were done!
What tragedies enacted 'neath the sun!
Her page is blurred with records of defeat

---

1. Read at the unveiling of the Freedman's monument in memory of
Abraham Lincoln on 14 April 1876 in New York City. The reading preceded a
speech by Frederick Douglass.

Of lives heroic lived in silence—meet
For the world's praise—of woe, despair, and tears—
The speechless agony of weary years!   40

Thou utterest the word, and Freedom fair
Rang her sweet bells on the clear winter air;
She waved her magic wand, and lo! from far
A long procession came! with many a scar
Their brows were wrinkled—in the bitter strife,
Full many had said their sad farewell to life.
But on they hasten'd—free—their shackles gone—
The aged, young—e'en infancy was borne
To offer unto thee loud paeons of praise—
Their happy tribute after saddest days.   50

A race set free! The deed brought joy and light!
It bade calm justice from her sacred height,
When faith, and hope, and courage slowly waned,
Unfurl the stars and stripes at last unstained!
The nations rolled acclaim from sea to sea,
And Heaven's vaults rang with Freedom's harmony.
The Angels, mid the amaranths must have hush'd
Their chanted cadence, as upward rush'd
The hymn sublime; and as the echoes pealed
God's ceaseless benison the action sealed.   60

As now we dedicate this shaft to thee,
True champion! in all humility
And solemn earnestness, we would erect
A monument invisible, undecked,
Save by our allied purpose to be true
To Freedom's loftiest precepts, so that through
The fiercest contest we may walk secure,
Fixed on foundations that may still endure
When granite shall have crumbled to decay
And generations passed from earth away.   70

Exalted patriot! illustrious chief!
Thy life's immortal work compels belief.
To-day in radiance thy virtues shine,
And how can we a fitting garland twine?
Thy crown most glorious is a ransomed race!
High on our country's scroll we fondly trace
In lines of fadeless light that softly blend;
Emancipation, hero, martyr, friend!

While Freedom may her holy sceptre claim,
The world shall echo with "Our Lincoln's" name.   80
read 1876, 1893)

To My Father

A leaf from Freedom's golden chaplet fair,
We bring to thee, dear father. Near her shrine
None came with holier purpose, nor was thine
Alone the soul's mute sanction; every prayer
Thy captive brother uttered found a share
In thy wide sympathy; to every sigh
That told the bondman's need thou didst incline.
No thought of guerdon hadst thou but to bear
A long part in Freedom's strife. To see
Sad lives illumined, fetters rent in twain,   10
Tears dried in eyes that wept for length of days—
Ah! was not that a recompense for thee?
And now where all life's mystery is plain,
Divine approval is thy sweetest praise.

(1910)

In Memoriam, Frederick Douglass

Shall the race falter in its courage now
That the great chief is fallen? Shall it bow
Tamely to aught of injury? Ah, nay!
For daring souls are needed e'en today.
Let his example be a shining light,
Leading through duty's paths to some far height
Of undreamed victory. All honored be
The silv'ry head of him we no more see!
Children unborn will venerate his name,
And History keep spotless his fair fame.   10

(1910)

from Verses to My Heart's Sister

So nearer clung we, sister,
And loved each other more;
The tendrils of our natures
Twined closer than before.
We could speak to each other
Of those sweet, holy things,
So tender yet so nameless
Which sorrow often brings.
. . . .
And shall not those sweet loved ones
Missed here so long! so long!   10
Join with us in the music
Of an all-perfect song?
We feel a gladder cadence
Will thrill their rapt'rous strain,
When we are with them, sister,
All, ne'er to part again?

(1910)

Lizette Woodworth Reese

1856–1935

Lizette Woodworth Reese's gift for writing sonnets, lyrics, and ballads earned her a faithful audience in her day. H. L. Mencken, editor of *The Smart Set*, declared Reese never wrote a bad poem and that her sonnet "Tears" was the finest since Shakespeare (Turnbull 9). Her fascination with the ever-changing landscape of her home and the preciousness of "common things" illumines much of her work ("In Praise of Common Things," line 33). Later poems include personal symbolism in which the color white acts as a paramount "loveliness" or aesthetic standard. Reese's emphasis on color, symbol, and image in poems treating the everyday reveal her as a poet striving to surpass the sentimental, often facile poetry of her day; intensity of feeling distinguishes her best work.

Lizette Woodworth Reese, daughter of a Welsh father and German mother, was born 9 January 1856, in Waverly, Maryland, two miles from Baltimore. Until age seventeen, Reese attended the Baltimore public schools and acquired an appreciation for Herrick, the Brownings, Emily Brontë, Poe, and Whittier. After graduating from high school in 1873, she embarked on a forty-five year career of teaching and poetry writing. Reese published her first poem, "The Deserted House," in *Southern Magazine* (1874) and contributed to the *New Republic*, *Harper's Bazaar*, *Virginia Quarterly Review*, and *Poetry*. Thomas Wentworth Higginson, William Dean Howells, and Edmund Clarence Stedman praised Reese's first volume, *A Branch of May* (1887), and after its success, Houghton Mifflin published *A Handful of Lavender* (1891) and *A Quiet Road* (1896). These three volumes established Reese as a successful poet. Seven other collections followed, including *White April* (1930), the volume that best illustrates her symbolic use of the color white. When Reese died on 17 December 1935, she had received numerous awards for her poetic achievement, including election as Maryland's poet laureate. She is buried at St. John's Church of Huntingdon.

Nature, love, memory, and mutability prove constant themes in Reese's work. "The Deserted House" describes the passage of a rural way of life while "Blackberry Blossoms" and "After the Rain" focus on a single image's metamorphosis from natural object to metaphor of beauty, time, or memory. Reese uses this language of landscape and time to reveal a lover's internal tension and longing for fulfillment in "Compensation" and "A Passing Mood." She further develops the landscape's role in love and artistic creation in poems such as "Spring Ecstasy" and "Before the Look of You," in which Nature's fierce beauty threatens to subdue, violate, or envelop the poet. These "Nature" poems illustrate the tension between the poet and her subject that is often necessary for creation. Part of Reese desires to let herself go with the intense feeling and vivid imagery so often found in her poetry. Yet even so, a cautioning voice in "Reserve" warns her:

> Keep back the one word more,
> Nor give of your whole store;
> For, it may be, in Art's sole hour of need,
> Lacking that word, you shall be poor indeed.
>
> (lines 1–4)

As Reese herself recognized throughout her career, should this tension between reserve and abandonment leave her, "I would vacant go, / And being naught, to nothing grow" ("In Praise of Common Things," lines 24–25).

Reese's popularity with writers and critics such as E. C. Stedman, Louise Imogen Guiney, H. L. Mencken, and Willa Cather reveals her importance to nineteenth-century literary circles and has encouraged critics to re-examine her as one of the stronger poetic voices of her generation—lost for awhile but not forgotten.

—*Mary K. Edmonds*

Suggestions for Further Reading

Dietrich, Mae. "Lizette Woodworth Reese." *Emily Dickinson Bulletin* 15 (Dec. 1970): 114–22.
Jones, Robert J., ed. *In Praise of Common Things: Lizette Woodworth Reese Revisited.* Westport, CT: Greenwood Press, 1992.
Kindilien, Carlin T. "The Village World of Lizette Woodworth Reese." *South Atlantic Quarterly* 56 (Jan. 1957): 91–104.
Turnbull, Grace H. "Miss Reese and Her Loyal Critic." *Menckeniana* 17 (Spring 1966): 9–11.
Walker, Cheryl. *The Nightingale's Burden: Women Poets and American Culture Before 1900.* Bloomington: Indiana UP, 1982.

TEXTS
A Branch of May: Poems. 1887.
A Handful of Lavender. 1891.
A Quiet Road. 1896.

Wild Cherry. Baltimore: Norman, Remington, 1923.
A Wayside Lute. Portland, ME: T. B. Mosher, 1929.

ꙮ

The Deserted House

The old house stands deserted, gray,
    With sharpened gables high in air,
And deep-set lattices, all gay
    With massive arch and framework rare;
And o'er it is a silence laid,
That feeling, one grows sore afraid.

The eaves are dark with heavy vines;
    The steep roof wears a coat of moss;
The walls are touched with dim designs
    Of shadows moving slow across;   10
The balconies are damp with weeds,
Lifting as close as streamside reeds.

The garden is a loved retreat
    Of melancholy flowers, of lone
And wild-mouthed herbs, in companies sweet,
    'Mid desolate green grasses thrown;
And in its gaps the hoar stone wall
Lets sprays of tangled ivy fall.

The pebbled paths drag, here and there,
    Old lichened faces, overspun   20
With silver spider-threads—they wear
A silence sad to look upon:
It is so long since happy feet
Made them to thrill with pressure sweet.

'Mid drear but fragrant shrubs there stands
    A saint of old made mute in stone,
With tender eyes and yearning hands,
    And mouth formed in a sorrow lone;
'Tis thick with dust, as long ago
'Twas thick with fairest blooms that grow.   30

Swallows are whirring here and there;
    And oft a little soft wind blows

A hundred odors down the air;
    The bees hum 'round the red, last rose
And ceaselessly the crickets shrill
Their tunes, and yet, it seems so still.

Or else, from out the distance steals,
    Half heard, the tramp of horses, or
The bleak and harsh stir of slow wheels
        Bound cityward; but more and more,   40
As these are hushed, or yet increase,
About the old house clings its peace.

                                            (1874, 1887)

Blackberry Blossoms

'Long sunny lane and pike, white, delicate,
    The blackberry blossoms are ablow, ablow,
Hiding the rough-hewn rails 'neath drift of snow,
Fresh-fallen, late. The opening pasture gate
Brushes a hundred of them loose, and shakes
Them down into the tall delicious grass:
Sometimes a little sudden wind doth pass,
And all the air is full of flying flakes.
It seems but yesterday they blew as sweet
Down old school ways, and thrilled me with delight;   10
And reaching out for them, I heard the fleet,
Glad creek go spinning o'er its pebbles bright.
Ah, well! Ah, me! Even now, long as they last,
I am a child again; Joy holds me fast.

                                            (1887)

Doubt

Creeds grow so thick along the way,
    Their boughs hide God; I cannot pray.

                                            (1887)

Truth

The old faiths light their candles all about.
　　　But burly Truth comes by and blows
　　　　　them out.

(1887)

After the Rain

Dripping the hollyhocks beneath the wall,
　　　Their fires half quenched, a smouldering red;
A shred of gold upon the grasses tall,
　　　A butterfly is hanging dead.

A sound of trickling waters, like a tune
　　　Set to sweet words; a wind that blows
Wet boughs against a saffron sky; all June
　　　Caught in the breath of one white rose.

(1887)

Compensation

All day I bar you from my slightest thought;
Make myself clear of you or any mark
Of our wrecked dawn and the uprising lark;
Am stern and strong, and do the thing I ought.
Yet ever are there moments with you fraught;
I hear you like some glad sound in the dark;
You wait like bloom outside my branches stark;
I dare not heed; else were my fight unfought.
But when the clamor and the heat are done,
And spent with both I come unto that door,　　　10
Sleep opens for me every setting sun,
The bitter lies behind, the sweet before.
We that are twain by day, at night are one.
A dream can bring me to your arms once more.

(1891)

A Passing Mood

You say not that you love me, yet 'tis so.
　Your mood is such the days in April wear,
　Driving their last flakes down the ashen air,
And yet with all their buds ready to blow;
Aye, with full-blossomed stalks in many a row,
Purpling the grass beneath the hedges bare.
　Therefore I wait. As sure as April fair,
Grown bolder, knows its boughs bear bloom, not snow;
So you, who halt betwixt the old and new,
　Will know your life's sweet, settled weather come,　10
　And marvel how the blessed thing befell—
How love from out the chill of friendship grew.
　Ah, then no longer, love, will you keep dumb;
　Caught to my heart you must your secret tell.

(1891)

Reserve

Keep back the one word more,
Nor give of your whole store;
For, it may be, in Art's sole hour of need,
Lacking that word, you shall be poor indeed.

(1896)

In Praise of Common Things

For stock and stone;
For grass, and pool; for quince tree blown
A virginal white in spring;
And for the wall beside,
Gray, gentle, wide;
For roof, loaf, everything,
I praise Thee, Lord;
For toil, and ache, and strife,
And all the commonness of life.

Hearty, yet dim,　　　　　　　　　　　　　10
Like country voices in a hymn,

The things a house can hold;
The memories in the air;
And down the stair
Fond footsteps known of old;
The chair, the book or two;
The little bowl of white and blue.

What would it be,
If loveliness were far from me?
A staff I could not take,   20
To hurry up and down,
From field to town;
Needs would my wild heart break;
Or, I would vacant go,
And, being naught, to nothing grow.

This is the best:
My little road from east to west,
The breadth of a man's hand,
Not from sky too far,
Nor any star,   30
Runs through the unwalled land;
From common things that be,
Is it but a step to run to Thee.

               (1909)

Tears

When I consider Life and its few years—
A wisp of fog betwixt us and the sun;
A call to battle, and the battle done
Ere the last echo dies within our ears;
A rose choked in the grass; an hour of fears;
The gusts that past a darkening shore do beat;
The burst of music down an unlistening street—
I wonder at the idleness of tears.
Ye old, old dead, and ye of yesternight,
Chieftains, and bards, and keepers of the sheep,   10
By every cup of sorrow that you had,
Loose me from tears, and make me see aright
How each hath back what once he stayed to weep;
Homer his sight, David his little lad!

             (1899, 1909)

Spring Ecstasy

Oh, let me run and hide,
    Let me run straight to God;
The weather is so mad with white
    From sky down to the clod!

If but one thing were so,
    Lilac, or thorn out there,
It would not be, indeed,
    So hard to bear.

The weather has gone mad with white;
    The cloud, the highway touch;   10
White lilac is enough;
    White thorn too much!

                         (1923)

Before the Look of You

I fear you, Loveliness;
    Before the look of you,
Your far yet intimate face,
    My song crumbles in two.

Less am I than a tower;
    Or a pool's thin, wrecked gold;
Or great bells loose at dusk;
    Or a shepherd and a fold;

Or a few violets—
    That straggle April-clear,   10
Within a tumbled wood
    At ending of the year.

Yet spend me at your will;
    Yet spend me low and high,
Though I am naught at all;
    For if you go, I die!

                         (1923)

Ben[jamin] [Franklin] King
1857–1894

Except for the occasional inclusion of two or three of his poems in anthologies, Ben King's poetry has received the most attention for his parody of the poem "If I Should Die Tonight" (Stevenson 127–42). Burton Stevenson's assessment of King's poetry as "mediocre humorous chaff" (141) echoes other twentieth-century notices of King's work. But King's poetry reproduces sensitive portraits of folk life in Chicago and the Midwest, portraying common scenes with common language and representing common folk and their dialects realistically.

Little information is available about Ben King's life. He was born on 17 March 1857, in St. Joseph, Michigan. He married Aseneth Belle Latham, of St. Joseph, on 27 November 1883, in Chicago; they had two sons. Apparently, King worked as a reporter in Chicago. He was a member of the famous Chicago Press Club, formed in 1880, and the infamous Whitechapel Club, a bizarre organization formed in 1889, comprised primarily of Chicago newspapermen and writers. Accounts of him as a club member refer to him as a poet-humorist. King died early on the morning of 8 April 1894 in Bowling Green, Kentucky, where he had performed the night before during an extended reading tour. On 10 April 1894, King was buried in St. Joseph, Michigan.

King published verse in newpapers and magazines, often using the psuedonym "Bow Hackley." *Century* magazine published Hackley's "De Bugle on De Hill" in June of 1891; according to a note made by King's editors, "this [was] the first poem by a Chicago author to be printed in 'The Century Magazine' " (McGovern). In June 1892, *Century* published another of King's poems, "Grave Matters," this time using his real name. After King's death, his friends from the Press Club assembled a volume of his poetry, *Ben King's Verse* (1894); from 1894 to 1923, this collection went through at least fourteen printings. By the turn of the century, with the sixth printing, thirteen thousand copies had been printed. Publishers also issued two gift books, *Jane Jones and Some Others* (1909), a selection from King's humorous scenes and dialogues, and *Ben King's Southland Melodies* (1911), a collection of his black dialect poems. King's work had popular appeal.

King was an acute observer, listener, and social critic; as a result, his poetry is diverse, ranging from regional folk humor to sensitive portraits in dialect. He wrote for the common reader, for the audience who would join him at a local club performance or in the town's Music Hall. Though most of his dialect poetry recreates either black or uneducated white speech, he spared no particular segment of the population, including Scandinavians, the Irish, and stuttering young men. In his poem "Say When, and Say It," King calls for a direct, original, "mirthy" poetry, and "The Pessimist" fulfills that call. But not all of his work is humorous. In black dialect poems such as "Decorate De Cabin," King offers sensitive renderings of nostalgic monologues that recall a painful past while preserving a black culture in language and memory. And in "Nobody Knows," he offers a pointed critique of a society unable to care for all of its members.

Chicago and the Midwest were undergoing great changes at the end of the century: frontier was changing to metropolis, an agrarian-based economy was shifting to manufacturing, and a rural populace was moving to cities. King's poetry records these scenes, revealing his audience to themselves and their neighbors; celebrating the common, the everyday, the local, the personal, the human; and preserving differences while portraying commonalities. King's poems democratize the common folk, pointing out that all of them speak a dialect of sorts, and all of them share frustrations, disappointments, and celebrations.

—*Glenn Blalock*

Suggestions for Further Reading

McGovern, John. "Introduction." *Ben King's Verse*. By Ben King. Ed. Nixon Waterman. 2nd ed. Chicago: Forbes, 1898. v–vii.
Stevenson, Burton. "If I Should Die Tonight." *Famous Single Poems and the Controversies Which Have Raged Around Them*. New York: Dodd, 1935. 127–42.

TEXT
Ben King's Verse. 1898.

꩜

If I Should Die

If I should die to-night
  And you should come to my cold corpse and say,

Weeping and heartsick o'er my lifeless clay—
If I should die to-night,
And you should come in deepest grief and woe—
And say: "Here's that ten dollars that I owe,"
   I might arise in my large white cravat
   And say, "What's that?"

   If I should die to-night
And you should come to my cold corpse and kneel,   10
Clasping my bier to show the grief you feel,
   I say, if I should die to-night
And you should come to me, and there and then
Just even hint 'bout payin' me that ten,
   I might arise the while,
   But I'd drop dead again.

              (1898)

Say When, and Say It

Write me a poem that hasn't been writ,
   Sing me a song that hasn't been sung yet,
String out a strain that hasn't been strung,
   And ring me a chime that hasn't been rung yet.

Paint me a picture but leave out the paint,
   Pile up a pile of old scenes of my schoolery,
Leave me alone; I would fain meditate
   And mourn o'er the moments I lost in tomfoolery.

Tell me a tale that dropped out of a star,
   Push me a pun that is pungent, not earthy.   10
I must have something sharp, strident, and strong
   To eke out a laugh or be moderately mirthy.

Give me a love that has never been loved,
   Not knowing the glance of the bold and unwary,
A cherub abreast with the saints up above,
   And I'll get along and be passably merry.

But come on the fly to me, come on the jump,
   Don't hang around on the outskirts and walk to me;
Throw out your chest well, and hold up your head;
   Say when, and *say* it, or else don't you talk to me.   20
              (1898)

Evolution

We seem to exist in a hazardous time,
   Driftin' along here through space;
Nobody knows just when we begun
   Or how fur we've gone in the race.
Scientists argy we're shot from the sun,
   While others we're goin' right back,
An' some say we've allers been here more or less,
   An' seem to establish the fact.
O' course 'at's somepin' 'at nobody knows,
   As far as I've read or cun see;   10
An' them as does know all about the hull scheme,
   Why, none of 'em never agree.

Now, why I think it's a perilous time,—
   What do we know 'bout them spots
Up there on that glorious orb of the day?
   Smart men has argyed an' lots
Of the brainiest folks has been cypherin' out,
   An' all sorts of stories has riz
'Bout what the sun's made of or how it's composed,
   An' lots of 'em think that it is.   20
O' course 'at's somepin' 'at nobody knows—
   Nobody under the sun;
Nary a body or bein', I s'pose;
   Nary a bein' but One.

Take Eva Lution, an' what does she say
   'Bout how we all sprung from a ape?
An' there's the goriller and big chimpanzee,
   Patterned exactly our shape.
An' I've seen some folks, an' I guess so have you,
   An' it ain't none of our bizness neither,   30
That actually looked like they sprung from a ape,
   An' didn't have fur to spring either.
Course 'at's somepin 'at every one knows;
   I don't see how you folks can doubt it;
S'posin' they have some resemblance to us,
   No use in a-writin' about it.

If a feller 'll take a geology book
   An' not go rushin' long through it,
But jes' sort o' figger the thing out hisself—
   What I mean is: 'ply hisself to it—   40

He'll see we've dug up folks ten thousand years old,
   Built on a ponderous plan;
Somehow this knocks Mr. Moses all out,
   An' Adam, the biblical man.
O' course 'at's somepin 'at nobody knows,
   Nobody under the sun;
Nary a body or bein I s'pose,
   Nary a bein' but One.

(1898)

De Bugle on De Hill

I doan like de noise ob de marchin' ob de boys,
   An' I 'low doan s'pose I evah will;
Er de trampin' ob de feet to de drum's wild beat,
   Er de sound ob de bugle on de hill.
Hit 'minds me ob de day when Gabe marched away
   En ole missus stood beside de cabin do';
Somepin' whispahed in my ear 'bout my little volunteer,
   An' said he nevah will come back no mo'.

I 'membah now de day jes' how he marched away,
   Wid de bright sun er climbin' up de sky,   10
Marched out en down de street to de drum's wild beat,
   Den dey fotched him home to die.
Oh, de sad en moanful way, po' old missus kneeled ter pray,
   When Gabe said: "Hit's gittin' mighty still."
But I rise en jine de boys when I hear de cannon's noise,
   Er de blowin' ob de bugle on de hill.

Hit 'pears es if I seen de ole plantation green,
   En sometimes I sho'ly think I hear
De regiment pars by, en 'low I hear de cry
   En de moan ob my little volunteer.   20
En I see de moanful way po' ole missus kneel to pray,
   En sometimes when all aroun' is still,
I kin hear de tread ob feet to de drum's wild beat
   En de blowin' ob de bugle on de hill.

Dar's a spot mighty dear to dis ole darky here,
   Whar de sunlight is peepin' froo de palms,
Wid his hands 'pon his breast, dar my soldier's gone to rest,
   Jes' peacefully er sleepin' in de calms.

Ben[jamin] [Franklin] King   459

En de drum's wild beat er de tread ob marchin' feet
No mo' kain't distrub 'im now until   30
De Lord gibs command, den I know he'll rise en stand
At de sound ob de bugle on de hill.

(1891, 1898)

Nobody Knows

Nobody knows when de col' winds am blowin',
Whar all de po' little chillun am a-goin'.
Nobody knows when de night time's hoverin'
How many little ones am des'tute ob coverin'.
Nobody sees, but de Lo'd done see 'em,
An' bime-by de Lo'd 'll tell humanity ter free 'em.

Nobody knows jes' how many am in rags,
A-sleepin' in de hot blocks an' 'roun' on de flags,
Nobody sees all dis poverty an' woe,
A-livin' on de emptyin's an' not a place ter go.   10
Nobody sees, but de Lo'd done see 'em,
An' bime-by de Lo'd 'll tell humanity ter free 'em.

Nobody knows whar dis poverty all comes—
How many po' folks am sleepin' in de slums.
Nobody knows jes' how few am befriendin',
But de good Lo'd knows dar mus' soon be an endin'.
Nobody sees, but de Lo'd done see 'em,
An' bime-by de Lo'd 'll tell humanity ter free 'em.

(1898)

Decorate De Cabin

I'se done gwine ter decorate mah cabin,
Wid all de brick-er-brack I'se been a-habbin',
Den I'se boun' ter hunt er wife,
'Deed I is, yo' bet yo' life.
Dar's nuffin like a woman roun' er blabbin'.

I'se gwine ter hang a coon skin on de do',
En hab some Turkey rugs roun' on de flo';
An' I nevah yet hab seen

De ole cabin look ser clean,
Ef yo' peep in dar some time yo'll fin' it so.   10

I los' mah wife las' summah, Jane Safras,
Kase she done got up 'n blew out de gas,
      An' eber since her leabin'
      I'se been sort o' greebin,
But I hope de one I'se ketchin' now 'll las'.

We's gwine ter start right in to decoratin',
An' yo' 'll be surprised at what I'm statin',
      She's six feet high en taperin',
      En out ob sight in paperin',
I'se mighty glad I'se been so long a-waitin'.   20

We's gwine ter 'range de pictures on de wall—
Yo' talk about a fine reception hall—
      Yo' ought to see de flowahs,
      En de chromios in ours,
W'y, de white man's house ain' in de thing at all.

(1898)

The Pessimist

Nothing to do but work,
      Nothing to eat but food.
Nothing to wear but clothes
      To keep one from going nude.

Nothing to breathe but air
      Quick as a flash 'tis gone;
Nowhere to fall but off,
      Nowhere to stand but on.

Nothing to comb but hair,
      Nowhere to sleep but in bed,   10
Nothing to weep but tears,
      Nothing to bury but dead.

Nothing to sing but songs,
      Ah, well, alas! alack!
Nowhere to go but out,
      Nowhere to come but back.

Ben[jamin] [Franklin] King   461

Nothing to see but sights,
    Nothing to quench but thirst,
Nothing to have but what we've got;
    Thus thro' life we are cursed.   20

Nothing to strike but a gait;
    Everything moves that goes.
Nothing at all but common sense
    Can ever withstand these woes.

(1898)

Horace Logo Traubel

1858–1919

Horace Traubel secured his place in literary history when he recorded Walt Whitman's daily conversations from March 1888 to January 1889. Traubel befriended Whitman when the poet first came to Camden to live in 1873, and in addition to his biographical work, Traubel helped Whitman prepare several late editions of his poetry, including the 1891–92 edition of *Leaves of Grass*. After Whitman's death, Traubel served as one of three literary executors, helped to edit *The Complete Writings of Walt Whitman* (1902), and published the first three volumes of his recorded conversations: *With Walt Whitman in Camden* (1906, 1909, 1914). Traubel failed to be one of those "Poets to Come" that Whitman addressed in "Inscriptions" in *Leaves of Grass*. With his early poems, his volume of poetic prose, *Chants Communal* (1904), and his volume of Whitmanesque free verse poetry, *Optimos* (1910), Traubel attempted to apply Whitman's expansive, universal aesthetic and political philosophy to specific causes and and local conditions, but his work was only a weak imitation of *Leaves of Grass*.

Horace Logo Traubel was born on 19 December 1858 in Camden, New Jersey. He was an early and avid reader, but he stopped attending school when he was twelve. Over the next twenty years, he worked for local newspapers as a delivery boy, as a pressman, and later as a reporter; he learned the printing trade; and he worked as a bank clerk and as a factory paymaster. Traubel's experiences as a wage-earner, his sensitivity to the overt injustices inherent in late nineteenth-century capitalism, and his close contact with Whitman's radical democracy and spiritual idealism contributed to his later support of socialism.

Traubel was publishing verse in the 1880s, but in 1890, he founded the *Conservator*, and for the next thirty years he edited the monthly, contributing essays and poetry regularly. The *Conservator* reflected Traubel's ideology, a mixture of explicit Marxist socialism and implicit poetic religiosity bordering on mysticism. He married Anne Montgomerie in 1891, and after 1892, he earned his living as a writer and editor. Traubel remained politically active until his death on 8 September 1919 in Ontario, Canada. He is buried in the same cemetery that holds Whitman's remains, the Harleigh Cemetery in Camden, New Jersey.

Traubel's early poetry, represented here by "Near You Is Sorrow and Plaint" (1892), was conventional in form and in subject; but beginning with "Cosmos" (1893), his poetry begins to reflect visible growth and development. Poems such as "Wild Rose" (1896) more closely resemble Whitman's in form. And Traubel expresses more openly his advocacy for political change in poems such as "I Saw a Thousand Singers Hand in Hand" (1894), "Face to Face" (1896), and "Before Time Was Woman" (1910).

Traubel cannot escape comparisons with Whitman. In his mature poetry, he attempts the free verse lines that Whitman mastered. And he relies on the same techniques that Whitman used to achieve the fullest poetic expression, including assonance, alliteration, repetition, inverse word order, naming, and listing. But Traubel's poetic vision is less expansive, and his language is less expressive. Because Whitman's poetry speaks timelessly, his work survives and flourishes. Because Traubel's poetry speaks to a reader in a specific time, in service of a specific ideology, his reputation as a poet suffers. Until his work is read in its historical context, Traubel will remain in the notes of Whitman studies.

—*Glenn Blalock*

Suggestions for Further Reading

Karsner, David. *Horace Traubel*. New York: Egmont Arens, 1919.
Walling, William English. *Whitman and Traubel*. New York: Albert and Charles Boni, 1916.

TEXTS
Conservator. 1890–1896.
Optimos. New York: B. W. Huebsch, 1910.

༄

Near You Is Sorrow and Plaint

Near you is sorrow and plaint:
Listen—yea, heed!
Fear not the craven croak
Who folds round him coward's cloak
And fain would make color faint
In the cheek of good deed!

Earth smells sweet to you?
Earth yet is Eden: we leap
Lower than hell, than heaven higher,
Consumed by desire,   10
Loth that one soul should reap
While one knows rue.

(1892)

Curse Not the Sleeping Past

Curse not the sleeping past!
Once it was sun and dew:
Out of its storehouse vast
Thou to thy stature grew!
Once it was health and fire—
Now it is mud and mire
To drag thee wearily down!
Brave traveller—wise of will—
The faith that fellowed thy heart
Out of midnight's frown   10
Now makes all fury still.
Thou mayst at peace depart:
Won and unwon the crown!
Curse not the hands that lift
Life in thee high on its hill:
But for the lost, estranged,
Thou wert not loved and changed!
Sea and earth interwrought—
Passion and sight have outrun
Couriers of darkness that brought   20
Gifts but at setting sun!
All were too late—yet had all
Blent in the joy of thy call!

(1893)

Cosmos

Hosts of evil beset me,
The darkness falls and doubt unwraps its cabal scroll,
While I, peaked nearest heaven, seek heaven's escape.

Outspread broad wings, O soul!
Defiantly pierce the spaces upward,

Carol for lower ears the victory and the hope,
And melt in skies eternal!

Flooded in light, outleaping ties sordid and black,
Mixing shadows to suns, ascending still and still,
Upborne in arms nerved to the ceaseless flight,   10
I, joyant, full circling day and night,
Sing all love's songs and live all thought and deed!

(1893)

I Saw a Thousand Singers Hand in Hand

I saw a thousand singers hand in hand,
Ages long the procession, the line unbroken,
Vulturous pedantries swooping and threatening,
The masters, the prophetic strong voices, defiantly
    continuous, measuring their tones with the infinite.
By these lips miracles: prison doors swung open, bonds of
    slaves vanishing, the blind seeing, the deaf hearing,
    silence given speech, the hungry fed, by no seen witness
    of grace.
This chorus is the rescue-dream of the innocent, it assuages
    the intermediate hours,
It is the open hand of nations and races, the light-beam
    bridging the abysses of stars, the dawn that withdraws
    gently the shadowy gray of death,
Knowing not offender and offended, knowing only man,
    woman, child, animal, life—
Of whom the song, of whom the singers chanting their ages
    long choral—
For whom the immortal line from perfect to perfect
    proceeding.   10

(1894)

Wild Rose

The new soul of earth, fresh from hidden confidences,
Knowing the will of the unseen as well as the whim and will
    of the seen,
Speaking by the lips of new-born men, not welcomed in
    places of power,
Makes announcement of the future.
At your doorstep forbidden,

Where men make sacrifice of men, where alchemy makes
  gold of betrayal,
Where priests chant the old truths to the new lie,
Where effete laws, throned in mask, dispense the judgments
  of inferiority,
There is the call uttered, there the courier, though rejected,
  stays.
Behold in him a protest: its flavor is of the color and sting of
  the rose,   10
Entangled upon him are thorns and brush, he is strong-
  savored of the earth,
He is not recognized, his voice is sweet-musical but is not
  scheduled in the schools,
Unmistakably he is god: as Jesus rebuked and summoned, so
  does he rebuke and summon—
His an equal sign, by his power the same potent old new
  demand:
Do you not see and hear?
Lo! he is your neighbor, he is your own heart,
He is not secreted in baffling by-ways, he is not the
  possession of a class, he is not folded in the leaves of
  the books of the library,
He is abroad on your great streets, going undisguised
  among men,
Though you are blind, he is that instant most with you,
  seeing for you, providing for your illumination.
The trade-shadows by his will must vanish,   20
That which you planned by your best skill doing injustice
  will avail nothing as against his will that justice shall
  acquit man of man everywhere:
He brings you this censure from the deep wood: into his
  charge he puts no sentence of death.
His rebuke is knowledge, his heartburst floods and bathes
  the earth.
Come, the trickeries, arts, sinister schemes, of your mart-
  places must be abolished,
That you may live all must be given equal life, full-measure,
This is the wood-dream, bestowing upon your cities light.
                                                    (1896)

Face to Face

Face to face, the house of the farm hand, the palace of the
  money king,
(The mails pass up and down the road, never across),

Though two men were seas apart they had not been farther
    separated,
I pass between—I take one hand from each.

(1896)

Before Time Was Woman

Before time was woman,
She brought the first day out of the day that was not first,
She was couched in motherhood and reaffirmed in her child
    and matched to virile delight.
Before space was woman,
Out of her distance came and habitable worlds and men
    who gave the earth its dreams.
Forthcoming, forthcoming,
Always giving her due to the hungering soil,
Always renewing the ever unappeased laws,
Always renowned, yet not always free,
Always revered, yet not always respected,   10
The unaccomplished ideal in her completeness ratified.

Who shall remove the veil from woman?
Who shall break the clouds before her radiant eyes?
Who shall be foremost to affront the dulled senses of her
    ancient slavemasters?
Who shall give woman to her child, in free treaty
    sanctioned?
The dream of woman grants suffrage to life and joy.
When you speak of your law woman shudders:
When you speak of your passion woman is humbled:
When you speak of your duty woman disdains:
When you speak of your love woman loves.   20
The hand that removes her veil will abolish chivalry forever:
It will be a man's ungloved hand, or her own, bearing no
    lace or flag.
Though you worshiped her face you worshiped it behind a
    cloud.
Now you may still worship, but you must worship as an
    equal born,
Conceding the august compact.

(1910)

Louise Imogen Guiney

1861–1920

Louise Guiney created a successful career as an editor, translator, literary critic, and poet. As an editor and critic, Guiney studied minor seventeenth-century English poets. Her poetic subjects include the popular cavalier lyrics (employing the attitudes and themes of seventeenth-century England), religious lyrics, "pagan" or naturalistic studies, and tributes to literary figures and friends. Louise Guiney's reputation today rests upon her work as a dedicated Catholic scholar and respected poet.

Louise Imogen Guiney was born on 7 January 1861 in Boston, Massachusetts, the daughter of Irish Catholic immigrants. Guiney exemplified in scholarship the same kind of energy that marked her father's swift rise in Boston society. General Patrick Robert Guiney, her father, distinguished himself during the Civil War and later as an assistant district attorney in Boston; her mother, Janet Margaret Doyle Guiney, was a typical Victorian matron.

Guiney's schooling at Elmhurst Academy in French, music, history, and literature enabled her to enter easily the writing profession and provided the groundwork for later research. The public's immediate, positive reception of her first volume of poetry, *Songs at the Start* (1884), introduced her to the Boston literary salons, where she met Ann Fields, Alice Brown, and others. The salon society contributed a stiff, "literary" feel to her second, less successful, book, *The White Sail and Other Poems* (1887). In 1893, Guiney published *A Roadside Harp*, her most unified and well-received book of mature poetry. Economic difficulties forced Guiney to work first as postmistress and then as a librarian, but she continued to write articles and poems, publishing *Martyrs' Idyl and Shorter Poems* in 1899.

Guiney left the United States permanently for Oxford, England, in 1890. She supported herself and three orphaned relatives with a stream of articles for American magazines and involved herself in English intellectual and religious circles. Guiney's research resulted in scholarly works on Henry Vaughan, Katherine Phillips, Robert Emmet, Hurrel Froude,

Edmund Campion, and Thomas Stanley. She also edited a collection of her own poetry, *Happy Ending* (1909). She industriously researched beleaguered Catholic poets from the time of Queen Elizabeth I and the Reformed Church of England. The first volume of *Recusant Poets: 1535–1745* was published posthumously in 1938; the second volume remains unpublished. Guiney finished the two-volume work in September 1920, two months before her death on 2 November 1920 in Gloucestershire, England. She is buried in Oxford.

In his 1894 review, Bliss Carman praised Guiney's "sincerity" and the passion of "these beautiful and pagan, perfectly pagan, lyrics." She promptly denied the paganism attributed to her by Carman, prefering the term "natural religion" (Fairbanks 46). The emotional quality of her attachment to nature influences many of her lyrics, including "Two Irish Peasant Songs." Guiney's strong lyric phrases and extended metaphors work best in the sonnet's controlled and compact form, as exemplified in the bells' "dark throats aching and outblown" in "Sunday Chimes in the City" (line 7). Cheryl Walker comments on the emotional tension of "Tarpeia," in which Guiney mourns Tarpeia's self-betrayal but credits the traitor as partly a victim of lustful Sabini warriors (132).

Later in her life, Guiney turned from a natural spirituality (similar to transcendentalism in its emotional response) to stronger expressions of faith in religious lyrics such as "Sanctuary." Through the figure of a cavalier, as in "The Kings," she combines her sense of a spiritual Christian mission with admiration for her father's heroic deeds. Although conventional by modern standards, these well-crafted and popular religious lyrics convey the energy of Guiney's personal convictions.

—*Taimi Olsen*

Suggestions for Further Reading

Brown, Alice. *Louise Imogen Guiney, a Study*. New York: Macmillan, 1921.
Carman, Bliss. "Miss Guiney's Verse." *The Chap-Book*. 15 Nov. 1894: 27–36.
Fairbanks, Henry. *Louise Imogen Guiney*. New York: Twayne, 1973.*
Tulley, Shelly. "Heroic Failures and the Literary Career of Louise Imogen Guiney." *The American Transcendental Quarterly* 48 (1980): 171–86.
Walker, Cheryl. *The Nightingale's Burden: Women Poets and American Culture Before 1900*. Bloomington: Indiana UP, 1982.

The White Sail and Other Poems. 1887.
A Roadside Harp. 1893.
The Martyrs' Idyl and Shorter Poems. 1899.

꒰ꙮ꒱

The Wild Ride

I hear in my heart, I hear in its ominous pulses,
All day, the commotion of sinewy, mane-tossing horses;
All night, from their cells, the importunate tramping and
*   neighing.*

Cowards and laggards fall back; but alert to the saddle,
Straight, grim, and abreast, vault our weather-worn,
    galloping legion,
With a stirrup-cup each to the one gracious woman that
    loves him.

The road is thro' dolor and dread, over crags and morasses;
There are shapes by the way, there are things that appal or
    entice us:
What odds? We are knights, and our souls are but bent on
    the riding!

I hear in my heart, I hear in its ominous pulses,   10
All day, the commotion of sinewy, mane-tossing horses;
All night, from their cells, the importunate tramping and
*   neighing.*

We spur to a land of no name, out-racing the storm-wind;
We leap to the infinite dark, like the sparks from the anvil.
Thou leadest, O God! All's well with Thy troopers that
    follow.

                                                        (1887)

Tarpeia

Woe: lightly to part with one's soul as the sea with its foam!
Woe to Tarpeia, Tarpeia, daughter of Rome!

Lo, now it was night, with the moon looking chill as she
    went:
It was morn when the innocent stranger strayed into the tent.

The hostile Sabini were pleased, as one meshing a bird;
She sang for them there in the ambush: they smiled as they
    heard.

Her sombre hair purpled in gleams, as she leaned to the light;
All day she had idled and feasted, and now it was night.

The chief sat apart, heavy-browed, brooding elbow on knee;
The armlets he wore were thrice royal, and wondrous to
    see: 10

Exquisite artifice, whorls of barbaric design,
Frost's fixed mimicry; orbic imaginings fine

In sevenfold coils: and in orient glimmer from them,
The variform voluble swinging of gem upon gem.

And the glory thereof sent fever and fire to her eye.
'I had never such trinkets!' she sighed,—like a lute was her
    sigh.

'Were they mine at the plea, were they mine for the token,
    all told,
Now the citadel sleeps, now my father the keeper is old,

'If I go by the way that I know, and thou followest hard,
If yet at the touch of Tarpeia the gates be unbarred?'   20

The chief trembled sharply for joy, then drew rein on his
    soul:
'Of all this arm beareth I swear I will cede thee the whole.'

And up from the nooks of the camp, with hoarse plaudit
    outdealt,
The bearded Sabini glanced hotly, and vowed as they knelt,

Bare-stretching the wrists that bore also the glowing great
    boon:
'Yea! surely as over us shineth the lurid low moon,

'Not alone of our lord, but of each of us take what he hath!
Too poor is the guerdon, if thou wilt but show us the path.'

Her nostril upraised, like a fawn's on the arrowy air,
She sped; in a serpentine gleam to the precipice stair,   30

They climbed in her traces, they closed on their evil swift
    star:
She bent to the latches, and swung the huge portal ajar.

Repulsed where they passed her, half-tearful for wounded
    belief,
'The bracelets!' she pleaded. Then faced her the leonine
    chief,

And answered her: 'Even as I promised, maid-merchant, I do.'
Down from his dark shoulder the baubles he sullenly drew.

'This left arm shall nothing begrudge thee. Accept. Find it
    sweet.
Give, too, O my brothers!' The jewels he flung at her feet,

The jewels hard, heavy; she stooped to them, flushing with
    dread,
But the shield he flung after: it clanged on her beautiful
    head.   40

Like the Apennine bells when the villagers' warnings begin,
Athwart the first lull broke the ominous din upon din;

With a 'Hail, benefactress!' upon her they heaped in their
    zeal
Death: agate and iron; death: chrysoprase, beryl and steel.

'Neath the outcry of scorn, 'neath the sinewy tension and
    hurl,
The moaning died slowly, and still they massed over the girl

A mountain of shields! and the gemmy bright tangle in links,
A torrent-like gush, pouring out on the grass from the
    chinks,

Pyramidal gold! the sumptuous monument won
By the deed they had loved her for, doing, and loathed her
    for, done.   50

Such was the wage that they paid her, such the acclaim:
All Rome was aroused with the thunder that buried her
    shame.

On surged the Sabini to battle. O you that aspire!
Tarpeia the traitor had fill of her woman's desire.

Woe: lightly to part with one's soul as the sea with its foam!
Woe to Tarpeia, Tarpeia, daughter of Rome!

(1887)

Two Irish Peasant Songs

I

I knead and I spin, but my life is low the while,
Oh, I long to be alone, and walk abroad a mile,
Yet if I walk alone, and think of naught at all,
Why from me that's young should the wild tears fall?

The shower-stricken earth, the earth-colored streams,
They breathe on me awake, and moan to me in dreams,
And yonder ivy fondling the broke castle-wall,
It pulls upon my heart till the wild tears fall.

The cabin-door looks down a furze-lighted hill,
And far as Leighlin Cross the fields are green and still;   10
But once I hear the blackbird in Leighlin hedges call,
The foolishness is on me, and the wild tears fall!

II

'Tis the time o' the year, if the quicken-bough be staunch,
The green, like a breaker, rolls steady up the branch,
And surges in the spaces, and floods the trunk, and heaves
In little angry spray that is the under-white of leaves;
And from the thorn in companies the foamy petals fall,
And waves of jolly ivy wink along a windy wall.

'Tis the time o' the year the marsh is full of sound,
And good and glorious it is to smell the living ground.
The crimson-headed catkin shakes above the pasture-bars,
The daisy takes the middle field and spangles it with stars,   10
And down the bank into the lane the primroses do crowd,
All colored like the twilight moon, and spreading like a
     cloud!

'Tis the time o' the year, in early light and glad,
The lark has a music to drive a lover mad;
The downs are dripping nightly, the breathèd damps arise,
Deliciously the freshets cool the grayling's golden eyes,
And lying in a row against the chilly north, the sheep
Inclose a place without a wind for tender lambs to sleep.

'Tis the time o' the year I turn upon the height
To watch from my harrow the dance of going light;   20
And if before the sun be hid, come slowly up the vale
Honora with her dimpled throat, Honora with her pail,
Hey, but there's many a March for me, and many and many a
    lass!
I fall to work and song again, and let Honora pass.

                            (1893)

The Kings

A man said unto his angel:
"My spirits are fallen thro',
And I cannot carry this battle;
O brother! what shall I do?

"The terrible Kings are on me,
With spears that are deadly bright,
Against me so from the cradle
Do fate and my fathers fight."

Then said to the man his angel:
"Thou wavering, foolish soul,   10
Back to the ranks! What matter
To win or to lose the whole,

"As judged by the little judges
Who hearken not well, nor see?
Not thus, by the outer issue,
The Wise shall interpret thee.

"Thy will is the very, the only,
The solemn event of things;
The weakest of hearts defying
Is stronger than all these Kings.   20

"Tho' out of the past they gather,
Mind's Doubt and Bodily Pain,
And pallid Thirst of the Spirit
That is kin to the other twain,

"And Grief, in a cloud of banners,
And ringletted Vain Desires,
And Vice, with the spoils upon him
Of thee and thy beaten sires,

"While Kings of eternal evil
Yet darken the hills about,   30
Thy part is with broken sabre
To rise on the last redoubt;

"To fear not sensible failure,
Nor covet the game at all,
But fighting, fighting, fighting,
Die, driven against the wall!"

(1893)

Summum Bonum[1]

Waiting on Him who knows us and our need,
Most need have we to dare not, nor desire,
But as He giveth, softly to suspire
Against His gift, with no inglorious greed,
For this is joy, tho' still our joys recede;
And, as in octaves of a noble lyre,
To move our minds with His, and clearer, higher,
Sound forth our fate; for this is strength indeed.

Thanks to His love let earth and man dispense
In smoke of worship when the heart is stillest,   10
A praying more than prayer: "Great good have I,
Till it be greater good to lay it by;
Nor can I lose peace, power, permanence,
For these smile on me from the thing Thou willest!"

(1893)

---

1. Latin for "the highest good."

Sunday Chimes in the City

Across dispeopled ways, patient and slow,
Saint Magnus and Saint Dunstan[2] call in vain:
From Wren's forgotten belfries, in the rain,
Down the blank wharves the dropping octaves go.

Forbid not these! Tho' no man heed, they shower
A subtle beauty on the empty hour,
From all their dark throats aching and outblown;
Aye in the prayerless places welcome most,
Like the last gull that up a naked coast
Deploys her white and steady wing, alone.

(1893)

In the Docks

Where the bales thunder till the day is done,
And the wild sounds with wilder odors cope;
Where over crouching sail and coiling rope,
Lascar and Moor along the gangway run;
Where stifled Thames spreads in the pallid sun,
A hive of anarchy from slope to slope;
Flag of my birth, my liberty, my hope,
I see thee at the masthead, joyous one!

O thou good guest! So oft as, young and warm,   10
To the home-wind thy hoisted colors bound,
Away, away from this too thoughtful ground,
Sated with human trespass and despair,
Thee only, from the desert, from the storm,
A sick mind follows into Eden air.

(1893)

Sanctuary

High above hate I dwell:
O storms! farewell.

---

2. London churches built by Sir Christopher Wren: St. Magnus Martyr
(1671–76, steeple 1705) and St. Dunstan in the East (1670–71, steeple 1697–99).

Though at my sill your daggered thunders play,
Lawless and loud to-morrow as to-day,
To me they sound more small
Than a young fay's footfall:
Soft and far-sunken, forty fathoms low
In Long Ago,
And winnowed into silence on that wind
Which takes wars like a dust, and leaves but love behind.   10

Hither Felicity
Doth climb to me,
And bank me in with turf and marjoram
Such as bees lip, or the new-weaned lamb;
With golden barberry-wreath,
And bluets thick beneath;
One grosbeak, too, mid apple-buds a guest
With bud-red breast,
Is singing, singing! All the hells that rage
Float less than April fog below our hermitage.

(1899)

Borderlands

Through all the evening,
All the virginal long evening,
Down the blossomed aisle of April it is dread to walk alone;
For there the intangible is nigh, the lost is ever-during;
And who would suffer again beneath a too divine alluring,
Keen as the ancient drift of sleep on dying faces blown?

Yet in the valley,
At a turn of the orchard alley,
When a wild aroma touched me in the moist and moveless
    air,
Like breath indeed from out Thee, or as airy vesture round
    Thee,   10
Then was it I went faintly, for fear I had nearly found Thee,
O hidden, O perfect, O desired! the first and the final Fair.

(1900)

Edith Newbold Jones Wharton
1862–1937

Although Edith Wharton's fiction established her place in American literature, R. W. B. Lewis has noted that her verse enhanced her reputation because it showed that she alone among her contemporary American novelists was capable of genuine poetic achievement (236). Her lyric poems and dramatic monologues exploring the conflicts between the individual's passionate will and society's expectations won praise for their refinement and technical finesse from her contemporaries, who seem to have overlooked Wharton's feminism. Today, few readers realize that Wharton wrote poetry. Unfortunately, only her last volume of poems has ever been reprinted.

Edith Newbold Jones, born into a distinguished New York family on 24 January 1862, grew up in a genteel environment and received an excellent private education at home. The precocious child attempted her first fiction at age eleven and published *Verses*, her first volume of poetry, at sixteen. Longfellow read some of her work, and upon his recommendation several of her poems appeared in the *Atlantic Monthly* in 1880. In 1885, she married Edward "Teddy" Wharton, a wealthy Bostonian thirteen years her senior. Their unhappy marriage, which ended in divorce in 1913, spurred Edith to turn to serious writing as an antidote to depression. Beginning with *The Greater Inclination* in 1899 and continuing until her death in France on 11 August 1937, she produced a steady stream of fiction works, winning a Pulitzer Prize in 1920 for *The Age of Innocence*.

Wharton once confessed, "Poetry is to me so august a thing that I always feel that I should be struck by lightning when I sidle up to the shrine" (qtd. in Lewis 236). Despite her sense of inadequacy as a poet, she wrote poems throughout her career. Her affair with Morton Fullerton from 1907 through 1910 inspired some of her most passionate poetry, much of which remained unpublished during her lifetime. After *Verses*, her poems appeared during the 1880s and 1890s in such magazines as *Harper's*, *Century*, and *Scribner's*. Two collections followed: *Artemis to Actaeon and Other Verses* (1909), favorably reviewed in the major literary magazines, and *Twelve Poems* (1926). She also published war poems, tributes and memorials to friends (among them, Theodore Roosevelt), and other occasional verse.

Wharton's talents as a lyricist manifested themselves in her favorite form, the sonnet. She wrote other forms of lyrics as well as a number of dramatic monologues that insightfully explore human psychology. Like Tennyson and Browning, she often drew her subjects from myth and history and explored crises in faith, the problem of failure, and instances of the human will striving to achieve the supreme moment. The conflict between personal desire and social or spiritual demands, especially as manifested in adultery, runs through much of her poetry, as it does her fiction. "The Mortal Lease," a sonnet sequence tracing Wharton's relationship with Fullerton, shows the speaker's struggle to justify giving in to illicit passion. "Margaret of Cortona," a blank verse dramatic monologue, presents the tortured expression of a woman saint who has renounced physical passion for the cloistered life. Those critics who charged Wharton's delicately-controlled poetry with lacking passion failed to understand that exploring passion was Wharton's chief poetic concern and one source of her enduring merit as a poet.

—*Ellen Giduz*

Suggestions for Further Reading

Lewis, R. W. B. *Edith Wharton: A Biography*. New York: Harper, 1975.
Sencourt, Robert. "Edith Wharton." *Cornhill Magazine* 157 (1938): 721–36.
———. "The Poetry of Edith Wharton." *The Bookman* 73 (1931): 478–86.

TEXTS
Verses (1878).
"Wants." *Atlantic Monthly* 45 (1880): 599.
"Chartres." *Scribner's Magazine* 14 (1893): 287.
"Margaret of Cortona." *Harper's Magazine* 103 (1901): 884–87.
Artemis to Actaeon, and Other Verse. New York: Scribner's, 1909.

༄

Some Woman to Some Man

We might have loved each other after all,
Have lived and learned together! Yet I doubt it;
You asked, I think, too great a sacrifice,

Or else, perhaps, I rate myself too dear.
Whichever way the difference lies between us,
Would common cares have helped to lessen it,
A common interest, and a common lot?
Who knows indeed? We choose our path, and then
Stand looking back and sighing at our choice,
And say: "Perhaps the other road had led   10
To fruitful valleys dozing in the sun."
Perhaps—perhaps—but all things are perhaps,
And either way there lies a doubt, you know.
We've but one life to live, and fifty ways
To live it in, and little time to choose
The one in fifty that will suit us best,
And so the end is, that we part, and say:
"We might have loved each other after all!"

(1878)

Wants

We women want so many things;
    And first we call for happiness,—
The careless boon the hour brings,
    The smile, the song, and the caress.

And when the fancy fades, we cry,
    Nay, give us one on whom to spend
Our heart's desire! When Love goes by
    With folded wings, we seek a friend.

And then our children come, to prove
    Our hearts but slumbered, and can wake;   10
And when they go, we're fain to love
    Some other woman's for their sake.

But when both love and friendship fail,
    We cry for duty, work to do;
Some end to gain beyond the pale
    Of self, some height to journey to.

And then, before our task is done,
    With sudden weariness oppressed,
We leave the shining goal unwon,
    And only ask for rest.

(1880)

Chartres[1]

I

Immense, august, like some Titanic bloom,
    The mighty choir unfolds its lithic core,
Petalled with panes of azure, gules and or,
    Splendidly lambent in the Gothic gloom,
And stamened with keen flamelets that illume
    The pale high-altar. On the prayer-worn floor,
By worshippers innumerous thronged of yore,
    A few brown crones, familiars of the tomb,
The stranded driftwood of Faith's ebbing sea—
    For these alone the finials fret the skies,   10
The topmost bosses shake their blossoms free,
    While from the triple portals, with grave eyes,
Tranquil, and fixed upon eternity,
    The cloud of witnesses still testifies.

II

The crimson panes like blood-drops stigmatise
    The western floor. The aisles are mute and cold.
A rigid fetich in her robe of gold,
    The Virgin of the Pillar, with blank eyes,
Enthroned beneath her votive canopies,
    Gathers a meagre remnant to her fold.   20
The rest is solitude; the church, grown old,
    Stands stark and grey beneath the burning skies.
Well-nigh again its mighty framework grows
    To be a part of nature's self, withdrawn
From hot humanity's impatient woes;
    The floor is ridged like some rude mountain lawn,
And in the east one giant window shows
    The roseate coldness of an Alp at dawn.

                        (1893, 1909)

---

1. Chartres, France, is the site of the Cathedral of Notre Dame. This thirteenth-century masterpiece of French Gothic architecture is renowned for its ornate triple doorway and its incomparably beautiful stained-glass windows.

from Margaret of Cortona[2]

But stay! Suppose my lover had not died?
(At last my question! Father, help me face it.)
I say: Suppose my lover had not died—
Think you I ever would have left him living,
Even to be Christ's blessed Margaret?
—We lived in sin? Why, to the sin I died to
That other was as Paradise, when God
Walks there at eventide, the air pure gold,
And angels treading all the grass to flowers!
He was my Christ—he led me out of hell—   10
He died to save me (so your casuists say!)—
Could Christ do more? Your Christ out-pity mine?
Why, *yours* but let the sinner bathe His feet;
Mine raised her to the level of his heart . . .
And then Christ's way is saving, as man's way
Is squandering—and the devil take the shards!
But this man kept for sacramental use
The cup that once had slaked a passing thirst;
This man declared: "The same clay serves to model
A devil or a saint; the scribe may stain   20
The same fair parchment with obscenities,
Or gild with benedictions; nay," he cried,
"Because a satyr feasted in this wood,
And fouled the grasses with carousing foot,
Shall not a hermit build his chapel here
And cleanse the echoes with his litanies?
The sodden grasses spring again—why not
The trampled soul? Is man less merciful
Than nature, good more fugitive than grass?"
And so—if, after all, he had not died,   30
And suddenly that door should know his hand,
And with that voice as kind as yours he said:
"Come, Margaret, forth into the sun again,

---

2. Margaret of Cortona (1247–1297), a Franciscan penitent canonized in 1728, left her father's farm in Tuscany as an adolescent and lived as the mistress of a nobleman for nine years, bearing him a son. Following her lover's murder, which Margaret perceived as a sign from God, she went to the Franciscan friars as a penitent, leading a life of severe self-mortification from 1274 until her death. Recipient of many mystical graces and founder of a hospital and an order of tertiary sisters, she nevertheless was accused of sexual improprieties and other sins during her years as a penitent. In Wharton's version of her story, Margaret was a young prostitute rescued from the streets by her noble lover. In this excerpt (lines 94–138 of a 168-line poem), the mature Margaret, who appears to be making her deathbed confession, faces the question that reveals her deep conflict between religious commitment and human love.

Back to the life we fashioned with our hands
Out of old sins and follies, fragments scorned
Of more ambitious builders, yet by Love,
The patient architect, so shaped and fitted
That not a crevice let the winter in—"
Think you my bones would not arise and walk,
This bruised body (as once the bruised soul)   40
Turn from the wonders of the seventh heaven
As from the antics of the market-place?
If this could be (as I so oft have dreamed),
I, who have known both loves, divine and human,
Think you I would not leave this Christ for that?

(1901, 1909)

from The Mortal Lease[3]

V

Yet for one rounded moment I will be
No more to you than what my lips may give,
And in the circle of your kisses live
As in some island of a storm-blown sea,
Where the cold surges of infinity
Upon the outward reefs unheeded grieve,
And the loud murmur of our blood shall weave
Primeval silences round you and me.

If in that moment we are all we are
We live enough. Let this for all requite.   10
Do I not know, some wingèd things from far
Are born along illimitable night
To dance their lives out in a single flight
Between the moonrise and the setting star?

(1909)

Survival

When you and I, like all things kind or cruel,
The garnered days and light evasive hours,

---

3. A sequence of eight sonnets composed during her affair with Morton
Fullerton.

Are gone again to be a part of flowers
And tears and tides, in life's divine renewal,

If some grey eve to certain eyes should wear
A deeper radiance than mere light can give,
Some silent page abruptly flush and live,
May it not be that you and I are there?

(1909)

Richard Hovey

1864–1900

Richard Hovey was best known
in his day for poems about vagabond life and comradeship. Like
Whitman, he was also among the first poets to advocate a more
liberal attitude toward sex and marriage. For his poems on Dart-
mouth College, the school regards him as its poet laureate.

Born 4 May 1864 in Normal, Illinois, Hovey grew up in Wash-
ington, D.C., where his mother educated him at home. After pri-
vately printing *Poems* in 1880, he entered Dartmouth in 1881, and
his experiences there, especially with the Psi Upsilon fraternity,
provided the material for some of his best-known poems about
comradeship, including "A Stein Song." Upon graduation in 1885,
Hovey tried his hand at acting in Washington and at a seminary
in New York, but neither fulfilled him. In 1887, Hovey met
poet Bliss Carman and artist Thomas Meteyard, and the three
conducted a walking tour of New England, out of which grew
Hovey's "Vagabondia."

On a train ride from Chicago to Bloomington, Illinois, on
New Year's Day 1889, Hovey committed himself to becoming a
poet. He resolved to begin by composing a cycle of dramas based
on the Arthurian legend. Hovey planned to write three parts,
each of which would contain a masque, a tragedy, and a romance;
however, he completed only part one and the masque of the sec-
ond part before his death. In these plays, Hovey considers the
individual's struggle between self and society, a theme which
pervades much of his other poetry.

In 1892, the *Independent* published Hovey's poem "Seaward."
Songs from Vagabondia, to which both Hovey and Carman con-
tributed, appeared in 1894. After a long affair, Hovey married
Mrs. Henrietta Russell, and they lived in England where he trans-
lated symbolist Maurice Maeterlinck's plays. His relationship
with Mrs. Russell doubtless prompted his praise of the inde-
pendent "new woman" of the age, as in "Her Valentine," and his
advocacy of true love and its physical expression, even outside of
marriage, as in "When the Priest Left" and "Love and Pity."

More Songs from Vagabondia, to which Carman contributed, ap-
peared in 1896. A rebel against the sordid commercialism of his

day, Hovey called on Americans to value spiritual freedom and emotional fulfillment above wealth and position. He believed that American participation in Cuba's fight for freedom in 1898 would help replace greed and materialism in the hearts of the American people with idealism and selflessness.

Hovey's early death on 24 February 1900 brought his work instant recognition, and his popularity rose until the 1930s. Since that time, however, most anthologies of American poetry have omitted Hovey's verse, and Allan Macdonald's recent book highlights the spirit and dedication of the man instead of the brilliance of his work.

—*E. Frances Frame*

Suggestions for Further Reading

Linneman, William R. *Richard Hovey*. Boston: Twayne, 1976.*
Macdonald, Allan H. *Richard Hovey: Man and Craftsman*. Durham, NC: Duke UP, 1957.*

TEXTS
More Songs from Vagabondia. 1896.
Along the Trail: A Book of Lyrics by Richard Hovey. 1898.
Last Songs from Vagabondia. Boston: Small, Maynard. 1901.
Songs from Vagabondia. Boston: Small, Maynard. 1907.
To the End of the Trail. New York: Duffield, 1908.

ঽ🙖ౘ

Vagabondia

Off with the fetters
That chafe and restrain!
Off with the chain!
Here Art and Letters,
Music and wine,
And Myrtle and Wanda,
The winsome witches,
Blithely combine.
Here are true riches,
Here is Golconda,   10
Here are the Indies,
Here we are free—
Free as the wind is,

Richard Hovey   *487*

Free as the sea,
Free!

Houp-la!

What have we
To do with the way
Of the Pharisee?
We go or we stay   20
At our own sweet will;
We think as we say,
And we say or keep still
At our own sweet will,
At our own sweet will.

Here we are free
To be good or bad,
Sane or mad,
Merry or grim
As the mood may be,—   30

Free as the whim
Of a spook on a spree,—
Free to be oddities,
Not mere commodities.
Stupid and salable,
Wholly available,
Ranged upon shelves;
Each with his puny form
In the same uniform,
Cramped and disabled;   40
We are not labelled,
We are ourselves.

Here is the real,
Here the ideal;
Laughable hardship
Met and forgot,
Glory of bardship—
World's bloom and world's blot
The shock and the jostle,
The mock and the push,   50
But hearts like the throstle
A-joy in the bush;
Wits that would merrily
Laugh away wrong,

Throats that would verily
Melt Hell in Song.

What though the dimes be
Elusive as rhymes be,
And Bessie, with finger
Uplifted, is warning   60
That breakfast next morning
(A subject she's scorning)
Is mighty uncertain!

What care we? Linger
A moment to kiss—
No time's amiss
To a vagabond's ardor—
Then finish the larder
And pull down the curtain.

Unless ere the kiss come,   70
Black Richard or Bliss come
Or Tom with a flagon,
Or Karl with a jag on—
Then up and after
The joy of the night
With the hounds of laughter
To follow the flight
Of the fox-foot hours
That double and run
Through brakes and bowers   80
Of folly and fun.

With the comrade heart
For a moment's play,
And the comrade heart
For a heavier day,
And the comrade heart
Forever and aye.

For the joy of wine
Is not for long
And the joy of song   90
Is a dream of shine;
But the comrade heart
Shall outlast art
And a woman's love
The fame thereof.

But wine for a sign
Of the love we bring!
And song for an oath
That Love is king!
And both, and both   100
For his worshipping!

Then up and away
Till the break of day,
With a heart that's merry
And a Tom-and-Jerry,
And a derry-down-derry—
What's that you say,
You highly respectable
Buyers and sellers?
We should be decenter?   110
Not as we please inter
Custom, frugality,
Use and morality
In the delectable
Depths of wine-cellars?

Midnights of revel,
And noondays of song!
Is it so wrong?
Go to the Devil!

I tell you that we,   120
While you are smirking
And lying and shirking
Life's duty of duties,
Honest sincerity,
We are in verity
Free!
Free to rejoice

In blisses and beauties!
Free as the voice
Of the wind as it passes!   130
Free as the bird
In the weft of the grasses!
Free as the word
Of the sun to the sea—
Free!

(1894)

A Stein Song

Give a rouse, then, in the Maytime
For a life that knows no fear!
Turn night-time into daytime
With the sunlight of good cheer!
For it's always fair weather
When good fellows get together,
With a stein on the table and a good song ringing clear.

When the wind comes up from Cuba
And the birds are on the wing,
And our hearts are patting juba   10
To the banjo of the spring,
Then it's no wonder whether
The boys will get together,
With a stein on the table and a cheer for everything.

For we're all frank-and-twenty
When the spring is in the air;
And we've faith and hope a-plenty,
And we've life and love to spare;
And it's birds of a feather
When we all get together,   20
With a stein on the table and a heart without a care.

For we know the world is glorious,
And the goal a golden thing,
And that God is not censorious
When his children have their fling;
And life slips its tether
When the boys get together,
With a stein on the table in the fellowship of spring.

                           (1896)

Harmonics

Truth is not a creed,
For it does not need
Ever an apology.
Truth is not an ology;
'Tis not part, but all.
Priests and savans shall

Never solve the mystic
Problem. The artistic
Mind alone of all can tell
What is Truth.   10

"Poet, thou art wisest;
Dogmas thou despisest—
Science little prizest.
Tell us, for thou knowest well,
What is Truth."

Spake the seekers to an holy
Bard, who answered, mild and lowly—
This, all this, was in the olden
Days when Saturn's reign was golden—

"Shall I read the riddle—   20
Tell you what is Truth?
Truth is not the first
Nor the last or middle;
'Tis the beautiful
And symmetric whole,
Embracing best and worst,
Embracing age and youth.

"All the universe
Is one mighty song,
Wherein every star   30
Chants out loud and strong
Each set note and word
It must aye rehearse.
Though the parts may jar,
The whole is as one chord."

(1900)

When the Priest Left

What did he say?
To seek love otherwhere
Nor bind the soul to clay?
It may be so—I cannot tell—
But I know that life is fair,

And love's bold clarion in the air
Outdins his little vesper-bell.

Love God? Can I touch God with both my hands?
Can I breathe in his hair and brush his cheek
He is too far to seek.   10
If nowhere else be love, who understands
What thing it is?
This love is but a name that wise men speak.
God hath no lips to kiss.

Let God be; surely, if he will,
At the end of days,
He can win love as well as praise.
Why must we spill
The human love out at his feet?
Let be this talk of good and ill!   20
Though God be God, art thou not fair and sweet?

Open the window; let the air
Blow in on us.
It is enough to find you fair,
To touch with fingers timorous
Your sunlit hair,—
To turn my body to a prayer,
And kiss you—thus.

(1900)

Her Valentine

What, send her a valentine? Never!
I see you don't know who "she" is.
I should ruin my chances forever;
My hopes would collapse with a fizz.

I can't see why she scents such disaster
When I take heart to venture a word;
I've no dream of becoming her master,
I've no notion of being her lord.

All I want is just to be her lover!
She's the most up-to-date of her sex,   10

And there's such a multitude of her,
No wonder they call her complex.

She's a bachelor, even when married,
She's a vagabond, even when housed;
And if ever her citadel's carried
Her suspicions must not be aroused.

She's erratic, impulsive and human,
And she blunders,—as goddesses can;
But if *she's* what they call the New Woman,
Then *I'd* like to be the New Man.   20

I'm glad she makes books and paints pictures,
And typewrites and hoes her own row,
And it's quite beyond reach of conjectures
How much further she's going to go.

When she scorns, in the L-road, my proffer
Of a seat and hangs on to a strap;
I admire her so much, I could offer
To let her ride up on my lap.

Let her undo the stays of the ages,
That have cramped and confined her so long!   30
Let her burst through the frail candy cages
That fooled her to think they were strong!

She may enter life's wide vagabondage,
She may do without flutter or frill,
She may take off the chains of her bondage,—
And anything else that she will.

She may take *me* off, for example,
And she probably does when I'm gone.
I'm aware the occasion is ample;
That's why I so often take on.   40

I'm so glad she can win her own dollars
And know all the freedom it brings.
I love her in shirt-waists and collars,
I love her in dress-reform things.

I love her in bicycle skirtlings—
Especially when there's a breeze—

I love her in crinklings and quirklings
And anything else that you please.

I dote on her even in bloomers—
If Parisian enough in their style—   50
In fact, she may choose her costumers,
Wherever her fancy beguile.

She may box, she may shoot, she may wrestle,
She may argue, hold office or vote,
She may engineer turret or trestle,
And build a few ships that will float.

She may lecture (all lectures but curtain)
Make money, and naturally spend,
If I let her have *her* way, I'm certain
She'll let me have *mine* in the end!   60

(1900)

Love and Pity

Are you too tender-hearted to be true?
True to your love, to me and your own soul?
Will you for pity give what is love's due
And leave love lorn and begging for a dole?
Then pity is a thief, that steals love's purse
To squander in dishonest charity;
Then love is outcast, with the exile's curse
Who sees his varlets loot his seigneury.
Is love so hard it recks not where I lie,
While pity melts at aught that he endures?   10
I deserve nothing, save that you ensky
No other with those vesper lips of yours—
    I deserve nothing; but your love of me
    Deserves of you the courage to be free.

(1908)

Richard Hovey   *495*

Madison Cawein
1865–1914

Madison Cawein, known as "the Kentucky poet," is best remembered for his nature poetry of the Kentucky woodlands. Although his subject matter often includes Arthurian legend and classical myth, the bulk of his nearly forty volumes of verse explores the relationship between man and the natural world.

Madison Julius Cawein was born on 23 March 1865 in Louisville, Kentucky, to William Cawein and Anne Christiana Stelsly Cawein. His father, a confectioner, accepted a job in 1874 as manager of a resort some twenty miles east of Louisville. There, Cawein recalled later, he first "came into contact with wild nature" (Rothert 121). After relocating to New Albany, Indiana, and living there for three years, the family returned to Louisville, where Cawein lived for the rest of his life. He attended Louisville Male High School, where he read Spenser, Coleridge, Keats, Shelley, Tennyson, and Browning. He began writing poetry as a junior, and was named class poet for the 1886 graduating class.

After graduation, he began work at the Newmarket Pool Hall. During his six years there, he published six volumes of poetry, beginning with *Blooms of the Berry* (1887), which received a favorable review from William Dean Howells. By 1892, Cawein had saved enough money from his books and investments to leave the pool hall and write full-time. During the next decade, he regularly issued volumes of verse, and his audience grew to include people on both sides of the Atlantic. Having achieved financial success, he married Gertrude Foster McKelvey in 1903. The couple's only child, Preston Hamilton Cawein, was born on 18 March 1904. Despite financial difficulties resulting from real-estate losses, Cawein continued to write poetry until his death on 8 December 1914 from a blood clot in the brain incurred in a bathroom fall.

Cawein was a highly conventional poet, following his southern precursors Timrod, Simms, Legare, Hayne, and Lanier in exploring the blurred boundary between man and nature. His landscapes transcend mere sensory experience; as Howells wrote in

1908, "He has the gift . . . of touching some smallest or common-est thing in nature, and making it live from the manifold associa-tions in which we have our being" (xv). In Cawein's more suc-cessful verse, this "penetralia" is evoked rather than asserted, although in many poems the speaker's contentment appears too complacent and unchallenged. Unlike Wordsworth's speaker in "The World Is Too Much with Us," who desperately longs to "[h]ave sight of Proteus rising from the sea," Cawein's speakers frequently encounter mythological figures emblematic of the un-broken bond between man and nature.

The modernist era, with its skepticism of the pathetic fallacy, was not kind to Cawein. By all accounts he wrote too much, and the resulting verse, although competent, often lacks energy. Probably he will continue to be viewed as a minor romantic talent.

—*Scott Romine*

Suggestions for Further Reading

Hart, Paula L. "Madison Cawein." *American Poets, 1880–1945*. Vol. 54 of *Dictionary of Literary Biography*. Ed. P. Quartermain. De-troit: Gale, 1987. 29–35.

Howells, William Dean. Foreward. *Poems*. By Madison Cawein. New York: Macmillan, 1911. xiii–xix.

Rothert, Otto A. *The Story of a Poet: Madison Cawein*. Louisville: J. P. Morton, 1921.

TEXT
The Poems of Madison Cawein. 5 vols. Boston: Small, Maynard. 1908.

ᗰᕏᑢ

Discovery

What is it now that I shall seek
Where woods dip downward, in the hills?—
A mossy nook, a ferny creek,
And May among the daffodils.

Or in the valley's vistaed glow,
Past rocks of terraced trumpet-vines,
Shall I behold her coming slow,
Sweet May, among the columbines?

With redbud cheeks and bluet eyes,
Big eyes, the homes of happiness,   10
To meet me with the old surprise,
Her hoiden hair all bonnetless.

Who waits for me, where, note for note,
The birds make glad the forest trees?
A dogwood blossom at her throat,
My May among th' anemones.

As sweetheart breezes kiss the blooms,
And dewdrops drink the moon's bright beams,
My soul shall drink her lips' perfumes,
And drain the magic of her dreams.   20

                                                    (1907)

Penetralia

I am a part of all you see
In Nature; part of all you feel:
I am the impact of the bee
Upon the blossom; in the tree
I am the sap,—that shall reveal
The leaf, the bloom,—that flows and flutes
Up from the darkness through its roots.

I am the vermeil of the rose,
The perfume breathing in its veins;
The gold within the mist that glows   10
Along the west and overflows
The heaven with light; the dew that rains
Its freshness down and strings with spheres
Of wet the webs and oaten ears.

I am the egg that folds the bird,
The song that beaks and breaks its shell;
The laughter and the wandering word
The water says; and, dimly heard,
The music of the blossom's bell
When soft winds swing it; and the sound   20
Of grass slow-creeping o'er the ground.

I am the warmth, the honey-scent
That throats with spice each lily-bud
That opens, white with wonderment,
Beneath the moon; or, downward bent,
Sleeps with a moth beneath its hood:
I am the dream that haunts it too,
That crystallizes into dew.

I am the seed within its pod;
The worm within its closed cocoon: 30
The wings within the circling clod,
The germ that gropes through soil and sod
To beauty, radiant in the noon:
I am all these, behold! and more—
I am the love at the world-heart's core.

                                                (1907)

The Wind of Spring

The wind that breathes of columbines
And celandines that crown the rocks;
That shakes the balsam of the pines
With music from his airy locks,
Stops at my city door and knocks.

He calls me far a-forest, where
The twin-leaf and the blood-root bloom;
And, circled by the amber air,
Life sits with beauty and perfume
Weaving the new web of her loom.   10

He calls me where the waters run
Through fronding ferns where wades the hern;
And, sparkling in the equal sun,
Song leans above her brimming urn,
And dreams the dreams that love shall learn.

The wind has summoned, and I go:
To read God's meaning in each line
The wildflow'rs write; and, walking slow,
God's purpose, of which song is sign,—
The wind's great, gusty hand in mine.   20
                                                (1907)

Beauty and Art

The gods are dead; but still for me
      Lives on in wildwood brook and tree
Each myth, each old divinity.

For me still laughs among her rocks
      The Naiad; and the Dryad's locks
Drop perfume on the wildflower flocks.

The Satyr's hoof still prints the loam;
      And, whiter than the wind-blown foam,
The Oread haunts her mountain home.

To him, whose mind is fain to dwell   10
      With loveliness not time can quell,
All things are real, imperishable.

To him—whatever facts may say—
      Who sees the soul beneath the clay,
Is proof of a diviner day.

The very stars and flowers preach
      A gospel old as God, and teach
Philosophy a child may reach;

That can not die; that shall not cease;
      That lives through idealities   20
Of Beauty, ev'n as Rome and Greece:

That lifts the soul above the clod,
      And, working out some period
Of art, is part and proof of God.

                            (1907)

Prototypes

Whether it be that we in letters trace
    The pure exactness of a woodbird's strain,
    And name it song; or with the brush attain
The high perfection of a wildflower's face;
Or mold in difficult marble all the grace

We know as man; or from the wind and rain
 Catch elemental rapture of refrain
And mark in music to due time and place:
The aim of art is Nature; to unfold
 Her truth and beauty to the souls of men   10
 In close suggestions; in whose forms is cast
Nothing so new but 'tis long eons old;
 Nothing so old but 'tis as young as when
 The mind conceived it in the ages past.

            (1907)

The Winds

Those hewers of the clouds, the Winds,—that lair
 At the four compass-points,—are out to-night;
 I hear their sandals trample on the height,
I hear their voices trumpet through the air:
Builders of storm, God's workmen, now they bear,
 Up the steep stair of sky, on backs of might,
 Huge tempest bulks, while,—sweat that blinds their
  sight,—
The rain is shaken from tumultuous hair:
Now, sweepers of the firmament, they broom,
 Like gathered dust, the rolling mists along   10
 Heaven's floors of sapphire; all the beautiful blue
Of skyey corridor and aëry room
Preparing, with large laughter and loud song,
For the white moon and stars to wander through.

            (1907)

Enchantment

The deep seclusion of this forest path,—
 O'er which the green boughs weave a canopy;
 Along which bluet and anemone
Spread dim a carpet; where the Twilight hath
Her dark abode; and, sweet as aftermath,
 Wood-fragrance roams,—has so enchanted me,
 That yonder blossoming bramble seems to be
Some Sylvan resting, rosy from her bath:

Has so enspelled me with tradition's dreams,
    That every foam-white stream that, twinkling, flows,   10
    And every bird that flutters wings of tan,
Or warbles hidden, to my fancy seems
    A Naiad dancing to a Faun who blows
    Wild woodland music on the pipes of Pan.

(1907)

William Vaughn Moody
1869–1910

W illiam Vaughn Moody devel-
oped as a poet in the creative lull between the death of Whitman
and his contemporaries and the evolution of twentieth-century
verse. In his day, Moody, whose technical skill and serious subject
matter set him apart from his contemporaries, was widely praised
for his poetry and his verse dramas. In both, Moody struggled
with a few central themes, chief among them his attempt to work
out his ambivalence about religion. From his earliest college
verses to his final play, Moody struggled with the nature of hu-
mankind's relationship to God.

William Vaughn Stoy Moody was born 8 July 1869 in Spencer,
Indiana. He grew up in New Albany, Indiana, taught briefly
there, then moved east to prepare for college. He entered Harvard
in 1889 and obtained undergraduate and graduate degrees before
joining the English faculty there in 1894. During his Harvard
years, Moody befriended a number of writers, including Bliss
Carman, George Santayana, and Robert Herrick. He also wrote
much imitative verse in the styles of various European masters.
Although he published regularly in the *Harvard Monthly*, Moody
knew that this work was only practice for his own career; he in-
cluded only three of these efforts in *Poems* (1901).

When Moody moved in 1895 to teach at the University of Chi-
cago, he broke free from the influences of his student days and
wrote from his own experiences. He taught and edited scholarly
editions in order to finance his literary career, although he hated
to waste his time on anything besides his own work. He published
The Masque of Judgment (1900), a verse "closet drama" not meant
for stage production. A year later, he published *Poems*, which se-
cured his literary reputation. Soon after this, Moody gave up his
teaching to write full-time. When he had abandoned his other
distractions, Moody was able to create the masterful verse and
prose dramas that mark his later career. *The Fire-Bringer* (1904),
unlike the earlier *Masque*, was clearly written for the stage. Moody
was able to gain control of the elements of the story and com-
press them into a manageable unit that the public could follow;

from this point on, his dramas became increasingly more polished and ambitious. Both *The Great Divide*, (1906), the first of two prose dramas, and *The Faith Healer*, his final completed play, were successful. After his success with the prose dramas, Moody turned again to verse and began *The Death of Eve*, which remained incomplete at his death on 17 October 1910. Grouped with *The Masque of Judgment* and *The Fire-Bringer*, *The Death of Eve* was the last piece in the puzzle of the poet's relationship to God.

Moody believed "evil, as a manifestation of an imperfect but evolving universe, springs from the same creative source as good; and it provides the condition of strife necessary for the good" to triumph in the end (Halpern 166). In the verse dramas and poems like "Good Friday Night" and "Second Coming," this struggle is most easily accessible. The two poems deal with incidents from the poet's travels in Europe; in each case, the poet identifies with a Christlike stranger and reflects on how that identification changes his perception of a religious ritual. *The Masque of Judgment* centers around a discussion between the archangels Raphael and Uriel; *The Fire-Bringer* puts the idea of the need for a changing view of God in the context of the Prometheus myth; *The Death of Eve* treats Eve's return to the garden in her old age. Where once she had been the source of evil through the Fall, she has transcended her earlier weakness and emerged as the bringer of all that is good. This central theme appears in such poems as "The Daguerreotype" and "Good Friday Night."

Moody's most famous poems are protest verses written in 1900 for publication in *Poems*: "Ode in Time of Hesitation," "On a Soldier Fallen in the Phillipines," and "The Menagerie." Still, the religious question is so pervasive that one must consider it first in a study of Moody's work. Although technically accomplished and experienced with complex poetic forms, Moody deserves to be remembered for his attempts to answer the universal question of humankind's relationship to God.

—William R. Nash

Suggestions for Further Reading

Brown, Maurice F. *Estranging Dawn: The Life and Works of William Vaughn Moody*. Carbondale: Southern Illinois UP, 1973.

Halpern, Martin. *William Vaughn Moody*. Ed. Sylvia E. Bowman. New York: Twayne, 1964.

Henry, David D. *William Vaughn Moody: A Study*. Boston: Bruce Humphries, 1934.

TEXT

The Poems and Plays of William Vaughn Moody in Two Volumes. 2
vols. New York: Houghton, 1912.

ꙅⲬꙅ

Good Friday Night

At last the bird that sang so long
In twilight circle, hushed his song:
Above the ancient square
The stars came here and there.

Good Friday night! Some hearts were bowed,
But some amid the waiting crowd
Because of too much youth
Felt not that mystic ruth;

And of these hearts my heart was one:
Nor when beneath the arch of stone   10
With dirge and candle flame
The cross of passion came,

Did my glad spirit feel reproof,
Though on the awful tree aloof,
Unspiritual, dead,
Drooped the ensanguined Head.

To one who stood where myrtles made
A little space of deeper shade
(As I could half descry,
A stranger, even as I),   20

I said, "These youths who bear along
The symbols of their Savior's wrong,
The spear, the garment torn,
The flaggel, and the thorn,—

"Why do they make this mummery?
Would not a brave man gladly die
For such a smaller thing
Than to be Christ and king?"

He answered nothing, and I turned.
Throned in its hundred candles burned   30

The jeweled eidolon
Of her who bore the Son.

The crowd was prostrate; still, I felt
No shame until the stranger knelt;
Then not to kneel, almost,
Seemed like a vulgar boast.

I knelt. The doll-face, waxen white,
Flowered out a living dimness; bright
Dawned the dear mortal grace
Of my own mother's face.   40

When we were risen up, the street
Was vacant; all the air hung sweet
With lemon-flowers; and soon
The sky would hold the moon.

More silently than new-found friends
To whom much silence makes amends
For the much babble vain
While yet their lives were twain,

We walked along the odorous hill.
The light was little yet; his will   50
I could not see to trace
Upon his form or face.

So when aloft the gold moon broke,
I cried, heart-stung. As one who woke
He turned unto my cries
The anguish of his eyes.

"Friend! Master!" I cried falteringly,
"Thou seest the thing they make of thee.
Oh, by the light divine
My mother shares with thine,   60

"I beg that I may lay my head
Upon thy shoulder and be fed
With thoughts of brotherhood!"
So through the odorous wood,

More silently than friends new-found
We walked. At the first meadow bound

His figure ashen-stoled
Sank in the moon's broad gold.

(1898, 1901)

from The Masque of Judgment

URIEL
Thou knowest what whispers are abroad in Heaven;
How God pines ever for his broken dream,
Broken by vague division, whence who knows!
And pangs of restless love too strong to quench
Save by the putting of creation forth,—
Quenched then but for a moment, since the worlds
He made to soothe Him only vex Him more,
Being compact of passion, violent,
Exceeding quarrelsome, and in their midst
Man the arch-troubler. Fainter whispers say   10
He ponders how to win his prodigal
By some extremity to render back
The heritage abused, to merge again
Each individual will into his will:
Till when, his pangs increase.

RAPHAEL
                        A nine day's tale.
I hold Him no such weakling! Yet . . . and yet . . .
I have beheld . . . I know not . . . pallor couched
On brows that wont to beacon; through the orbs
Quivers of twilight, hints and flecks of change. . . .   20
We cannot be, we would not be, I deem,
The same as ere space was, or time began
To trellis there life's wild and various bloom.
—We linger. Let me hear.

URIEL
                Some things He made
Out of his wistfulness, his ecstasy,
And made them lovely fair; yet other some
Out of his loathing, out of his remorse,
Out of chagrin at the antinomy
Cleaving his nature; these are monstrous shapes,   30
Whereof the most abhorred one dwells below
Within the caves and aged wells of dark

William Vaughn Moody   507

Toward which this Valley plunges. There it waits
Hoarding its ugly strength till time be full.

(1900)

from Jetsam

I wonder can this be the world it was
At sunset? I remember the sky fell
Green as pale meadows, at the long street-ends,
But overhead the smoke-wrack hugged the roofs
As if to shut the city from God's eyes
Till dawn should quench the laughter and the lights.
Beneath the gas flare stolid faces passed,
Too dull for sin; old loosened lips set hard
To drain the stale lees from the cup of sense;
Or if a young face yearned from out the mist   10
Made by its own bright hair, the eyes were wan
With desolate fore-knowledge of the end.
My life lay waste about me; as I walked,
From the gross dark of unfrequented streets
The face of my own youth peered forth at me,
Struck white with pity at the thing I was;
And globed in ghostly fire, thrice-virginal,
With lifted face star-strong, went one who sang
Lost verses from my youth's gold canticle.
Out of the void dark came my face and hers   20
One vivid moment—then the street was there;
Bloat shapes and mean eyes blotted the sear dusk;
And in the curtained window of a house
Whence sin reeked on the night, a shameful head
Was silhouetted black as Satan's face
Against eternal fires. I stumbled on
Down the dark slope that reaches riverward,
Stretching blind hands to find the throat of God
And crush Him in his lies. The river lay
Coiled in its factory filth and few lean trees.   30
All was too hateful—I could not die there!
I whom the Spring had strained unto her breast,
Whose lips had felt the wet vague lips of dawn.
So under the thin willows' leprous shade
And through the tangled ranks of riverweed
I pushed—till lo, God heard me! I came forth
Where, 'neath the shoreless hush of region light,

Through a new world, undreamed of, undesired,
Beyond imagining of man's weary heart,
Far to the white marge of the wondering sea   40
This still plain widens, and this moon rains down
Insufferable ecstasy of peace.

                                                    (1897, 1901)

from The Daguerreotype

This, then, is she,
My mother as she looked at seventeen,
When she first met my father. Young incredibly,
Younger than spring, without the faintest trace
Of disappointment, weariness, or tean
Upon the childlike earnestness and grace
Of the waiting face.
These close-wound ropes of pearl
(Or common beads made precious by their use)
Seem heavy for so slight a throat to wear;   10
But the low bodice leaves the shoulders bare
And half the glad swell of the breast, for news
That now the woman stirs within the girl.
And yet,
Even so, the loops and globes
Of beaten gold
And jet
Hung, in the stately way of old,
From the ears' drooping lobes
On festivals and Lord's-day of the week,   20
Show all too matron-sober for the cheek,—
Which, now I look again, is perfect child,
Or no—or no—'tis girlhood's very self,
Moulded by some deep, mischief-ridden elf
So meek, so maiden mild,
But startling the close gazer with the sense
Of passions forest-shy and forest-wild,
And delicate delirious merriments.

As a moth beats sidewise
And up and over, and tries   30
To skirt the irresistible lure
Of the flame that has him sure,
My spirit, that is none too strong to-day,

Flutters and makes delay,—
Pausing to wonder on the perfect lips,
Lifting to muse upon the low-drawn hair
And each hid radiance there,
But powerless to stem the tide-race bright,
The vehement peace which drifts it toward the light
Where soon—ah, now, with cries   40
Of grief and giving-up unto its gain
It shrinks no longer nor denies,
But dips
Hurriedly home to the exquisite heart of pain,—
And all is well, for I have seen them plain,
The unforgettable, the unforgotten eyes!
Across the blinding gush of these good tears
They shine as in the sweet and heavy years
When by her bed and chair
We children gathered jealously to share   50
The sunlit aura breathing myrrh and thyme,
Where the sore-stricken body made a clime
Gentler than May and pleasanter than rhyme,
Holier and more mystical than prayer.

God, how thy ways are strange!
That this should be, even this,
The patient head
Which suffered years ago the dreary change!
That these so dewy lips should be the same
As those I stooped to kiss   60
And heard my harrowing half-spoken name,
A little ere the one who bowed above her,
Our father and her very constant lover,
Rose stoical, and we knew that she was dead.
Then I, who could not understand or share
His antique nobleness,
Being unapt to bear
The insults which time flings us for our proof,
Fled from the horrible roof
Into the alien sunshine merciless,   70
The shrill satiric fields ghastly with day,
Raging to front God in his pride of sway
And hurl across the lifted swords of fate
That ringed Him where he sat
My puny gage of scorn and desolate hate
Which somehow should undo Him, after all!

(1901)

from The Fire-Bringer

PROMETHEUS
Be comforted; it is established sure.
Light shall arise from light, day follow day,
Season meet season, with all lovely signs
And portents of the year. These shall not fail;
From their appointed dance no star shall swerve,
Nor mar one accent of one whirling strophe
Of that unfathomed chorus that they sing
Within the porch and laughing house of Life,
Which Time and Space and Change, bright caryatids,
Do meanwhile pillar up. These shall not fail;   10
But O, these were the least I brought you home!
The sun whose rising and whose going down
Are joy and grief and wonder in the heart;
The moon whose tides are passion, thought, and will;
The signs and portents of the spirit year,—
For these, if you would keep them, you must strive
Morning and night against the jealous gods
With anger, and with laughter, and with love;
And no man hath them till he brings them down
With love, and rage, and laughter from the heavens,—   20
Himself the heavens, himself the scornful gods,
The sun, the sun-thief, and the flaming reed
That kindles new the beauty of the world.

(1904)

from Second Coming

"Yea, it is I, 'tis I indeed!
        But who art thou, and plannest what?
Beyond all use, beyond all need!
        Importunate, unbesought,

"Unwelcome, unendurable!
        To the vague boy I was before—
O unto him thou camest well;
        But now, a boy no more,

"Firm-seated in my proper good,
        Clear-operant in my functions due,   10

William Vaughn Moody   511

Potent and plenteous of my mood,—
    What hast thou here to do?

"Yes, I have loved thee—love thee, yes;
    But also—hear'st thou?—also him
Who out of Ida's wilderness
    Over the bright sea-rim,

"With shaken cones and mystic dance,
    To Dirce and her seven waters[1]
Led on the raving Corybants,[2]
    And lured the Theban daughters   20

"To play on the delirious hills[3]
    Three summer days, three summer nights,
Where wert thou when these had their wills?
    How liked thee their delights?

"Past Melos, Delos, to the straits,
    The waters roll their spangled mirth,
And westward, through Gibraltar gates,
    To my own under-earth,

"My glad, great land, which at the most
    Knows that its fathers knew thee: so   30
Will spend for thee nor count the cost;
    But follow thee? Ah, no!

"Thine image gently fades from earth!
    Thy churches are as empty shells,
Dim-plaining of thy words and worth,
    And of thy funerals!

"But oh, upon what errand, then,
    Leanest thou at the sailor's ear?
Hast thou yet more to say, that men
    Have heard not, and must hear?"   40
                (1903, 1912)

---

1. Dirce, a devotee of Dionysus, was killed by the vengeful sons of her nemesis, Antiope. Dionysus caused a spring (the "seven waters") to flow from the ground where Dirce died. This reference establishes the pattern of allusions to Dionysus, the Greek god of wine; these allusions stand as a contradiction to conventional Christian imagery.

2. The Corybants were male devotees of Cybele, the Phrygian goddess who cured Dionysus of his madness, inflicted on him by Hera, the wife of Zeus.

3. In vengeance for their rejection of his divinity, Dionysus drove all the women of Thebes mad.

Paul Laurence Dunbar

1872–1906

The complexity of Paul Laurence Dunbar's poetic ouvre mirrors that of his personality. He has always been best known as a writer of poems in dialect—one of the most accomplished. Yet he wrote an equal number of poems in standard English, and at times scorned his reputation as a dialect writer. Inevitably considered a poetic spokesperson for black people, Dunbar sometimes embraced this role, producing anguished, bitter protests against racial oppression, while at other times he seemingly endorsed prevailing racial stereotypes.

The son of former Kentucky slaves, Dunbar was born on 27 June 1872, and raised in Dayton, Ohio. His father, Joshua Dunbar, had escaped to Canada via the Underground Railroad and returned to fight for the Union in the Civil War. After the war, the elder Dunbar married Mathilda Murphy, whose first husband had been killed in the Union cause.

Though Dunbar distinguished himself in high school and published several poems in the *Dayton Herald*, he worked as an elevator operator after graduating, having searched unsuccessfully for more desirable employment. Almost all the poems in his first book, *Oak and Ivy* (1892), were composed on the elevator.

As his regional reputation increased, Dunbar gave readings in various Midwestern towns. In 1893, he read his poems to Frederick Douglass, an experience he treasured all his life. By 1895, national magazines, particularly *Century*, were publishing his poems. With his second book, *Majors and Minors* (1896), Dunbar vaulted into national notoriety almost overnight after a favorable review from the influential arbiter of taste, William Dean Howells.

Both Dunbar's activities and his poetic production accelerated thereafter. He gave extensive reading tours in the United States and in England, and moved from small Ohio publishers to a New York house, Dodd, Mead. In 1898, he married Alice Ruth Moore, also a poet, to whom he had proposed at their first meeting. He also produced novels, short stories, lyrics to several black musicals, and two more books of poems: *Lyrics of Lowly Life* (1895), which includes many of the poems in the first two books plus some new ones, and *Lyrics of the Hearthside* (1899).

This heavy pace took its toll; in 1899, Dunbar collapsed with a nearly-fatal case of pneumonia that worsened into tuberculosis. He moved to Florida, then to the Catskills, and to Colorado in search of a healthy climate, before returning to Dayton to live with his mother in 1902. Tortured by his illness and the belief that he had stagnated as a poet, and beset by financial difficulties, Dunbar spent his last years embittered and separated from his wife. Nevertheless, he managed to write two more volumes of poetry, *Lyrics of Love and Laughter* (1903) and *Lyrics of Sunshine and Shadow* (1905), as well as two books of short stories and a novel— a heroic achievement under such circumstances. He died of tuberculosis on 9 February 1906 in Dayton, Ohio, where he is buried.

Dunbar wrote poems both in standard English (conventionally called the "literary" poems) and in various dialects. He had grown up with the speech and stories of Southerners, and he had a keen ear; he reproduces several regional dialects—both black and white—accurately enough that linguists have studied them. Howells' estimation that Dunbar showed his talent most distinctively in dialect poems cast the die for Dunbar's reception: these poems were always his most highly esteemed.

Dunbar's attitude toward his dialect work was ambivalent. He wanted to be considered a serious poet and resented the acclaim that consistently went only to the dialect poems, which Howells had praised especially for their "humorous quality." His biting reference in "The Poet" to "a jingle in a broken tongue" voices this frustration (line 8). Yet at other times, he spoke favorably of these poems, once calling them his "fondest love." Whatever his reservations may have been, he never stopped writing them.

As Dunbar surely knew, a number of the dialect poems— many of which are set in the antebellum South—perpetuate unsavory myths of blacks as comfort-loving and simple, happy with a good meal or a banjo tune, and satisfied with their subservient lot. "Chrismus on the Plantation," in which former slaves agree that "Mistah Lincum" can "tek his freedom back" if they must desert their old, now destitute former master, affords an example. But in other poems, such as "Accountability," Dunbar's tone mirrors that of his speakers: superficially conformist while ironically undercutting white authority.

As a group, the dialect poems are probably the most enigmatic in content. And by their nature, they necessarily escape the flaws that beset the more conventional of the literary poems: standard imagery, too-sentimental themes, and inflated diction—all apparent in Dunbar's numerous love poems. On the other hand, the literary poems evince considerably more formal innovation. Dunbar experimented extensively and well with stanzaic forms, line lengths, and rhyme schemes. Among others, "Sympathy" and "We Wear the Mask" exemplify Dunbar's ability to wed form and content with powerful effect.

Dunbar's reputation declined as later generations found the dialect poems distasteful, akin to minstrel shows or Amos 'n' Andy routines. Interest revived in the late 1960s, and has continued to this day. Critical attention has focused, as it will probably continue to do, on arriving at an assessment of Dunbar that plausibly incorporates his contradictory sides. However he is eventually redefined, he was an accomplished craftsman and a careful student of language, both spoken and written.

—*Harry Crockett*

Suggestions for Further Reading

Braxton, Joanne M., ed. *The Collected Poetry of Paul Lawrence Dunbar*. Charlottesville: UP of Virginia, 1993.*
Cunningham, Virginia. *Paul Laurence Dunbar and His Song*. New York: Biblo & Tannen, 1969.
Gayle, Addison, Jr. *Oak and Ivy: A Biography of Paul Laurence Dunbar*. Garden City, NY: Doubleday, 1971.
Martin, Jay, ed. *A Singer in the Dawn: Reinterpretations of Paul Laurence Dunbar*. New York: Dodd, 1975.
Rexell, Peter. *Paul Laurence Dunbar*. Boston: Twayne, 1979.
Wegner, Jean. *Black Poets of the United States from Paul Laurence Dunbar to Langston Hughes*. Trans. Kenneth Douglas. Urbana: U of Illinois P, 1973. See esp. 39–125.

TEXTS
Lyrics of Lowly Life. 1895.
Lyrics of the Hearthside. 1899.
Lyrics of Love and Laughter. New York: Dodd, 1903.
Lyrics of Sunshine and Shadow. New York: Dodd, 1905.

Ode to Ethiopia

O Mother Race! to thee I bring
This pledge of faith unwavering,
    This tribute to thy glory.
I know the pangs which thou didst feel,
When Slavery crushed thee with its heel,
    With thy dear blood all gory.

Sad days were those—ah, sad indeed!
But through the land the fruitful seed
   Of better times was growing.
The plant of freedom upward sprung,   10
And spread its leaves so fresh and young—
   Its blossoms now are blowing.

On every hand in this fair land,
Proud Ethiope's swarthy children stand
   Beside their fairer neighbor;
The forests flee before their stroke,
Their hammers ring, their forges smoke,—
   They stir in honest labour.

They tread the fields where honour calls;
Their voices sound through senate halls   20
   In majesty and power.
To right they cling; the hymns they sing
Up to the skies in beauty ring,
   And bolder grow each hour.

Be proud, my Race, in mind and soul;
Thy name is writ on Glory's scroll
   In characters of fire.
High 'mid the clouds of Fame's bright sky
Thy banner's blazoned folds now fly,
   And truth shall lift them higher.   30

Thou hast the right to noble pride,
Whose spotless robes were purified
   By blood's severe baptism.
Upon thy brow the cross was laid,
And labour's painful sweat-beads made
   A consecrating chrism.[1]

No other race, or white or black,
When bound as thou wert, to the rack,
   So seldom stooped to grieving;
No other race, when free again,   40
Forgot the past and proved them men
   So noble in forgiving.

Go on and up! Our souls and eyes
Shall follow thy continuous rise;

---

1. A liquid used for anointing in church sacraments, such as baptism.

Our ears shall list thy story
From bards who from thy root shall spring,
And proudly tune their lyres to sing
Of Ethiopia's glory.

(1892)

Accountability

Folks ain't got no right to censuah othah folks about dey
    habits;
Him dat giv' de squir'ls de bushtails made de bobtails fu' de
    rabbits.
Him dat built de gread big mountains hollered out de little
    valleys,
Him dat made de streets an' driveways wasn't shamed to
    make de alleys.

We is all constructed diff'ent, d'ain't no two of us de same;
We cain't he'p ouah likes an' dislikes, ef we'se bad we ain't
    to blame.
Ef we'se good, we needn't show off, case you bet it ain't
    ouah doin'
We gits into su'ttain channels dat we jes' cain't he'p pu'suin'.

But we all fits into places dat no othah ones could fill,
An' we does the things we has to, big er little, good er ill.   10
John cain't tek de place o' Henry, Su an' Sally ain't alike;
Bass ain't nuthin' like a suckah, chub ain't nuthin' like a pike.

When you come to think about it, how it's all planned out
    it's splendid.
Nuthin's done er evah happens, 'dout hit's somefin' dat's
    intended;
Don't keer whut you does, you has to, an' hit sholy beats de
    dickens,—
Viney, go put on de kittle, I got one o' mastah's chickens.

(1896)

An Anti-Bellum Sermon

We is gathahed hyeah, my brothahs,
    In dis howlin' wildaness,

Fu' to speak some words of comfo't
To each othah in distress.
An' we chooses fu' ouah subjic'
Dis—we'll 'splain it by an' by;
"An' de Lawd said, 'Moses, Moses,'
An' de man said, 'Hyeah am I.' "

Now ole Pher'oh, down in Egypt,
Was de wuss man evah bo'n,   10
An' he had de Hebrew chillun
Down dah wukin' in his co'n;
'Twell de Lawd got tiahed o' his foolin',
An' sez he: "I'll let him know—
Look hyeah, Moses, go tell Pher'oh
Fu' to let dem chillun go."

"An' ef he refuse to do it,
I will make him rue de houah,
Fu' I'll empty down on Egypt
All de vials of my powah."   20
Yes, he did—an' Pher'oh's ahmy
Wasn't wuth a ha'f a dime;
Fu' de Lawd will he'p his chillun,
You kin trust him evah time.

An' yo' enemies may 'sail you
In de back an in de front;
But de Lawd is all aroun' you,
Fu' to ba' de battle's brunt.
Dey kin fo'ge yo' chains an' shackles
F'om de mountains to de sea;   30
But de Lawd will sen' some Moses
Fu' to set his chillun free.

An' de lan' shall hyeah his thundah,
Lak a blas' f'om Gab'el's ho'n,
Fu' de Lawd of hosts is mighty
When he girds his ahmor on.
But fu' feah some one mistakes me,
I will pause right hyeah to say,
Dat I'm still a-preachin' ancient,
I ain't talkin' 'bout to-day.   40

But I tell you, fellah christuns,
Things'll happen mighty strange;
Now, de Lawd done dis fu' Isrul,
An' his ways don't nevah change,

An' de love he showed to Isrul
    Wasn't all on Isrul spent;
Now don't run an' tell yo' mastahs
    Dat I's preachin' discontent.

'Cause I isn't; I'se a-judgin'
    Bible people by deir ac's;   50
I'se a-givin' you de Scriptuah,
    I'se a-handin' you de fac's.
Cose ole Pher'oh b'lieved in slav'ry,
    But de Lawd he let him see,
Dat de people he put bref in,—
    Evah mothah's son was free.

An' dah's othahs thinks lak Pher'oh,
    But dey calls de Scriptuah liar,
Fu' de Bible says "a servant
    Is a-worthy of his hire."   60
An' you cain't git roun' nor thoo dat,
    An you cain't git ovah it,
Fu' whatevah place you git in,
    Dis hyeah Bible too'll fit.

So you see de Lawd's intention,
    Evah sence de worl' began,
Was dat His almighty freedom
    Should belong to evah man,
But I think it would be bettah,
    Ef I'd pause agin to say,   70
Dat I'm talkin' 'bout ouah freedom
    In a Bibleistic way.

But de Moses is a-comin',
    An' he's comin', suah an' fas'
We kin hyeah his feet a-trompin',
    We kin hyeah his trumpit blas'.
But I want to wa'n you people,
    Don't you git too brigity;
An' don't you git to braggin'
    'Bout dese things, you wait an' see.   80

But when Moses wif his powah
    Comes an' sets us chillun free,
We will praise de gracious Mastah
    Dat has gin us liberty;
An' we'll shout ouah halleluyahs,
    On dat mighty reck'nin' day,

Paul Laurence Dunbar

When we'se reco'nised ez citiz'—
Huh uh! Chillun, let us pray!

(1896)

We Wear the Mask

We wear the mask that grins and lies,
It hides our cheeks and shades our eyes,—
This debt we pay to human guile;
With torn and bleeding hearts we smile,
And mouth with myriad subtleties.

Why should the world be over-wise,
In counting all our tears and sighs?
Nay, let them only see us, while
    We wear the mask.

We smile, but, O great Christ, our cries   10
To thee from tortured souls arise.
We sing, but oh the clay is vile
Beneath our feet, and long the mile;
But let the world dream otherwise,
    We wear the mask!

(1896)

Angelina

When de fiddle gits to singin' out a ol' Vahginny reel,
An' you 'mence to feel a ticklin' in yo' toe an' in yo' heel;
Ef you t'ink you got 'uligion an' you wants to keep it, too,
You jes' bettah tek a hint an' git yo'self clean out o' view.
Case de time is mighty temptin' when de chune is in de
    swing,
Fu' a darky, saint or sinner man, to cut de pigeon-wing.
An' you couldn't he'p f'om dancin' ef yo' feet was boun' wif
    twine,
When Angelina Johnson comes a-swingin' down de line.

Don't you know Miss Angelina? She's de da'lin' of de place.
W'y, dey ain't no high-toned lady wif sich mannahs an' sich
    grace.   10

She kin move across de cabin, wif its planks all rough an'
    wo';
Jes' de same's ef she was dancin' on ol' mistus' ball-room
    flo'.
Fact is, you don't see no cabin—evaht'ing you see look
    grand,
An 'dat one ol' squeaky fiddle soun' to you jes' lak a ban';
Cotton britches look lak broadclof an' a linsey dress look
    fine,
When Angelina Johnson comes a-swingin' down de line.

Some folks say dat dancin's sinful, an' de blessed Lawd, dey
    say,
Gwine to punish us fu' steppin' w'en we hyeah de music play.
But I tell you I don't b'lieve it, fu' de Lawd is wise and good,
An' he made de banjo's metal an' he made de fiddle's
    wood,   20
An' he made de music in dem, so I don' quite t'ink he'll keer
Ef our feet keeps time a little to de melodies we hyeah.
W'y, dey's somep'n' downright holy in de way our faces
    shine,
When Angelina Johnson comes a-swingin' down de line.

Angelina steps so gentle, Angelina bows so low,
An' she lif' huh sku't so dainty dat huh shoetop skacely
    show:
An' dem teef o' huh'n a-shinin', ez she tek you by de han'—
Go 'way, people, d' ain't anothah sich a lady in de lan'!
When she's movin' thoo de figgers er a-dancin' by huhse'f,
Folks jes' stan' stock-still a-sta'in', an' dey mos' nigh hol's
    dey bref;   30
An' de young mens, dey's a-sayin', "I's gwine mek dat
    damsel mine,"
When Angelina Johnson comes a-swingin' down de line.
                                                          (1899)

Chrismus on the Plantation

It was Chrismus Eve, I mind hit fu' a mighty gloomy day—
Bofe de weathah an' de people—not a one of us was gay;
Cose you'll t'ink dat's mighty funny 'twell I try to mek hit
    cleah,
Fu' a da'ky's allus happy when de holidays is neah.

But we wasn't, fu' dat mo'nin' Mastah'd tol' us we mus' go,
He'd been payin' us sence freedom, but he couldn't pay no
    mo';
He wa'n't nevah used to plannin' 'fo' he got so po' an' ol',
So he gwine to give up tryin', an' de homestead mus' be sol'.

I kin see him stan'in' now erpon de step ez cleah ez day,
Wid de win' a-kind o' fondlin' thoo his haih all thin an'
    gray;   10
An' I 'membah how he trimbled when he said, "It's ha'd fu'
    me,
Not to mek yo' Chrismus brightah, but I 'low it wa'n't to
    be."

All de women was a-cryin', an' de men, too, on de sly,
An' I noticed somep'n shinin' even in ol' Mastah's eye.
But we all stood still to listen ez ol' Ben come f'om de crowd
An' spoke up, a-try'n' to steady down his voice and mek it
    loud:—

"Look hyeah, Mastah, I's been servin' yo' fu' lo! dese many
    yeahs,
An' now, sence we's got freedom an' you's kind o' po', hit
    'pears
Dat you want us all to leave you 'cause you don't t'ink you
    can pay.
Ef my membry hasn't fooled me, seem dat whut I hyead you
    say.   20

"Er in othah wo'ds, you wants us to fu'git dat you's been
    kin',
An' ez soon ez you is he'pless, we's to leave you hyeah
    behin'.
Well, ef dat's de way dis freedom ac's on people, white er
    black,
You kin jes' tell Mistah Lincum fu' to tek his freedom back.

"We gwine wo'k dis ol' plantation fu' whatevah we kin git,
Fu' I know hit did suppo't us, an' de place kin do it yit.
Now de lan' is yo's, de hands is ouahs, an' I reckon we'll be
    brave,
An' we'll bah ez much ez you do w'en we has to scrape an'
    save."

Ol' Mastah stood dah trimblin', but a-smilin' thoo his teahs,
An' den hit seemed jes' nachul-like, de place fah rung wid
    cheahs,   30

An' soon ez dey was quiet, some one sta'ted sof' an' low:
"Praise God," an' den we all jined in, "from whom all
    blessin's flow!"

Well, dey wasn't no use in tryin', ouah min's was sot to stay,
An' po' ol' Mastah couldn't plead ner baig, ner drive us 'way,
An' all at once, hit seemed to us, de day was bright agin,
So evahone was gay dat night, an' watched de Chrismus in.

(1899)

Sympathy

I know what the caged bird feels, alas!
    When the sun is bright on the upland slopes;
When the wind stirs soft through the springing grass,
And the river flows like a stream of glass;
    When the first bird sings and the first bud opes,
And the faint perfume from its chalice steals—
I know what the caged bird feels!

I know why the caged bird beats his wing
    Till its blood is red on the cruel bars;
For he must fly back to his perch and cling   10
When he fain would be on the bough a-swing;
    And a pain still throbs in the old, old scars
And they pulse again with a keener sting—
I know why he beats his wing!

I know why the caged bird sings, ah me,
    When his wing is bruised and his bosom sore,—
When he beats his bars and he would be free;
It is not a carol of joy or glee,
    But a prayer that he sends from his heart's deep core,
But a plea, that upward to Heaven he flings—   20
I know why the caged bird sings!

(1899)

The Haunted Oak

Pray why are you so bare, so bare,
    Oh, bough of the old oak tree;

And why, when I go through the shade you throw,
    Runs a shudder over me?

My leaves were green as the best, I trow,
    And sap ran free in my veins,
But I saw in the moonlight dim and weird
    A guiltless victim's pains.

I bent me down to hear his sigh;
    I shook with his gurgling moan,   10
And I trembled sore when they rode away,
    And left him here alone.

They'd charged him with the old, old crime,
    And set him fast in jail:
Oh, why does the dog howl all night long,
    And why does the night wind wail?

He prayed his prayer and he swore his oath,
    And he raised his hand to the sky;
But the beat of hoofs smote on his ear,
    And the steady tread grew nigh.   20

Who is it rides by night, by night,
    Over the moonlit road?
And what is the spur that keeps the pace,
    What is the galling goad?

And now they beat at the prison door,
    "Ho, keeper, do not stay!
We are friends of him whom you hold within,
    And we fain would take him away

"From those who ride fast on our heels
    With mind to do him wrong;   30
They have no care for his innocence,
    And the rope they bear is long."

They have fooled the jailer with lying words,
    They have fooled the man with lies;
The bolts unbar, the locks are drawn,
    And the great door open flies.

Now they have taken him from the jail,
    And hard and fast they ride,
And the leader laughs low down in his throat,
    As they halt my trunk beside.   40

Oh, the judge, he wore a mask of black,
   And the doctor one of white,
And the minister, with his oldest son,
   Was curiously bedight.

Oh, foolish man, why weep you now?
   'Tis but a little space,
And the time will come when these shall dread
   The mem'ry of your face.

I feel the rope against my bark,
   And the weight of him in my grain,   50
I feel in the throe of his final woe
   The touch of my own last pain.

And never more shall leaves come forth
   On a bough that bears the ban;
I am burned with dread, I am dried and dead,
   From the curse of a guiltless man.

And ever the judge rides by, rides by,
   And goes to hunt the deer,
And ever another rides his soul
   In the guise of a mortal fear.   60

And ever the man he rides me hard,
   And never a night stays he;
For I feel his curse as a haunted bough,
   On the trunk of a haunted tree.

                                        (1900)

The Poet

He sang of life, serenely sweet,
   With, now and then, a deeper note.
   From some high peak, nigh yet remote,
He voiced the world's absorbing beat.

He sang of love when earth was young,
   And Love, itself, was in his lays.
   But ah, the world, it turned to praise
A jingle in a broken tongue.

                                        (1902)

CONTRIBUTORS

❦

INDEX OF AUTHORS, TITLES,
AND FIRST LINES OF POEMS

❦

SUBJECT INDEX

Contributors

ROBERT BAIN, professor emeritus of American literature at the University of North Carolina at Chapel Hill, edited with George F. Horner *Colonial and Federalist American Writing* (1966) and with Dennis G. Donovan *The Writer and the Worlds of Words* (1975). With Joseph M. Flora, he edited *Fifty Southern Writers Before 1900* (1987), *Fifty Southern Writers After 1900* (1987), *Contemporary Fiction Writers of the South* (1993), and *Contemporary Poets, Dramatists, Essayists, and Novelists of the South* (1994). With Flora and Louis D. Rubin, Jr., he edited *Southern Writers: A Biographical Dictionary* (1979). With Beverly Taylor, he edited *The Cast of Consciousness: Concepts of the Mind in British and American Romanticism* (1987). He is author of *H. L. Davis* (1974) and wrote the introduction to *H. L. Davis: Collected Essays and Stories* (1986). He received a Tanner Award for excellence in undergraduate teaching and a Bowman and Gordon Gray Professorship of Undergraduate Teaching (1987–90).

SUSAN BALES taught secondary school for nine years. She is now teaching at Central Carolina Community College at Pittsboro, North Carolina, and working at Davis Library at the University of North Carolina at Chapel Hill.

GLENN BLALOCK is an assistant professor of English at Stephen F. Austin State University, Nacogdoches, Texas, where he teaches composition and American literature. He has edited a collection of readings for composition teachers published by Bedford Books, and has presented papers on writing-across-the-curriculum and teaching writing to bilingual students. He has delivered conference papers on colonial American newspapers and on nineteenth-century literary annuals. Currently, he is working on a book about eighteenth-century Caribbean writing.

LISA CARL teaches English at Pratt Institute in Brooklyn, New York, and is a freelance book editor in Manhattan. She delivered a paper on the revisionist fictions of J. M. Coetzee and Sherley Anne Williams to the College English Association in 1994, and is at work on a book on contemporary revisionist fiction. She also reads from her poetry and fiction at New York City colleges. She has published chapters on Mary Lee Settle and Nikki Giovanni in *American Women Writers: A Critical Reference Guide* (1994). Her first novel, *Slicing the Nerve*, is being considered for publication.

HARRY CROCKETT is a research associate at a high-technology research firm in Loveland, Colorado. His current projects include a study of Western exploration writing, and a chapter on rivers, dams, and water projects for *State of the State: The Colorado Environmental Report* (forthcoming). Most recently, he was co-author (with Allison Wallace) of an essay on Rocky Mountain nature writing for the *Literary History of the American West* (forthcoming). He and his family live in Loveland.

PAUL CRUMBLEY teaches American literature at Utah State University in Logan, Utah. He contributed a chapter titled "The Dialogic Voice" to *The Emily Dickinson Handbook*, published by the University of Massachusetts Press. He is completing a book tentatively titled *Emily Dickinson and the Voices of Her Mind*.

MARY K. EDMONDS is a doctoral candidate at the University of North Carolina at Chapel Hill. She has published in *American Literary Realism*, and her research interests include American studies and late nineteenth-century American fiction. At present she is writing on aspects of social ritual, theatricality, and consumer culture in Edith Wharton's novels.

E. FRANCES FRAME is completing her doctoral degree at the University of South Carolina in Columbia, South Carolina. She also teaches composition at Midlands Technical College and computer courses at the University's Computer Services Division. Her research areas include nineteenth-century British literature and nineteenth-century American literature.

ELLEN GIDUZ is a doctoral candidate in English at the University of North Carolina at Chapel Hill. She has taught English courses at Davidson College, where she has also worked as a librarian, and at the Chapel Hill and Charlotte branches of the University of North Carolina. Her dissertation focuses on the treatment of moral evil in selected British and American romantic fiction.

WILLIAM R. NASH, assistant professor of American literature at Middlebury College, specializes in American and African-American literature. His research focuses on contemporary African-American fiction. He has written an essay on Charles Johnson for a forthcoming collection, as well as several essays for both *The Oxford Companion to Women's Writing* and *The Oxford Companion to African-American Literature.* He has presented papers on Charles Johnson's language, Ernest Gaines's fiction, and on the evolution of character in Mark Twain's novels.

TAIMI OLSEN is completing her doctorate in American and twentieth-century literature at the University of North Carolina at Chapel Hill, where she has taught composition and introductions to drama and fiction. She has published articles on Pearl S. Buck and E. E. Cummings, and has delivered papers on Gertrude Stein and on E. E. Cummings. Her dissertation considers language experimentation, metonymy, and metaphor in Henry David Thoreau's *Walden,* E. E. Cummings' *The Enormous Room,* and John Barth's *Lost in the Funhouse.*

TERRY ROBERTS is the author of *Self and Community in the Fiction of Elizabeth Spencer* (1993) as well as numerous articles and papers on American and southern literature. He is executive director of the National Paideia Center, a school reform organization based at the University of North Carolina at Chapel Hill.

SCOTT ROMINE, a doctoral candidate at the University of North Carolina at Chapel Hill, has published notes and essays on James Mathewes Legare, George Santayana, W. B. Yeats, James Joyce, Lady Gregory, Richard Wright, Lillian Smith, and John Crowe Ransom. He is currently completing his dissertation on interpretive paradigms in southern narrative.

WILSON SOMERVILLE lives in Winston-Salem, North Carolina, where he is a medical editor in the Department of Anesthesia of the Bowman Gray School of Medicine of Wake Forest University. His book, *The Tuesday Club of Annapolis (1745–1756) as Cultural Performance,* is being published by the University of Georgia Press.

Index of Authors, Titles, and First Lines of Poems

Subject Index

Irving, Washington, xxvii
Is It Poetry? (Holland), 182
Israfel (Poe), xxix, 111, 112
Isreal Potter (Melville), 189
Italy, 65

Jackson, Amelia, 127
Jackson, Blyden, 26
Jackson, Helen Hunt, 302–3
Jackson, Lidia (Lidian), 43
Jackson, William Sharpless, 302
James, Henry, 351,401
Jane Jones and Some Others (King), 455
Jest 'Fore Christmas (Field), 419
Jewish Problem, The (Lazarus), 401
Jim Bludso of the Prairie Bell (Hay), 351
Joaquin Miller's Poems (Miller), 341
John Brown and the Heroes (Channing), 162
John Burns of Gettysburg (Harte), 365
John Marr and Other Sailors (Melville), 189
Johnson, Thomas H., xxxiii, 394
Jones, Hannah Lucinda, 210
Journal (Thoreau), 156
Journals (Emerson), 43
Justice and Expediency (Whittier), 86

Kathrina (Holland), 182
Keats, John, 247, 496
"Kentucky poet" (Cawein), 496
Keramos and Other Poems (Longfellow), 66
Key to the Casket, A (Jackson), 302
King, Ben[jamin] [Franklin], xxvii, 455–56
Kings, The (Guiney), 470
King's Bell, The (Stoddard), 246
King's Missive, The (Whittier), 86
Kipling, Rudyard, 411
Klondike, 341
Knickerbocker Magazine, 145, 246
Kreymborg, Alfred, 236

labor reform, 435
Ladies' Magazine, 35
Lancaster [Massachusetts] *Gazette*, 25
Landmarks and Other Poems (Piatt), 318
landscape, 290, 448
language, indefiniteness of, xxx, xxxi
Lanier, Mary Day, 379
Lanier, Sidney, xxi, xxv, xxix, 358, 373, 379–81, 393, 496
Last Night that She Lived, The (Dickinson), 227
Later Lyrics (Tabb), 394
Later Poems (Tabb), 394
Latham, Aseneth Belle, 455
Lays of My Home (Whittier), 86
Lazarus, Emma, xxvii, xxix, 312, 401–2
Learning to Read (Harper), 255

Leaves of Grass (Whitman), xxxii, 42, 86, 290, 352, 380, 463
Lectures on Poetry (Bryant), xxx, 12
Legare, Hugh Swinton, 496
Legends of New-England (Whittier), 86
Leisure-Day Rhymes (Saxe), 145
L'Envoi (Read), 219
Leslie's Weekly, 425
Letters and Social Aims (Emerson), 43
Lewis, R. W. B., 479
Lewis, Sinclair, 412
Liberia, 25
Liberty of American Literature, A (Stedman), 312
Life Among the Modocs: Unwritten History (Miller), 341
Lifted Over (Jackson), 302
Ligeia, (Poe), 112
Light Beyond Darkness (Harper), 255
Light-Winged Smoke, Icarian Bird (Thoreau), 157
Lincoln, Abraham, xxiii, 13, 351, 436
Lincoln and Other Poems (Markham), 436
Lincoln Memorial, 436
Links (Lazarus), 401
Lion's Cub, The (Stoddard), 246
Lippincott's Magazine, 379, 401
Literature in the South (Timrod), 275
Little Boy Blue (Field), 418, 419
Little New World Idyls (Piatt), 318
Little Orphant Annie (Riley), 412
Little Review, xxxiv
Liverpool, 188
London, 43
London *Times*, 425
Longfellow, Henry Wadsworth, xxi, xxvi, xxvii, xxviii, xxix, xxx, xxxiv, 1, 65–67, 85, 86, 169, 219, 246, 289, 330, 479
Longfellow, Stephen, 65
Lord, The (Harris), 435
"Lost Cause," xxiii, 358
Lost Earl and Other Poems, The (Trowbridge), 264
Lost Farm, The (Piatt), 319
Lost Hunting Ground in Illinos, The (Piatt), 319
Louisville Jounal, 318
love, xxix, 35, 36, 275, 352, 412, 426, 441
Love and Pity (Hovey), 486
Lover's Diary, A (A. Cary), 202
Lowell, Amy, xxxiv
Lowell, James Russell, xxi, xxiii,, xxviii, xxxi, xxxiv, 85, 169–70, 246, 330, 411
Luck, The (Harte), 365
Luck of Roaring Camp, The (Harte), 365
lyceum lectures, 43, 145, 146
lynching, 255
Lyra and Other Poems (A. Cary), 202

Poe, Edgar Allan, xxi, xxviii, xxix, xxx, xxxi, xxxii, xxxiv, 35, 36, 86, 111–13, 169, 201, 220, 246, 290, 312, 380, 447

poems: abolitionist, 85; ballads, 66, 86, 170, 189, 227, 330, 447; cavalier lyrics, 469; dialect, xxvi, 169, 352, 365, 380, 411, 412, 418, 455, 456, 513, 514, 515; didactic narratives, 189; dramatic monologues, 189, 265, 479, 480; elegies, 2, 66; epigrams, 189; epitaphs, 189; hymns, 66, 170, 227; local-color romance, 302; masques, 486; moralistic, 182, 202, 425, 426; nature, xxviii, 85, 290, 496; occasional, 85, 127, 128, 136, 169, 312, 313, 480; odes, 66, 170, 189, 210; parodies, 226, 227, 365, 411; pastoral, xxvi, 290, 411; political, 394, 418; romance, 486; sonnets, 66, 136, 170, 210, 275, 290, 303, 312, 330, 402, 447, 480. *See also* poetry; verse

Poems (Aldrich), 331
Poems (Bryant), 12
Poems (Channing), 161
Poems (Emerson), 43
Poems (Harper), 254
Poems (Hay), 352
Poems (Hayne), 289, 290
Poems (Holmes), 127
Poems (Hovey), 486
Poems (Lowell, 1843), 169
Poems (Lowell, 1849), 170
Poems (Moody), 503, 504
Poems (Read), 219
Poems (Sigourney), 1
Poems (Tabb), 393, 394
Poems (Timrod), 274, 289
Poems (Tuckerman), 211
Poems (S. Whitman), 36
Poems (Whittier), 86
Poems and Essays (Very), 136
Poems and Parodies (P. Cary), 226
Poems and Translations (Lazarus), 401
Poems by Edgar A. Poe, 111
Poems here at Home (Riley), 411
Poems of Alice and Phoebe Cary, 201, 226
Poems of Faith, Hope, and Love (P. Cary), 226
Poems of Passion (Wilcox), 425
Poems of Richard Henry Stoddard, The, 246
Poems of Sidney Lanier, 380
Poems of the Orient (Taylor), 235, 236
Poems of the War (Hayne), 290
Poems of Thomas Bailey Aldrich, 331
Poems of Two Friends (Piatt), 318
Poems of William Cullen Bryant, 12
Poems on Miscellaneous Subjects (Harper), 254

Poems on Slavery (Longfellow), 66
Poems: Patriotic, Religious, and Miscellaneous (Ryan), 358
Poems: Second Series (Channing), 161
Poems: Second Series (Lowell), 169
poet, role of, xxviii, xxxi, xxxii, 136, 162, 380
Poet, The (Bryant), 14
Poet, The (Dunbar), 514
Poet, The (Emerson), xxxi, xxxii, 42
Poet at the Breakfast-Table, The (Holmes), 127
Poetess of Passion (Wilcox), 425
Poetic Principle, The (Poe), xxx, xxxi, 111, 112, 275
Poetical Works of George M. Horton, The, 26
Poetical Works of John Townsend Trowbridge, The, 264
Poetical Works of William Cullen Bryant, 13
poetics, 12
"Poet-Priest of the South" (Ryan), 358
poetry: didactic, 264, 425; domestic, xxx, 202, 236; as edification, 66; as entertainment, xxxii; experimental, 210; lyric, 65, 66, 127, 162, 169, 201, 226, 227, 236, 247, 254, 312, 313, 330, 393, 447, 479, 480; as music, xxxii, 112, 379, 380; narrative, 65, 85, 254, 264, 265, 402, 425; patriotic, 365; propaganda, 364; protest, 504; religious, 85, 425, 436, 469, 470; sentimental, xxx, 1, 202, 219, 237, 246, 247, 265, 275, 303, 330, 365, 373, 411, 418, 425, 447; social functions of, 86; theories of, xxix–xxxiv; traditional, 210. *See also* poems; verse
Poetry Magazine, xxxiv, 447
poets: Fireside, xxxiv, 12, 290; genteel, 86, 236; laureate, xxiii, 274, 275, 418, 447; New England, 331; post–Civil War, 373, 394; Schoolroom, xxxiv, 86; Vermont, 145; women, xxiv, 1, 201, 402
Poets of America (Stedman), 312
pogroms, 401
Poland, 351
pony express, 340
Portent, The (Melville), 189
Potter, Mary Storer, 65
Pound, Ezra, xxxiv
Power, Susan Anna, 36
Prairies, The (Bryant), xxxi, 13, 14
Presence, The (Very), 136
Professor at the Breakfast-Table, The (Holmes), 127
Progress (Saxe), 146
Progress: A Satirical Poem (Saxe), 145
Proud Miss MacBride, The (Saxe), 146

psyche, 113
puerperal fever (childbed fever), 127
Pulitzer Prize, 479
Puritan's Guest, The (Holland), 182

Quaker conscience, 86
Quaker Widow, The (Taylor), 236
Quakers, 85, 135, 235, 236, 302
Quiet Road, A (Reese), 447
Quips and Quiddits (Tabb), 394

race relations, 364
railroads, 162
Raven, The (Poe), 35, 112, 113
Raven and Other Poems, The (Poe), 112
Ray, Charlotte, 441
Ray, Florence, 441, 442
Ray, Henrietta Cordelia, xxvi, 441–42
Read, Thomas Buchanan, 219–20, 246
Realism (Aldich), 331
realistic fiction, 312
Reconstruction, 379, 380
Recusant Poets: 1535–1745 (Guiney), 470
Redburn (Melville), 188
Redpath Lyceum Bureau, 411
Reese, Lizette Woodworth, xxv, 312,
    447–48
Reformed Church of England, 470
religion, xxii, xxiv, 136, 352, 372, 435,
    504
Representative Men (Emerson), 43
Republic, 226
Republican Party, 13, 364
Reserve (Reese), 448
Resistance to Civil Government (Civil
    Disobedience) (Thoreau), 156
Retrospective (S. Whitman), 35
reunion, following Civil War, xxiii
Reynolds, David S., xxi
rhyme schemes, xxxii, 2, 14, 66, 146,
    170, 202, 254, 264, 341, 358, 394, 436
Rhymes of Travel, Ballads, and Poems
    (Taylor), 235
rhythm xxxii, 112, 379
Richmond, Annie, 112
Riley, James Whitcomb, xxvi, xxxii,
    411–12
Ripley, George, 36
Roach, Chevilette Eliza, 59
Roadside Harp, A (Guiney), 469
Robinson, Edwin Arlington, xxxiv, 312
romance (subject), 435
Rome, 43, 219
Roosevelt, Theodore, 394, 480
Rosary in Rhyme, The (Tabb), 394
Roughing It (Twain), xxvii
Rover, 246
Rubin, Louis D., Jr., 26, 60, 274
Rural Poems (Read), 220
Russell, Henrietta, 486

Russell's Bookshop Group, 274
Russell's Magazine, 274
Ryan, Abram Joseph, xxiii, 358–59

Sabini warriors, 470
Saint Gregory's Guest (Whittier), 86
St. Mary's Seminary, 393
St. Paul's School for Boys, 393
Same Old Story Told Again, The
    (Riley), 411
Sanctuary (Guiney), 470
Santayana, George, 236, 503
Sargsso Weed (Stedman), 313
Saturday Evening Post, 235
Sauverneur School of Languages, 441
Sawin, Birdofredum, 170
Saxe, John Godfrey, 145–46
Say When, and Say It (King), 456
Science of English Verse, The (Lanier),
    xxxii, 380
Scott, Sir Walter, 60
Scribner's Magazine, 182, 479
Scudder, Horace E., 170
Sea of Fire, The (Miller), 340
Seaside and the Fireside, The (Longfel-
    low), 66
Seawall, Ellen, 156
Seaward (Hovey), 486
Second Coming (Moody), 504
secretary of state, 351
self, the, 157
self and society, xxii, xxix
sentimental novels, 226
sexuality, xxix, 486
Shadows of Shasta (Miller), 341
Shakespeare, William, 379, 425, 441, 447
Sharps and Flats (Field), 418
Shaw, Elizabeth, 189
Shelley, Percy Bysshe, 236, 496
Shells (Wilcox), 425
Sheridan, Philip, 219
Sheridan's Ride (Read), 219, 220
Sherman, Joan R., 26, 442
Shoes in the Desert, The (Miller), 341
Ship of Earth, The (Lanier), 380
Shoes of Happiness, The (Markham), 436
Sigourney, Lydia Huntley, xxi, xxii,
    xxv, xxx, 1–2, 85
Sill, Edward Rowland, 372–73
Simms, William Gilmore, xxvii, 59–60,
    274, 289, 496
Singer, The (Whittier), 202
Skelton, John, 157
Sketches of Southern Life (Harper), 255
Skipper Ireson's Ride (Whittier), 86
Slave Mother, a Tale of the Ohio (Har-
    per), 255
slavery, xxii, xxiii, 13, 35, 156, 169, 170,
    255
Smart Set, The, 447

Thurman, Kelly, 352
Tide Rises, the Tide Falls, The (Longfellow), 66
Tidewater, 59
Tiger-Lillies (Lanier), 379
Timoleon (Melville), 189
Timrod, Henry, xxi, xxiii, 59, 274–76, 289, 358, 496
Titcomb, Timothy, 182
To ——— (Poe), 35
To a Locomotive in Winter (Whitman), xxvi
To a Shred of Linen (Sigourney), 2
To a Waterfowl (Bryant), xxv, 13, 14
To hear an Oriole sing (Dickinson), xxv
To Helen (Poe), xxix, 35, 111, 112
To J. L. (Lanier), 380
To One Complaining (Channing), 162
To Walt Whitman, the Man (Piatt), 319
Tollmen, The (Tabb), 394
Tom Deadlight (Melville), 189
transcendentalism, 35, 36, 43, 111, 135, 136, 146, 157, 161, 372, 401, 470
translations, 65, 66, 236, 401, 402, 418, 419
Traubel, Horace Logo, 463–64
travel writing, 235, 236
Trowbridge, John Townsend, xxvi, 264–65
Trumpet, 201, 226
Truthful James (Harte), xxvii
Tucker, Ellen, 42
Tuckerman, Frederick Goddard, 210–11
Turkey, 351
Twain, Mark (Samuel Clemens), xxvii, 86, 351, 365, 411
Twelve Poems (Wharton), 479
Two Irish Peasant Songs (Guiney), 470
Two Lyrics (Tabb), 394
Two Offers, The (Harper), 255
Typee (Melville), 188

Ultima Thule (Longfellow), 66
unconscious, the, xxviii, 43, 66, 111
Under the Willows and Other Poems (Lowell), 170
Underground Railroad, 513
Union army, 26, 393, 513
Union of Parties, The (Horton), 27
Union Seminary, 254
U.S. Military Academy (West Point), 111
Universalists, 201
universities, 12, 65, 111, 145, 169, 254, 312, 318, 351, 358, 372, 379, 425, 441, 503. *See also* colleges; Harvard College
Unknown Dead, The (Timrod), 275
Uriel (Emerson), xxix
Utilitarian View of the Monitor's Fight, A (Melville), xxvi, 189

Vagabondia (Hovey), 486
Vagabonds, The (Trowbridge), 264, 265
Vagabonds and Other Poems, The (Trowbridge), 264
Van Tassel, Katrina, xxvii
Variety Is the Spice of Life (Tabb), 394
Vaughan, Henry, 469
Venus of Milo and Other Poems, The (Sill), 372
Venus of the Louvre (Lazarus), 402
verse: bawdy, 418, 419; blank, 2, 14, 66, 170, 254, 436, 480; children's, 227, 246, 247, 412, 418, 419; closet drama, 503; dramas, 66, 503; dramatic, 66; English, 379; epistles, 189; fables, 247; forms, 112; free, 380; light mod")oodh, 128, 145, 313; medleys, 189; paragraph, 66; satirical, 312, 313, 418; society, 330; western, 418; women's, xxiv, xxx. *See also* poems; poetry
Verses (Jackson), 302
Verses (Wharton), 479
Verses to My Heart's Sister (Ray), 442
Very, Jones, 135–37, 210
Vienna, 351
Views A-Foot (Taylor), 235
Virginia Quarterly Review, 447
Vision of Echard, The (Whittier), 86
Vision of Sir Launfal (Lowell), 169
Vogel, Dan, 401
Voice of the Pines, The (Hayne), xxv
Voices of Freedom (Whittier), 86
Voices of the Night (Longfellow), 65

Wadsworth, Zilpah, 65
Waggoner, Hyatt, 42
Walden (Thoreau), 156
Walden Pond, 156
Walden Spring (Channing), 162
Walker, Cheryl, xxi, xxiv, xxx, 2, 426, 470
Wall Street, 312
Wallace, Lew, 219
Walser, Richard, 26
Wanderer, The (Channing), 162
Wanderlieder (Hay), 352
Washington, Booker T., 394
Watkins, William J., 254
Watts, Emily Stipes, xxiv, 1, 2
Waverly Magazine, 425
We Wear the Mask (Dunbar), xxvi, 515
Weaver, Gordon, 358
Webster, Daniel, 86
Week on the Concord and Merrimack Rivers, A (Thoreau), 156
West, The, 318, 340, 341
West Chester [Pennsylvania] *Register*, 235
western archetypes, 341
western myths, 341
western stories, 365

westward expansion, xxiii, xxvii
Wharton, Edith Newbold Jones, xxix,
  479–80
Wharton, Edward "Teddy," 479
What Is Poetry? (Timrod), 275
When the Priest Left (Hovey), 486
Whipple, S. G., 364
Whirlwind Road, The (Markham), 436
White, Maria, 169
White April (Reese), 447
White Sail and Other Poems (Guiney),
  469
Whitechapel Club, 455
White-Jacket (Melville), 189
Whitman, John Winslow, 35
Whitman, Sarah Helen, 35–36, 112, 202
Whitman, Walt, xxi, xxii, xxiii, xxiv,
  xxv, xxvi, xxvii, xxviii, xxix, xxxii,
  xxxiii, xxxiv, 2, 13, 14, 42, 66, 112,
  146, 182, 183, 210, 165, 274, 290,
  303, 312, 313, 318, 319, 341, 351, 352,
  380, 402, 425, 426, 436, 463, 464,
  486, 503
Whitman studies, 464
Whittier, Elizabeth, 86
Whittier, John Greenleaf, xxi, xxiii,
  xxvii, xxviii, xxxi, xxxiv, 85–87,
  201, 202, 289, 447
Wilcox, Ella Wheeler, xxi, 425–26
Wilcox, Robert, 425, 426
Wild Nights—Wild Nights! (Dickin-
  son), xxix
Wild Rose (Traubel), 464
Wild West, The, xxvii

Wilder, Thornton, 412
Williams, Andrew, 364
Williams, William Carlos, xxxiv
Wimsatt Mary Ann, 59
Winters, Yvor, 211
Witchcraft (Stedman), 313
With Walt Whitman in Camden
  (Traubel), 463
Woman's Conclusions, A (P. Cary), 227
Woman's Death Wound, A (Jackson), 303
Woman's Journal, 201
Woman's Love, A (Hay), 352
Woman's Poem, A (Stoddard), 247
women, pursuit of, 419
women's issues, xxii, xxiii, xxiv, 1, 2,
  146, 201, 202, 226, 255, 401, 426
Woodlands (plantation), 59
Woodman and Other Poems, The (Chan-
  ning), 161
Woof of the Sun, Ethereal Gauze
  (Thoreau), 157
Wordsworth, William, 43, 247, 319, 497
World Is Too Much with Us
  (Wordsworth), 497
World War I, xxiv, xxxiv, 65, 426
Wright brothers, xxvi
Wynken, Blynken, and Nod (Field), 419

Ximmena (Taylor), 235

Years Life, A (Lowell), 169

Zimmer, Giles Henry, 393
Zolaistic movement, 331